Thinking Politically

Thinking Politically

Essays in Political Theory

Michael Walzer

Selected, Edited, and with an Introduction by
David Miller

Yale University Press   New Haven & London

Designed by James J. Johnson
Set in Ehrhardt by Keystone Typesetting, Inc.
Printed in the United States of America by Vail Ballou Press, Binghamton, N.Y.

Library of Congress Cataloging-in-Publication Data
Walzer, Michael.
Thinking politically : essays in political theory / Michael Walzer ; selected, edited, and with
an introduction by David Miller.
p. cm.
Includes bibliographical references and index.
ISBN 978-0-300-11816-2 (alk. paper)
1. Political science. I. Miller, David, 1946– II. Title.
JA71.W25 2007
320.01—dc22   2007023115

A catalogue record for this book is available from the British Library.
The paper in this book meets the guidelines for permanence and durability of the
Committee on Production Guidelines for Book Longevity of the Council on
Library Resources.

10 9 8 7 6 5 4 3 2 1

Contents

Introduction

DAVID MILLER

When I proposed to Michael Walzer that I should edit a collection of his essays in political theory, I had two ambitions. The first, more mundane, was simply to bring together in one place a number of important papers, for the benefit of readers who might otherwise have to hunt for them in places that were not always easily accessible. The second was loftier. I thought that by publishing them together, new connections would appear, and we would begin to have a better sense of the underlying vision that informs Walzer's response to particular issues. Whether this second ambition has been fulfilled, the reader must judge. But the process of selecting, arranging, and rereading these essays has been remarkably illuminating, and my understanding of Walzer's political thought has changed materially and, I hope, improved. This introduction is intended to set out what I take to be the central ideas contained in these essays as well as in his many other books and articles. But first I shall explain the principles on which the selection has been made.

Michael Walzer has written prolifically on political questions for more than half a century, and these lectures, articles, and books were aimed at many audiences, some academic, others not (as is well known, he has been a contributing editor of the left political magazine *Dissent* for more than thirty years). To collect all of them in one place would have meant a very large volume indeed. My choice has been biased in three directions. First, I have focused attention on Walzer's more recent work: with one exception (chapter 17), these essays were composed over a twenty-five-year period from 1980 to 2005. Second, I have steered away from pieces that were later developed to be incorporated into books by Walzer himself or that have appeared in earlier collections of his essays and are therefore accessible in that form; in particular I chose not to include essays on Jewish questions, in anticipation of a projected volume that will collect his extensive writing in this area, on American Jewish identity, Zionism, and so forth. Third, where I had to choose between overlapping essays on particular topics, I chose whichever seemed to me to provide the fullest and deepest treatment of that topic: my bias, in other words, has been toward political theory and against political commentary. For readers whose appetites have been whetted, I have included an extensive bibliography of his work, giving original places of publication. The selection was nonetheless difficult: Michael offered encouragement and gave a few suggestions but made absolutely no attempt to dictate my choice. He also offered an unpublished paper on human rights, which appears here as chapter 15. He has been generous with his time in responding to numerous questions of the "What do you really think about. . . .?" kind. I should also like to record my thanks to Zosia Stemplowska, who helped me very considerably by reading everything and proposing a short-list; and to Ame Dyckman, Sarah Fine, and Emre Ozcan for their excellent work in preparing the final manuscript. The essays are arranged thematically rather than chronologically, and my introduction follows the same pattern.

PHILOSOPHY AND POLITICS

Michael Walzer was originally trained in the disciplines of political science and history rather than in philosophy, but in the 1960s he fell into the company of philosophers—among them John Rawls, Robert Nozick, and Ronald Dworkin—while working at Harvard, and ever since then has wrestled with the question of the relationship between the philosopher and the citizen: what contribution, if any, can philosophical thought about politics make to political activity itself? He is not a political philosopher in the conventional sense. He does not, in other words, believe that detached, abstract thought can yield principles that tell us how we should act politically. Indeed, as the first essay published here indicates, he sees the philosophical enterprise as involving a conscious distancing of oneself from the political opinions that prevail in any particular community. The philosopher brackets all of these received opinions and seeks to establish, by reason alone, political principles that are true and therefore universally valid. This enterprise Walzer describes as heroic. But, he claims, the heroic philosopher is doomed to disappointment because when he returns to the political community carrying his principles, he finds that the citizens are unwilling to accept them—since they do not connect to local traditions and ways of thinking about politics.

There is one particular version of heroic political philosophy that Walzer considers at greater length in chapter 2: the contractarian version that seeks to derive valid political principles from the agreements that people would reach under certain specified ideal conditions (Bruce Ackerman, Jürgen Habermas, and Rawls are the main figures considered here). Walzer highlights the gulf that separates the imagined discourse of the participants in these thought experiments from the real political debate that occurs between people with opposing interests and beliefs. Agreement is achieved in the contractarian setting only by severely limiting what the participants can know or what they can say, and so the discussion proceeds to its predetermined conclusion without any real dissent. What we have here, Walzer claims, is philosophical argument masquerading as political discourse.

All of this might suggest that political philosophy in this mode is irrelevant but essentially harmless, since its conclusions are bound to be rejected by citizens engaged in real political debates about the direction their society should take. But Walzer thinks it can nevertheless have a corrupting influence, even in democracies. It helps to foster two tendencies especially. One is for judicial decision making to displace popular democracy. If an expanding list of rights can be established by philosophical reasoning, and if judges are empowered to enforce these rights against a democratically elected legislature, then the space that remains for democratic politics will steadily shrink (this argument, when first made by Walzer, might have seemed to apply specifically to the American tradition of judicial enforcement of constitutional rights, but the more recent proliferation of human rights charters in Europe and elsewhere suggests the phenomenon he identifies is becoming more widespread). The second tendency is for democratic decision making itself to be understood in a way that brings it closer to philosophical discourse. Walzer finds this tendency evident in much recent writing about "deliberative democracy," especially that strand that draws upon the work of Habermas. Deliberative democrats are tempted to reduce political engagement to the kind of discussion that might go on in a philosophical seminar, where the participants try to move each other toward a consensus by rational argument alone. Against this temptation, Walzer insists that politics is a complex activity in which reasoned argument has to take its place alongside other forms of interaction—bargaining, coalition building, mobilizing supporters through appeals to loyalty, and so forth—hence the title of chapter 9, "Deliberation, and What Else?"

So do philosophers have anything to contribute to political life or must they set aside their philosophical commitments and participate simply as ordinary citizens in the debates of the day? Walzer thinks it is possible to be an engaged philosopher who contributes to these debates by speaking in the language of the political community, playing, as he puts it, the role of "sophist, critic, publicist, or intellectual." But in what sense, then, is the engaged philosopher still a philosopher? Can he or she claim any kind of epistemological superiority vis-à-vis the opinions of fellow citizens? Here we need to look to Walzer's several discussions of the idea of social criticism, in his books *Interpretation and Social Criticism* and *The Company of Critics* and in the third essay included here, "Objectivity and Social Meaning." Two forms of social criticism are relatively uncontroversial. In the first, the critic contrasts a society's underlying values with its existing practices and the behavior of its members. He or she calls upon fellow citizens to be true to their deeper commitments. In the second, the critic takes a received idea or value and develops it, applying it to new areas of social life or to groups that have up to now not been included in its scope (consider, for instance, how the idea of political equality was extended over time to embrace propertyless workers, women, and ethnic minorities). In both cases the critic remains connected and speaks the language of the society but urges greater consistency in the way the society's values are implemented. But what should we say if a value that seems repugnant from the outside is nevertheless deeply embedded in the society's value system and not obviously inconsistent with anything else its members believe? Can the critical philosopher claim that, objectively, the society has got it wrong, that the ideas being invoked are simply false? Walzer grapples with this question in chapter 3, taking as his example a society in which women are regarded as objects of exchange and treated as such. His answer turns on whether the women, too, "agree to the construction of themselves as objects of exchange" or whether they are forcibly silenced by men. No one can be denied the status of an agent who can play a part in constructing the world of meanings in which he or she lives. But if they do agree, then the scope for philosophical criticism is limited, pending changes in social life that would allow new conceptions of women's role in society to challenge the idea they are merely commodities.

There are many questions arising from this view of the limits of objectivity that cannot be pursued here. What is clear, however, is that Walzer offers the philosopher only a severely chastened role vis-à-vis the political community. He or she cannot criticize that community simply by holding it up against principles claimed to be universally valid without regard to the members' own understanding of their way of life and the values it embodies. And even in the case in which the philosopher acts as a connected critic and produces an interpretation of those values that serves to condemn much of what the community currently does, still this interpretation carries no special authority. The philosopher casts it into the political debate and waits to see whether the people accept or reject the gift that is being offered.

LIBERALISM

Politically, Michael Walzer is a liberal; he is also what Europeans would call a social democrat—a liberal who believes that the state should play an extensive role in promoting welfare and social justice. For the moment, however, I want to focus attention less on specific political commitments than on the peculiar character of Walzer's liberalism. For Walzer has also frequently been described as a communitarian, in contexts in which liberalism and communitarianism are being contrasted. In hindsight, this contrast looks increasingly unilluminating, and Walzer's own reading of the so-called liberal-communitarian debate can be found in chapter 7 below. Nonetheless there is no smoke without fire, and Walzer's liberalism is indeed of a very different character from much that has passed under that name in recent political theory.

The difference can perhaps be summed up in the following way. For many liberals, the core of liberalism can be found in a view about the limits of political authority and state activity. A liberal society is one that recognizes an inviolable private sphere in which people are free to pursue their own plans of life without interference by the state. This is often expressed in the language of rights: people have rights to engage in a range of activities that are essentially their own business and nobody else's, and the state must respect these rights—rights that ought to be laid down in a constitution that sets limits to what legislatures and executives can do.

Walzer is not opposed to the idea that there are areas of life that are properly regarded as private and off-limits to the state. But he finds the heart of liberalism elsewhere—in the idea of separation, of a society made up of different spheres, each of which preserves its autonomy and counterbalances the rest. Private life is one such sphere, but the line that divides public from private is no more important than the line that divides church and state or the economic market and the welfare state. A free society is not one that removes power from everyday life by concentrating it in the hands of the (suitably constituted) state, but one that recognizes its omnipresence and then tries to tame it by setting power against power—the power of the church against the power of the state, and so forth. The ensuing separation, Walzer thinks, is a fragile achievement because the spheres contain institutions that attempt to dominate society as a whole—the church at one time, the state at another, the corporation at yet another—but a central aim of liberal politics is to preserve it.

Why is this understanding of liberalism superior to the conventional view? Essentially because it is sociologically more realistic. It recognizes the pervasiveness of power, whereas conventional liberalism focuses its attention on controlling the coercive power of the state, thereby often losing sight of other forms of power that can dominate the lives of individuals, especially perhaps in the contemporary world economic power. It also has a more realistic understanding of freedom. Conventional liberalism emphasizes *individual* autonomy—the self-made person choosing his or her own path through life—thereby failing to recognize the degree to which people are unavoidably shaped by the particular milieux in which they are raised (and in which in some cases they are compelled to remain, by reason of gender or ethnicity, for example). What matters more, therefore, is collective autonomy—the freedom of institutions and social groups to organize their internal affairs without external constraint. So in place of an individualist liberal vision of a society made up of autonomous individuals freely contracting with one another to form social institutions of various kinds, Walzer offers a social liberalism in which we recognize the extent to which people are already embedded in groups and institutions and understand freedom primarily as the protection of these collective bodies from external domination.

Successful separation confers not only liberty but also equality: this is the argument famously set out in Walzer's book *Spheres of Justice*. I have examined it at some length in an earlier contribution (*Pluralism, Justice, and Equality*, coedited with Michael Walzer), so I will not repeat myself here but only emphasize that Walzer's liberalism is not only philosophically unconventional but also politically radical. Some of the measures it entails are presented in the account of social justice in chapter 5, "Justice Here and Now": these include an extensive welfare state and widespread industrial democracy. Equality is not the aim but rather the by-product of public policy whose purpose is not only to ensure that within each social sphere goods are distributed according to the principles appropriate to that sphere, but also to combat domination—the subordination of one sphere to the power and distributive requirements of another.

Walzer's liberalism has little to say about rights, an idea that features so prominently in many rival versions. He does not, of course, want to argue that individuals should be denied the protection of legal rights, and he recognizes that the language of rights is unavoidably central to political debate in contemporary liberal societies, but he still resists giving rights any fundamental role in liberal political theory. I believe that this resistance has at least three sources. First, a rights-based theory mirrors the individualist model of society he wants to reject in favor of a sociologically informed liberalism. Second, such a theory also encourages the displacement of democratic politics by judicial decision making, as we saw in the previous section. Third, policies justified by appeal to rights may nullify local diversity and therefore opportunities for local self-government. Rights to welfare, for example, may entail that everyone everywhere is entitled to exactly the same medical treatment in case of illness or exactly the same educational provision, thereby removing from local communities the power to decide what priorities to pursue in their hospitals and schools. Does this, however, reveal some tension between Walzer's commitment to social pluralism and his commitment to equality? I explore this question in the following section.

CIVIL SOCIETY AND THE STATE

Walzer often writes admiringly about civil society and the opportunities it offers for political engagement. He interprets the concept broadly to include all forms of voluntary association, whether these are formed to meet the immediate material or spiritual needs of the associates, to advance their interests against outsiders, or to embrace political causes. Thus on Walzer's conception neighborhood associations, churches, labor unions, political parties, charities, and pressure groups like Greenpeace and Human Rights Watch all belong within civil society. A good society for him is above all one in which a multitude of such associations flourish. Their importance is, first, that they draw people out of social isolation and into groups whose members offer one another mutual support; second, that they are agents of social justice, helping to ensure that different goods are distributed by the proper principles (for example, welfare to those who need it most, religious offices to those who are best qualified to hold them, etc.); third, that they provide people with the means and the incentive to act politically at the local level and on issues that really concern them—in contrast to national politics, which is often too remote to engage their attention.

This vision of civil society and its possibilities places Walzer recognizably (and self-avowedly) in an American tradition of political pluralism—which also means that his analysis and the proposals that flow from it may be less directly relevant elsewhere. But he does not embrace pluralism uncritically, as did some of his predecessors in that tradition, who believed that democracy meant essentially allowing the state to become the creature of civil society, its policies determined by the balance of power between the pressure groups that sought to influence it. Walzer, by contrast, is keenly aware of the limitations as well as the virtues of civil society and sees independent state action as vital to overcome these limitations, bringing him here closer to European social democratic thought.

What are these limitations? A flourishing civil society, Walzer argues, is not something we can take for granted. It is threatened, in particular by what in chapter 7 he calls the "four mobilities"—geographic, social, marital, and political—which often bring personal freedom to individuals but at the cost of weakening those social ties that make voluntary association possible. People who move away from their neighborhood, their family, or their political associates are more likely to become disengaged and to live an essentially private existence. To counteract this tendency the state must be willing to support the associations of civil society, by granting them rights or privileges, by funding them to provide services, and so forth.

Another limitation is that voluntary associations are inevitably imperfect agents of social justice; in particular, they may redistribute resources internally among their own members but fail to counteract inequality on a wider scale. They may be poorly placed to tackle social exclusion—the focus of Walzer's discussion in chapter 6—because where an underclass exists, its members are far less likely to be involved in these associations. Social justice, then, requires a delicate balance between civil society and state: civil society associations are needed to check the state, to prevent it from intruding in areas in which (according to liberal principles) it has no proper business, but the state must oversee and correct the distribution of resources and opportunities that civil society creates. How this balance is to be achieved remains one of the principal dilemmas of Walzer's political theory

Finally, civil society is not proof against attempts at domination. Religious groups, in particular, may attempt to impose their principles on the political community as a whole, bypassing the normal process of political deliberation and compromise. This question is discussed in chapter 10, in which Walzer argues against the rigid separation of religion and politics and against strict state neutrality in matters of religion but maintains nonetheless that coercive power must always remain in the hands of the state, where it can be made subject to democratic contestation, and never be allowed to drift toward churches, parties, or other sectional associations.

This means, of course, that for democratic politics to continue, people have to think and act as citizens first and as members of civil society groups second. But how is this possible? Walzer is quite critical of the republican tradition (recently revived in the work of Quentin Skinner, Philip Pettit, and others), holding that republicanism (at least in its Rousseauian version) makes sense only in small, homogenous communities. It is asking too much of citizens in modern liberal societies to set aside their personal interests and convictions and to work single-mindedly for the common good, even if the scale of such societies did not make direct political involvement impractical. Nevertheless, citizenship remains a key idea in Walzer's thought. So the next question one must ask is: what can bind people together with sufficient strength that their commitment to one another as citizens overrides their sectional loyalties of class, gender, ethnicity, or religion?

NATIONALISM AND MULTICULTURALISM

Walzer has addressed this question in numerous places, and the answer he gives is not straightforward. On the one side, he recognizes both the practical power and the moral value of national allegiances; on the other, he is strongly committed to respecting cultural differences, including those between the majority community and minority groups within nation-states. But can one consistently be both a nationalist and a multiculturalist? or should one advocate an idea of citizenship that divorces it from nationality in the cultural sense? Walzer's solution involves not only discriminating between forms of nationalism, but also contemplating a variety of ways in which cultural differences can be accommodated. The common element here is the weight he attaches to cultural autonomy—to the opportunity for men and women to work together to create a distinctive way of life free from outside interference. This is the value that justifies nationalism, or, more specifically, national self-determination, but it is also the value that justifies cultural groups in resisting assimilation to the dominant national culture of the society to which they belong—hence the practical dilemma.

Walzer has written at length about different regimes of toleration of cultural diversity in his book *On Toleration,* the main idea of which is presented in chapter 11 here, "The Politics of Difference." Leaving aside for present purposes the first two regimes discussed (the multinational empire and the consociational state), I want to consider the contrast Walzer draws between nation-states and those, like the United States, that he describes as "immigrant societies." In the former case, "a single dominant group organizes the common life in a way that reflects its own history and culture," and minorities are tolerated only within the limits set by that common life, whereas in the latter case no group is dominant and the state operates on the principle, not of complete cultural neutrality, but of equal treatment of the various cultural groups that make up the society. It is implied here that immigrant societies can be multicultural but not national in character. But is this really so? It seems rather that immigrant societies have evolved a distinct form of national identity, one that relies less on inherited cultural traditions and more on political principles and institutions (including institutions whose purpose is to assist immigrant groups and help them to integrate). Indeed Walzer has himself written about this question at some length in *What It Means to be an American,* in which he concedes that American nationality exists and that what distinguishes it most clearly from nationality as understood in the older European countries is its open and inclusive character: anyone, in principle, can become an American. But if common citizenship, as the idea that binds people together across divisions of class, gender, and so forth, does require a shared national identity to sustain it, then support for multicultural policies must be selective: we should favor those whose effect is to integrate people in common institutions and promote the shared identity, while opposing those whose effect is to segregate people into what are often now called parallel societies.

Walzer's support for nationalism is, then, significantly qualified. He believes that some societies can manage with a thinner version of national identity that allows for hyphenation (Italian-American, etc.); and he is acutely aware of the destructive power of nationalism as well as its integrative power. For all that, he is a passionate defender of the right of political communities to manage their own affairs, even in cases where the management is not conducted through formally democratic channels. In chapter 12, "Nation and Universe," he argues that a defensible nationalism must be "reiterative"—that is, it must allow other communities the same freedom to pursue their own distinctive paths as the nation claims for itself. This principle must extend to national minorities living within the borders of established states, who must be given sufficient political autonomy to do this, albeit not necessarily states of their own. Where nationalism is not reiterative, it becomes imperialist, seeking to impose a single model of national culture on communities who would reject it if they could. "The proper judgement of nationalism," Walzer writes, "has to do with the attitudes and practices it adopts towards other nations."

But, we must still ask, under what circumstances is national self-determination genuine, as opposed to merely the successful imposition of the values of a cultural elite on the rest of society? This is the problem Walzer wrestles with in the essay reprinted here as chapter 13, "The Moral Standing of States," responding to the criticism that the doctrine of nonintervention put forward in his book *Just and Unjust Wars* is too statist in character, in the sense that it seeks to protect states from external intervention even in cases where those states are not democratic. Walzer argues in reply that there can be a natural fit between government and people, such that government can embody and pursue national values without being formally answerable to the community it governs; the history and culture of some communities may be such that they prefer authoritarian regimes to other political forms. In any case, he continues, outsiders are in no position to judge whether or not a regime is legitimate in the eyes of its subjects. If the community is divided, then internal political struggle (which may take the form of revolution) is the only way for a people to determine how it will be governed in the future.

There are exceptions to this rule—regimes that massacre or enslave their own citizens. I shall discuss the principles Walzer applies to these cases in the following section. But we can now see the common thread that runs through the various themes already considered: the idea that men and women are entitled to work together to create their own form of social life; that this work is essentially political, though it can occur at many levels, not just the national; that when they do this, the outcome will in each case be a distinctive set of cultural values, ideas of justice, social practices; and that it is always wrong for outside agents to attempt to dictate some uniform solution—whether these agents are heroic philosophers or lawyers clutching charters of rights or imperial powers imposing "civilization" on barbarians or well-meaning liberals seeking to spread democracy worldwide.

HUMANITARIAN INTERVENTION AND HUMAN RIGHTS

For the reasons just given, Walzer is opposed in general to interference by one state in the internal affairs of another, even if the motives behind the intervention are good ones. But over time he has become more willing to accept the case for humanitarian intervention, understood to mean forcible intervention aimed at preventing genocides, ethnic cleansing, or other gross violations of human rights. In this section I explore the grounds on which such interventions are justified and ask what implications this has for Walzer's political theory as a whole.

In some cases, interventions occur in circumstances in which political order has been shattered by civil war or by rivalries between local warlords and their supporters and in which, as a result, there is no political community whose self-determination the intervention might undermine. But in other cases, the intervention is aimed at a reasonably well-functioning state whose actions involve the violent suppression or expulsion of a minority group—as, for example, the NATO action against Serbia in 1999–2000. If such interventions are justified, it must be on grounds that trump claims to national self-determination. Walzer argues that the only relevant grounds are large-scale violations of basic human rights. Here he appeals to a moral principle that, unlike the principles that feature in his account of distributive justice, is not tied to any particular political community but can be justified independently.

The underpinning for this position can be found in his book *Thick and Thin,* in which he argues in defence of "moral minimalism," the idea that there are certain moral rules common to all societies—rules such as those prohibiting murder, deception, and gross cruelty—that exist alongside the thicker morality that each society has evolved to govern its distributive practices and other areas of social life. The moral minimum can be expressed as the injunction to respect a set of basic human rights, although Walzer freely concedes that the *language* of human rights comes more easily to some cultures than to others. So when humanitarian intervention takes place, it does so in the name of a principle that (if Walzer is correct) the intervened-against society must already recognize. Of course, its leaders will claim that their actions are justified by the need to preserve public order or territorial integrity, goals which they will claim are sufficiently important to override human rights. But they cannot dismiss the moral basis on which the intervention is being launched.

How long or short should the list of human rights be, for this purpose? Walzer argues, in chapter 15, "Beyond Humanitarian Intervention," that it must be limited in two respects. First, the rights in question must be those without which no kind of decent human life is possible—rights to life, liberty, and minimal levels of subsistence. Second, we should speak of rights and rights violations only when some collective agency, usually a government, is involved in creating them, so that although we might say that not only mass murder but also famine violates human rights, we would here be assuming that the famine was caused deliberately or negligently by the government in question. This, evidently, is a much more restricted conception than the one that has been employed in recent decades to generate various charters of human rights—in which human rights are extended to cover much of what the citizens of liberal democracies expect their governments to provide for them (generous welfare services, for example). Whatever the merits of this wider conception, it is clearly precluded by Walzer's appeal to human rights solely as a way of setting limits to the communal autonomy he otherwise applauds.

Humanitarian intervention also raises the question of which states, or coalitions of states, are entitled to undertake it—indeed, in the literature on the topic, this question of proper authority is often taken to be the main issue intervention poses. Walzer is clear that the right answer, in general, is, "Whoever can, should"—the problem is not one of selecting between many potential interveners but of finding any state willing to bear the costs of intervention. The more difficult question, he believes, is whether we can properly speak of an *obligation* as well as a right to intervene in the face of a genocidal or other such threat. If we say there is an obligation, then we have also to say that democracies are entitled to expose their soldiers to significant risks in defense of the human rights of outsiders—something that in practice they are very reluctant to do. And there is the further problem that the obligation is one that must fall on every state that has the capacity to intervene, giving rise to the problem of deciding who in particular is required to act. These are reasons for not imposing a strict obligation to intervene. Nevertheless, Walzer is willing to say that there is a more general obligation to work toward an international order in which all states are rights-protecting states, however different they may be in other respects. This, then, sets the limits of pluralism in international society.

POLITICAL MORALITY

I have ended my selection of Walzer's writing with two essays of a character rather different from all the rest (they are also the last and first to be published, but that is coincidence). They are about the moral responsibilities of the individual who engages in political action; more narrowly, they are about political violence: when it may be used, what moral consequences follow from its use. Walzer has, of course, written extensively about the ethics of war, in his book *Just and Unjust Wars* and in the essays collected in *Arguing About War*. But the issues addressed here are rather different.

Chapter 16, "Terrorism and Just War," considers both the morality of terrorism and the morality of responses to terrorism—of what we may and may not do as part of the so-called war on terrorism. Walzer approaches these questions through the just war tradition, though the problem, it turns out, is that terrorism stands outside of the rules and conventions embodied in that tradition.

The terrorists seek deliberately to blur the crucial distinction between combatants and noncombatants by considering everybody belonging to the designated group (nation, class, etc) a legitimate target. And in responding to terrorism it may be difficult to draw that very line: are terrorists to be treated like enemy soldiers in a war? If so, how do we separate the man who plants a bomb from his supporters and accomplices, who help plan the operation, offer him refuge, etc.?

Walzer's provocative thesis in this essay is that what distinguishes terrorism from other forms of political violence is the intention to "destroy or remove or radically subordinate" the whole group at which the acts of terror are directed; its wrongness, correspondingly, lies not just in the use of violence, horrible though that is, but in the attitude it expresses toward the target group. This means that politically motivated campaigns of violence that were directed more narrowly against the armed forces or political opponents and attempted to limit the damage inflicted on ordinary citizens wouldn't qualify as terrorism in Walzer's account (the IRA campaign in Northern Ireland, he suggests, came close to this description, although it also involved random killings and other acts that took it closer to terrorism proper). The effect is to widen the gulf between terrorism and politics: the terrorist is not simply somebody who has raised the political stakes by employing the threat of violence, but someone who signals his unwillingness to deal politically at all with those he regards as his enemies. Although Walzer is certainly right to contrast politics and terror, there are also some dangers in this way of thinking about terrorism. For defeating it always involves, in the end, engaging politically with the terrorists—treating them as potential partners in political negotiation and as in principle able to consent to a political solution that accommodates (some of) their demands. As Walzer points out, this is sometimes achieved by drawing a semifictitious distinction between the political and military wings of the movement and talking to the political wing. But if terrorists were, by definition, uniformly motivated in the way Walzer describes—unwilling to recognize their target group as "candidates for equality or even co-existence"—none of this would be possible.

Chapter 17, "Political Action: The Problem of Dirty Hands," looks at the question from the other side, so to speak—from the point of view of the politician who has to engage in immoral acts, especially acts of violence, for the greater good of his political community. Some ways of responding to terrorism, such as targeted killings, are a good example of this. It is an essay about political guilt: are the good consequences themselves sufficient to lift the burden of guilt from the politician's shoulders? or must he be left to wrestle privately with his conscience? Walzer thinks that neither of these answers (which he attributes to

Niccolò Machiavelli and Max Weber, respectively) is satisfactory, and he leans toward a third position (which he associates with Albert Camus): the politician with dirty hands ought to be punished for the wrongs he has done, even as he is honored for the good he has achieved. Of course, Walzer observes, there is no mechanism available for doing this.

Having begun by considering the separation of politics from philosophy, the book thus ends by contemplating cases in which politics and morality appear to conflict. I have added an interview which lets the reader see how Walzer applies his ideas to the political issues of the day, including, as it happens, cases in which the dirty hands problem becomes a very real one. Although, as I have indicated, my aim in editing this book has been to present Michael Walzer as a political theorist with a clear and coherent vision of the political community as it should be, engagement with the much messier issues of contemporary politics has been a constant feature of his writing throughout. In this way, he has been an exemplary "connected critic," not only of American political life, but of the politics and international relations of the Western world as a whole.

CHAPTER ONE

Philosophy and Democracy

[1]

The prestige of political philosophy is very high these days. It commands the attention of economists and lawyers, the two groups of academics most closely connected to the shaping of public policy, as it has not done in a long time. And it claims the attention of political leaders, bureaucrats, and judges, most especially judges, with a new and radical forcefulness. The command and the claim follow not so much from the fact that philosophers are doing creative work, but from the fact that they are doing creative work of a special sort—which raises again, after a long hiatus, the possibility of finding objective truths, "true meaning," "right answers," "the philosopher's stone," and so on. I want to accept this possibility (without saying very much about it) and then ask what it means for democratic politics. What is the standing of the philosopher in a democratic society? This is an old question; there are old tensions at work here: between truth and opinion, reason and will, value and preference, the one and the many. These antipodal pairs differ from one another, and none of them quite matches the pair "philosophy and democracy." But they do hang together; they point to a central problem. Philosophers claim a certain sort of authority for their conclusions; the people claim a different sort of authority for their decisions. What is the relation between the two?

I shall begin with a quotation from Wittgenstein that might seem to resolve the problem immediately. "The philosopher," Wittgenstein wrote, "is not a citizen of any community of ideas. That is what makes him into a philosopher."[1] This is more than an assertion of detachment in its usual sense, for citizens are surely capable, sometimes, of detached judgments even of their own ideologies, practices, and institutions. Wittgenstein is asserting a more radical detachment. The philosopher is and must be an outsider; standing apart, not occasionally (in judgment) but systematically (in thought). I do not know whether the philosopher has to be a political outsider. Wittgenstein does say *any* community, and the state (polis, republic, commonwealth, kingdom, or whatever) is certainly a community of ideas. The communities of which the philosopher is most importantly not a citizen may, of course, be larger or smaller than the state. That will depend on what he philosophizes about. But if he is a political philosopher—not what Wittgenstein had in mind—then the state is the most likely community from which he will have to detach himself, not physically, but intellectually and, on a certain view of morality, morally too.

This radical detachment has two forms, and I shall be concerned with only one of them. The first form is contemplative and analytic; those who participate in it take no interest in changing the community whose ideas they study. "Philosophy leaves everything as it is."[2] The second form is heroic. I do not want to deny the heroic possibilities of contemplation and analysis. One can always take pride in wrenching oneself loose from the bonds of community; it is not easy to do, and many important philosophical achievements (and all the varieties of philosophical arrogance) have their origins in detachment. But I want to focus on a certain tradition of heroic action, alive, it seems, in our own time, where the philosopher detaches himself from the community of ideas in order to found it again—intellectually and then materially too, for ideas have consequences, and every community of ideas is also a concrete community. He withdraws and returns. He is like the legislators of ancient legend, whose work precludes ordinary citizenship.[3]

In the long history of political thought, there is an alternative to the detachment of philosophers, and that is the engagement of sophists, critics, publicists, and intellectuals. To be sure, the sophists whom Plato attacks were citiless men, itinerant teachers, but they were by no means strangers in the Greek community of ideas. Their teaching drew upon, was radically dependent upon, the resources of a common membership. In this sense, Socrates was a sophist, though it was probably crucial to his own understanding of his mission, as critic and gadfly, that he also be a citizen: the Athenians would have found him less irritating had he not been one of their fellows. But then the citizens killed Socrates, thus demonstrating, it is sometimes said, that engagement and fellowship are not possible for anyone committed to the search for truth. Philosophers cannot be sophists. For practical as well as intellectual reasons, the distance that they put between themselves and their fellow citizens must be widened into a breach of fellowship. And then, for practical reasons only, it must be narrowed again by deception and secrecy. So that the philosopher emerges, like Descartes in his *Discourse,* as a separatist in thought, a conformist in practice.

He is a conformist, at least, until he finds himself in a position to transform practice into some nearer approximation to the truths of his thought. He cannot be a participant in the rough and tumble politics of the city, but he can be a founder or a legislator, a king, a nocturnal councillor, or a judge—or, more realistically, he can be an advisor to such figures, whispering in the ear of power. Shaped by the very nature of the philosophical project, he has little taste for bargaining and mutual accommodation. Because the truth he knows or claims to know is singular in character, he is likely to think that politics must be the same: a coherent conception, an uncompromising execution. In philosophy as in architecture, and so in politics, wrote Descartes: What has been put together bit by bit, by different masters, is less perfect than the work of a single hand. Thus, "those old places which, beginning as villages, have developed in the course of time into great towns, are generally . . . ill-proportioned in comparison with those an engineer can design at will in an orderly fashion."⁴ Descartes himself disclaims any interest in the political version of such a project—perhaps because he believes that the only place where he is likely to reign supreme is his own mind. But there is always the possibility of a partnership between philosophical authority and political power. Reflecting on that possibility, the philosopher may, like Thomas Hobbes, "recover some hope that one time or other, this writing of mine may fall into the hands of a sovereign, who will . . . by the exercise of entire sovereignty . . . convert this truth of speculation into the utility of practice."⁵ The crucial words in these quotations from Descartes and Hobbes are "design at will" and "entire sovereignty." Philosophical founding is an authoritarian business.

[2]

A quick comparison may be helpful here. Poets have their own tradition of withdrawal and engagement, but radical withdrawal is not common among them. One might plausibly set alongside Wittgenstein's sentences the following lines of C. P. Cavafy, written to comfort a young poet who has managed after great effort to finish only one poem. That, Cavafy says, is a first step, and no small accomplishment:

> To set your foot upon this step you
> must rightfully be a citizen of the
> city of ideas.[6]

Wittgenstein writes as if there were (as there are) many communities, while Cavafy seems to suggest that poets inhabit a single, universal city. But I suspect that the Greek poet means in fact to describe a more particular place: the city of Hellenic culture. The poet must prove himself a citizen there; the philosopher must prove that he is not a citizen anywhere. The poet needs fellow citizens, other poets and readers of poetry, who share with him a background of history and sentiment, who will not demand that everything he writes be explained. Without people like that, his allusions will be lost and his images will echo only in his own mind. But the philosopher fears fellowship, for the ties of history and sentiment corrupt his thinking. He needs to look at the world from a distance, freshly, like a total stranger. His detachment is speculative, willful, always incomplete. I do not doubt that a clever sociologist or historian will detect in his work, as readily as in any poem, the signs of its time and place. Still, the philosopher's ambition (in the tradition that I am describing) is extreme. The poet, by contrast, is more modest—as Auden has written:

> A poet's hope:
> to be like some valley cheese,
> local, but prized elsewhere.[7]

The poet may be a visionary or a seer; he may seek out exile and trouble; but he cannot, short of madness, cut himself off from the community of ideas. And perhaps for that reason, he also cannot aspire to anything quite like sovereignty over the community. If he hopes to become a "legislator for mankind," it is rather by moving his fellow citizens than by governing them. And even the moving is indirect. "Poetry makes nothing happen."[8] But that is not quite the same thing as saying that it leaves everything as it is. Poetry leaves in the minds of its readers some intimation of the poet's truth. Nothing so coherent as a philosophical statement, nothing so explicit as a legal injunction: a poem is never more than a partial and unsystematic truth, surprising us by its excess, teasing us by its ellipsis, never arguing a case. "I have never yet been able to perceive," wrote Keats, "how anything can be known for truth by consecutive reasoning."[9] The knowledge of the poet is of a different sort, and it leads to truths that can, perhaps, be communicated but never directly implemented.

[3]

But the truths discovered or worked out by political philosophers can be implemented. They lend themselves readily to legal embodiment. Are these the laws of nature? Enact them. Is this a just scheme of distribution? Establish it. Is this a basic human right? Enforce it. Why else would one want to know about such things? An ideal city is, I suppose, an entirely proper object of contemplation, and it may be the case that "whether it exists anywhere or ever will exist is no matter"—that is, does not affect the truth of the vision. But surely it would be better if the vision were realized. Plato's claim that the ideal city is "the only commonwealth in whose politics [the philosopher] can ever take part" is belied by his own attempt to intervene in the politics of Syracuse when an opportunity arose, or so he thought, for philosophical reformation.[10] Plato never intended, of course, to become a citizen of the city he hoped to reform.

The claim of the philosopher in such a case is that he knows "the pattern set up in the heavens." He knows what ought to be done. He cannot just do it himself, however, and so he must look for a political instrument. A pliable prince is, for obvious practical reasons, the best possible instrument. But in principle any instrument will do—an aristocracy, a vanguard, a civil service, even the people will do, so long as its members are committed to philosophical truth and possessed of sovereign power. But clearly, the people raise the greatest difficulties. If they are not a many-headed monster, they are at least many-headed, difficult to educate and likely to disagree among themselves. Nor can the philosophical instrument be a majority among the people, for majorities in any genuine democracy are temporary, shifting, unstable. Truth is one, but the people have many opinions; truth is eternal, but the people continually change their minds. Here in its simplest form is the tension between philosophy and democracy.

The people's claim to rule does not rest upon their knowledge of truth (though it may, as in utilitarian thought, rest upon their knowledge of many smaller truths: the account that only they can give of their own pains and pleasures). The claim is most persuasively put, it seems to me, not in terms of what the people know but in terms of who they are. They are the subjects of the law, and if the law is to bind them as free men and women, they must also be its makers. This is Rousseau's argument. I do not propose to defend it here but only to consider some of its consequences. The argument has the effect of making law a function of popular will and not of reason as it had hitherto been understood, the reason of wise men, sages, and judges. The people are the successors of gods and absolutist kings, but not of philosophers. They may not know the right thing to do, but they claim a right to do what they think is right (literally, what pleases them).[11]

Rousseau himself pulled back from this claim, and most contemporary democrats would want to do so too. I can imagine three ways of pulling back and constraining democratic decisions, which I will outline briefly, drawing on Rousseau, but without attempting any explicit analysis of his arguments. First, one might impose a formal constraint on popular willing: the people must will generally.[12] They cannot single out (except in elections for public office) a particular individual or set of individuals from among themselves for special treatment. This is no bar to public assistance programs designed, say, for the sick or the old, for we can all get sick and we all hope to grow old. Its purpose is to rule out discrimination against individuals and groups who have, so to speak, proper names. Second, one might insist on the inalienability of the popular will and then on the indestructibility of those institutions and practices that guarantee the democratic character of the popular will: assembly, debate, elections, and so on. The people cannot renounce now their future right to will (or, no such renunciation can ever be legitimate or morally effective).[13] Nor can they deny to some group among themselves, with or without a proper name, the right to participate in future willing.

Clearly, these first two constraints open the way for some kind of review of popular decision-making, some kind of enforcement, against the people if necessary, of non-discrimination and democratic fights. Whoever undertakes this review and enforcement will have to make judgments about the discriminatory character of particular pieces of legislation and about the meaning for democratic politics of particular restrictions on free speech, assembly, and so on. But these judgments, though I do not want to underestimate either their importance or their difficulty, will be relatively limited in their effects compared to the sort of thing required by the third constraint. And it is on the third constraint that I want to focus, for I do not believe that philosophers in the heroic tradition can possibly be satisfied with the first two. Third, then, the people must will what is right. Rousseau says, must will the common good, and goes on to argue that the people will will the common good if they are a true people, a community, and not a mere collection of egoistic individuals and corporate groups.[14] Here the idea seems to be that there exists a single set—though not necessarily an exhaustive set—of correct or just laws that the assembled people, the voters or their representatives, may not get right. Often enough, they get it wrong, and then they require the guidance of a legislator or the restraint of a judge. Rousseau's legislator is simply the philosopher in heroic dress, and though Rousseau denies him the right to coerce the people, he insists on his right to deceive the people. The legislator speaks in the name of God, not of philosophy.[15] One might look for a parallel deception among contemporary judges. In any case, this third constraint surely raises the most serious questions about Rousseau's fundamental argument, that political legitimacy rests on will (consent) and not on reason (rightness).

[4]

The fundamental argument can be put in an appropriately paradoxical form: it is a feature of democratic government that the people have a right to act wrongly—in much the same way they have a right to act stupidly. I should say, they have a right to act wrongly within some area (and only, following the first two constraints, if the action is general over the area and does not preclude future democratic action within the area). Sovereignty is always sovereignty somewhere and with regard to some things, not everywhere and with regard to everything. The people can rightfully, let us say, enact a redistributive income tax, but they can only redistribute their own income, not those of some neighboring nation. What is crucial, however, is that the redistributive pattern they choose is not subject to authoritative correction in accordance with philosophical standards. It is subject to criticism, of course, but insofar as the critic is a democrat he will have to agree that, pending the conversion of the people to his position, the pattern they have chosen ought to be implemented.

Richard Wollheim has argued in a well-known article that democratic theory conceived in this way is not merely paradoxical in some loose sense; it is a strict paradox.[16] He constructs the paradox in three steps:

(1) As a citizen of a democratic community, I review the choices available to the community and conclude that *A* is the policy that ought to be implemented.
(2) The people, in their wisdom or their willfulness, choose policy *B*, the very opposite of *A*.
(3) I still think that policy *A* ought to be implemented, but now, as a committed democrat, I also think that policy *B* ought to be implemented. Hence, I think that both policies ought to be implemented. But this is incoherent.

The paradox probably depends too much upon its verbal form. We might imagine a more modest first person—so that the first step would go like this:

(1) I conclude that *A* is the policy the people ought to choose for implementation.

Then there would nothing incoherent about saying:

(3) Since the people didn't choose *A*, but chose *B* instead, I now conclude that *B* ought to be implemented.

This is not very interesting, but it is consistent, and I think it makes sense of the democratic position. What underlies Wollheim's version of the first step is a philosophical, and probably an antidemocratic, argument that has this form:

(1) I conclude that *A* is the right policy, and that it ought to be implemented *because it is right*.

But it is not at all obvious that a policy's rightness is the right reason for implementing it. It may only be the right reason for hoping that it will be implemented and so for defending it in the assembly. Suppose that there existed a push-button implementation system, and that the two buttons, marked *A* and *B*, were on my desk. Which one should I push, and for what reasons? Surely I cannot push *A* simply because I have decided that *A* is right. Who am I? As a citizen of a democratic community, I must wait for the people's decision, who have a right to decide. And then, if the people choose *B*, it is not the case that I face an existential choice, where my philosophical arguments point toward *A* and my democratic commitments point toward *B*, and there is no way to decide between them. There is a way to decide.

The distinction that I am trying to draw here, between having a right to decide and knowing the right decision, might be described in terms of procedural and substantive justice. Democrats, it might be said, are committed to procedural justice, and can only hope that the outcomes of just procedures will also be substantively just. But I am reluctant to accept that formulation because the line between procedure and substance seems to me less clear than it suggests. What is at stake in discussions about procedural justice is the distribution of power, and that is surely a substantive matter. No procedural arrangement can be defended except by some substantive argument, and every substantive argument (in political philosophy) issues also in some procedural arrangement. Democracy rests, as I have already suggested, on an argument about freedom and political obligation. Hence it is not only the case that the people have a procedural right to make the laws. On the democratic view, it is right that they make the laws—even if they make them wrongly.

Against this view, the heroic philosopher might argue that it can never be right to do wrong (not, at least, once we know or can know what is right). This is also, at least incipiently, an argument about the distribution of political power, and it has two implications. First, that the power of the people ought to be limited by the rightness of what they do; and second, that someone else ought to be empowered to review what the people do and step in when they move beyond those limits. Who else? In principle, I suppose, anyone who knows the truth about rightness. But in practice, in any ongoing political order, some group of people will have to be found who can be presumed to know the truth better or more consistently than the people as a whole do. This group will then be awarded a procedural right to intervene, grounded on a substantive argument about knowledge and moral truth.

Popular legislation might be reviewed democratically: in ancient Athens, for example, citizens concerned about the legitimacy of a particular decision of the assembly could appeal from the assembly as a whole to a smaller group of citizens, selected by lot and empanelled as a jury. The jury literally put the law on trial, with individual citizens acting as prosecutors and defense attorneys, and its verdict took precedence over the legislative act itself.[17] In this case, obviously, no special wisdom was claimed; the same argument or the same sort of argument would justify both the act and the verdict. More often, however, groups of this sort are constituted on aristocratic rather than democratic grounds. The appeal is from popular consciousness, particular interests, selfish or shortsighted policies to the superior understanding of the few: Hegel's corps of civil servants, Lenin's vanguard party, and so on. Ideally, the group to which the appeal is made must be involved in the community of ideas, oriented to action within it, but attuned at the same time to philosophers outside. In but not wholly in, so as to provide a match for the philosopher's withdrawal and return.

[5]

In the United States today, it is apparent that the nine judges of the Supreme Court have been assigned something like this role. The assignment is most clearly argued in the work of a group of contemporary law professors, all of whom are philosophers too or, at least, much influenced by political philosophy.[18] Indeed, the revival of political philosophy has had its most dramatic impact in schools of law—and for a reason that is not difficult to make out. In a settled democracy, with no revolution in prospect, judges are the most likely instruments of philosophical reformation. Of course, the conventional role of Supreme Court judges extends no further than the enforcement of a written constitution that itself rests on democratic consent and is subject to democratic amendment. And even when the judges act in ways that go beyond upholding the textual integrity of the constitution, they generally claim no special under-standing of truth and rightness but refer themselves instead to historical prece-dents, long-established legal principles, or common values. Nevertheless, the place they hold and the power they wield make it possible for them to impose philosophical constraints on democratic choice. And they are readily available (as the people are not) for philosophical instruction as to the nature of those constraints. I am concerned here with judges only insofar as they are in fact instructed—and with philosophers before judges because a number of philoso-phers seem so ready to provide the instruction. The tension between judicial review and democracy directly parallels the tension between philosophy and democracy. But the second is the deeper tension, for judges are likely to expand upon their constitutional rights or to sustain a program of expansion only when they are in the grip of a philosophical doctrine.

Now, judges and philosophers are (mostly) different sorts of people. One can imagine a philosopher-judge, but the union is uncommon. Judges are in an important sense members of the political community. Most of them have had careers as officeholders, or as political activists, or as advocates of this or that public policy. They have worked in the arena; they have participated in debates. When they are questioned at their confirmation hearings, they are presumed to have opinions of roughly the same sort as their questioners—commonplace opinions, much of the time, else they would never have been nominated. Once confirmed, to be sure, they set themselves at some distance from everyday politics; their special standing in a democracy requires a certain detachment and thoughtfulness. They don the robes of wisdom, and those robes constitute what might be called a philosophical temptation: to love wisdom better than the law. But judges are supposed to be wise in the ways of a particular legal tradition, which they share with their old professional and political associates.

The stance of the philosopher is very different. The truths he commonly seeks are universal and eternal, and it is unlikely that they can be found from the inside of any real and historic community. Hence the philosopher's withdrawal: he must deny himself the assurances of the commonplace. (He does not have to be confirmed.) To what sort of a place, then, does he withdraw? Most often, today, he constructs for himself (since he cannot, like Plato, discover for him-self) an ideal commonwealth, inhabited by beings who have none of the particu-lar characteristics and none of the opinions or commitments of his former fellow-citizens. He imagines a perfect meeting in an "original position" or "ideal speech situation" where the men and women in attendance are liberated from their own ideologies or subjected to universalizing rules of discourse. And then, he asks what principles, rules, constitutional arrangements these people would choose if they set out to create an actual political order.[19] They are, as it were, the philosophical representatives of the rest of us, and they legislate on our behalf. The philosopher himself, however, is the only actual inhabitant of the ideal commonwealth, the only actual participant in the perfect meeting. So the principles, rules, constitutions, with which he emerges are in fact the products of his own thinking, "designed at will in an orderly fashion," subject only to whatever constraints he imposes upon himself. Nor are any other participants required, even when the decision procedure of the ideal commonwealth is conceived in terms of consensus or unanimity. For if there were another person present, he would either be identical to the philosopher, subject to the same constraints and so led to say the same things and move toward the same conclusions, or he would be a particular person with historically derived characteristics and opinions and then his presence would undermine the universality of the argument.

The philosopher returns from his retreat with conclusions that are different from the conclusions of any actual democratic debate. At least, they have, or he claims for them, a different status. They embody what is right, which is to say for our present purposes, they have been agreed upon by a set of ideal representatives, whereas the conclusions reached through democratic debate are merely agreed upon by the people or by their actual representatives. The people or their representatives might then be invited to revise their own conclusions in the light of the philosopher's work. I suppose that this is an invitation implicitly extended every time a philosopher publishes a book. At the moment of publication, at least, he is a proper democrat: his book is a gift to the people. But the gift is rarely appreciated. In the political arena, the philosopher's truths are likely to be turned into one more set of opinions, tried out, argued about, adopted in part, repudiated in part, or ignored. Judges, on the other hand, may well be persuaded to give the philosopher a different sort of hearing. Their special role in the democratic community is connected, as I have already said, to their thoughtfulness, and thoughtfulness is a philosophical posture: judicial status can only be enhanced by a little real philosophy. Moreover, judges are admirably placed to mediate between the opinions (temporarily) established in the democratic arena and the truths worked out in the ideal commonwealth. Through the art of interpretation, they can do what Rousseau's legislator does through the art of divination.[20]

[6]

Consider the case of "rights." Our ideal representatives in philosophical seclusion come up with a list of rights that attach to each individual human being. Let us assume that the list is, as it commonly is among contemporary philosophers, deeply meditated and serious. The enumerated rights form a coherent whole, suggesting what it might mean to recognize in another man or woman the special qualities of moral agency and personality. The philosophical list differs from the list currently established in the law, but it also overlaps with the law and with what we can think of as the suburbs of the law, the cluster of opinions, values, and traditions to which we escape, if we can, whenever we find the inner city of the law constraining. Now the philosopher—I mean still the heroic philosopher, the philosopher as founder—invites the judges to attempt a more organized escape, from the law, through the suburbs, to the ideal commonwealth beyond. The invitation is all the more urgent in that rights are at stake. For rights have this special characteristic: their violation requires immediate relief or reparation. And judges are not merely the available, they are also the appropriate instruments of relief and reparation.[21]

In effect, the philosopher proposes a decision procedure for judges modeled on that of the ideal commonwealth. This is in part flattery, but it also has a factual rationale. For the discussions of judges among themselves really do resemble the arguments that go on in the ideal commonwealth (in the mind of the philosopher) much more closely than democratic debate can ever do. And it seems plausible to say that rights are more likely to be defined correctly by the reflection of the few than by the votes of the many.[22] So the philosopher asks the judges to recapitulate in their chambers the argument he has already worked out in solitary retreat, and then to give that argument "the utility of practice" first by locating it in the law or in the traditions and values that surround the law and then by deciding cases in its terms. When necessary, the judges must preempt or overrule legislative decisions. This is the crucial point, for it is here that the tension between philosophy and democracy takes on material form.

The legislature is, if not the reality, then at least the effective representation of the people assembled to rule themselves. Its members have a right to act within an area. Judicially enforced rights can be understood in two different but complementary ways with regard to this area. First, they are boundaries circumscribing it. From this view, a simple equation follows: the more extensive the list of rights, the wider the range of judicial enforcement, the less room there is for legislative choice. The more rights the judges award to the people as individuals, the less free the people are as a decision-making body. Or, second, rights are principles that structure activities within the area, shaping policies and institutions. Then judges do not merely operate at the boundaries, however wide or narrow the boundaries are. Their judgments represent deep penetration raids into the area of legislative decision.[23] Now, all three of the constraints on popular willing that I described earlier can be conceived in either of these ways, as defense or as penetration. But it is clear, I think, that the third constraint simultaneously narrows the boundaries and permits deeper raids. As soon as the philosophical list of rights extends beyond the twin bans on legal discrimination and political repression, it invites judicial activity that is radically intrusive on what might be called democratic space.

But this, it can be objected, is to consider rights only in the formal sense, ignoring their content. And their content may well enhance rather than circumscribe popular choice. Imagine, for example, a philosophically and then judicially recognized right to welfare.[24] The purpose of such a right is plain enough. It would guarantee to each citizen the opportunity to exercise his citizenship, and that is an opportunity he could hardly be said to have, or to have in any meaningful fashion, if he were starving to death or desperately seeking shelter for himself and his family. A defensible right, surely, and yet the argument I have just sketched still holds. For the judicial enforcement of welfare rights would radically reduce the reach of democratic decision. Henceforth, the judges would decide, and as cases accumulated, they would decide in increasing detail, what the scope and character of the welfare system should be and what sorts of redistribution it required. Such decisions would clearly involve significant judicial control of the state budget and, indirectly at least, of the level of taxation—the very issues over which the democratic revolution was originally fought.

This sort of thing would be easier for committed democrats if the expanded list of rights were incorporated into the constitution through a popularly controlled amending process. Then there would exist some democratic basis for the new (undemocratic) power of philosophers and judges. The people would, I think, be ill-advised to agree to such an incorporation and to surrender so large a part of their day-to-day authority. In the modern state, however, that authority is exercised so indirectly—it is so far, in fact, from being day-to-day authority—that they might feel the surrender to be a minor matter. The rights they gain as individuals (in this case, to welfare services from a benevolent bureaucracy) might in their view far outweigh the rights they lose as members. And so it is not implausible to imagine the constitutional establishment of something like, say, Rawls's two principles of justice.[25] Then the entire area of distributive justice would effectively be handed over to the courts. What a range of decisions they would have to make! Imagine a class action suit testing the meaning of the difference principle. The judges would have to decide whether the class represented in the suit was really the most disadvantaged class in the society (or whether all or enough of its members fell within that class). And if it was (or if they did), the judges would then have to decide what rights followed from the difference principle under the material conditions currently prevailing. No doubt, they would be driven to consult experts and officials in making these decisions. It would make little sense for them to consult the legislature, however, for to these questions, if rights are really at issue, there must be a right answer— and this answer is more likely to be known by philosophers, judges, experts, and officials than by ordinary citizens or their political representatives.[26]

Still, if the people came to feel oppressed by the new authorities that they had established, they could always disestablish them. The amending process would still be available, though it might be the case that the gradual erosion of legislative energy would make it less available in practice than it was in principle.[27] Partly for this reason, and partly for reasons to which I will now turn, I want to argue that philosophers should not be too quick to seek out the judicial (or any other) instrument, and that judges, though they must to some extent be philosophers of the law, should not be too quick to turn themselves into political philosophers. It is a mistake to attempt any extensive incorporation of philosophical principles into the law either by interpretation or amendment. For that is, in either case, to take them out of the political arena where they properly belong. The interventions of philosophers should be limited to the gifts they bring. Else they are like Greeks bringing gifts, of whom the people should beware, for what they have in mind is the capture of the city.

[7]

"The philosopher is not a citizen of any community of ideas. That is what makes him into a philosopher." I have taken these sentences to mean that the political philosopher must separate himself from the political community, cut himself loose from affective ties and conventional ideas. Only then can he ask and struggle to answer the deepest questions about the meaning and purpose of political association and the appropriate structure of the community (of every community) and its government. This kind of knowledge one can have only from the outside. Inside, another kind of knowledge is available, more limited, more particular in character. I shall call it political rather than philosophical knowledge. It answers the questions: What is the meaning and purpose of *this* association? What is the appropriate structure of *our* community and government? Even if we assume that there are right answers to these last questions (and it is doubtful that the particular questions have right answers even if the general questions do), it is nevertheless the case that there will be as many right answers as there are communities. Outside the communities, however, there is only one right answer. As there are many caves but only one sun, so political knowing is particular and pluralist in character, while philosophical knowing is universalist and singular. The political success of philosophers, then, would have the effect of enforcing a singular over a pluralist truth, that is, of reiterating the structure of the ideal commonwealth in every previously particularist community. Imagine not one but a dozen philosopher kings: their realms would be identically fashioned and identically governed, except for those adjustments required by an ineradicably particularist geography. (If God were a philosopher king, He would have allocated to each community an identical or equivalent set of geographic conditions.) The case would be the same with a dozen communities founded in the original position: there is only one original position. And it would be the same again with a dozen communities shaped by undistorted communication among an idealized set of members: for it is a feature of undistorted communication, as distinct from ordinary talk, that only a very few things can be said.[28]

Now, we may or may not be ready to assign value to particularism and pluralism. It is not easy to know how to decide. For pluralism implies a range of instances—a range of opinions, structures, regimes, policies—with regard to each of which we are likely to feel differently. We might value the range or the idea of a range and yet be appalled by a large number of the instances, and then search for some principle of exclusion. Most pluralists are in fact constrained pluralists, and the constraints they defend derive from universal principles. Can it still be said that they value pluralism? They merely like variety, perhaps, or they are not ready yet to make up their minds about every case, or they are tolerant, or indifferent. Or they have an instrumentalist view: many social experiments will lead one day (but that day is far off) to a single truth. All these are philosophical perspectives in the sense that they require a standpoint outside the range. And from that standpoint, I suspect, pluralism will always be an uncertain value at best. But most people stand differently. They are inside their own communities, and they value their own opinions and conventions. They come to pluralism only through an act of empathy and identification, recognizing that other people have feelings like their own. Similarly, the philosopher might come to pluralism by imagining himself a citizen of every community rather than of none. But then he might lose that firm sense of himself and his solitude that makes him a philosopher, and the gifts he brings might be of less value than they are.

I do not mean to underestimate those gifts. But it is important now to suggest that the value of universal truth is as uncertain when seen from inside a particular community as is the value of pluralism when seen from outside every particular community. Uncertain, I mean to say, not unreal or negligible: for I do not doubt that particular communities improve themselves by aspiring to realize universal truths and by incorporating (particular) features of philosophical doctrine into their own ways of life. And this the citizens also understand. But from their standpoint, it will not always be obvious that the rights, say, of abstract men and women, the inhabitants of some ideal commonwealth, ought to be enforced here and now. They are likely to have two worries about any such enforcement. First of all, it will involve overriding their own traditions, conventions, and expectations. These are, of course, readily accessible to philosophical criticism; they were not "designed at will in an orderly fashion" by a founder or a sage; they are the result of historical negotiation, intrigue, and struggle. But that is just the point. The products of a shared experience, they are valued by the people over the philosopher's gifts because they belong to the people and the gifts do not—much as I might value some familiar and much-used possession and feel uneasy with a new, more perfect model.

The second worry is more closely connected to democratic principle. It is not only the familiar products of their experience that the people value, but the experience itself, the process through which the products were produced. And they will have some difficulty understanding why the hypothetical experience of abstract men and women should take precedence over their own history. Indeed, the claim of the heroic philosopher must be that the first sort of experience not only takes precedence over but effectively replaces the second. Wherever universal truth has been established, there is no room for negotiation, intrigue, and struggle. Hence, it looks as if the political life of the community is to be permanently interrupted. Within some significant part of the area over which citizens had once moved freely, they are no longer to move at all. Why should they accept that? They might well choose politics over truth, and that choice, if they make it, will make in turn for pluralism. Any historical community whose members shape their own institutions and laws will necessarily produce a particular and not a universal way of life. That particularity can be overcome only from the outside and only by repressing internal political processes.

But this second worry, which is the more important of the two, is probably exaggerated. For philosophical doctrine, like the law itself, requires interpretation before it can be enforced. Interpretations must be particular in character, and they invite real and not merely hypothetical argument. Unless the philosopher wins "entire sovereignty" for himself, then, his victory will not in fact interrupt or cut off political activity. If his victory were to take the form that I have been imagining, it would merely shift the focus of political activity from legislatures to courts, from law-making to litigation. On the other hand, insofar as it is a victory at all, it has to have some universalizing tendencies; at least, it has to impose some constraints on the pluralizing tendencies of a freewheeling politics. The more the judges are "strict constructionists" of philosophical doctrine, the more the different communities they rule will look alike and the more the collective choices of the citizens will be confined. So the exaggeration makes a point: the citizens have, to whatever degree, lost control over their own lives. And then they have no reason, no democratic reason, for obeying the decrees of the judges.

[8]

All this might be avoided, of course, if the judges adopted a policy of "judicial restraint," preempting or overruling legislative decisions only in rare and extreme cases. But I would suggest that judicial restraint, like judicial intervention, draws its force from some deeper philosophical view. Historically, restraint has been connected with skepticism or relativism.[29] It is, of course, true that philosophical views change, and judges must be wary of falling in with some passing fashion. But I am inclined to think that judicial restraint is consistent with the strongest claims that philosophers make for the truths they discover or construct. For there is a certain attitude that properly accompanies such claims, and has its origins in the ideal commonwealth or the perfect meeting from which the claims derive. This attitude is philosophical restraint, and it is simply the respect that outsiders owe to the decisions that citizens make among themselves and for themselves. The philosopher has withdrawn from the community. It is precisely because the knowledge he seeks can only be found outside this particular place that it yields no rights inside.

At the same time, it has to be said that since the philosopher's withdrawal is speculative only, he loses none of the rights he has as an ordinary citizen. His opinions are worth as much as any other citizen's; he is entitled like anyone else to work for their implementation, to argue, intrigue, struggle, and so on. But when he acts in these ways, he is an engaged philosopher, that is, a sophist, critic, publicist, or intellectual, and he must accept the risks of those social roles. I do not mean that he must accept the risk of death; that will depend upon the conditions of engagement in his community, and philosophers, like other citizens, will hope for something better than civil war and political persecution. I have in mind two different sorts of risks. The first is the risk of defeat, for though the engaged philosopher can still claim to be right, he cannot claim any of the privileges of rightness. He must live with the ordinary odds of democratic politics. The second is the risk of particularism, which is, perhaps, another kind of defeat for philosophy. Engagement always involves a loss—not total but serious enough—of distance, critical perspective, objectivity, and so on. The sophist, critic, publicist, or intellectual must address the concerns of his fellow citizens, try to answer their questions, weave his arguments into the fabric of their history. He must, indeed, make himself a *fellow* citizen in the community of ideas, and then he will be unable to avoid entirely the moral and even the emotional entanglements of citizenship. He may hold fast to the philosophical truths of natural law, distributive justice, or human rights, but his political arguments are most likely to look like some makeshift version of those truths, adapted to the needs of a particular people: from the standpoint of the original position, provincial; from the standpoint of the ideal speech situation, ideological.

Perhaps we should say that, once engaged, naturalized again into the community of ideas, the philosopher is like a political poet, Shelley's legislator, not Rousseau's. Though he still hopes that his arguments reach beyond his own community, he is first of all "local." And so he must be ready to forsake the prerogatives of distance, coherent design, and entire sovereignty, and seek instead with "thoughts that breathe and words that burn," to reach and move his own people. And he must give up any more direct means to establish the ideal commonwealth. That surrender is philosophical restraint.

Judicial restraint follows (and so does vanguard restraint and bureaucratic restraint). The judges must hold themselves as closely as they can to the decisions of the democratic assembly, enforcing first of all the basic political rights that serve to sustain the character of that assembly and protecting its members from discriminatory legislation. They are not to enforce rights beyond these, unless they are authorized to do so by a democratic decision. And it does not matter to the judges as judges that a more extensive list of rights can be, or that it has been, validated elsewhere. Elsewhere does not count.

Once again, I do not want to deny that rights can be validated elsewhere. Indeed, the most general truths of politics and morality can only be validated in the philosophical realm, and that realm has its place outside, beyond, separate from every particular community. But philosophical validation and political authorization are two entirely different things. They belong to two entirely distinct spheres of human activity. Authorization is the work of citizens governing themselves among themselves. Validation is the work of the philosopher reasoning alone in a world he inhabits alone or fills with the products of his own speculations. Democracy has no claims in the philosophical realm, and philosophers have no special rights in the political community. In the world of opinion, truth is indeed another opinion, and the philosopher is only another opinion-maker.

NOTES

1. Ludwig Wittgenstein, *Zettel*, ed. G. E. M. Anscombe and G. H. von Wright (Berkeley: University of California Press, 1970), 455.

2. Ludwig Wittgenstein, *Philosophical Investigations*, trans. G. E. M. Anscombe (New York: Macmillan, 1958), para. 124.

3. For an account of this special form of philosophical heroism, see Sheldon S. Wolin, *Hobbes and the Epic Tradition of Political Theory* (Los Angeles: University of California Press, 1970).

4. René Descartes, *Discourse on Method*, trans. Arthur Wollaston (Harmondsworth: Penguin, 1960), 44–45.

5. Thomas Hobbes, *Leviathan*, pt. II, chap. 31.

6. C. P. Cavafy, "The First Step," in *The Complete Poems of Cavafy*, trans. Rae Dalven (New York: Harcourt Brace Jovanovich, 1976), 6.

7. W. H. Auden, "Shorts II," in *Collected Poems*, ed. Edward Mendelson (New York: Random House, 1976).

8. "In Memory of W. B. Yeats," in *The English Auden: Poems, Essays and Dramatic Writings, 1927–1939*, ed. Edward Mendelson (New York: Random House, 1977).

9. *The Letters of John Keats*, ed. M. B. Forman (London: Oxford University Press, 1952), 67.

10. *The Republic of Plato*, trans. F. M. Cornford (New York: Oxford University Press, 1945), 591A–592B.

11. Thus an Athenian orator to the assembly: "It is in your power, rightly, to dispose of what belongs to you—well, or, if you wish, ill." Quoted in K. J. Dover, *Greek Popular Morality in the Time of Plato and Aristotle* (Berkeley: University of California Press, 1974), 290–91.

12. Jean-Jacques Rousseau, *The Social Contract*, bk. 2, chaps. 4, 6.

13. This follows, I think, from the argument that the general will is inalienable, though Rousseau wants to make even more of inalienability than this—as in his attack on representation, bk. 3, chap. 15.

14. Ibid., bk. 2, chap. 3 and *passim*.

15. Ibid., chap. 7.

16. Richard Wollheim, "A Paradox in the Theory of Democracy," in *Philosophy, Politics and Society* (2d ser.), ed. Peter Laslett and W. G. Runciman (Oxford: Basil Blackwell, 1962), 71–87. I should stress that the argument here is about implementation, not obedience. What is at issue is how or for what reasons policies should be chosen for the community as a whole. Whether individual citizens should uphold this or that policy once it has been chosen, or assist in carrying it out, is another question.

17. A. H. M. Jones, *Athenian Democracy* (Oxford: Basil Blackwell, 1960), 122–23.

18. See, for example, Ronald Dworkin, *Taking Rights Seriously* (Cambridge: Harvard University Press, 1977); Frank Michelman, "In Pursuit of Constitutional Welfare Rights," *University of Pennsylvania Law Review* 121:5 (May 1973), 962–1019; Owen Fiss, "The Forms of Justice," *Harvard Law Review* 93:1 (November 1979), 1–58; Bruce Ackerman, *Social Justice in the Liberal State* (New Haven: Yale University Press, 1980).

19. In this mode of argument, John Rawls is obviously the great pioneer. But the specific use of the new philosophy with which I am concerned is not advocated by him in *A Theory of Justice* (Cambridge: Harvard University Press, 1971) or in any subsequent articles.

20. Like Rousseau's legislator again, the judges have no direct coercive power of their own: in some ultimate sense, they must always look for support among the people or among alternative political elites. Hence the phrase "judicial tyranny," applied to the enforcement of some philosophically but not democratically validated position, is always a piece of hyperbole. On the other hand, there are forms of authority, short of tyranny, that raise problems for democratic government.

21. The special invitation and the sense of urgency are most clear in Ronald Dworkin, *Taking Rights Seriously* (Cambridge: Harvard University Press, 1977). But Dworkin seems to believe that the ideal commonwealth actually exists, so to speak, in the suburbs. The set of philosophically validated rights can also be validated, he argues, in terms of the constitutional history and the standing legal principles of the United States, and when judges enforce these rights they are doing what they ought to be doing, given the sort of government we have. For a different reading of our constitutional history, see Richard Ely, *Democracy and Distrust* (Cambridge: Harvard University Press, 1980). Ely argues for something very much like the two constraints that I have defended. For him, too, the ideal commonwealth lies somewhere beyond the U.S. Constitution. It is the proper goal of parties and movements, not of courts.

22. For a careful and rather tentative argument to this effect, see T. M. Scanlon, "Due Process" in *Nomos* 22, ed. R. Pennock and J. Chapman (New York: New York University Press, 1977), 120–21.

23. Fiss provides some clear examples in "The Forms of Justice."

24. Cf. Michelman "Welfare Rights," and also "On Protecting the Poor Through the Fourteenth Amendment," *Harvard Law Review* 83: 1 (November 1969).

25. For a proposal to this effect, see Amy Gutmann, *Liberal Equality* (Cambridge: Cambridge University Press, 1980), 199.

26. Dworkin, *Taking Rights Seriously*, esp. chaps. 4, 13.

27. Judicial interventions on behalf of individual rights broadly understood may also lead to an erosion of popular energies—at least on the left. For a brief argument to this effect, see my article "The Left and the Courts," *Dissent* (Spring 1981).

28. Even if we were to connect philosophical conclusions to some set of historical

circumstances, as Habermas does when he imagines "discursive will-formation" occurring "at a given stage in the development of productive forces," or as Rawls does when he suggests that the principles worked out in the original position apply only to "democratic societies under modern conditions," it remains true that the conclusions are objectively true or right for a range of particular communities, without regard to the actual politics of those communities. See Jürgen Habermas, *Legitimation Crisis* (Boston: Beacon, 1975), 113; Rawls, "Kantian Constructivism in Moral Theory," *Journal of Philosophy* 77:9 (September 1980), 518.

29. See, for example, Ely, *Democracy and Distrust*, 57–59.

CHAPTER TWO

A Critique of Philosophical Conversation

[1]

I am not concerned in this paper with the fact that philosophers talk to one another; there is nothing to worry about in that. Nor am I concerned with the fact that ordinary people sometimes talk about "philosophical" questions—necessity, freedom, justice, the meaning of life and death. I assume that conversations of these sorts are normal and innocent. They go on for a while; they are sometimes interesting and sometimes not; they do not reach any firm conclusions; and at some point they just stop. People get tired or bored, or they want to eat lunch, or they think of something else they have to do or someone else to whom they want to talk. These conversations have no authoritative moments, and they generate no authoritative claims; they lie outside my interests here. I want to examine constructed or designed conversations, where the whole purpose of the construction or design is to produce conversational endings, finished arguments, agreed-upon propositions—conclusions, in short, whose truth value or moral rightness the rest of us will be obliged to acknowledge.

Implicit in the constructed conversation is the value of agreement. There may be stronger foundations for truth or rightness claims, but this is the most obvious one—indeed, how would we know that any other was stronger unless we (or some of us, talking things through) agreed that it was? Even the agreement of one other person, who had begun by disagreeing, makes a strong impression; for we know how hard it is to get two intelligent people fixed on one conclusion. The force of Plato's dialogues derives in part from this knowledge. The dialogues begin with contention and end with a virtually total agreement. At the end, they have hardly any dialogical qualities; they are monologues interrupted by the affirmations of a one-man chorus—here played by Glaucon in the *Republic*, responding to a succession of arguments presented at some length by Socrates:

> Certainly.
> Of course.
> Inevitably.
> Yes, that is bound to be so.
> It must.
> Well, that is certainly a fact.
> Yes.
> No, tell me.
> I entirely agree.[1]

Affirmations of this sort add to the force of a philosophical argument or, at least, they make the argument seem more forceful (why else would philosophers write dialogues?) because the acquiescent interlocutor speaks not only for himself but for the reader as well. Plato has built our agreement into his discourse, and while we can always refuse to agree, we feel a certain pressure to go along, to join the chorus. And yet we know that philosophical dialogues do not really end in this way, with one of the protagonists on his verbal knees, desperately searching for new ways to say yes. Agreements do arise among philosophers and, more generally, across societies; they develop very slowly, over long periods of time; they are always rough and incomplete; and the processes through which they arise are only in part conversational. I shall have more to say about these processes later on; right now I need only note that the conversations they include never really end. Choral affirmations make nothing firm.

Still, there is something engaging in the spectacle of the philosophical hero who triumphs over his opponents by reducing them to helpless agreement (the philosophical equivalent of surrender and captivity in time of war). More give and take in the dialogue would make for greater realism but probably not for greater persuasiveness. If we are not wholly persuaded, it is because of our own experience of argument where, even when we think we have done very well, we do not reach to, we only dream about, Platonic triumphalism. Certain sorts of arguments in the real world do have conventionally fixed endings, and these endings often represent victories of one sort or another; but these are not victories that carry philosophical certainty with them. Consider, for example, the debates that go on in a political assembly (where the right policy is at issue) or the deliberations of a jury (where truth itself is at issue). The debates end at some point with a vote, and the policy that commands majority support is then enforced; but its opponents are unlikely to concede that it is the right policy simply because the majority supports it. They will concede only that it is, for the moment, the policy that it is right to enforce. The deliberations of a jury are closer to philosophical argument, in part because the jurors (unlike the members of the assembly) are supposed to have no direct or material interest in the outcomes they determine. They deliberate until they reach a *verdict*, that is, a true speech, and we enforce the verdict as if it were really true. In fact, it is true only by convention (in virtue of previous agreements). It is not the truth of the verdict which lends authority to the jury system, but the system that makes the verdict authoritative. We know that juries make mistakes even when their deliberations are genuinely disinterested and their conclusions unanimous.[2] And, similarly, we know that philosophers, even when they succeed in persuading their immediate opponents, are often wrong—at least, other philosophers always come along who tell us so.

Plato's mistake, we might say, was to write dialogues which lay claim to verisimilitude—with real locations and well-known protagonists—but which do not in fact resemble our own arguments about philosophical (or any other) questions. Anyone who writes a dialogue (rather than a design for a dialogue), anyone who imagines and reports an argument between or among philosophical characters, faces a difficult dilemma. For literary if not philosophical reasons, he must make some claim on his readers' sense of what good talk is really like, and then either his conclusions and choral affirmations will not ring true or he must end inconclusively. There are not many examples of inconclusive endings, but David Hume's *Dialogues Concerning Natural Religion* demonstrate the possibility. Hume's skepticism seems to create a kind of "negative capability"—a readiness to resist philosophical triumph and forgo choral affirmation. The result is that people come away from reading the *Dialogues* unsure who it is among the characters who speaks for Hume.[3] His readers resemble men and women in an actual conversation who disagree the next day about who said what, and with what intent. It is obvious that no sure truths about natural religion have been delivered to them.

Is there some way of delivering truth (or moral rightness) through conversation? Not, I think, through actual and not through literary conversations. Real talk, even if it is only imagined, makes for disagreement as often as for agreement, and neither one is anything more than temporary. Moreover, the motives for the one are as suspect as the motives for the other: if people often disagree only because of interest, pride, or spite, they also often agree only because of weakness, fear, or ignorance. Agreement in actual conversations is no more definitive, no more foundational, than disagreement. What we require for the sake of truth is a hypothetical (which is not the same as a literary) conversation whose protagonists are protected against both bad agreements and bad disagreements. Hence the need for a design, a set of rules which will determine who exactly the protagonists are and what they can say. Working out the design is a major enterprise in contemporary moral and political philosophy. Curiously, once one has a conversational design, it is hardly necessary to have a conversation.

[2]

There are by now a number of available designs. I want to write about them in general terms, though also with some particular references. I acknowledge in advance that the particular references will not do justice to the complexity and sophistication of the theories involved. It takes a big theory to replace real talk. In one way or another, each of the theories must cope with the chief causes of disagreement—particular interests, relationships, and values; and it must cope with the chief causes of inauthentic or false agreement—inequality and misinformation. Since all these causes occur regularly in the real world, theorists are driven to design an ideal conversational setting and then an ideal speaker and/or an ideal set of speech acts. Consider now the possible forms of this idealism.

The setting obviously cannot be the assembly or the jury room or any other actual social or political environment. All these presuppose some institutional arrangements, but what institutional arrangements are morally preferable is one of the things that the conversation is supposed to decide. What is necessary is a change of venue, as when a jury moves from the neighborhood of a crime to some more distant place, where the jurors will be less exposed to rumor, prejudice, and fear. In this case, however, no known venue is suitable. Hypothetical conversations take place in asocial space. The speakers may be provided with information about a particular society (and a particular historical moment: "a given stage," as Jürgen Habermas says, "in the development of productive forces"[4]), but they cannot *be there*, even hypothetically, lest they gather information for themselves and make mistakes. As with jurors, ideal speakers are denied access to newspapers, magazines, television, other people. Or, rather, only one paper or magazine is allowed, which provides the best available account of whatever the speakers need to know—much as a certain set of facts is stipulated by the opposing attorneys in a courtroom (though these facts do not necessarily add up to "the best available account").

The speakers themselves are also idealized, designed or programmed in such a way that certain words, and not others, will come naturally to their lips. First of all, they are one another's equals, and they must know themselves to be one another's equals; arrogance and pride of place, deference and humility, are rooted out of their minds. This can be accomplished by stipulation: they are to speak as if (with the understanding that) all relationships of subordination have been abolished. Conversational equality reflects a hypothetical social equality (but is not the conversation supposed to produce, among other things, an argument for or against social equality?). Alternatively, the equality of speakers can be accomplished without the "as if," by dropping the Rawlsian "veil of ignorance" and denying them any knowledge of their own standing in the actually existing hierarchy of class and status. They are then equally ignorant of their sociological place and of the feelings that it engenders.[5] Or equality can be given effect later on, as we will see, by policing what they can say once the conversation begins.

Second, the speakers are fully and identically informed about the real world —about what Habermas calls "the limiting conditions and functional imperatives of their society."[6] One body of knowledge, uniform and uncontroverted, is possessed in common by all speakers; now they are equally knowledgeable; they share a sociology, perhaps also a cosmology.

Third, they are set free from their own particular interests and values. This is the most complex of the idealizations, and its precise form varies with the philosophical goal of the hypothetical conversation. In Rawls's model, the ideal speakers know that they have interests and values of their own and that they will want to assert them, but they do not know anything at all about the content of these interests and values. Their conversations will therefore produce a world safe for individual men and women who plan a life of self-assertion, who intend, that is, to maximize their own interests and values, whatever these are. In Habermas's model, by contrast, the ideal speakers have full self-knowledge but are internally committed to assert only those interests and values which can be universalized; all others are somehow repressed. Their conversations will produce something more like a sense of the general interest or the common good and then a set of principles for a community of cooperating citizens. The contrast suggests the dominance of design over discourse. "One extracts from the ideal speech situation," writes Seyla Benhabib of the Habermasian model, "what one has . . . put into it."[7] The case is the same with the original position.

Whatever one does not "put into" the speakers one must put into their speech. Before anyone says anything, the speech act must be described so as to fix limits on what can be said. Habermas argues for "unconstrained communication," but he means only (!) to exclude the constraints of force and fraud, of deference, fear, flattery, and ignorance. His speakers have equal rights to initiate the conversation and to resume it; to assert, recommend, and explain their own positions; and to challenge the positions of other speakers. But the universalization requirement is a powerful constraint. Habermas insists that it is no more than the mutually understood requirement of actual speech—"demanding," indeed, but also "pre-theoretical."[8] In fact, universalization has a theoretical purpose, which stands in sharp contrast to the purpose of many actual conversations: it is intended to rule out bargaining and compromise (the negotiation of particular interests) and to press the speakers toward a preordained harmony. Justice is not, on Habermas's view, a negotiated settlement, a *modus vivendi*, fair to all its egoistic and rational subjects. It is a common life, the terms of which are fixed by the general will of a body of citizens—"what all can will in agreement to be a universal norm."[9] Habermas defends a position that is very much like Rousseau's, though Rousseau wisely renounced the hope that one could reach that position conversationally. We discover the general will, he wrote, if, when the people deliberate, the citizens "have no communication one with another."[10] But it probably does not make much difference whether there are no speech acts at all (but only internal reflection on the common good) or none but universalizing speech acts.

Bruce Ackerman's account of "liberal dialogue," by contrast, calls for external restraint rather than an internal commitment to universalization. Any claims his speakers make for the precedence of their own interests or the superiority of their own values are simply disallowed, stricken from the conversational record. If we control speech from the outside, he argues, then it will not be necessary to idealize the speakers or even the speech acts. The participants in his dialogues are real people (or better, they are typical people, with names like Democrat, Elitist, Advantaged, Disadvantaged, and so on—Ackerman's scripts are allegorical dramas), and they talk, more or less, the way real people talk. But their conversation is patrolled by a policewoman (whose name is Commander).[11] This is supposed to make the actual words of the speakers and their exchanges with one another more important than they are for Rawls or Habermas, who are focused on design rather than exchange. If one knows the mandate of the policewoman, however, and if one accepts the reasons for the mandate, it is easy to write the conversational scripts, just as Ackerman does. The scripts are merely illustrative, and the argument they illustrate is probably best defended monologically. But Ackerman's idea of a patrolled conversation points to an important fact about all these philosophical efforts: they are armed, one way or another, against the indeterminacy of natural conversation. The talk proceeds by design to a designated end. Agreement at the end is certain, and once it is reached it is equally certain, so long as the design is in place, that it will be sustained (or, if the conversation is resumed, that it will be reproduced). New speakers will not have much more to say than "That sounds right," or "I can think of no objections," or "I entirely agree." In an Ackermanian dialogue, the speakers might try to object, but their objections will regularly be disallowed by the Commander, and so the end will be, as it often is in Ackerman's scripts, "(silence)."[12]

[3]

I said earlier that the conversational project presupposes the value of agreement; it also presupposes the possibility of agreement. Acquiescence is not enough, nor a readiness to go along, make no trouble, think about other things. What is required is rational and explicit agreement; Ackerman's "silence" is an acknowledgment of philosophical defeat and so stands in for full consent to the victor's position. Rawls guarantees agreement with his veil of ignorance, which separates the speakers from any reasons they might have for disagreeing. The policewoman in Ackerman's account plays an analogous role. But Habermas takes a larger risk and makes a more radical assumption. He apparently believes that conversation subject to the universalization constraint will produce among the speakers what Steven Lukes calls "an endogenous change of preferences . . . such that preferences, tastes, values, ideals, plans of life, etc., will to some large degree (to what degree?) be unified and no longer conflict."[13] But what possible reason do we have for joining in this belief? Perhaps Habermas also thinks that there are knock-down arguments (about distributive justice, for example) just waiting to be made. Or perhaps he thinks that such arguments have already been made but not in ideal conditions, and so they have been denied their proper response, that is, the Platonic chorus of affirmation. Both these views are highly unlikely.

We can best see the unlikelihood of philosophical agreement by consulting what I have already described as the actual and inconclusive conversations of living (rather than hypothetical) philosophers. For these conversations bear some resemblance to Habermas's ideal speech: the participants think of themselves as rough equals, though some of them speak with greater authority and are listened to with greater respect than others; they share a body of information, though always with marginal disagreements; and they aim fairly steadily, except for a few renegades, at universalization. Yet they reach no agreement among themselves; they produce again and again the philosophical equivalents of hung juries. Some philosophers, earnestly carrying on an internal dialogue, reach agreement within themselves, but that does not have the weight of an external consensus. The "others" are always a problem.

Why are they a problem? I suppose that the reasons can always be met (or avoided) by further idealization. Among philosophers, for example, there is the desire to carve out one's own position, to find the way by oneself, to make an original argument.[14] So each speaker criticizes, amends, or rejects the claims of the previous speaker: What would be the point of agreeing? Perhaps Rawls's veil would conceal from the speakers this intensely felt interest in notice and praise; and then they might meekly join the chorus of support for the most persuasive speech. Habermas insists that speakers must always be bound by the better argument—the tightest constraint of all so long as we can recognize the better argument. But most speakers quite honestly think that their own arguments are the better ones. Sometimes they might acknowledge that they are not making the better argument then and there: so the conversation ends or one of the speakers walks out (like Demea in Hume's *Dialogues,* who "did not at all relish the latter part of the discourse; and . . . took occasion, soon after, on some pretense or other, to leave the company").[15] But such people are commonly saved by the brilliant afterthought, "I should have said . . ."—and that, they tell themselves, would have turned the argument around. How can it ever be certain that the better argument in any particular conversation is the best possible argument? It rarely happens among philosophers, but it is always possible to agree too soon.

Perhaps none of this matters; ideal speech is a thought experiment, and we can abstract from all human infirmities. If conversation itself serves to bring out our infirmities, we can abstract from that, too, Thus Rawls, who acknowledges that, for his purposes, no more than one speaker is necessary. What we hear from behind the veil of ignorance is really a philosophical soliloquy.[16] The argument does not depend on any exchange of views; if we in turn step behind the veil we will simply agree.[17]

But Ackerman claims to be describing the way liberals ought to talk to one another. And Habermas's conception of ideal speech is meant to be "compatible with a democratic self-understanding." This is the way citizens would talk to one another, he insists, in a fully realized democracy. So ideal speech reaches back toward actual speech.[18] But what is the strength and extent of its reach? What do we know about actual liberal and democratic speech?

The first thing we know, surely, is that agreement is less likely among liberals and democrats than among the subjects of a king, say, or a military dictator or an ideological or theocratic vanguard. That is why Ackerman's policewoman is necessary; she is a benevolent stand-in for authoritarian censors, though what she enforces is not deference to the ruler but universal deference—toleration for all (tolerant) ways of life. She presses the mass of diverse and discordant speakers toward a special sort of agreement: they must agree to disagree about conceptions of the good. But that agreement simply suspends the argument, and sometimes at least it is necessary to reach a conclusion. What we know about liberal and democratic conclusions is that they are unpredictable and inconclusive. They reflect the indeterminacy of any nonideal and unpatrolled (natural) conversation, in which rhetorical skill, or passionate eloquence, or insidious intensity may carry the day (but only the day). Or, it may be that none of these has any effect at all; the give and take of the conversation, the constant interruptions of one speaker by another, make it impossible for anyone to develop a persuasive argument, and people end where they began, voting their interests or defending an entrenched ideological position.

As Plato's dialogues suggest, the philosopher requires a largely passive interlocutor if he is to make a coherent argument. And since coherent arguments are important in democracies, too (though Plato did not think so), while democratic interlocutors are rarely passive, political debate among citizens cannot always take conversational forms. "Conversation," Emerson wrote, "is a game of circles."[19] But there are times when we need to listen to a sustained argument, a linear discourse. Then what is necessary is a certain freedom from interlocution, a suspension of dialogue, so that someone can make a speech, deliver a lecture, preach a sermon (or write a book). All these are standard forms of liberal and democratic communication—just as whispering in the ear of the prince is standard in royal courts. The speaker in front of (not in the midst of) his audience, speaking to (not with) the people, making a case: this picture is central to any plausible account of democratic decision making. The speech is public, and speakers take responsibility for what they say; listeners are invited to remember what they say and to hold them responsible. Who, by contrast, is responsible for the outcome of an ideal conversation? The author or designer, I suppose, who seeks however to implicate the rest of us. If we all agree, then there is no one who can be held responsible later on. But democratic politics in all its versions, ancient and modern, depends on "holdings" of just this sort.

If liberalism and democracy sometimes require freedom from interlocution so that arguments can be made, they also require radical subjection, so that arguments (and speakers) can be tested. Hence the importance of judicial cross-examinations, congressional hearings, parliamentary question periods, press conferences, and so on. None of these is conversational in style. They are governed by more or less strict conventions that have little in common with the principles of Habermasian ideal speech. One or more people ask questions; one person, standing alone, must answer the questions—though he can always answer evasively or claim one of the conventional exceptions: ignorance, self-incrimination, the requirements of national security. All answers and refusals to answer are subject to popular judgment.

Democratic citizens speak, listen, and ask questions; they play different roles on different occasions—not all roles together on a single occasion. We might think of communication in a democracy the way Aristotle thinks of citizenship: ruling and being ruled, speaking and listening, in turn. Ideal speech, by contrast, is more like Rousseau's understanding of citizenship, where the citizens "give the law to themselves," all of them ruling, all of them being ruled, simultaneously. I do not mean that ideal speakers all speak at once—though that is not impossible if they are reciting the same soliloquy. They speak and listen on the same occasion and in a setting that, in principle at least, rules out both the lecture and the cross-examination. We can, of course, imagine a dialogue across occasions, in which citizens take their Aristotelian turns: I write a book, you write a critique of the book, I write a response to the critique, you write a reply to the response. Let us assume an egalitarian society: there is no relation of subordination or dependency between us. And let us assume that we are honest writers, trying as best we can to get at the truth. It is still an open question whether the exchange will bring us closer together or drive us into polar opposition. Perhaps we will exchange concessions and draw closer—to one another, not necessarily to the truth. Perhaps we will defend, with growing irritation, our starting points. In either case, our decisions will be at least partly strategic: democratic speech, in the turn-taking sense, has an adversarial quality; we take turns in front of an audience whose support is crucial to both of us. We seek popular support because it seems to confirm our account of the truth and—this is at least equally important—because it serves to make our account effective in the world.

Ideal speech abstracts from all this, creating thereby a more intimate conversation, a political version, perhaps, of Martin Buber's I–Thou dialogue. Something like this is suggested by Hans-Georg Gadamer, a defender of actual rather than ideal speech, whose defense, however, requires a fairly radical idealization: "Coming to an understanding in conversation presupposes that the partners . . .

try to allow for the validity of what is alien and contrary to themselves. If this happens on a reciprocal basis and each of the partners, while holding to his own ground simultaneously weighs the counter-arguments, they can ultimately achieve a common language and a common judgment in an imperceptible and non-arbitrary transfer of viewpoints. (We call this an exchange of opinions.)"[20] The parenthetical remark has a certain comic quality; we smile because we know that an "exchange" of the sort Gadamer describes may well leave neither partner any the wiser; also that many conversational partnerships, with the best will in the world, will not reach even this far. In any case, the resolute avoidance of antagonism which Gadamer defends hardly reflects a "democratic self-understanding." It does not usefully account for what happens or even for what might (ideally) happen in the political arena where parties and movements, not only individual speakers, confront one another. Gadamer is describing something closer to deliberation than debate, and he simply assumes the success of the deliberative encounter.[21]

[4]

Common language and judgment, agreements and understandings, strong and extensive meetings of minds, are nonetheless necessary to any human society. It is not the case, obviously, that people agree on this or that policy, but they must agree at a deeper level on the rough contours of a way of life and a view of the world. Some things they must understand together or else their disagreements will be incoherent and their arguments impossible. They can have no politics unless they also have what political scientists call a "consensus" on institutional arrangements and lines of authority. They cannot sustain a common life without a set of shared conceptions about the subjects of that life—themselves—and their character, interests, and aspirations. But conversation is only one among many features of the complex social process that produces consensus and shared understandings. That process includes political struggle (settled, at best, by the force of numbers, not arguments), negotiation and compromise, law making and law enforcement, socialization in families and schools, economic transformations, cultural creativity of all sorts. The understandings that come to be shared will never have been rationally defended by a single speaker who managed to see them whole. Nor do they arise in the course of a debate among many speakers who contribute different pieces of the whole, and who argue until a conclusion is reached incorporating all the pieces. Nothing like that: for no conclusion is imaginable without authority, conflict, and coercion (socialization, for example, is always coercive). And yet the conclusions have some sort of binding force, which derives from the common life that is sustained on the basis they provide.

Ideal speech might be conceived as a way of testing these conclusions, but I am not sure that they are of a sort that can readily be tested. Consider, for example, one of our own deepest understandings: our conception of a human life (social, not biological) as a career, a project, an individual undertaking. The idea of a "life plan" is crucial to Rawls's theory of justice.[22] But that is not an idea that can be confirmed or disconfirmed in the original position. Rawls simply assumes that individuals plan their lives, and without that assumption he could not begin to tell us what goes on, what is thought and said and agreed to, by his ideal speakers as they maximize their opportunities and minimize their risks. The idea of a career is, so to speak, pre-original. We know that it has a history, but in the original position it is simply given. How could it ever be the subject of a rational agreement? We would have to imagine human beings who knew nothing at all, literally nothing, about the shape of a human life. And then on what basis would they decide to have careers rather than, say, inherited stations or a succession of spontaneous acts? The actual process through which the idea of a career came to be central to our self-understanding has its beginning in the breakup of traditional communities; it is the product of force and fraud as much as of philosophical argument. And yet, today, we can hardly begin a philosophical argument about social arrangements or theories of justice without assuming the existence of individuals who plan their lives—and who have a right to plan their lives—in advance of living them.

The case is the same with the external conditions of human existence as with its conceptual shape. Men and women who find themselves in the original position or the ideal speech situation will not be able to argue coherently with one another unless they share some understanding of what the world is like and where they are within it. How does their economy work? What are the constraints of scarcity in their particular time and place? What are their political options? What opportunities are offered, what choices are posed, by the current state of science and technology? These are some of the questions covered by Habermas's claim that, for any effort to construct a society or morality through discourse, there are "limiting conditions" and "functional imperatives" that must be taken into account. If the speakers start by disagreeing about the social and economic parameters within which the meaning of justice, say, is to be worked out, they are unlikely to reach an agreement, later on, about what justice means. Hence, any philosopher who wants to design an ideal conversation will have to assume the existence of, perhaps he will have to specify, a single body of knowledge: the best available social scientific information, certified, I suppose, by the most authoritative economists, psychologists, political scientists, and so on.[23] But how is such knowledge generated? By what means does it come into the philosopher's hands?

The production and delivery of knowledge is, again, a complex social process. Conversation certainly plays a part in that process; we like to imagine that it plays the largest part. In the community of scholars, good talk is all-important; argument is the essential form of scholarly communion. Maybe so; but scholarly communion is not the whole of knowledge production. No one who has sat on a university committee, helped to edit a scholarly journal, fought with colleagues over the content of the curriculum, or reviewed proposals for funding research, will doubt the centrality of politics even in the academy. Here, too, negotiation and compromise precede agreement; here, too, authority has its prerogatives, pressure can be brought to bear, patterns of dominance emerge; here, too, there are interests at work besides the interest in truth. Michel Foucault, who is wrong about many things, is surely right to argue for the symbiosis of power and knowledge.[24] The constitution of professional authority and the development of scientific disciplines go hand in hand.

None of this, obviously, produces definitive results, but knowledge production does have *results*. In some academic fields, some of the time, there is a professional establishment and a reigning wisdom (sometimes the reign is brief). In other fields, in other times, there is a determinate set of competing doctrines, each with its expert advocates who, since they cannot reign, reluctantly share power. The competition will always be encompassed within a larger agreement that establishes the boundaries of power sharing. So men and women in the original position or the ideal speech situation will be told, for example, that there are systematic connections between the economy and the political order. But what will they be told about the nature of the connections? That capitalist markets make for a liberal and democratic politics? Or that a really democratic politics is incompatible with market-generated inequalities? Each of these claims is urged with considerable force by rival authorities, who assemble much the same sort of historical and sociological evidence. They are in fact working within a single "paradigm." Ideal speakers will hardly be able to test the paradigm—they have to be given *some* authoritative view of the politics/economics relation. And it is not clear that they could resolve the debate about markets and democracy (though they could certainly join it) unless they were also presented with a single set of historical and sociological "facts." But whoever made them such a present would thereby determine the resolution of the debate, and that resolution would determine, in turn, the shape of whatever agreement they reached about, say, distributive justice.

The pre-original idea of a career goes a long way toward explaining Rawlsian outcomes. In much the same way, the pre-ideal theory of society (whatever it is) will go a long way toward explaining Habermasian outcomes. Once again, the end of philosophical conversation depends on its beginnings. To say this is not to deny the value of conversation, but only the value of conversational design; it requires us to repudiate the dream of endings that are anything like full stops. We will never be brought to the point where the only thing we can do is to play the part of the Platonic chorus. Design cannot help us, since all its elements, formal and substantive, necessarily precede hypothetical speech; they have to be worked out (and are worked out) independently of any ideal procedure. We can and should talk about the elements; they have an immediate importance; they raise deep questions about freedom and equality and the nature of a human life and the structure of social arrangements. But this is real talk, not hypothetical talk, not ideal speech, not philosophical soliloquy. Hypothetical talk can only begin when real talk has been concluded, when we know what free speech is and in what way ideal speakers are one another's equals and what kind of a life they will have and how their social arrangements work. But real speech is always inconclusive; it has no authoritative moments. I began by saying that I was not interested in speech of this sort. It may be the case, however, that nothing else is more interesting.

But if ideal speech cannot serve as a test of received ideas, perhaps it can serve as a test of the processes (including the real talk) through which such ideas are generated. Should we aim, for example, at a more open debate and a more egalitarian politics? Probably we should, but the reasons for doing so precede ideal speech rather than emerge from it; the freedom and equality of all speakers is the first assumption of Rawls, Habermas, Ackerman, and, so far as I know, of every other philosopher who has written along similar lines.[25] At the same time, all these writers also assume the existence of scientific authorities, policewomen, and speech designers like themselves—who must also have their real-life counterparts. Exactly what the role of such people should be is something we are likely to disagree about and to go on arguing about for as long as we argue about anything at all. And that means that there is no safe and sure conversational design that will protect us against bad agreements and bad disagreements. The continuing argument provides our only protection.

Real talk is the conscious and critical part of the processes that generate our received ideas and reigning theories—reflection become articulate. Arguing with one another, we interpret, revise, elaborate, and also call into question the paradigms that shape our thinking. So we arrive at some conception of a just society (say) through a conversation that is constrained, indeed, by the ordinary constraints of everyday life: the pressure of time, the structure of authority, the discipline of parties and movements, the patterns of socialization and education, the established procedures of institutional life. Without any constraints at all, conversation would never produce even those conventional (and temporary) stops which we call decisions or verdicts; because of the constraints, every stopping point will appear, to some of the speakers, arbitrary and imposed. They will seek to renew the conversation and, despite the constraints, will often succeed in doing so. In another sense, however, these same conversations are radically unconstrained, for while there may be ideas that are taken for granted by all the speakers, there are no stipulated ideas, none that has to be taken for granted if the conversation is to proceed (nor are the constraints taken for granted). There is no design. Real talk is unstable and restless, hence it is ultimately more radical than ideal speech. It reaches to reasons and arguments that none of its participants can anticipate, hence to reasons and arguments undreamt of (for better and for worse) by our philosophers.

NOTES

1. Plato, *The Republic,* trans. F. M. Cornford (New York: Oxford University Press, 1945), 312–15 (585c–588a).

2. At the same time, we support the jury system, because we believe that disinterested jurors are more likely to get at the truth than anyone else. So why not make this a model for all truth-seeking and even for all right-seeking inquiries? The replacement of political debate with an idealized version of judicial deliberation is in fact the goal of a number of contemporary philosophers.

3. See Henry David Aiken's "Introduction" to Hume, *Dialogues Concerning Natural Religion* (New York: Hafner, 1951), vii–xvii. On "negative capability," see *The Letters of John Keats,* ed. M. B. Forman, 4th ed. (London: Oxford University Press, 1952), 71.

4. Jürgen Habermas, *Legitimation Crisis,* trans. Thomas McCarthy (Boston: Beacon, 1975), 113.

5. John Rawls, *A Theory of Justice* (Cambridge: Harvard University Press, 1971), 136–42.

6. Habermas, *Legitimation Crisis,* 113.

7. Seyla Benhabib, *Critique, Norm, and Utopia: A Study of the Foundations of Critical Theory* (New York: Columbia University Press, 1986), 292–93.

8. Jürgen Habermas, "A Reply to My Critics," in *Habermas: Critical Debates,* ed. John B. Thompson and David Held (Cambridge: MIT Press, 1982), 254–55.

9. This is Thomas McCarthy's formula, accepted by Habermas in "Reply," 257.

10. Rousseau, *Social Contract*, bk. 2, chap. 3.

11. Bruce Ackerman, *Social Justice in the Liberal State* (New Haven: Yale University Press, 1980), 24.

12. See, for example, ibid., 169.

13. Steven Lukes, "Of Gods and Demons: Habermas and Practical Reason," in *Critical Debates*, 144.

14. Cf. Descartes' account of his desire "to build on a foundation which is wholly my own." *Discourse on Method*, trans. F. E. Sutcliffe (Harmondsworth: Penguin, 1968), 38.

15. Hume, *Dialogues*, 81.

16. "Therefore we can view the choice in the original position from the standpoint of one person selected at random." Rawls, *A Theory of Justice*, 139.

17. Perhaps that is why Rawlsian theory appeals so much to law professors, who imagine themselves writing briefs that judges, recognizing their impartial wisdom, will instantly accept (and enforce).

18. Ackerman, *Social Justice*, chap. 1; Benhabib, *Critique, Norm, and Utopia*, 283, describing Habermas's program.

19. Ralph Waldo Emerson, "Circles," in *Complete Essays and Other Writings*, ed. Brooks Atkinson (New York: Modern Library, 1940), 284.

20. Quoted in Georgia Warnke, *Gadamer: Hermeneutics, Tradition, and Reason* (Stanford: Stanford University Press, 1987), 101.

21. For a description of what "democratic talk" is like, see Benjamin Barber, *Strong Democracy: Participatory Politics for a New Age* (Berkeley: University of California Press, 1984), 173–98.

22. Rawls, *A Theory of Justice*, 92–93, 407–16.

23. "It is taken for granted," writes Rawls, that the persons in the original position "know the general facts about human society. They understand political affairs and the principles of economic theory; they know the basis of social organization and the laws of human psychology." Ibid., 137.

24. See Michel Foucault, *Power/Knowledge: Selected Interviews and Other Writings, 1972–1977*, ed. Colin Gordon (New York: Pantheon, 1980).

25. For example, Agnes Heller, *Beyond Justice* (New York: Blackwell, 1987), chap. 5.

CHAPTER THREE

Objectivity and Social Meaning

[1]

Iprobably do not have an objective view of objectivity. Having been accused so often of disdaining it, I come to it now with some trepidation; I want to make a cautious approach, repressing for a while the uneasy sense that the conjunction in my title misrepresents the likely outcome of my argument. Let me begin with a strong, simplistic, and usefully wrong definition of objectivity: a given perception, recognition, or understanding can be called "objective" if its content is wholly or largely determined by its object—so that a range of human subjects, differently placed, with different personalities and different, even conflicting, interests, would agree on the same content so long as they attended to the same object. The table determines the objective perception of the table. What makes for objectivity is simply this: the object imposes itself. The subject is passive and undiscriminating, a promiscuous consumer of available "data."

For reasons philosophers have long understood, that cannot be right. Human beings are active subjects. Our faculties of perception and cognition help to determine whatever it is that we finally see or recognize or understand. But we are still inclined to call the perception "objective" so long as these faculties are so widely shared as to constitute what we might call a normal subject. Then perception is objective when it is jointly determined by the object and the normal subject. If someone without depth perception reports on the existence of a table different from the one the rest of us see, his is the subjective report. The table and the normal person looking at the table (who represents "the rest of us") together determine what the table objectively is (looks like). The object still imposes itself, but perception is conditioned by the character of the receptive organism, and the idea of "objectivity" incorporates the results of this conditioning.

But that cannot be right either, and this time for reasons that have generated a long series of complex, difficult, and sometimes high-flying philosophical arguments. We do not come to the object with faculties alone but with interests and ideas too. And what we see, recognize, and understand depends (with a strong but not absolute dependency) on what we are looking for, our cognitive *concerns,* and the ways we have of describing what we find, our conceptual *schemes.* Given our concerns and our schemes, what opportunity is there now for the object to impose itself? We seem armoured against imposition, shaping the world to our own purposes.

But I do not mean to surrender objectivity so quickly—indeed, it is the scientific perception of the world, driven by a strong purposefulness and structured by elaborate and highly speculative schemes, that makes the most insistent claim these days to be called an objective perception. The claim takes many different forms, but in all its forms it must hold that if the object does not impose itself it is still recalcitrant to conceptual and purposive impositions. Scientific concepts must accommodate the object—not as the object appears, perhaps, but as it *really* is. I am not going to comment on that last assertion, except to say that for most of us, at least, appearance is an important aspect of reality. But I want to accept the claim that objectivity hangs (somehow) on the accommodation of the object by a knowing, inquiring subject. The knowing subject shapes the object, but he cannot shape it however he likes; he cannot just decide that a table, say, has a circular or a square shape without reference to the table. Similarly, someone self-confidently applying a conceptual scheme that divided the world into friends, enemies, reading matter, and edible plants would get the table wrong (objectively wrong), or he would miss the table entirely, and deny its reality, and that would be a merely idiosyncratic (subjective) denial.

This is still a very simple account of objectivity, a rough, commonsensical approach to philosophical difficulties that lie beyond my immediate cognitive concerns and possibly also beyond the conceptual schemes at my disposal. But the account works, more or less well, for simple objects-in-the-world. The question that I want to ask now is whether it works at all for objects to which we assign use and value, objects that carry "social meanings."[1] This term, borrowed from anthropology, seems to cast a cloud over all claims to objective knowledge. Social meanings are constructions of objects by sets of subjects, and once such constructions are, so to speak, in place, the understanding of the object has been and will continue to be determined by the subjects. New sets of subjects learn the construction and then respect or revise it with only a minimal accommodation of the object. The object may or may not limit the constructive work in which they are engaged. Obviously, the table cannot be constructed as an intercontinental ballistics missile. But it can become a desk, a workbench, a butcher's block, or an altar, and each of these can take on meanings to which the "mere" table gives us no positive clue. Can perceptions of objects like these, objects-with-meanings, ever be called objective? It is easy enough to imagine situations in which one person's altar is another person's butcher's block. But we do accept reports on social constructions. Now objectivity (in the reports) hangs on an acknowledgment of the construction. Our shared understanding of what an altar is, what we have made it for, determines our perception of the table-that-is-an-altar. The holiness of the altar is similarly objective, since it is part of the same construction. All normal persons living within the system of social meanings would deliver similar reports on the objective reality of tables-that-are-altars-that-are-holy.

But this may go too far. Suppose that there are dissenting voices within the society where some tables are holy altars, people who deny the construction, who announce, "There's nothing there but an old table." That is also an objective report of a kind. Can we say that it is an incomplete report, that it misses something of real importance? Imagine a fuller report: "Some people claim that it's an altar and treat it as if it were holy, but there's nothing there but an old table." No incompleteness now, and now only the disagreement can be objectively reported: "*I think* there's nothing there but an old table." Nothing in the nature of the table will lead us to say that it is or is not a holy altar. The altar is objectively there only for those who understand it to be objectively there. It is holy only for those who acknowledge its holiness. And what they will have to say, if they are to report objectively, is that it is holy *for them*.

Believers will want to say more than that. They will want to say that God has sanctified the table and made it into a holy altar; hence everyone who knows how things really are in the world will acknowledge its holiness. But I shall take it as given that altars and holiness are alike human creations. The believers are wrong, then, to take the holiness of their altar as a universally recognizable (objective) fact. The altar is holy only because and only in so far as they have made it so. With regard to such creations, the rest of us are not bound by majority rule; only the voice of the people as a whole resembles the voice of God. Social constructions must reflect a general agreement—or, better, since no vote is ever taken, there must be a consensus—if there is ever to be an unqualified objectivity, an objectivity without pronouns, in our reports about them. (Reports from outside observers will always need pronouns: "their altars" or, in more extended form, "these tables, which they use as altars.") The more complex and specific the construction the more surprising it is when a consensus is actually reached. The social processes that make this possible are mixed processes, involving force and fraud, debate and consent, long periods of habituation; overall, they remain mysterious.

Compared to "altar," "table" is both uncomplicated and indeterminate; hence its meanings will rarely provoke significant or stirring dissent. Someone who says, "That's not a table," while pointing to a flat piece of wood with a supporting structure of appropriate height, will probably lead us to talk about mistakes, not disagreements. (I will not stop here to imagine bizarre cases of table-like objects that are rarely not tables.) We would suspect some failure of normal understanding. A table is indeed a social construction, as well as a physical construction, but the socially constructive work is so rudimentary that we are unlikely to recognize much more in it than the assignment of a general name to the object. And then we expect people of normal understanding to remember the name. Nothing much follows from remembering it; the construction of the flat piece of wood, etc., as a table does not require us to use or to value the table in a certain way. More specific constructions, by contrast, have normative consequences.

Tables-that-are-altars-that-are-holy must be treated in accordance with certain principles and rules. I cannot use the altar, for example, as a desk on which to write profane essays on social meaning—not because the altar will resist the use or God strike me dead, but because it would be wrong to do that given what an altar is in my society (for me and my fellow members). Nor can I chop it up for firewood, even if the church is very cold; or trade it for personal profit—a new suit, say, or a season ticket to the opera, or a place on the Stock Exchange: it would be the wrong thing to do. But would it be objectively wrong? It seems to me that it is possible to ask questions like that too soon. Clearly the rules of use and value are not determined by the "mere" table; nor are they jointly determined by the table and a normal person looking at the table; nor do they represent an accommodation of the table by a knowing subject or a scientific observer. The rules follow from the social construction of the table as a holy altar and they would seem to be objective rules only for those men and women who join in the construction or acknowledge its results. The other might be bound by some notion of "decent respect" for the opinions of their fellows, but not by the idea of holiness.

But perhaps we can go a little further than this. If we think of the holiness of the altar not as an isolated construction but as one feature of a more complex whole, a cultural system or a way of life, then the force of the rules is considerably enhanced. Imagine the table-that-is-an-altar-that-is-holy within a set of connected constructions: socially meaningful occasions (holy days), spaces (churches), officials (priests and bishops), performances (religious services), texts (scriptures, prayers, homilies, catechisms), and beliefs (theologies or cosmologies), and the result is something from which individuals cannot so easily opt out. Some day there will be alternative occasions, spaces, officials, performances, texts, and beliefs, arising out of a long process of social change ("secularization," say); and then people will be able to explain to their fellows why the altar is not (really) holy. But now the refusal of some dissident or rebel to treat the altar in accordance with its rules of use and value is probably not a straightforward denial of its holiness but a specific act of desecration literally, an effort to reverse the process through which this particular altar has been consecrated. And the religious rebel committed to desecration is likely to appeal, in much the same way as the early Protestants appealed, to other features of the existing cultural system or way of life, features that give him reasons, so he says, for what he does. The system as a whole still has objective value for him; he lives within the set of social constructions. Where else can he live?

[2]

We can still ask whether this is objectively the best place to live. But I want, again, to postpone that question in order to explore more fully the crucial implication of my argument thus far: that social construction is also moral legislation. The meanings with which we invest objects have normative consequences. I have been calling these norms "rules of use and value;" they are also rules of distribution, that is, they regulate our relations not only with things but also with other people. Any number of philosophers have argued that morality is a human invention, writing mostly as if what we invent are the rules that govern a moral life. We leap to principles like equality before God or personal autonomy or the greatest happiness; and then we make lists, like the *Decalogue*. Maybe we do that, sometimes; but the thickness of the moral world and the density of our relationships suggest a radically different kind of invention. One of the ways we reach that thickness and density is through the social construction of objects (of all kinds). Social construction makes for a complex and rich world, many features of which will seem so obvious to us that we will not be prompted to ask whether they are, of all possible features of all possible worlds, objectively best. They will have a more immediate objectivity. So we will use and value objects in accordance with the meaning they have in our world, and we will exchange, share, and distribute them in accordance with their use and value. We will know what objects we owe to other people as soon as we understand what those objects (really) are and what they are for. And a great part of our conduct towards other people will be governed by these distributive entailments of social meanings.

At this point, it will be useful to take up another example, even though the difficulties of the table-that-is-an-altar-that-is-holy have by no means been exhausted. I want to consider the construction of a human life—not a biological but a social life, not a life span but a life course in a particular society, namely, our own. What we have constructed is a life-that-is-a-career-that-is-open-to-talents. Obviously, there is nothing in the nature of a human life that determines its construction as a career. Any given version of the life course is conditioned by the life span, so that youth, maturity, and age give rise to a pattern like training, professional practice, and retirement; but these latter three do not by themselves constitute a career. A career is an individual achievement; it is constituted by choice and qualification. Though career patterns may be collectively established and repetitively enacted, a career is none the less a projection of the self into a chosen and uncertain future. What makes this projection possible is the opening up of certain sorts of places and positions (professional or bureaucratic), which I will call "offices." Offices are the objects of careers. The social construction of the two goes hand in hand, like altars and offerings. If careers are open to talents, then offices must be distributed on meritocratic principles to qualified persons. If we imagine individual men and women planning careers-open-to-talents, we must also imagine competitions for office. If there are competitions, there must be rules protecting the competitors, not only against violence but also against discrimination, that is, against any refusal to attend honestly to their qualifications.

Once careers and offices are in place, nepotism becomes a wrongful practice. It would be wrong for me, the member of some search committee, say, to favour my brother over a more qualified candidate. It does not matter that I have a very strong, and to my mind overriding, belief in family loyalty; I am caught up in a complex set of social constructions that has normative entailments. Someone who fails to respect the table-that-is-an-altar-that-is-holy does no injury to the table, and in so far as the failure is private he does no injury (causes no offence) to other men and women either. His is one of the minor sins. But once constructions determine distributions, private refusals make for a more serious wrong. And when behaviour is in question, general agreement is no longer a necessary condition of rightness or wrongness; the rule against nepotism, for example, is binding even on individuals who argue that offices are family holdings and not objects of careers. There will not be many people, however, who will actually *argue* that offices are family holdings—except in the unlikely case that a strong familial idealism is part of the same set of social constructions as the career-open-to-talents, and then we might well recognize the public nepotist as a conscientious objector. Acts of refusal and opposition commonly have a basis of this sort, in the coexistence of contradictory constructions. Then people have to choose, guided only by their best understanding of the complex social world they inhabit.

I want to stress that it would not be objectively wrong to adopt the argument for offices-as-family-holdings. Majority rule does not govern arguments about social meaning; it only governs behaviour. The rules of behaviour, then, are objectively right relative to the prevailing meanings, but the prevailing meanings are not objectively right (or wrong). They are only objectively *there*, the objects, that is, of more or less accurate reports. The life-that-is-a-career could, over time, be constructed in an entirely different way, and offices could be reconstructed to match the difference, and no wrong would have been done. It would not be the case that lives or offices had somehow been misunderstood; nor would the men and women leading lives and holding (or not holding) offices under the new dispensation have been treated unjustly.

It is not my claim that the whole of morality is objectively relative (relatively objective?) in this way, only whatever part of it is entailed by the social construction of objects. Even here we might plausibly ask whether there are cases where construction is jointly determined by its objects and its human agents in such a way that the same normative entailments appear again and again, in all or almost all human societies. Then the same behaviour would be wrongful for the same reasons in all human societies; morality would lose its particularist character without ceasing to be relative to social construction. The easiest case has to do with the things we call "food:" given the human body, the construction of edible objects is not an entirely free construction though people in different cultures do choose different things to eat and not eat, edibility itself is (in part) socially determined. In any case, the experience or expectation of hunger and the possibility of eating certain things work together to turn some of those things into human provisions, and it would seem to follow from this that provisions should be provided for those in need; food belongs to the hungry. (Who should do the providing and at whose expense are questions not so easily answered.) More complex and specific constructions will still be culturally relative: we save certain food for festive occasions or we burn it before the gods or we waste it at extravagant banquets. But the original construction of things-that-are-food-for-the-hungry entails certain distributive rules that have, I suspect (this could be checked), always been recognized. Hoarders in time of famine act wrongly, for example, given what food is for.

I shall assume that reiterated social construction rather than diffusion from an authoritative center is the preferred explanation for the appearance of identical or similar used and valued objects in different societies. There is no authoritative centre, no Jerusalem from which meanings go forth. The list of similarly constructed uses and values, then, constitutes what we might think of as a universal and objective morality—relative to social construction where construction repetitively takes the same form, relative to the prevailing argument where the same argument always prevails. We could go on to further explanations: if certain things-in-the-world are constructed in the same way again and again, presumably there is something in the nature of the things and / or something in the nature of the human agents that accounts for the construction. As the example of food suggests, the account is likely to be a naturalistic one. But I doubt that the list of similar constructions would be very long; nor would it include the complex and specific constructions that make for the thickness of moral life: food for eating would get on the list, not food for offerings. This is what it means to say that complexity is free: the more complex the construction the more room there is for cultural difference. Complex constructions do not turn up again and again, and they do not have plausible or satisfying naturalistic explanations.

There is no universal model for social construction, and the range of difference among actual outcomes is very wide. It might be argued, however, that this is so only because the constructive work takes place under a great variety of adverse and advantageous (mostly adverse) conditions. Only a common necessity, like the need for nourishment, makes for sameness. But if we imagine social construction in ideal conditions (and if ideal conditions are a single set of conditions), then we will get a model outcome, that is, a free construction that is at the same time the best construction. I am afraid that this is an impossible dream. For we can replace actual with hypothetical social construction only if we know, and not hypothetically, what conditions are ideal. And if we know that, then we already know the model outcome. We simply pull into our account of the imagined (ideal, original, natural) conditions all those materials, and only those materials, out of which we want society constructed. We might as well draw a blueprint of the good society and give up the idea that construction is free.

[3]

But if we do not have a model outcome, how can we ever criticize actual outcomes? This question is motivated, I think, by a misunderstanding of what an actual outcome is. Social construction is first of all conceptual in character. Holy altars and careers-open-to-talents are ideas, and the distributive norms that follow from them are also ideas. These ideas are never more than partially instantiated in the world; holiness and openness are more often than not honoured in the breach. What social critics commonly do is to hold the idea, or some more or less elaborated interpretation of the idea, over against the instance of the idea. Or, just as commonly, they hold some other idea or complex set of ideas, also the product of social construction, over against this idea and its instances. They say, if careers are open to talents, then why are they not open to the talents of Jews, or blacks, or women? Or, if our society is a union of families or a democratic and co-operative community of citizens, how can we tolerate the intense competitiveness generated by careers-open-to-talents?

Criticism of this sort depends on objective values, where objectivity is a true report on social meaning. The criticism itself, however, is not objectively true or false, for it also depends on an interpretation of social meaning, and interpretations are (except at the margins) only more or less persuasive and illuminating. But surely there are times when we want to say something stronger than this. We want to say that though the report is objectively true, the meaning is wrong (and not just *wrong for us*). Or we want to say that that is not the way we ought to think about altars or careers or whatever. Or even, that is not what an altar or a career *really is*.

Is it possible for a whole society to get things wrong in this fundamental way? This is the question that I have been postponing, and it is time now to try to deal with it. I want to make sure, though, that we understand exactly what the question is. Clearly, it is possible for individuals within a society to get things wrong, even fundamentally wrong, and it is also possible for groups of individuals to do the same thing. We should think of the Nazi case in these terms. It would strain the imagination to describe a fully elaborated world of complex meanings of a Nazi sort; in any case, no such world has ever existed. Within German or European or Western culture, the Nazis were an aberration, and in so far as we can make out their distributive principles—air for Aryans, gas for Jews—we can readily say that these are objectively wrong, immoral, monstrous. All the resources necessary for a judgement of this sort are already available, the products of a long history of social construction. It is a great mistake to make of the Nazis a hard case. The hard case comes when we begin to think that a long history of social construction has somehow gone awry.

Consider, then, those societies where women (all women) seem to have been socially constructed as objects of exchange and where rules of exchange follow from the construction. I will not attempt an internal account of the exchanges that actually take place or of the meanings attached to them. Perhaps our understanding of an "object" and even of an "exchange" is not available to the participants. All I will say about the social construction at this point is that women are transferred among households, from one patriarchal jurisdiction to another, as if they were objects of exchange. What should we think of that? Are exchanges conducted in accordance with the rules objectively just?

There are a number of possibilities here: either women have or have not played a part in the constructive work; either they agree or they do not agree to its outcomes. Or, in a language less marked by our own conceptions of moral agency and lives-as-careers, they acquiesce or do not acquiesce, go along or do not go along with the outcomes. If they have played no part and do not go along, then the exchanges cannot be described as just. We can only report on the disagreement. Or perhaps we can say, as I would be inclined to say, that the exchanges are unjust, because in this case the objects are also human subjects, capable (as tables and lives are not) of going along or not, and the resistance of the constructed object nullifies the construction. It does not matter if the resistance is inarticulate, passive, hidden, or private. So long as we can in one way or another discover it, so long as we have probable cause to believe in its reality, the social construction fails.

The women involved may or may not be able to describe themselves as persons-engaged-in-social-construction; the vocabulary that I have deployed here is presumably not their own vocabulary. But we can see how their resistance "works" in the world and why the construction fails. The unanimity or consensus principle plays a part in explaining this failure, but something more is involved. Constructions of persons are not free—and not only in the obvious sense that we cannot make women or men into intercontinental ballistics missiles. The theory of social construction implies (some sort of) human agency and requires the recognition of women and men as agents (of some sort). We might say, looking at the idea itself as something we have made, that the construction of social-construction-with-human-agents has certain moral entailments. Among these is the right of subjective nullification, the right of the agents to refuse any given object status—as commodities, "hands," slaves, or whatever.[2]

But what if women, for whatever reasons, actually agree that they are objects of exchange and live willingly by the rules of exchange? The phrase "for whatever reasons" conceals a problem here, which philosophers who are quick with hypothetical examples are prone to ignore. What reasons could these women possibly have? We can easily see the reasons they might have for concealing disagreement, for stifling anger, for expressing resentment only in private or only in the company of other women. But if the experience of being treated as an object of exchange is the sort of experience we think it is, and if the women being exchanged are beings like us, what reasons could they have for agreeing? If, on the other hand, the experience does not match our understanding of it, and if these hypothetical women are beings of a different sort, then what is the philosophical issue here? What can we say, why should we want to say anything at all, about experiences and beings of which we are entirely ignorant?

Still, let us accept the hypothesis in its strongest form: here is a society in which women really do agree to the construction of themselves as objects of exchange. They do not agree because they have been brainwashed, because some chemical process or some hitherto unknown social process has turned them into moral robots or made servitude a reflex—for then, whatever they did or said, it would not constitute agreeing. Nor do they agree because they have no choice or because they are physically coerced or because they find themselves in desperate difficulties from which agreement is the only escape—like the woman who sells herself into slavery in order to feed her children. For their agreement in these circumstances would not count as the construction of themselves as objects of exchange; it would represent only a reluctant and resentful acceptance of a pretence, a role that they could not refuse or escape. We must imagine reasons of a different sort: that the exchange of women brings some benefits to at least some women (even if the benefits are much greater for men); that it is only one part of a larger pattern of relationship, fitted to a system of beliefs, symbolically represented, ritually enacted and confirmed, handed down from mothers to daughters over many generations. So women accept the construction, even participate in it. What normative consequences follow?

One possible response is that no consequences follow, for agency is inalienable. This is Rousseau's argument, not applied by him to the self-subordination of women but obviously applicable: "To renounce liberty is to renounce being a man, to surrender the rights of humanity and even its duties. . . . Such a renunciation is incompatible with man's nature; to remove all liberty from his will is to remove all morality from his acts."[3] Since human beings are agents by nature, and necessarily responsible for the worlds they make, the surrender of agency simply does not count; it is a gesture without effect. The argument from social construction is harder than this since it cannot refer to a universal and unconditioned *moral* agency. Now agents are socially produced, themselves involved in the production. It is still true that we (with our perceptions, understandings, theories) can recognize the woman-who-is-an-object-of-exchange as a social construction with moral entailments only if we also recognize the same woman as a moral agent capable of agreeing (or not) to the construction. She can only be (morally) an object if she is simultaneously a subject confirming her object status. She is constituted by a contradiction in so far as her subordinate status depends (morally) on her own agreement or acquiescence and is therefore inconsistent with subordination itself—and therein lies her freedom. She can never become just an object of exchange; the proof of this is that if she ever repudiates her object status, she is immediately and wholly a subject; the rules of exchange instantly lose their force. But so long as she confirms them (and even if her confirmation takes, as it commonly will, some other form than explicit agreement), they retain their force: she is partly an object.[4] There is nothing in the nature of a woman, or a man, that rules out contradictions of this sort. (The case is somewhat similar, I think, to Kant's means-ends polarity. We do not have to treat every person we meet, on every occasion, as an end-in-himself, for persons can agree to be means, like good civil servants who make themselves into the instruments of their fellow citizens, even surrendering some of their civil rights. But they can always resign from instrumentality.)

So long as the woman-who-is-an-object-of-exchange confirms her object status, the contradiction in her being is an objective contradiction. We can give a true account of it. Someone who claims that she is wholly an object is wrong. But so is someone who claims that she is wholly a subject (this would be roughly analogous to insisting that we must always, on every occasion, treat the civil servant as an end-in-himself). This last turn of the argument may well seem to many readers too relativistic, a surrender to what Marxists call "false consciousness." But once we have ruled out brainwashing and coercion, I see no morally acceptable way of denying the woman-who-is-an-object-of-exchange her own reasons and her own place in a valued way of life. That does not mean that we cannot argue with her, offering what we take to be better reasons for the repudiation of (what we take to be) object status. It does mean that, once the argument begins, she has to choose what *she* thinks are the better reasons, without any certainty as to which ones are objectively best. But we can say, and this seems to me all that we should want to say, that the choice is truly hers.

Is this not a plausible account of social construction seemingly gone awry? If nature provided a blueprint for construction, the process would not go awry as often as it does (seems to do). If something like gender equality were a simple entailment of the constructive process and every internal contradiction were ruled out a priori, then arguments for equality would be much easier than they are. When we encounter a complex set of social meanings, we enter a moral world, and it is no tribute to the creators of that world to deny its reality. Social meanings are constructed, accepted, and revised for reasons, and we have to engage those reasons. When we engage them from the outside, as in the case of women-who-are-objects-of-exchange, we are like missionaries preaching a new way of life to the natives, and we would do best, morally and politically, to try to work out what they find valuable or satisfying in their old way of life. More often, and more importantly, criticism of the old ways comes from within, as the result of long processes of social change. For the construction of objects-with-meanings and thus of moral worlds goes on and on; it is a continuous process in which we are all engaged. Conservatives try to freeze the process, but that effort is only one more instance of constructive activity (it has its reasons), one more expression of human agency. Criticism is no different in form.

Consider, for example, the construction of lives-that-are-careers-that-are-open-to-talents in a society where women are still objects of exchange. Over a period of time, institutions and practices take shape that make it possible (or necessary) for some members of the society, mostly men, to plan their lives—and, over the same period, lives of this sort are discussed, argued about, rendered meaningful. In the course of this process women will find that they have a new reason to repudiate their object status, for only by doing so can they undertake careers of their own. Some of them will seize upon this reason, and then more and more of them; at some point women-who-are-objects-of-exchange will be relics, sad memories, their agreement to subordination hard to understand. If a few people try to act out the rules of exchange, they will appear quixotic, not so much defenders of old ways as fools of time. In similar fashion, an archaeological guide might say to us: "These were the holy altars of Xanadu, in the days when holiness reigned in the city."

[4]

I come back at last to my initial reservations. The kind of objectivity that I have attached to social meanings is probably not the kind that philosophers seeking objectivity are interested in. They are in search of things as they really are or as they must be. But I know very little about things as they really are, social construction apart. It is true (we can give objective reports) that particular constructions are reiterated in one social setting after another. The extent of the reiteration and the reasons for it—these are empirical matters. Exactly what evidence would lead us to say that such and such a construction could not or should never be otherwise, I do not know; in any case, that sort of evidence will not often be available. Interesting objects, all the more complex constructions, can always be otherwise. Tables need not be altars; lives need not be careers.

But is it not objectively true that meanings are always constructed? Men and women who claimed to have discovered meaning in nature, say, would surely be misreporting (misconstructing) their own activity—as if they were telling us that it was not Adam but God who named the animals. Even if no particular meaning were objectively true or right or necessary, it would still be the case that the construction of meaning is a real process. Men and women really have made tables into holy altars and lives into careers. This has been the presupposition of my argument, and I have even pointed to its possible moral entailments; I do not want to run away from it now. But it is a strange "objectivity" that leaves us adrift in a world we can only make and remake and never finish making or make correctly.

NOTES

In this chapter I have tried to sketch an account of "social meaning" that might underpin and uphold the theory of distributive justice presented a few years ago in my book *Spheres of Justice* (New York: Basic Books, 1983). My views on objectivity have been guided, stimulated, and provoked by recent philosophical and anthropological work that I can only acknowledge in a general way by listing a few crucial books: Hilary Putnam, *Reason, Truth and History* (Cambridge: Cambridge University Press, 1981) and *The Many Faces of Realism* (La Salle, Ill.: Open Court, 1988); Nelson Goodman, *Ways of Worldmaking* (Indianapolis: Hackett, 1978); Thomas Nagel, *The View from Nowhere* (Oxford: Oxford University Press, 1986); Clifford Geertz, *Local Knowledge* (New York: Basic Books, 1986); and the essays collected in *Rationality and Relativism*, ed. Martin Hollis and Steven Lukes (Cambridge: MIT Press, 1982) and in *Objectivity and Cultural Divergence*, ed. S. C. Brown (Cambridge: Cambridge University Press, 1984). I am grateful to Ruth Anna Putnam, Alan Wertheimer, John Goldberg, and Thomas Nagel, who read the paper in an earlier version and told me what was wrong with it. Martha Nussbaum suggested that I write the paper and provided its title, but she is responsible only for its existence, not for its argument.

1. Are there any objects without social meaning? Perhaps the phrase "simple objects-in-the-world" names a null set. But I am going to assume that there are such things, which we accommodate and shape directly, without any necessary reference to their sociological

significance. Stones are, for my purposes, simple objects-in-the-world—until they are made into cornerstones, tombstones, grindstones, milestones, steppingstones, or doorsteps (or, more dramatically, until they are used for coronations or set up as markers for a sacred history). As for tables, see the argument below.

2. A friend writes in criticism of this "right" that some participants in any social system "will resist or resent or reject the position or identity they are given. . . . Not all resistance nullifies." So we have to decide in each case whether the resistance is legitimate or not, and this requires standards that are extrinsic to the business of social construction. Yes, we will have to decide whether the resistance is just a way of avoiding particular obligations incurred by particular men or women. Agency itself cannot be denied, and promises made by agents are not subject to unilateral repudiation. But the denial of agency can always be repudiated, with the consequences described further on in the text. The right of nullification is simply the agent's right to claim her agency against any social process of objectification—and it does follow, I think, from the view of objectification as the work of human agents.

3. Jean-Jacques Rousseau, *The Social Contract*, trans. G. D. H. Cole (London: Dent), 9.

4. I do not mean to say more than this. I do not mean that the construction is right because the woman confirms it, only that it is effective and consequential in the moral world. Her agreement (or acquiescence) had evidentiary, not legitimizing, force. Agreement makes for rightness only within moral systems where it is understood to do that, and in such systems it is commonly hedged with qualifications as to the freedom of subjects, the knowledge available to them, and so on. Hence women-who-are-objects-of-exchange can be exchanged justly or unjustly; but the objectification itself is not justified by their agreement.

CHAPTER FOUR

Liberalism and the Art of Separation

[1]

I suggest that we think of liberalism as a certain way of drawing the map of the social and political world. The old, preliberal map showed a largely undifferentiated land mass, with rivers and mountains, cities and towns, but no borders. "Every man is a piece of the continent," as John Donne wrote— and the continent was all of a piece. Society was conceived as an organic and integrated whole. It might be viewed under the aspect of religion, or politics, or economy, or family, but all these interpenetrated one another and constituted a single reality. Church and state, church-state and university, civil society and political community, dynasty and government, office and property, public life and private life, home and shop: each pair was, mysteriously or unmysteriously, two-in-one, inseparable. Confronting this world, liberal theorists preached and practiced an art of separation. They drew lines, marked off different realms, and created the sociopolitical map with which we are still familiar. The most famous line is the "wall" between church and state, but there are many others. Liberalism is a world of walls, and each one creates a new liberty.

This is the way the art of separation works. The wall between church and state creates a sphere of religious activity, of public and private worship, congregations and consciences, into which politicians and bureaucrats may not intrude. Queen Elizabeth was speaking like a liberal, though a minimalist one, when she said that she would not "make a window into men's souls, to pinch them there."[1] Believers are set free from every sort of official or legal coercion. They can find their own way to salvation, privately or collectively; or they can fail to find their way; or they can refuse to look for a way. The decision is entirely their own; this is what we call freedom of conscience or religious liberty.

Similarly, the line that liberals drew between the old church-state (or state-church) and the universities creates academic freedom, leaving professors as free to profess as believers are to believe. The university takes shape as a kind of walled city. In the hierarchical world of the middle ages, universities were legally walled, that is, students and professors were a privileged group, protected from penalties and punishments meted out to ordinary men. But this was a function of the integration of the universities and the church (students and professors had clerical status) and then of the church and the state. Precisely because of this integration, scholars did not enjoy the privilege of heretical thought. Today the universities are intellectually though not legally walled; students and professors have no legal privileges, but they are, in principle at least, absolutely free in the sphere of knowledge.[2] Privately or collectively, they can criticize, question, doubt, or reject the established creeds of their society. Or, what is more likely in any relatively stable society, they can elaborate the established creeds, most often in conventional, but sometimes in novel and experimental ways.

Similarly, again, the separation of civil society and political community creates the sphere of economic competition and free enterprise, the market in commodities, labor, and capital. I will focus for now on the first of these three and adopt the largest view of market freedom. On this view, the buyers and sellers of commodities are entirely at liberty to strike any bargain they wish, buying anything, selling anything, at any price they can agree upon, without the interference of state officials. There is no such thing as a just price, or at least there is no enforcement of a just price; and, similarly, there are no sumptuary laws, no restrictions on usury, no quality or safety standards, no minimum wage, and so on. The maxim *caveat emptor,* let the buyer beware, suggests that market freedom entails certain risks for consumers. But so does religious freedom. Some people buy unsafe products and some people are converted to false doctrines. Free men and women must bear such risks. I have my doubts about the analogy, since unsafe products pose actual, and false doctrines only speculative, risks, but I won't pursue this argument here. My immediate purpose is not to criticize but only to describe the map the liberals drew, and on that map the commodity was given at least as much room as the creed.

Another example: the abolition of dynastic government separates family and state and makes possible the political version of the "career-open-to-talents," the highest form, we might say, of the labor market. Only the eldest male in a certain line can be a king, but anyone can be a president or prime minister. More generally, the line that marks off political and social position from familial property creates the sphere of office and then the freedom to compete for bureaucratic and professional place, to lay claim to a vocation, apply for an appointment, develop a specialty, and so on. The notion of one's life as one's project probably has its origin here. It is to be contrasted with the notion of one's life as one's inheritance—on the one hand, the predetermination of birth and blood; on the other, the self-determination of struggle and achievement.

Finally, the separation of public and private life creates the sphere of individual and familial freedom, privacy and domesticity. Most recently, this has been described as a sphere of sexual freedom; so it is, but it isn't originally or primarily that; it is designed to encompass a very wide range of interests and activities—whatever we choose to do, short of incest, rape, and murder, in our own homes or among our friends and relatives: reading books, talking politics, keeping a journal, teaching what we know to our children, cultivating (or, for that matter, neglecting) our gardens. Our homes are our castles, and there we are free from official surveillance. This is, perhaps, the freedom that we most take for granted—the two-way television screens of Orwell's *1984* are a particularly frightening piece of science fiction—so it is worth stressing how rare a freedom it is in human history. "Our homes are our castles" was first of all the claim of people whose castles were their homes, and it was for a very long time an effective claim only for them. Now its denial is an occasion for indignation and outrage even among ordinary citizens. We greatly value our privacy, whether or not we do odd and exciting things in private.[3]

[2]

The art of separation has never been highly regarded on the left, especially the Marxist left, where it is commonly seen as an ideological rather than a practical enterprise. Leftists have generally stressed both the radical interdependence of the different social spheres and the direct and indirect causal links that radiate outwards from the economy. The liberal map is a pretense, on the Marxist view, an elaborate exercise in hypocrisy, for in fact the prevailing religious creeds are adapted to the ideological requirements of a capitalist society; and the universities are organized to reproduce the higher echelons of the capitalist work force; and the market position of the largest companies and corporations is subsidized and guaranteed by the capitalist state; and offices, though not legally inheritable, are nevertheless passed on and exchanged within a capitalist power elite; and we are free in our homes only so long as what we do there is harmless and without prejudice to the capitalist order. Liberals draw lines and call them walls, as if they had the material force of brick or stone, but they are only lines, one-dimensional, doctrinal, insubstantial. The contemporary social world is still an organic whole, less different from feudalism than we might think. Land has been replaced by moveable wealth as the dominant good, and while that replacement reverberates through all the spheres of social life, it doesn't alter their deep connectedness.

And yet Marx also believed that the liberal art of separation had been all too successful, creating, as he wrote in his essay on the Jewish question, "an individual separated from the community, withdrawn into himself, wholly preoccupied with his private interest and acting in accordance with his private caprice."[4] I shall want to come back to this argument later on for it makes an important point about the theoretical foundations of the liberal enterprise. For now, however, it is enough to say that in Marx's eyes even the egotism of the separated individual was a social product—required, indeed, by the relations of production and then reproduced in all the spheres of social activity. Society remained an organized whole even if its members had lost their sense of connection. It was the goal of Marxist politics to restore that sense, or, better, to bring men and women to a new understanding of their connectedness and so enable them to take control of their common life. For Marx, separation, insofar as it was real, was something to be overcome. Separated institutions—churches, universities, even families—have no part in his program; their distinctive problems will be solved only by a social revolution. Society, for Marx, is always ruled as a whole, now by a single class, ultimately by all of its members working together.

The leftist critique of liberal separation might, however, take a different form, holding that liberalism served particular social interests and limited and adapted its art to that service. What is necessary is to make the art impartial—or, if that is a utopian project, at least to make it serve a wider range of interests. As the institutions of civil society were protected from state power, so now they must be protected, and the state too, from the new power that arises within civil society itself, the power of wealth. The point is not to reject separation as Marx did but to endorse and extend it, to enlist liberal artfulness in the service of socialism. The most important example of the extended art of separation has to do with private government and industrial democracy, and I mean to defend that extension at some length. But it is important to insist first that the separations already achieved, in principle if not always in fact, have their value too. Even the career-open-to-talents is a leftist as well as a liberal requirement. For socialism will never be a success so long as socialist parties and movements are led, as in Robert Michel's account, by a gerontocratic oligarchy whose members, drawn from the educated and professional middle class, coopt their own successors.[5] One wants energetic, politically skillful workers and intellectuals to rise to positions of leadership, and so there must be room for such people to develop their talents and plan their careers. More generally, Marx's vision of individual and collective self-determination requires (though he himself did not understand the requirement) the existence of a *protected space* within which meaningful choices can be made. But space of that sort can only exist if wealth and power are walled in and limited.

Society is indeed all of a piece, at least in this sense: that its various parts bear a family resemblance to one another, the outward reflection of an internal genetic (sociological, not biological) determination. But this family resemblance leaves a great deal of room for the sociological versions of sibling rivalry and marital discord and grown-up children with apartments of their own. So the bishops of the church criticize national defense policy, the universities harbor radical dissidents, the state subsidizes but also regulates corporate activity, and so on. In each case, institutions are responsive to their own internal logic even while they are also responsive to systemic determinations. The play of internal logic can only be repressed by tyrannical force, crossing the lines, breaking through the walls established by the art of separation. Liberalism is best understood as an argument against that sort of repression. It would be a meaningless argument, and tyranny a superfluous politics, unless independent churches and universities, and autonomous states, really existed or might really exist in the world. But they can and sometimes do exist. The art of separation is not an illusory or fantastic enterprise; it is a morally and politically necessary adaptation to the complexities of modern life. Liberal theory reflects and reinforces a long-term process of social differentiation. I shall want to argue that liberal theorists often misunderstand this process, but at least they recognize its significance.

Marxist writers tend to deny the significance of the process. It is, on their view, a transformation that doesn't make a substantial difference, an event or a series of events that takes place largely in the world of appearances. Liberal freedoms are, all of them, unreal. As the formal freedom of the worker is only a mask for wage slavery, so religious liberty, academic freedom, free enterprise, self-determination, and privacy are masks for continued or reiterated subjection: the forms are new, but the content is old. The difficulty with this view is that it doesn't connect in any plausible way with the actual experience of contemporary politics; it has a quality of abstraction and theoretical willfulness. No one who has lived in an illiberal state is going to accept this devaluation of the range of liberal freedoms. The achievement of liberalism is real even if it is incomplete. But the recognition of this achievement is difficult within a Marxist framework: for the commitment to organic wholeness and deep structural transformation doesn't readily accommodate separated spheres and autonomous institutions. Nor is it my purpose here to try to work out such an accommodation. I want instead to pursue the alternative criticism that liberals have not been serious enough about their own art. And I want to suggest that where they have been serious they have been guided by an inadequate and misleading theory. As with other forms of social life and political action, the liberal enterprise lends itself to more than one interpretation.

[3]

The art of separation doesn't make only for liberty but also for equality. Consider again, one by one, the examples with which I began. Religious liberty annuls the coercive power of political and ecclesiastical officials. Hence it creates, in principle, the priesthood of all believers, that is, it leaves all believers equally free to seek their own salvation; and it tends to create, in practice, churches dominated by laymen rather than by priests. Academic freedom provides theoretical, if not always practical, protection for autonomous universities, within which it is difficult to sustain the privileged position of rich or aristocratic children. The free market is open to all comers, without regard to race or creed; alien and pariah groups commonly exploit its opportunities; and though it yields unequal results, these results never simply reproduce the hierarchy of blood or caste or, for that matter, of "merit." The "career open to talents," if it is really open, provides equal opportunities to equally talented individuals. The idea of privacy presupposes the equal value, at least so far as the authorities are concerned, of all private lives; what goes on in an ordinary home is as much entitled to protection, and is entitled to as much protection, as what goes on in a castle.

Under the aegis of the art of separation, liberty and equality go together. Indeed, they invite a single definition: we can say that a (modern, complex, and differentiated) society enjoys both freedom and equality when success in one institutional setting isn't convertible into success in another, that is, when the separations hold, when political power doesn't shape the church or religious zeal the state, and so on. There are, of course, constraints and inequalities within each institutional setting, but we will have little reason to worry about these if they reflect the internal logic of institutions and practices (or, as I have already argued in *Spheres of Justice,* if social goods like grace, knowledge, wealth, and office are distributed in accordance with shared understandings of what they are and what they are for).[6] But, all too often, the separations don't hold. The liberal achievement has been to protect a number of important institutions and practices from political power, to limit the reach of government. Liberals are quick to see the danger to freedom and equality when the police repress a minority religion in the name of theoretical truth, or shut down petty-bourgeois enterprises in the name of economic planning, or invade private homes in the name of morality or law and order. They are right in all these cases, but these are not the only cases, or the only kinds of cases, in which liberty and equality are threatened. We need to look closely at the ways in which wealth, once political tyranny is abolished, itself takes on tyrannical forms. Limited government is the great success of the art of separation, but that very success opens the way for what political scientists call *private* government, and it is with the critique of private government that the leftist complaint against liberalism properly begins.

The line between political community and civil society was meant to mark off coercive decision making from free exchange. That's why the sale of offices was banned and the old baronial right to do justice and conscript soldiers was transferred to state officials. And that's why those same officials were denied the right to interfere in market transactions. But it is a false view of civil society, a bad sociology, to claim that all that goes on in the marketplace is free exchange and that coercion is never an issue there. Market success overrides the limits of the (free) market is three closely related ways. First of all, radical inequalities of wealth generate their own coerciveness, so that many exchanges are only formally free. Second, certain sorts of market power, organized, say, in corporate structures, generate patterns of command and obedience in which even the formalities of exchange give way to something that looks very much like government. And third, vast wealth and ownership or control of productive forces convert readily into government in the strict sense: capital regularly and successfully calls upon the coercive power of the state.[7]

The problem here is less importantly a failure of nerve than a failure of perception. Liberal theorists literally did not "see" individual wealth and corporate power as social forces, with a political weight, as it were, different from their market value. They aimed to create a free market, and thought that they had done enough when they opposed state intervention and set entrepreneurs free. But a free market, in which the three kinds of coercion that I listed above are (largely) ineffective, requires a positive structure. Free exchange won't maintain itself; it needs to be maintained by institutions, rules, mores, and customary practices. Consider for a moment the religious analogy. The art of separation worked against state churches and church states not only by disestablishing the church but also by divesting it of wealth and power. Nor did it do this in the name of private faith alone, but also in the name of congregational self-government. Congregationalism is by no means the natural or the only possible institutional arrangement once church and state have been separated, but it is the cultural form best adapted to and most likely to reinforce the separation. Similarly in the economic sphere: The art of separation should work against both state capitalism and the capitalist state, but it won't work successfully unless it is accompanied by disestablishment and divestment—and unless appropriate cultural forms develop within the economic sphere. The analogue to private conscience is individual enterprise; the analogue to congregational self-government is cooperative ownership.

Without divestment and without cooperative ownership, the market is bound to take shape in ways that defy the art of separation. New connections are quickly established. As I have already indicated, these are most importantly connections with the state, originating now from the market side rather than the state side, but deep and powerful nonetheless. In addition, unlimited wealth threatens all the institutions and practices of civil society—academic freedom, the career open to talents, the equality of "homes" and "castles." It is less overt, more insidious than state coercion, but no one can doubt the ready convertibility of wealth into power, privilege, and position. Where are the walls that wall in the market? In principle, perhaps, they already exist, but they will never be effective until private governments are socialized, just as established churches were socialized, that is, turned over to their participants. Religious democracy must find its parallel in industrial democracy. I won't try here to specify any particular set of institutional arrangements; there are many possible arrangements compatible with the two crucial requirements: that there should be room for the entrepreneur and the new company, just as there is room for the evangelist and the "gathered" church; and that there should not be room for the kind of economic power that shapes and determines public policy, any more than for the high ecclesiastical authority that routinely calls upon the "secular arm."

With this analogy, we can glimpse a consistent liberalism—that is, one that passes over into democratic socialism. But this is still a democratic socialism of a liberal sort; it does not require the abolition of the market (nor does it require the abolition of religion) but rather the confinement of the market to its proper space. Given an illiberal socialism, where the state takes total control of economic life, the same imperative would work in the opposite way, not to confine the market but to reassert its independence from the political realm. In the United States, then, the art of separation requires the restraint and transformation of corporate power. In the Soviet Union the same art would require, among other things, the liberation of individual enterprise.

[4]

Distributive justice is (largely) a matter of getting the lines right. But how do we do that? How do we draw the map of the social world so that churches and schools, states and markets, bureaucracies and families each find their proper place? How do we protect the participants in these different institutional settings from the tyrannical intrusions of the powerful, the wealthy, the well born, and so on? Historically, liberals have taken as their foundation a theory of individualism and natural rights. They mark out the lines so as to guarantee the secure existence and free activity of the individual. Conceived in this way, the art of separation looks like a very radical project: It gives rise to a world in which every person, every single man and woman, is separated from every other. Thus Marx: "the so-called rights of man . . . are simply the rights . . . of egoistic man, separated from other men and from the community."[8] Institutional autonomy is an intermediate, not an end point in the process of separation. The end is the individual, free within his or her circle of rights, protected from every sort of external interference. Liberal society, ideally, is simply a collection of these circles, held together by all the tangential connections and actual overlappings that their solitary inhabitants voluntarily establish.[9] Churches, schools, markets, and families are all the products of willful agreements among individuals, valuable because of the agreement they embody but at the same time subject to schism, withdrawal, cancellation, and divorce. Religious freedom is the right of the individual to worship his God (the pronoun is important, not because it is masculine, it can as easily be feminine, but because it is singular and possessive) publicly or privately, however and with whomever else he chooses; it has nothing to do, nothing in particular to do, with the doctrinal and institutional character of Judeo-Christian religiosity. Academic freedom has nothing in particular to do with the university as a social setting; it is simply the right of the individual to study, to speak, to listen as he or she pleases. All other freedoms are accounted for in similar ways.

Individual agreement is indeed an important source of our institutions, and individual rights of our freedoms. But taken together, with nothing more said, they make again for a bad sociology. They do not provide either a rich or a realistic understanding of social cohesion; nor do they make sense of the lives individuals actually live, and the rights they actually enjoy, within the framework of on-going institutions. The goal that liberalism sets for the art of separation—every person within his or her own circle—is literally unattainable. The individual who stands wholly outside institutions and relationships and enters into them only when he or she chooses and as he or she chooses: This individual does not exist and cannot exist in any conceivable social world. I once wrote that we could understand a person's obligations by studying his biography, the history of his agreements and relationships.[10] That is right, but only so long as one acknowledges that personal history is part of social history; biographies have contexts. The individual does not create the institutions that she joins; nor can she wholly shape the obligations she assumes. The individual lives within a world she did not make.

The liberal hero, author of self and of social roles, is a mythic invention: It is Shakespeare's Coriolanus, that aristocratic warrior and anti-citizen, who claims (and fails) to live "as if he were the author of himself and knew no other kin."[11] Turned into a philosophical ideal and a social policy, this claim has frightening implications, for it is endlessly disintegrative, reaching a kind of culmination, perhaps, in recent discussions about the rights of children to divorce their parents and parents their children. But this is individualism in extremis and not likely, I think, to be sustained for long. The liberal hero is more important as a sociological pretense than as a philosophical ideal. He or she opens the way for sham descriptions of churches, schools, markets, and families, as if institutions of this sort were in fact created, and wholly created, through the voluntary acts of individuals. The sham serves a practical purpose: It rules out state interference in institutional life, since the state is in its nature coercive; and it makes it very difficult to recognize other, more subtle sorts of interference (including that imitation of the state that I have already referred to as private government). More concretely, it limits the uses of political power and sets money free, for what power takes by force, money merely purchases, and the purchase has the appearance of a voluntary agreement between individuals. In fact, it is often something different than that, as we can see if we place the purchase in its context and examine its motives and effects. And then we are likely to conclude that, just as there are things the state cannot do, so there must be things that money cannot buy: votes, offices, jury decisions, university places—these are relatively easy—and also the various sorts of national influence and local domination that go along with the control of capital. But to get the limits right requires an understanding of institutional life more complex than the one that liberal individualism provides.

Churches, schools, markets, and families are social institutions with particular histories. They take different forms in different societies, forms that reflect different understandings of faith, knowledge, commodities, and kinship obligations. In no case are they shaped wholly by individual agreements, for these agreements always take place within, and are always constrained by, particular patterns of rules, customs, and cooperative arrangements. It follows from this that the art of separation is not rooted in or warranted by individual separateness (which is a biological, not a social, phenomenon); it is rooted in and warranted by social complexity. We do not separate individuals; we separate institutions, practices, relationships of different sorts. The lines we draw encircle churches and schools and markets and families, not you and me. We aim, or we should aim, not at the freedom of the solitary individual but at what can best be called institutional integrity. Individuals should be free, indeed, in all sorts of ways, but we don't set them free by separating them from their fellows.

And yet the separated individual looks more fundamental than institutions and relationships, a firmer foundation for political and social philosophy. When we build from the individual we build, so it seems to the liberal eye, from the ground up. But in fact the ground is always social: persons-in-societies, not persons-by-themselves. We never encounter persons-by-themselves, and the effort to invent them, a strenuous exercise, has no agreed-upon outcome. We do not know ourselves as strangers to one another, absolute aliens, or isolates, and there is no way to specify or understand what it would mean for such "individuals" to be free. Men and women are free when they live within autonomous institutions. We might take as our model the idea of a free state, one that is not a colony or a conquered land, a state ruled by internal rather than external forces. The inhabitants of such a state are free only in a special and limited sense, but that sense, as anyone who has endured a military conquest knows, is real and important. And if those same individuals live within a state that is internally free (I will try to say what that means in a moment) and if they participate in free churches, free universities, free firms and enterprises, and so on, we will at some point want to say that they are free generally. Freedom is additive; it consists of rights within settings, and we must understand the settings, one by one, if we are to guarantee the rights. Similarly, each freedom entails a specific form of equality or, better, the absence of a specific inequality—of conquerors and subjects, believers and infidels, trustees and teachers, owners and workers—and the sum of the absences makes an egalitarian society.

[5]

On the liberal view, men and women are not free in the state so much as from it; and they are equal under the law. So they are protected from political power, conceived as a monopoly of physical force, immensely threatening to the solitary individual. It is immensely threatening, and I want to say again that the limitation of power is liberalism's historic achievement. But if we turn from individuals to institutions, it is clear that political power itself requires protection—not only against foreign conquest but also against domestic seizure. The state is unfree when power is seized and held by a set of family members, or clergymen, or office-holders, or wealthy citizens. Dynastic, theocratic, bureaucratic, and plutocratic control all make for unfreedom—and for inequality too. Meritocratic control would have the same effect, though I don't believe it has ever been realized. Compared to family, church, office, and corporation, universities and professional schools are relatively weak, though the men and women they license are not without political pretensions. A free state, in a complex society, is one that is separated from all other institutions, that is to say, a state that is in the hands of its citizens generally—just as a free church is in the hands of believers, a free university in the hands of scholars, a free firm in the hands of workers and managers. And then citizens are free in the state as well as from it (in fact, it is not as citizens that they are free from the state but as believers, scholars, entrepreneurs, workers, parents, and so on); and they are equal in the making of the law and not only under the law.

The art of separation works to isolate social settings. But it obviously doesn't achieve, and can't achieve, anything like total isolation, for then there would be no society at all. Writing in defense of religious toleration, John Locke claimed that "the church . . . is a thing absolutely separate and distinct from the commonwealth. The boundaries . . . are fixed and immovable."[12] But this is too radical a claim, deriving, I think, more from a theory of the individual conscience than from an understanding of churches and religious practices. What goes on in one institutional setting influences all the others; the same people, after all, inhabit the different settings, and they share a history and a culture—in which religion plays a greater or lesser role. The state, moreover, always has a special influence, for it is the agent of separation and the defender, as it were, of the social map. It is not so much a night watchman protecting individuals from coercion and physical assault as it is the builder and guardian of the walls, protecting churches, universities, families, and so on from tyrannical interference. The members of these institutions also, of course, protect themselves as best they can, but their ultimate resort when they are threatened is an appeal to the state. This is so even when the threat comes from the state itself: Then they appeal from one group of officials or one branch of government to another, or they appeal against the government as a whole to the body of citizens.

One way of judging the actions of the state is to ask whether they uphold institutional integrity—including the integrity of the state itself. Consider the relatively minor example of safety regulation. *Caveat emptor,* let the buyer beware, is, as I said earlier, a rule of the market, but it covers only a certain range of wariness. It has to do with disappointment ("I don't look as handsome as I thought I would look in my new clothes"), frustration ("The blurb says this book is 'accessible to the intelligent layman,' so I bought it, but now I can't seem to understand it"), and even known and foreseeable risks ("These cigarettes are dangerous to my health"). Clothes and books and cigarettes are properly market commodities. But the range of wariness doesn't extend to unknown and un-foreseeable risks or to collective risks—as in the case, say, of unsafe cars or of cars that contaminate the air. The degree of risk that we live with on our highways and in our common environment is a matter for political decision; it belongs, so to speak, to the state and its citizens, not to the market and its buyers and sellers. At least that is so on our current understanding, as I understand it, of states and markets. The art of separation is properly artful when it draws a line that leaves the risk of disappointment on one side and the risk of disaster on the other.

But this artfulness, when it comes to concrete cases, is always controversial. There are problems of information and problems of interpretation. What goes on in this or that institutional setting? And what is the internal logic of what goes on? These questions have to be debated, first in particular institutional settings and then in the general setting of the state. The art of separation is a popular, not an esoteric, art. Liberals, however, have not always recognized its popular character, for if individual rights are at stake then philosophers and judges can claim some special understanding of its requirements. It is the courts that define and patrol the circle of rights.[13] To focus on institutions, practices, and relationships is to shift the location of agency, to socialize the art of separa-tion. Believers, scholars, workers, and parents establish and guard the lines— and then the citizens as a body do so, through the political process. Liberalism passes definitively into democratic socialism when the map of society is socially determined.

But what if some political majority misunderstands or overrides the auton-omy of this or that institutional setting? That is the unavoidable risk of democ-racy. Since the lines do not have the clear and distinct character that Locke thought them to have, they will be drawn here and there, experimentally and sometimes wrongly. The line between politics and exchange has, as I have suggested, been wrongly drawn for a long time now: And we suffer from the abuse of market power. We have to argue, then, about the location of the line and fight (democratically) to draw it differently. Probably we will never get it exactly right, and the changing character of states and markets requires, in any case, its continual revisions, so the arguing and the fighting have no visible end.

And what if tyrants seize control of this or that church or university or company or family? Michel Foucault has recently contended that a dark and rigid discipline has been clamped down upon a whole series of institutions—and that this is the work of internal elites, professional men and women with claims to scientific knowledge, not of political officials.[14] But I think that he exaggerates the success of these elites and their ability to sustain their discipline without calling upon state power. It is only in authoritarian states, which systematically violate institutional integrity, that Foucault's "disciplinary society" is likely to be realized in anything like the form that he describes. Among ourselves, the risks are of a different sort; they include but are not limited to professional pretension and aggrandizement; we also have to worry about internal corruption, bureaucratic privilege, popular fearfulness, and passivity.

All of these risks will be reduced, perhaps, insofar as the different institutional settings have themselves been socialized, so that their participants enjoy a rough equality and no group of believers, knowers, or owners is capable of reaching for political power. If men and women enjoy their different social roles, they are more likely to respect the settings within which the roles are played. This is the socialist form of the old liberal hope that individuals secure in their own circles won't invade the circles of others. It is still a problematic but also I think a more realistic hope, for it is lonely in those circles; the life of institutions is more lively and more satisfying.

NOTES

1. J. E. Neale, *Queen Elizabeth* (New York: Harcourt Brace Jovanovich, 1934) 174.

2. Draft exemptions for college students represent, perhaps, a modern version of the medieval liberties. They breach the liberal wall between state and university—not because they violate academic freedom but rather because they violate political integrity (the equal standing of citizens).

3. The art of separation remains an important feature of contemporary liberalism, as in John Rawls's *A Theory of Justice* (Cambridge: Harvard University Press, 1971). His two principles, Rawls writes, "presuppose that the social structure can be divided into two more

or less distinct parts, the first principle applying to the one, the second to the other. They distinguish between those aspects of the social system that define and secure the equal liberties of citizenship and those that specify and establish social and economic inequalities." *A Theory of Justice,* 61. Rawls redraws the old line between the state and the market, though in a rather different way than I shall suggest below.

4. Karl Marx, *Early Writings,* trans. T. B. Bottomore (London: C. A. Watts, 1963), 26.

5. Robert Michels, *Political Parties,* trans. Eden Paul and Cedar Paul (New York: Dover, 1959).

6. Michael Walzer, *Spheres of Justice: A Defense of Pluralism and Equality* (New York: Basic Books, 1983).

7. The best recent account of the transformation of market power into political power is Charles E. Lindblom, *Politics and Markets* (New York: Basic Books, 1977), esp. pt. 5.

8. Marx, *Early Writings,* 24.

9. I omit here any discussion of the early twentieth-century pluralists, some of whom are plausibly called liberals, since their arguments never attained the high philosophical respectability of the doctrine of individual rights.

10. Michael Walzer, *Obligations: Essays on Disobedience, War, and Citizenship* (Cambridge: Harvard University Press, 1970), x.

11. William Shakespeare, *Coriolanus,* 5.3.

12. John Locke, *A Letter Concerning Toleration,* ed. Patrick Romanell (Indianapolis: Bobbs-Merrill, 1950), 27.

13. For a strong statement of the role of courts in defense of rights, see Ronald Dworkin, *Taking Rights Seriously* (Cambridge: Harvard University Press, 1977).

14. See especially Michel Foucault's *Discipline and Punish: The Birth of the Prison,* trans. Alan Sheridan (New York: Vintage, 1979). The argument works best for institutions like prisons, hospitals, and asylums, where the subjects of discipline are civically, physically, or mentally incapacitated, but Foucault means it to apply also to schools and factories: 293ff.

CHAPTER FIVE

Justice Here and Now

For most intellectual purposes, we draw a line between philosophical speculation about politics and actual political debate. It is conceivably a useful line, but it is also an artificial and sometimes a misleading line. For philosophy reflects and articulates the political culture of its time, and politics presents and enacts the arguments of philosophy. Of course, one-eyed philosophers distort what they reflect, and simpleminded and partisan politicians mutilate what they enact, but there can be no doubt about the two-way movement. Philosophy is politics reflected upon in tranquillity, and politics is philosophy acted out in confusion. The link between the two, the connection of theory to practice, was once thought to be a special concern of the left: it was the goal of the left to overcome the division of labor between philosophers and politicians, to impose upon philosophers something of the immediacy of political struggle so as to give them a chance at something like the pleasure of political victory. Leftist writers were prepared to intensify present confusions for the sake of future tranquillities. But the clearest contemporary example of the connection between philosophy and politics comes from the right: market ideology and its immediate companion, the new politics of laissez-faire.

This same example also provides wonderful material for the study of one-eyed philosophers and simpleminded and partisan politicians. For market ideology is a highly distorted reflection of our political culture, ignoring or repressing examples of communal cooperation and state action and denying the significance of political struggles for public health, industrial democracy, workplace safety, environmental control, and so on. And laissez-faire politics has taken the form of a crude attack on the welfare state, leaving the large-scale public subsidy of capitalist enterprise untouched. But I don't want to elaborate these commonplace criticisms except incidentally in the course of a rather different and more positive project. I shall try to address some of the issues that figure in current political debates and to describe what I take to be the necessary features of distributive justice in the United States today. It is important to stress that last prepositional phrase: in the United States today, that is, among ourselves, given our lives, values, and common practices. It is my purpose here not to make universal pronouncements but to reflect upon the real and particular pluralism of American culture and to suggest the pattern of social policy that follows from that pluralism. How must we live together if we are not to oppress and injure one another?

[I]

The first requirement of distributive justice is a shared economic, social, and cultural infrastructure, a public sector that both enlarges the scope of and gives some determinate shape to our private lives: roads, bridges, mass transit, national parks, communication systems, schools, museums, and so on. It may be that the great age of construction in these areas lies behind us; certainly we have lost our sense of the necessary collective base of our everyday social life and of the political decisions and economic costs required to sustain that base. At the moment we are not sustaining it; we stand and watch its slow decay. In itself, I suppose, the decay of the infrastructure is a matter not of justice or injustice but rather of wisdom and foolishness—though contemporary foolishness imposes costs on future generations, and that may be an unjust imposition. Among ourselves, at any rate, we have every right to choose public impoverishment for the sake of private affluence, so long as the choice reflects a democratic decision and so long as the impoverishment and the affluence are shared across the society. But these conditions are rarely met.

The purpose of the infrastructure is to enable the mass of citizens to participate in necessary or valued social activities. Hence its construction and repair, when they are decided upon in some more or less democratic fashion, provide a rough index of contemporary understandings of those activities. Again and again, over long periods of time, money must be appropriated and costs distributed. Should we, to take an easy and obvious example, subsidize the highways and the suburbs or the subways and the cities? How much are we prepared to invest in safety? in recreation? in high culture? These decisions give concrete shape to a way of life. The decay of the infrastructure and its replacement by private facilities has the effect of disabling or excluding some citizens, but not others, from participating in that way of life. Or it has the effect of undercutting the democratic process by which our common ways are shaped.

Let me illustrate that last effect by considering a proposal put forward by the president of a California research institute in the wake of the collapse of a bridge in Connecticut. (The locations of the institute and the bridge are not without significance.) It would be better, the institute president tells us, to sell our highways and bridges "to private firms that would operate them as competing, self-financed business ventures." Travel would then be safer than it is today because "the prospect of a multi-million dollar liability in the event of a bridge collapse would lead the new owners to make rapid, major investments in re-building."[1] This is an interesting argument—though not, as it pretends to be, a laissez-faire argument. The safety record of private enterprise has never been very good except when safety is imposed by the state, and so it would be under this proposal, in the form of "multi-million dollar liability." In effect, the proposal to sell highways and bridges to private companies is a proposal to rely on the courts rather than the legislature to set safety standards and user costs.[2] Government is still crucial, but now the least democratic rather than the most democratic branch of government would play the decisive role. If the standards were set very high, the price of maintenance and insurance would be passed on to the men and women who used the roads; if it became impossible to meet those standards and still maintain a respectable profit margin, the "new owners" would quickly apply to the state for a subsidy. Then, indeed, the legislature would have to make a decision, but it would decide under severe (and by now familiar) constraints—for aren't these owners providing essential services? At the same time, whatever profits were made would be invested at the sole discretion of the owners. How, then, would we decide what new roads and bridges to build? It is false to assume that these are merely market decisions; they determine patterns of development, habitation, and work as well as patterns of travel and recreation. And they affect the lives of people whom the owners don't know and will never consult. Nor will the courts consult these people, for though judicial decisions on liability will, at least initially, determine the whole pattern of costs, they will do so with reference only to the entitlements of particular individuals. Even if we assume that justice is done to these individuals, the subsequent shaping of the infrastructure would be unjust to all the rest of us.

The injustice in this case would be political, a failure of democracy (in a country explicitly committed to democratic politics). But this sort of failure may well lead to injustices of another sort. When we decide to subsidize subways, for example, we do so because we want to live in a city of a certain kind, where movement is easy and cultural facilities are generally available, and where individuals are not trapped in their neighborhoods. If such a vision is widely shared, then the decay of the subway system (through public inadvertence) or the lapse of the subsidy (through privatization) is likely to make full participation in the urban economy and culture impossible for some people, who will then plausibly claim that they are being treated unjustly. One can imagine a city, divided, say, into ethnic "quarters," each with its own internal life, where the absence or failure of public transportation would merely confirm the shared understanding of urbanity and injure no one. But we don't live in cities of that sort, and among ourselves the injury would be palpable. Indeed, I can leave the conditional mood behind: the injury is palpable. In an inegalitarian society, the decay of the infrastructure has differential effects, constraining the activities, limiting the scope of some people and not others. These constraints have never been ratified democratically, and they are, in any case, inconsistent with a democratic social life.

[2]

The second requirement of distributive justice is a system of communal provision. The infrastructure is enabling, but not everyone is able, and we need to care for the ill, the aged, the infirm, the destitute, the unemployed, and so on. The state has to be a welfare state. This is, I think, a general truth about all states, a moral fact. Every state that I have ever encountered in the study of history and comparative politics is in some sense committed, or at least claims to be committed, to the welfare of its own people (though not necessarily of conquered or captive peoples). Its officials secure the trade routes and the grain supply, organize the irrigation of the fields, appease the gods, ward off hostile foreigners, look after public health, care for widows and orphans, and so on. Or they bustle about importantly pretending to do these things. And these are the sorts of things they ought to do. What in particular they ought to do will depend on the local political culture and the shared understanding of social life. The emphasis of our own welfare state, for example, is overwhelmingly on physical well-being and long life. The amount of money that we spend on health care is probably without precedent in the history of human civilization. That emphasis isn't simply a matter of justice; it would not be unjust, for example, if we spent more of our money on housing, or schooling, or even on science and the arts. Given the prevailing emphasis, however, justice requires that the protection we provide be provided across the class of citizens, to everyone who is ill. I have argued elsewhere that this requires in turn something like a national health service and the enlistment or conscription of physicians for the sake of that service.[3] I won't repeat that argument here; the important claim is simply that the state should respond to the socially recognized needs of its members. That is what the state is for.

The response can take different forms. "A system of communal provision" doesn't necessarily mean a single centralized and uniform system. The requirements of justice are not exact. They do not derive from a doctrine of individual rights such that every individual is entitled, given similar illnesses, say, to exactly the same treatment. If that were the case, then every hospital would have to be organized in the same way, with the same equipment and the same medical procedures. Local differences would be ruled out, even if they were shaped by democratic decisions about budgets, bond issues, hospital government, and so on. Similarly, every schoolchild would have to attend the same sort of school, similarly furnished and equipped, and work through the same curriculum under the guidance of similarly trained teachers and along with an identical mix of other children. None of this is necessary, for the rights in question are social rights; they have their origin in a shared social life, and they partake of the rough and ready character of that life. We make a great mistake when we acquiesce in descriptions of the welfare state as a kind of war against the inevitable and ultimately comfortable messiness of human society: a systematic effort to turn society into "a clean, well-lighted place." No doubt our hospitals should be clean and our urban streets well lit. But there is plenty of room in a welfare state that meets the requirements of justice for chance and risk, for local and diverse arrangements, for voluntary as well as coercive organization, for amateur warmth alongside professional coolness.

The contemporary right-wing demand that government "get off our backs" is entirely legitimate whenever governmental agents interfere with ethnic or religious or regional efforts at collective self-help. But the demand isn't legitimate when it represents (as it most often does) an effort to evade the responsibilities of the collective. This evasion is often masked as a defense of voluntarism and pluralism, but it is also justified, sometimes, in a more direct and forthright way. The responsibilities of the collective have become too onerous, it is said; the costs of the welfare state are too high; and, after all, private life and even private affluence are also central values of American culture. I shall leave aside the standard liberal-left response to this sort of thing, though it is an important and largely true response, namely, that we already run our welfare state on the cheap and that levels of taxation and expenditure are relatively low compared with those of other Western countries. It may be the case that communal sentiment and practical solidarity are so attenuated in American society as to make it difficult to justify higher levels of taxation. But if the costs of welfare are too high in the United States today, then they have to be cut in ways that respect the equal standing of citizens. It is obviously unjust to reduce communal provision only for politically vulnerable men and women and children—so obviously unjust that government officials who do so are compelled to lie about what they are doing.

A more general reduction—not only in funds targeted to desperate individuals and depressed areas but also in medicare, unemployment insurance, and social security—would never command popular support. Is this because we have created a dependent population, men and women with their hands held out, unwilling, perhaps unable, to stand on their own?[4] The description is both condescending and false. We would do better to say that, after long political struggles, the mass of citizens have come to understand the democratic state as a cooperative enterprise and to assert their claim to the fruits of that enterprise. It is not the purpose of the democratic state, rightly understood, to uphold the power of the few or to redistribute wealth to the wealthy—though this is what states have commonly done: the rich have always had their hands out—but to sustain equally the lives and minimal well-being of all its citizens. Even if we were to fall on collective hard times, even if the people were to decide on a lower level of communal provision, this purpose would remain paramount. Hence reductions would have to begin, so to speak, at the top, and they would have to be carried out in ways that did not weaken the position of the weakest citizens. This is a version of Rawls's difference principle that commands not only hypothetical but actual consent. It is expressed in the idea of a "safety net," and were this idea taken seriously, it would probably rule out any reductions at all in current welfare standards: for those reductions that are morally possible are politically impossible, and those that are politically possible are morally barred.

The idea of the "safety net" is a more powerful idea than is commonly thought. It means that the first commitment of the welfare state is to its weakest members; nothing else can be done until their position is secured. What counts as security is a matter for political debate: how high do we hang the net? But answers to this question are not arbitrary; security is a relative term, which has to be understood together with the values of the society and the common expectations of its members. The better-off members are entitled to protect their private lives—as they will anyway be inclined to do in a liberal society—but only so long as they recognize the extent to which those lives are themselves protected by the community as a whole and only so long as they are prepared to extend communal protection to all the other members. In the United States today that extension would require a considerable restructuring of the welfare state for the sake of equal protection. Whether it would also require a refinancing of the welfare state is a question I can leave aside. I suspect that restructuring would entail, for reasons of political if not moral logic, greater expenditure, but if we were prepared to spend less money enhancing the lives of the rich and the merely prosperous, we could probably spend less money simply. The crucial point is that the safety net be constructed so as to secure for everyone whatever it is we collectively believe to be the central values of our culture, the needs that must be met if we are to stand to one another as *fellow* citizens.

[3]

The third requirement of distributive justice is nicely stated in the classical liberal slogan about "equality of opportunity." But this slogan is not well understood when it is taken to legitimize the familiar forms of competition—as if the goals of the competitive race are given, and only the number and the handicaps of the runners are at issue. In fact, the three words "equality of opportunity" tell us nothing about what opportunities ought to be available. It's not the case that opportunities are fixed forever in the prevailing set; nor are they necessarily responsive, even in a liberal society, to individual preference. We need not set about opening career paths to feudal lordship or political tyranny, for example, even if there are people around who long to be lords and tyrants. We discourage such ambitions, forcibly if necessary; and the discouragement is in no sense unjust. Nor would it be unjust if we were to discourage ambitions for the higher forms of capitalist ownership. We tell ambitious bureaucrats that they can climb the institutional ladder only so far: unlimited power is not within their reach. Similarly, we might tell ambitious entrepreneurs that they can enrich themselves only so far: unlimited wealth (ownership of the major means of production, say) is not within their reach. What the range of opportunities should be is something, again, that can only be decided politically and that always has to be decided with reference to a particular set of cultural values and social understandings.

In the United States today, there are three social goods to which equality of opportunity is relevant: the first is office (in both bureaucracies and the professions); the second is money or market power; the third is political power. With regard to all three, strong anti-authoritarian tendencies are at work, and have been at work for some time, reflecting the deepest values of a liberal and demo-cratic culture. We can think of these tendencies as imposing limits on available opportunities. Review boards, consent requirements, collective bargaining, grievance procedures, government licensing of radio and television stations, democratic politics itself—all these instrumentalities restrict what one can do with office, wealth, and power. Conceivably, these restrictions make the goods less *good*, less attractive to the men and women who seek or hold them; certainly, the restrictions make the goods less dangerous to the men and women who don't seek or hold them. In any case, the nature of the competition changes as the nature of the opportunities change. It is easier to succeed and less disastrous to fail when goods are limited (not in number but) in value. Equality of oppor-tunity is more likely when the slope of ambition and advantage is less steep.

This rule holds for two reasons. First, unlimited office, wealth, and power make it possible for those who win such goods to close off opportunities to everyone else. Indeed, the failure of limits in any one sphere endangers equality of opportunity in all the others—for unlimited wealth can buy office and power, unlimited power can control the market and shape the professions, and so on. This is the common historical pattern, and it explains most of the standard inequalities. Today's inequalities of opportunity derive from yesterday's victo-ries and defeats; they are inherited from the past, carried not by genetic but by social structures, by organized power, wealth, and professional standing. But the rule holds for a second reason also. When we open old opportunities to new groups of competitors, the immediate effect is to intensify the competition, to generate the classical rat race. And the rat race is not an ideal setting for equality of opportunity. One might say that the rat race provides opportunities only for rats. An exaggeration, perhaps, but the statement is not wholly untrue. When competition is too fierce (because the stakes are too high), all sorts of social and psychological mechanisms come into play to foster aggressive and ruthless behavior among some people and withdrawal and resignation among others. To some extent, the resulting pattern will overlap with older patterns of class or group subordination; to some extent, its shape will be new. But if we imagine equality of opportunity as it was conventionally imagined among liberals and democrats, as a way of creating an open, fluid, and lively social life, the rat race represents a defeat. There isn't, so to speak, enough room on the steep slope of ambition and advantage.

Equality of opportunity won't work unless the slope is flattened—and that is what the democratic understanding of office, wealth, and power also requires.

Hence it is what justice requires. It must still be possible, in a society like ours, to exercise professional authority, make money in the marketplace, win political power. These are legitimate opportunities—so long as they are available only in ways that don't establish positions of privilege, social strongholds that other men and women can take only by storm and that are always desperately defended. Since many opportunities are both attractive and exclusive, competition is inevitable, and so is winning and losing; nor will winning ever lose its sweetness or losing its bitterness. But it is possible to describe a society—different from but also deriving from our own society—in which winning doesn't breed arrogance and domination and losing doesn't breed servility and subjection, and in which winners and losers can imagine themselves in each other's places. This is, after all, the actual experience of democratic politics. Powerful men and women lose elections and surrender their power. They must be ready to do that and then to return to private life, for otherwise opposition would be too dangerous and the right of opposition never fully established or widely exercised. Similarly, equality of opportunity requires a (relatively) easy mobility up and down the scale of professional and financial standing. That mobility is not easily established, either for individuals or for families, but its acceptance is more likely if the advantages that go with office and money are less far-reaching than they are today.

If we are committed to equal opportunity, then, we would do best to reduce the steepness of the slope of advantage. This is not the goal that is served by contemporary affirmative action programs; they aim instead at making the existing scramble for office and money more accessible to women and to minority groups and, by virtue of that new accessibility, more fair. The scramble should be more fair; such programs, so long as they avoid rigid quotas, are readily defensible. I would argue, however, that they will have only a limited and local effect if the men and women they advance merely take over established positions. The point is to change the nature of the positions, and so offer to the men and women who come next the prospect of a scramble that is at once more lively and less fierce, for a wider range of opportunities.

[4]

The fourth requirement of distributive justice is a strong democracy. In a sense, equality of opportunity encompasses the argument for democracy because it requires that political power be widely available to citizens. This requirement is important for two reasons: first, because power is a good thing to have (it is even a good thing to share, that is, to have in something less than the strongest sense of the word "have"); second, because power is the crucial instrument for determining infrastructural and welfare state priorities and for shaping available opportunities in other fields. It has intrinsic and instrumental value, and the experience of these values should be common and readily accessible in a democratic society.

Justice, however, requires not only the openness of the sphere of power but also its integrity. Wherever the exercise of power takes on political forms, wherever it is sustained, serious, and extensive, it must be subject to the distributional rules of democratic politics. For now I shall simply assume the existence and importance of these rules—free speech, free assembly, periodic elections, and so on. The question I want to raise has to do with the area over which they are enforced. In a capitalist society, historically, enforcement is barred from the marketplace; entrepreneurs and property owners are exempt from the requirements of democracy; a line is drawn between economy and polity. The establishment of unions and collective bargaining under the sponsorship or at least the protection of the state blurs that line. So does the steady growth of governmental regulation. It is time now to think about the reasons for unions and for regulations and to attempt a more explicit and radical boundary revision.

The reasons have to do with what goes on in the economic sphere. If we focus narrowly on entrepreneurial activity and on petty-bourgeois enterprise, we can, perhaps, describe a "pure" economy: all transactions, or by far the greater number of transactions, can plausibly be talked about in the language of free exchange. But if we focus on the modern corporation, all such plausibility vanishes. For corporations are—this is now a commonplace of American political science—private governments; their transactions are significantly political in character, taking the form of command and obedience rather than free exchange; their owners and agents make decisions that determine the costs and the risks that other people must live with.[5] It is the experience of private government that prompts the internal opposition of unions and the external interventions of the state. The unions represent men and women directly subject to corporate power; the state represents men and women radically affected by corporate decisions. But these two forms of representation are only sometimes effective, and effective then only to a limited degree, because corporate power at its core remains exempt from the rules of democracy. The exemption is defended, these days, not with an argument that private government is after all legitimate, but with a denial that private government exists: there is no one out here but us entrepreneurs. Since the denial is false, justice requires that we challenge the exemption and explore systematically the alternatives to private government: public ownership and workers' control and various combinations of the two.

Marxists have long argued that the fundamental moral problem of the capitalist economy (if there is a *moral* problem at all) is exploitation, not domination, the extraction of surplus value through the productive process, not the tyrannical control of production.[6] The theory of exploitation, at least as it has commonly been understood, makes a strong claim: that workers are literally robbed of value that they and only they create. They work but don't reap the full benefits of their work; someone else benefits who hasn't worked at all. The injustice is plain, at least if one accepts Marx's account of the creation of value. Conceivably, the injustice would still be plain even if one recognized a wider creativity than Marx allows for: it might still be said that workers don't get their "fair share" of the surplus they help to create. That, indeed, is what workers commonly say when they demand higher wages. But the complaint about *unfair shares* isn't the most important of their complaints. For exploitation is merely one consequence of the failure of democracy in economic life. When wages are very low, it looks like the crucial consequence and the necessary focus of working-class militancy. It isn't, however, an issue that can be addressed by itself. Private government is a prior issue—not only in theory: it always, in fact, comes first. The earliest and sharpest form of class struggle is the struggle against the tyranny of owners and foremen, the daily discipline of the workplace, the arbitrary layoffs and firings; and the earliest and greatest working-class victories are the victories that bring union recognition, grievance procedures, seniority rules, and so on. It is the distribution of power, not of surplus value, that is crucial. Power is instrumental to the acquisition of surplus value, but that is never the only reason for seeking it; citizenship and self-respect are also at stake.

As a political economist, not a moralist, Marx argued that capitalism had created vast collective enterprises that would necessarily come under collective control. I don't know if that argument is right; I'm not a political economist. But the argument has a moral analogue, in which "should" substitutes for "would"—and the analogue is certainly right. Collective enterprises should be governed collectively, in accordance with the shared understanding of how such government works. Among ourselves, that understanding is democratic: hence, again, the requirement of industrial democracy.

Industrial democracy will make for "fair shares," but only in this special sense: that some particular idea of fairness will be chosen over some other idea, and the idea that is chosen will command widespread support. There are, indeed, many claims on surplus value—entrepreneurial profits and capital costs; investment; the social costs of welfare, safety, environmental protection; management costs; research costs; worker shares, which can be paid in money or in time; and so on—and many different proposals for an equitable or a prudent division. Though market considerations are relevant to all these claims, we must also make political choices. The theory of exploitation does not help us much to make these choices, for there is no division of surplus value, so much here, so much there, that is just in itself. But a division that is the work of democratic citizens will at least reflect current understandings of justice, and it will leave the way open for better understandings.

Throughout this chapter I have emphasized the importance of politics. The social infrastructure, the pattern of communal provision, the range of opportunities, the division of surplus value: all these must be decided politically, though always with reference to shared understandings that are themselves worked out through deeper social processes. Hence political justice, or democracy, is the immediate form of justice. But democracy, though it rests ultimately upon a substantive distribution of power—one citizen, one vote—takes in practice the form of a procedural allocation of power—chiefly through free elections. And elections have unpredictable outcomes; the resulting distributive decisions are, sometimes, unjust. So justice requires that justice itself be democratically at risk. This means that your favored conception, or mine, of infrastructural priorities, or the necessary forms of welfare, or the nature of available opportunities, or the division of this or that factory's profits, may be rejected. Justice is not likely to be achieved by the enactment of a single philosophy of justice, but rather of this philosophical view and then of that one, insofar as these views seem to the citizens to capture the moral realities of their common life. And the enactment is always, as I said at the beginning, "in confusion"—justice is not an instant and exact order; it isn't the end of political contention.

The contention is endless, but it isn't philosophically uncontrolled. Political argument is not a matter of searching randomly for whatever claims, examples, or precedents will help us on our way to victory; it is not a matter of rhetorical gesture or mere expedience. Individuals and groups will, of course, defend their particular interests as best they can, but they must also refer themselves to the common interests and the shared values of their society. They are participants in a process not only of egoistic assertion but also of collective interpretation. In the United States today, that process has its beginning in an account of the meaning of citizenship. I have been assuming such an account, and it has provided me with an egalitarian baseline: for citizenship in a democratic state entails equality. But citizenship doesn't reproduce equality in all the spheres of social life—not even in politics itself, where the allocation of power through elections makes some citizens more powerful than others. How much equality is appropriate to each sphere is a difficult question, for it depends on interpretations that lack certainty and on decisions that lack finality. We can get things wrong. Indeed, it has been my claim in this chapter that we have gotten things wrong and made our citizens more unequal than they ought to be. We have not sustained the infrastructure that our social life requires. We have not made a sufficient commitment to communal provision. We have not provided a wide enough range of opportunities. We have not challenged the power of private governments. Justice requires that we do all these things, but it also requires that we do them democratically. Hence the burden that egalitarian philosophers must accept: to provide a persuasive interpretation of democratic citizenship and then of the goods and opportunities that citizens distribute to one another— I mean American citizens, here and now, who rightly have the authoritative (but never the final) word.

NOTES

1. Robert Poole, "How Should We Fix I-95's Ailing Bridges? By Selling Them Off," *New York Times* (July 9, 1983), op ed page.

2. Robert Nozick provides a full-scale philosophic defense of this position in *Anarchy, State, and Utopia* (New York: Basic Books, 1974), chap. 4.

3. Michael Walzer, *Spheres of Justice: A Defense of Pluralism and Equality* (New York: Basic Books, 1983), chap. 3.

4. This is a common charge against the welfare state; see, for example, George Gilder, *Wealth and Poverty* (New York: Basic Books, 1981), especially pt. 2.

5. There is a large literature on private government; for a recent and especially useful discussion. see Charles E. Lindblom, *Politics and Markets* (New York; Basic Books, 1977). chaps. 13, 14.

6. Robert Tucker argues for the centrality of the idea of domination, in the economy as well as the state, in *The Marxian Revolutionary Idea* (New York; Norton, 1969). Marxist views of justice have been much debated in recent years; for some of the best statements, see Marshall Cohen, Thomas Nagel, and Thomas Scanlon, eds., *Marx, Justice, and History* (Princeton; Princeton University Press, 1980).

CHAPTER SIX

Exclusion, Injustice, and the Democratic State

[1]

W ho is in and who is out?—these are the first questions that any
political community must answer about itself. Particular communities are constituted by the answers they give or, better, by the
process through which it is decided whose answers count. This is true even if
the decision isn't definitive, doesn't draw an absolute line between insiders
and outsiders. In fact, absolutism is rarely possible here. Ancients Greeks and
Israelites, for example, distinguished themselves from foreigners on relatively
straightforward kinship lines. But their political communities included, alongside citizens and brethren, an intermediate group of resident aliens, *metics* or
ge'rim—not kin, but not foreign either, sharing some but not all of the rights and
duties of members. What may be more important, divisions of class and gender
cut across all these categories, so that there were in both Greece and Israel
powerless members and powerful strangers: the formal rules of inclusion and
exclusion did not determine the actual process of political (or everyday social
and economic) decision making. Nor would it have bothered Greek philosophers or Jewish sages that women, slaves, urban workers, and "people of the
land" (*am ha-aretz*)—even if they were native born and genealogically correct—
had little or no say in the government of their communities. The exclusion of
such people was probably less problematic than that of resident aliens.

Among ourselves, with our huge populations of guest workers and illegal
immigrants, we have reproduced the old intermediate class. We have our own
resident aliens, in but not of the political community, their rights and obligations as disputed today as they were two thousand years ago. The other kind of
exclusion, however, we at least pretend to have overcome. We have expanded the

ancient understanding of citizenship and brotherhood, abolishing class and gender barriers, incorporating women, slaves, and workers, producing the modern, inclusive *demos*. All the people, every man and woman, are or are supposed to be equal participants in all the spheres of justice, sharing, as members, in the distribution of welfare, security, wealth, education, office, political power, and so on—and also joining in the debates about what that sharing involves and how it ought to be managed.

It was the argument of my book *Spheres of Justice* that this participation (with a little luck!) would give rise to a "complex equality" of members.[1] Not that all goods would be distributed equally to all members: given the nature, that is, the social meaning and customary use, of the goods, equal distribution is neither desirable nor possible. Rather, different goods would be distributed for different reasons by different agents to different people—so that no single group of people would be dominant across the spheres; nor would the possession of one good, like wealth or power or familial reputation, bring all the others in train. People who fared badly in one distributive sphere would do better in another, and the result would be a horizontal and socially extended version of Aristotle's "ruling and being ruled in turn." No one would rule or be ruled all the time and everywhere. No one would be radically excluded.

But this is an ideal picture, a critical standard, describing how things would turn out if people actually joined in the distributive work and successfully defended the autonomy of the spheres. Defense is always necessary, since any socially significant good—money in a capitalist society is the obvious example—is likely to be convertible into all the other goods and so to serve as a medium of domination for those who possess it. Inequality is always worked through some such medium. Land or money or political power or racial or religious identity (or some subset of these) become the means of access to the entire range of social goods. The agents of autonomous distributions are effectively disempowered. And then poor people, members of racial or religious minorities, heterodox men and women share only minimally in their country's good times, bear the brunt of economic decline, are shut out of the better schools and offices, carry everywhere the stigma of failure. We thus reproduce the internal exclusions of the ancient world: disenfranchised, powerless, unemployed, and marginalized members.

We don't quite know what to call these people—the dispossessed, the underclass, the truly disadvantaged, the socially isolated, the estranged poor—and this confusion about their classification reflects a deeper embarrassment about their existence. For the whole tendency of modern (welfarist or social) democracy, so we once thought, is to make the reproduction of marginality and exclusion increasingly difficult. Civil service exams and laws requiring "fair employment practices" open available careers to talented citizens, whoever they are—blocking the distribution of offices and jobs through a network of relatives, ethnic or religious kin, or "old boys." Public schools and meritocratic admissions policies guarantee the distribution of educational opportunities without regard to race or religion. Universal entitlement programs preclude the use of welfare as a form of political patronage. The public defender, the ban on bribery, and the new limits on campaign contributions protect the judicial system and the political process against the corruptions of wealth. Religious toleration and cultural pluralism allow individual men and women to worship and live independently, unconventionally, without fear of political or economic penalty. In all these, and many other, ways we defend the boundaries of the spheres of justice. Why, then, are we still so far from complex equality?

[2]

I want to make two arguments in response to this question: first, that the convertibility of social goods and the domination it makes possible take increasingly subtle and indirect forms in modern societies; they have hardly yet been subjected to democratic control. And second, that given the continued existence of excluded groups, the state must play a larger role in advancing the cause of complex equality than I envisaged for it when I wrote about these matters ten years ago. The first argument deals with an overestimation of the justice of contemporary distributions, the second with an underestimation of the state as an agent of distributive justice.

The old accounts of inequality and exclusion, focused on dominant goods and ruling classes, still carry a lot of weight, but they have tended in recent years to produce among excluded and marginal groups theories of systematic oppression, tales of conspiracy, that can not sustain empirical analysis. In fact, active domination is less in evidence today; democratic membership brings with it significant protections that no one is prepared to challenge openly. Individual members of excluded groups, thus protected, make their way forward or upward, winning at least a small share of social goods. And so an insidious myth is born, a counter-myth to all the conspiracies, which holds that the remaining exclusions are no longer unjust, that they are indeed the unexpected product of justice itself. Excluded men and women get what they deserve, or what they have chosen, or they are the victims of bad luck; no one else is responsible for

their fate. The assignment of responsibility is at stake here—with large consequences for social policy.

The myth of just or justified exclusion looks back, I think, to Michael
Young's *Rise of the Meritocracy*, the classic dystopia of contemporary social
science.[2] What Young wrote was, in fact, a savage critique of meritocratic distributions absent any sort of socialist solidarity. Equality of opportunity, he
argued, would divide society into two classes—those who are capable and those
who are incapable of seizing their opportunities. The second group would be a
lower class without precedent in human history: not enslaved, not oppressed,
not exploited; standing exactly where their own efforts (or lack thereof) had
brought them; deprived even of a cause to rally around. Young's argument is
repeated today without its critical thrust. Subordination and exclusion, it is
said, are more the result of incapacity, apathy, or disinterest than of domination.
The excluded are simply the class of men and women deficient across the range
of qualities, so that distributive processes working autonomously, exactly as they
are supposed to work, bring them no goods or no goods that they can profitably
use. Subtlety and indirection have nothing to do with their fate, for we have
largely replaced the collective exclusion of women or workers or blacks or Jews
with a new exclusion of individuals chosen, as it were, for the right reasons.

The triumph of equality, the democratic expansion of citizenship, turns out
(on this view) to be a cruel hoax. It has simply made visible what was once
concealed by the false abstractions of gender, race, and class: the presence of
men and women who cannot (or will not) meet the standard, or even the
pluralized standards, of citizenship. Those who can, do—barring bad luck,
which is always someone's fate. Failure in all the spheres is no longer the result
and therefore the visible sign of oppression and injustice. Hence the only motive
we have for helping those who fail is sympathy or humane feeling. About this we
must be careful, for it may well lead us to act unjustly, limiting the autonomous
distribution of goods (as in cases of affirmative action or "reverse discrimination") and overbuilding the welfare system. All that humane feeling requires is
humanitarian relief—a "safety net" so that those who are justly denied the most
desirable social goods are not callously denied subsistence itself.

My own claim that exclusion is still unjust has to be defended against this
neo-Youngian argument. Also, perhaps, against its libertarian variant, which
holds that the last vestiges of domination won't be eliminated until we have
curtailed the welfare system, deregulated the market, and given up affirmative
action. Only when everyone is exposed to the harsh incentives as well as the
golden opportunities of meritocracy and "free enterprise" will we know who the

justly (or the not-unjustly) excluded really are. They will fall into two groups: those who work at low-paying jobs and survive on the social margins and those who can't or won't work and land in the safety net. A fixed determination not to accept any further responsibility for such people underlies, I think, the conservative social policies of the 1980s. We can find it articulated (though rarely as openly as in Young's satire) in recent academic literature dealing with intelligence, crime, poverty, and welfare. Also in a more popular style—in the columns of local newspapers, on radio talk shows, and in everyday conversation —often thought to express nothing but egotism and mean-spiritedness: but behind this too there is a view of justice, according to which everything has been done for "those people" that ought to be done. This is the argument that I need to address, but first it will be useful to provide a model description of one of "those people" as seen from the neo-Youngian perspective.

Imagine, then, a man or woman who is a citizen, a full member as this is legally defined; who has been on the welfare rolls but was never enabled by the assistance he received to lead an independent life, a passive client of the state incapable of self-help or mutual aid, who is now pushed out of the system by (justified) budget cuts; who brings no skills or resources to the market, is only intermittently employed, displaying no entrepreneurial competence or energy; who has had a standard public education, up to the legally required minimum, which was largely ineffective, never engaging either his mental or material interests; who is therefore unqualified for the places on offer in the civil service or the professions or in the institutions that train their members; who is likely to do much more than his share of hard or dirty work; who has time on his hands since he is often out of work or (with good reason) in prison—but not much of the sort of time that we call "leisure;" who lives in a broken family or altogether without familial support, alone, sometimes literally homeless; who receives neither recognition nor respect from his fellow citizens and suffers, as a result, from a loss of self-respect; who is politically powerless despite his suffrage, because he is numbered among those who need not be counted, a mass of unorganized, inarticulate, and therefore unrepresented men and women; and finally, who is probably not even saved, though salvation is the social good most readily available to him, at the hands of itinerant (or radio and television) evangelists.

Has this person been treated unjustly? Isn't his story simply a sad story of individual misfortune and failure, with all the distributive agencies doing the work they are supposed to do, as best they can, and always in accordance with the principles of justice? Social workers and teachers have tried to help him; personnel managers have attended to his talents or lack of talent; democratic politicians have labored, unsuccessfully, to "build a base" among people like himself; and so on. He has not been treated like a foreigner; he has not been excluded without first being attended to. Given the attentiveness, what grounds of complaint can he possibly have for the exclusion? An individual in this situation can only complain, like Job, to God. His is a case, perhaps, of a good man suffering undeserved pain—but this is divine, not human, injustice.

[3]

I can imagine a social world in which such an account might have some plausibility, and I want to come back, later on, to the difficulties this might raise for the theory of justice. Can it be our aim to create a society where the poor and the powerless have no grounds of complaint? Is that the definition of a *just* society? In any case, we do not now live in a society like that. Among ourselves, excluded men and women are not a random series of failed individuals, rejected one by one, sphere by sphere. Failure is not randomly distributed across the multicultural range of American society. Instead, the excluded mostly come in groups whose members share common experiences and, often enough, a family (racial, ethnic, gender) resemblance. Failure pursues them from sphere to sphere in the form of stereotyping, discrimination, and disregard, so that their condition is not in fact the product of a succession of autonomous decisions but rather of a single systemic decision or of an interconnected set. And for their children, exclusion is an inheritance; the qualities that supposedly produce it (and that might give it legitimacy) are now its products.

Groups like this take shape and reproduce themselves only under pressure. But the pressure, in order to be effective, need not take the form of organized and premeditated oppression—like the slavery that American blacks once endured, say, or the restraints that would be imposed on blacks today by white supremacists. Something less will do the job, as the black example suggests. The knowledge that white supremacists are still politically active has some effect, I suppose, on the everyday life of black Americans, but what is more important in explaining their (partial) exclusion from the American mainstream is the continuum of attitudes and practices that starts with racism at one end and has a long way to go before it reaches to a thoroughgoing egalitarian civility or friendship at the other. The greater number of people whose attitudes and practices are represented along this continuum would certainly repudiate racism if they were asked, but their own habits, expectations, and unspoken fears carry, as it were, the residues of racial prejudice and constitute a significant social force—even if this is a force whose consequences no one intends. Many of these people are agents of distribution, at work in welfare agencies or in school counseling offices or on admission and search committees or in political parties and movements. All of them are voters; all of them hold in their hands, or, better, in their minds and eyes the power of recognition. When I suggested that the contemporary use of dominant goods across boundaries and the resulting forms of exclusion are subtle and indirect, I had in mind these people, myself, of course, among them. Because of what we do, even though there is no master plan directing what we do, and even though we do it in different ways and to different degrees—as we stand more to the right or more to the left on the continuum—the plight of an excluded man or woman is still today a social and not only a personal responsibility: ours, not only his or hers.

This argument is equally strong if exclusion is—as I suspect it most often is—as much a matter of class as of race (or ethnicity or religion). Describing domination in *Spheres of Justice*, I focused on how it worked for those individuals or groups who were able to wield the dominant good—to use their wealth, for example, to purchase goods that should never be up for sale. Consider now the people whose lack of wealth renders them liable to lose all those goods that are in fact being sold: market poor, they find themselves impoverished everywhere. In this case, too, their exclusion can take subtle and indirect forms. It does not depend upon the literal transfer for cash in hand of school places, or offices in the civil service, or political influence, or justice in the courts. The power of money is revealed in the way its owners are trained and tutored, the way they dress and talk, the generosity they are capable of, the services they can command, the attention they draw to themselves. And here again, all of us are complicit, to greater or lesser degree, in allowing these things to matter in our own and other people's distributive decisions.

No doubt, the exclusions of a class society, and even of a racist society, are structural in character and not merely attitudinal. But the impact of structures on what structuralists call "real life" is mediated by the ideas and actions of individuals, and that impact must vary significantly depending on the prevailing distribution of individuals along the attitudinal continuum from racism or snobbery to civic friendship. Established structures are more likely to be scrutinized and challenged by men and women inclined, as it were, to the left side of the continuum. But the greater number of individuals (at least in America today) are content with the established structures—precisely because the people they exclude or marginalize are "those people," black or poor or somehow stigmatized.

I don't make this argument in order to inspire guilt. The kinds of "doing" and "allowing" that I have attributed to large numbers of my fellows seem to me largely guilt-free. I doubt that many of us possess the capacity to purge ourselves of the residual prejudices of race or class. What follows from my argument is not private regret or remorse but social obligation. Given the existence of excluded groups, justice requires a sustained public effort to enable their members to re-enter society and to function independently in all the distributive spheres. Indeed, this is the central purpose of two closely related social goods: welfare and education. Let me consider these two in turn, for they reveal the extent to which we are committed, despite our continued ineffectiveness and denial, to the creation of an inclusive society.

Welfare is sometimes understood as mere relief: the state as soup kitchen. This is the view of those contemporary writers and politicians who think that excluded men and women are responsible, insofar as anyone is responsible, for their own fate. Expecting them to fail, we set a safety net in place—for their sakes or for ours, it doesn't matter. But I don't think that this has ever been the general understanding or the best reading of actual welfare practices (as distinct, say, from almsgiving). With regard to the able-bodied poor, from earliest times, the aim was never relief simply; state officials did what they could to coax or compel such people to re-enter the work force and make their own way. The chosen means were often punitive; I don't want to recommend them. But the project seems to fit well, without the punitiveness, into democratic conceptions of membership.

I have described in *Spheres of Justice* how the Jewish communities of medieval Europe designed a welfare system with this specific project in mind. The Jews were pioneers here, driven by their situation as a persecuted minority not to democracy but to a very strong version of mutuality. The resources of the communities were mobilized against exclusion, used, therefore, to provide schools, dowries, business loans and jobs, religious artifacts, as well as food and clothing—so that effective membership could be maintained. And while the explicit purpose of the mobilization was not to create a just society, the responsibility of each individual member was thought to be a matter of justice. It seems to me, however, that a society from which no one is excluded is more just than a society that includes, so to speak, excluded or marginalized men and women, non-participants in a world to which they willy-nilly belong. The contemporary critique of "welfare dependency," whatever its political motives, supports this view: the goal of public assistance is to produce active participants in the economy and the polity, not to maintain a permanent clientage.

But this last claim assumes that all the excluded are capable of participation; they have the appropriate ambitions and latent talents; they can take their turn, with only a little help, in at least some of the distributive spheres. This is also the underlying assumption of our own commitment to universal public education: that the children we force to attend school really can benefit from the experience and become active citizens and useful, self-reliant workers. We owe it to one another to reproduce these sorts of citizens and workers; the obligation follows from our agreement to sustain a society of people like ourselves, within which a secure and decent life is possible. But we also owe it to the children, because we, or some of us, have brought them into the world and because we will be responsible for the pain and unhappiness of their exclusion, insofar as we could have prevented it.

But maybe it can't be prevented. Maybe the only realizable purpose of public education is to sort out the children, distinguishing the included from the excluded in as fair a way as possible. Certainly many inner-city schools these days don't seem to be doing anything else, and without much concern for fairness: the children picked for exclusion come overwhelmingly from the same "families." But since these schools, like all schools in a democratic society, are educating *citizens*, even the strictest fairness in exclusion would represent a terrible defeat. Democratic education is a wager on universal or near-universal competence—or, better, democracy itself is the wager and education is the crucial means of winning. Of course, individuals are more or less competent; victories are always partial; and schools do a lot of sorting out in ways that verge on, though they need not establish or reinforce, the radical dichotomy of in and out. But teachers have to make the democratic wager; it is the moral prerequisite of their job.

It follows, then, that massive failure in the spheres of welfare and education or, more specifically, failure that massively impacts on particular groups, ought to suggest (if not a positive will to fail) a massive undercommitment of material and mental resources: not enough money, not enough people, not enough faith in the enterprise, not enough inventiveness and experiment. What constitutes a deficiency of resources changes over time. The more complicated modern political and economic life become, the greater the necessary commitment. Social reproduction and rescue today require large-scale resources—a requirement that has no precedent in the recent or distant past, when both these enterprises were sustained mostly by family members and communal volunteers, without professional training or much in the way of organizational support. I suspect that relatives and volunteers can still do a great deal of the necessary work, though they will work best within organizational frameworks: schools, hospitals, nursing homes, and so on. The frameworks themselves depend on the helping professions. Any modern society that devalues these professions (as most modern societies do, in part because so many citizens don't want to think about the social problems that make professional help necessary), and fails as a result to recruit talented men and women to teaching, nursing, counseling, and social work, is going to produce and reproduce exclusion. And it will be *unjust exclusion:* for then the excluded won't have received the attention that is due to every member of a democratic society.

I want to stress that though this is a matter of justice, it isn't necessarily a matter for direct state action. The role of the state is very important, and I shall have more to say about it later on; but many of the difficulties of excluded men and women are best handled within civil society, where the state can at most provide incentives and subsidies. Every voluntary association—church, union, co-op, neighborhood club, interest group, society for the preservation or prevention of this or that, philanthropic organization, and social movement—is an agency of inclusion. Alongside their stated purpose, whatever that is, the associations of civil society provide recognition, empowerment, training, and even employment. They serve to decentralize the spheres, multiplying settings and agents and guaranteeing greater diversity in the interpretation of distributive criteria. (Consider, for example, the different understandings of "merit" in churches, social movements, sports clubs, and the administrative apparatus of a modern state.) The officials and staff of all the associations taken together constitute an informal civil service, a social bureaucracy, and though it is in the nature of a democratic society that one can't assign tasks to these people, it is nonetheless important to acknowledge their centrality. The state can't direct their work, but it can, and therefore should, facilitate it. All the spheres of justice are implicated in the activity of voluntary associations; complex equality, under modern conditions, depends in large measure upon their success.

[4]

So we can re-describe excluded men or women, who lose out in every sphere, as victims. Anyone who claims this status makes a major political (and perhaps also a psychological) mistake, but the word is nonetheless accurate: these people have not received the attention or help that justice requires in the spheres of welfare and education, and their defeats there have carried over into market, polity, and family, producing the reiterated losses whose sum is exclusion itself. This is not to say that individuals bear no responsibility for their own situation, or that they have been treated unjustly everywhere, or that they are the literal prey of an oppressive or exploitative ruling class. They are not, as we might say of slaves or concentration camp prisoners or stateless refugees, pure victims. Their situation is more complicated, and we can ask a great deal of them—so long as we recognize them as fellow-members, who can ask a great deal of us.

But the question persists: what if we were to provide all that they can legitimately ask, and it still didn't help or didn't help enough? There are bound to be some people who can't be helped, who can't or won't help themselves. They don't study at school or their studying is without intellectual effect; they don't work hard or the work they do is badly done; they are clumsy or cruel in personal relationships; they avoid the political arena or act incoherently within it; they seek the available opportunities or the quick success of a criminal life; they choose marginality because it looks like freedom. At some point, we might want to turn away from these people, acknowledging only minimal obligations to them. I don't think it is crazy to imagine a just society as one in which turning away would not be unjust—so long as we kept the safety net in place. Only kindness or compassion would lead (some of) us to do more. But I cannot imagine a just society in which there were large numbers of such people. Poverty and alienation are idiosyncratic, not popular, choices; and at least some of the incapacities of the poor and the alienated are remediable.

The myth of just or justified exclusion, transferred to some hypothetical future time, is still a myth. It derives from or depends upon a thin view of the individual person, according to which all his qualities are of a kind, flatly described. Either he is competent and willing across the board, though no doubt with strengths and weaknesses that get sorted out in the different spheres of justice, or he is incompetent and passive across the board, a failure everywhere. Complex equality merely reflects the sorting out: if distributive processes are working autonomously, competent men and women will be each other's equals in the way this ideal suggests. But the incompetent will be excluded from both complexity and equality; their lives will be simple and their social position uniformly subordinate. Justice is governed by this radical dichotomy between those who are eligible for complex equality and those who are not.

But this radical dichotomy is an ideological invention. Complex equality is matched (not only to a differentiation of goods but also) to a differentiation of persons and then of qualities, interests, and capacities within persons. There aren't only two sorts of persons; nor is any single person of one gross "sort." The range of qualities, interests, and capacities is very wide, and I don't know of any evidence—certainly my own experience provides no evidence—of any radical clustering of positive or negative versions of these in particular individuals. This brilliant mathematician is a political idiot. This talented musician doesn't have the faintest idea about how to deal with other people. This skillful and loving parent has no business sense. This adventurous and successful entrepreneur is a moral coward. This beggar on the street or criminal in prison is a competent craftsman, or a secret poet, or a superb orator. These easy contrasts are commonplace and obvious, but they hardly reach to the real complexity of individual men and women, for each of whom we could put together a long list not only of different but also of contradictory qualities, interests, and capacities. That is why the outcome of autonomous distributions is so utterly unpredictable, at least with regard to individuals. We can be sure, however, that these distributions won't divide any set of individuals into two radically distinct groups of "haves" and "have-nots"—unless autonomy itself has been corrupted in some major way.

If individual men and women were not complexly constituted, divided selves, then complex equality would be an example of bad utopianism—a false ideal that served in fact to justify an unattractive reality. For it would then follow that the radical exclusion of flatly incompetent people was not unjust. They would have, as I have already suggested, nothing to complain about; it would be very difficult to organize a social movement on their behalf, for the organizers would not be able to appeal to the moral conscience of their fellow citizens. But there are no flatly incompetent people or, at least, no class of such people. The anxiety about just or justified exclusion is misplaced. The democratic wager is, in fact, a safe bet as bets go, though it is certainly not a bet that will be won, or even partly won, without a serious and sustained effort to win it. In any society where goods are differentiated and distributive processes putatively autonomous, across-the-board exclusion is and must be called unjust—a legitimate occasion, then, for political protest.

[5]

Political protest is aimed at the state; it is a call for state action (sometimes for an end to state action) of one sort or another. Public officials must do this or that (or stop doing this or that). In *Spheres of Justice,* the sorts of things that I imagined them doing were largely related to defending the boundaries of the spheres, as in the list that I have already provided: requiring meritocratic admission and appointment procedures, enforcing anti-discrimination laws, maintaining the integrity of the judicial system. The state also defends its own integrity, polices its own borders, by outlawing the sale of votes, for example, or by regulating campaign contributions or setting limits on the lobbying activities of former civil servants. Acting on its own behalf, it reveals the dual character of the political sphere. On the one hand, this is simply the bounded field or arena within which one highly valued social good—political power—is distributed. On the other hand, it is the base from which this power is deployed along all the social boundaries—and sometimes, of course, across them. When we protest against exclusion, we are working toward a redistribution and a redeployment of political power. The two go together in ways that I did not grasp in my earlier analysis, and this union of the two aspects of politics has far-reaching consequences.

Exclusion is a condition reiterated in each of the spheres, the sphere of politics one among the others. Hence the first goal of the protesters is to mobilize excluded men and women and bring them into the state. Because they are already citizens, this means to win for them a share of political power. And the first demand on the state is that it assist in this process—as the federal government did in the United States, for example, when it enforced voting rights on behalf of black Americans. We can understand this enforcement as a defense of political autonomy, in accordance with the principle, internal to democratic politics, that power is to be distributed with the consent of all the state's citizens and not by some racially marked subset of citizens. But the point of redistributing power to black Americans was not mere possession and enjoyment (though power is indeed enjoyable) but also use, a very specific use in this case: to open all the other spheres to these same hitherto excluded men and women. When citizens and officials act to reform the state, they are also acting to reform the larger society. They are advocates and agents of complex equality.

Once power has been redistributed, it will also be redeployed—and not just to defend the boundaries of the spheres. For the existence of an excluded group of men and women means that the boundaries have been violated to such a degree that they must now be redrawn before they can be defended. And they must be redrawn from within, with reference to the social meaning of the goods at stake. Arguments about affirmative action, for example, must deal with the idea of office-holding and the sorts of competence it has come to encompass. The result may be a call for changes in what it means to "qualify" for an office, but these can't be merely arbitrary changes, politically expedient for this or that party to the argument. Nonetheless, state agents—citizens and officials acting politically—will now play a part in interpreting the relevant meanings and in designing appropriate distributive arrangements. They will not play the only part, for they cannot usurp the authority of people more locally and directly involved: social workers, teachers, doctors and nurses, entrepreneurs, union members, parents, and so on. But citizens have an authority of their own, which derives from the fact that the boundaries of the spheres are not given but contested. Exclusion is a sign that the contests have gone badly—an invitation, therefore, to the state to set them right. Political protesters deliver the invitation.

Politics is implicated in all distributive disputes; the state cannot disregard what is going on in the different spheres of justice. Its role is limited only by the success of autonomy. If the "wall" between church and state is in place and effective, for example, state officials have nothing to say about the distribution of church offices (the criteria can be hereditary, meritocratic, elective, or whatever) or of religious goods like salvation and eternal life. They can defend only some version of a minimalist morality, intervening, say, against polygamy or animal (or perhaps only human?) sacrifice. Similarly, if the market is operating within appropriate bounds, the state must limit itself to laws like those that protect children against exploitation or consumers against unsafe products. But where the church controls marriage and divorce and uses the control to repress heterodox opinions, or where market relations determine the distribution of nonmarket goods, then the state is likely to find itself, under pressure from protesting citizens, engaged in maximalist work: defining the meaning, if only in order to limit the extent, of religious authority and exchange relationships.

Nor does this exhaust the area of legitimate, perhaps even necessary, state action. For the best way to deal with exclusion may be to enlarge the amounts of some available good rather than to redistribute whatever already exists. Teacher-student ratios and school places are obvious examples: the decision to build more schools or hire more teachers or open new universities cannot be made from within the sphere of education; it is a political decision, whether national or local governments are constitutionally authorized to make it. The extension and reform of welfare services cannot be accomplished by a vote of social workers and their clients; it is the political responsibility of citizens generally. Efforts to expand markets and increase the number of jobs are similarly political, requiring decisions about infrastructural investment, tax incentives, foreign trade, and so on.

Many motives play a part in such decisions. When third world governments enlarge their own bureaucracies so as to guarantee jobs to college graduates, for example, they are aiming at political stability, not at any sort of egalitarianism. State power dominates the sphere of office, and academic degrees displace actual qualifications. The people who lose out in such transactions are those who can't afford to go to school or who depend upon the competence of public officials: they are pushed toward the margins of social life. There is little hope, in the third world or the first, of bringing such people into the mainstream of society unless state officials and active citizens make that their explicit goal. The state—or, at least, the modern democratic state—must defend the values of complexity and equality on behalf of all its citizens. It can't, then, be neutral or uncommitted with regard to the meaning of disputed social goods: decisions about the size of the bureaucracy depend upon a particular view of offices and their purposes; decisions about the scope of the market depend upon a view of commodities and entrepreneurial success; decisions about the number of school places depend upon a view of education. And all these decisions are, in something close to a foundational sense, warranted and (partly) determined by an understanding of citizenship.

Inclusion begins with citizenship, which then serves as a value reiterated through democratic political activity in all the spheres of justice. The reiteration is qualified by the nature of the goods at stake; participation in the different spheres takes different forms. But what marks a democratic political community is the recognition that all those social transactions that drive citizens toward the margins, that produce a class of excluded men and women—uneducated, unemployed, unrecognized, and powerless—are everywhere and always in the life of the community unjust.

NOTES

1. Michael Walzer, *Spheres of Justice* (New York: Basic Books, 1983).
2. Michael Young, *The Rise of the Meritocracy* (London: Thames and Hudson, 1958).

CHAPTER SEVEN

The Communitarian Critique of Liberalism

[1]

Intellectual fashions are notoriously short-lived, very much like fashions in popular music, art, or dress. But there are certain fashions that seem regularly to reappear. Like pleated trousers or short skirts, they are inconstant features of a larger and more steadily prevailing phenomenon—in this case, a certain way of dressing. They have brief but recurrent lives; we know their transience and expect their return. Needless to say, there is no afterlife in which trousers will be permanently pleated or skirts forever short. Recurrence is all.

Although it operates at a much higher level (an infinitely higher level?) of cultural significance, the communitarian critique of liberalism is like the pleating of trousers: transient but certain to return. It is a consistently intermittent feature of liberal politics and social organization. No liberal success will make it permanently unattractive. At the same time, no communitarian critique, however penetrating, will ever be anything more than an inconstant feature of liberalism. Someday, perhaps, there will be a larger transformation, like the shift from aristocratic knee-breeches to plebeian pants, rendering liberalism and its critics alike irrelevant. But I see no present signs of anything like that, nor am I sure that we should look forward to it. For now, there is much to be said for a recurrent critique, whose protagonists hope only for small victories, partial incorporations, and when they are rebuffed or dismissed or coopted, fade away for a time only to return.

Communitarianism is usefully contrasted with social democracy, which has succeeded in establishing a permanent presence alongside of and sometimes conjoined with liberal politics. Social democracy has its own intermittently fashionable critics, largely anarchist and libertarian in character. Since it sponsors certain sorts of communal identification, it is less subject to criticism than liberalism is. But it can never escape such criticism entirely, for liberals and social democrats alike share a commitment to economic growth and cope (although in different ways) with the deracinated social forms that growth produces. Community itself is largely an ideological presence in modern society; it has no recurrent critics of its own. It is intermittently fashionable only because it no longer exists in anything like full strength, and it is criticized only when it is fashionable.

The communitarian critique is nonetheless a powerful one; it would not recur if it were not capable of engaging our minds and feelings. In this essay, I want to investigate the power of its current American versions and then offer a version of my own—less powerful, perhaps, than the ones with which I shall begin, but more available for incorporation within liberal (or social democratic) politics. I do not mean (I hardly have the capacity) to lay communitarianism to rest, although I would willingly wait for its reappearance in a form more coherent and incisive than that in which it currently appears. The problem with communitarian criticism today—I am not the first to notice this—is that it suggests two different, and deeply contradictory, arguments against liberalism. One of these arguments is aimed primarily at liberal practice, the other primarily at liberal theory, but they cannot both be right. It is possible that each one is partly right—indeed, I shall insist on just this partial validity—but each of the arguments is right in a way that undercuts the value of the other.

[2]

The first argument holds that liberal political theory accurately represents liberal social practice. As if the Marxist account of ideological reflection were literally true, and exemplified here, contemporary Western societies (American society especially) are taken to be the home of radically isolated individuals, rational egotists, and existential agents, men and women protected and divided by their inalienable rights. Liberalism tells the truth about the asocial society that liberals create—not, in fact, *ex nihilo* as their theory suggests, but in a struggle against traditions and communities and authorities that are forgotten as soon as they are escaped, so that liberal practices seem to have no history. The struggle itself is ritually celebrated but rarely reflected on. The members of liberal society share no political or religious traditions; they can tell only one story about themselves and that is the story of *ex nihilo* creation, which begins in the state of nature or the original position. Each individual imagines himself absolutely free, unencumbered, and on his own—and enters society, accepting its obligations, only in order to minimize his risks. His goal is security, and security is, as Marx wrote, "the assurance of his egoism." And as he imagines himself, so he *really is*, "that is, an individual separated from the community, withdrawn into himself, wholly preoccupied with his private interest and acting in accordance with his private caprice. . . . The only bond between men is natural necessity, need, and private interest."[1] (I have used masculine pronouns in order to fit my sentences to Marx's. But it is an interesting question, not addressed here, whether this first communitarian critique speaks to the experience of women: Are necessity and private interest their only bonds with one another?)

The writings of the young Marx represent one of the early appearances of communitarian criticism, and his argument, first made in the 1840s, is powerfully present today. Alasdair MacIntyre's description of the incoherence of modern intellectual and cultural life and the loss of narrative capacity makes a similar point in updated, state-of-the-art, theoretical language.[2] But the only theory that is necessary to the communitarian critique of liberalism is liberalism itself. All that the critics have to do, so they say, is to take liberal theory seriously. The self-portrait of the individual constituted only by his willfulness, liberated from all connection, without common values, binding ties, customs, or traditions—sans eyes, sans teeth, sans taste, sans everything—need only be evoked in order to be devalued: It is already the concrete absence of value. What can the real life of such a person be like? Imagine him maximizing his utilities, and society is turned into a war of all against all, the familiar rat race, in which, as Hobbes wrote, there is "no other goal, nor other garland, but being foremost."[3] Imagine him enjoying his rights, and society is reduced to the coexistence of isolated selves, for liberal rights, according to this first critique, have more to do with "exit" than with "voice."[4] They are concretely expressed in separation, divorce, withdrawal, solitude, privacy, and political apathy. And finally, the very fact that individual life can be described in these two philosophical languages, the language of utilities and the language of rights, is a further mark, says MacIntyre, of its incoherence: Men and women in liberal society no longer have access to a single moral culture within which they can learn how they ought to live.[5] There is no consensus, no public meeting-of-minds, on the nature of the good life, hence the triumph of private caprice, revealed, for example, in Sartrean existentialism, the ideological reflection of everyday capriciousness.

We liberals are free to choose, and we have a right to choose, but we have no criteria to govern our choices except our own wayward understanding of our wayward interests and desires. And so our choices lack the qualities of cohesion and consecutiveness. We can hardly remember what we did yesterday; we cannot with any assurance predict what we will do tomorrow. We cannot give a proper account of ourselves. We cannot sit together and tell comprehensible stories, and we recognize ourselves in the stories we read only when these are fragmented narratives, without plots, the literary equivalent of atonal music and nonrepresentational art.

Liberal society, seen in the light of this first communitarian critique, is fragmentation in practice; and community is the exact opposite, the home of coherence, connection, and narrative capacity. But I am less concerned here with the different accounts that might be provided of this lost Eden than I am with the repeated insistence on the reality of fragmentation after the loss. This is the common theme of all contemporary communitarianisms: neoconservative lamentation, neo-Marxist indictment, and neoclassical or republican hand-wringing. (The need for the prefix "neo" suggests again the intermittent or recurrent character of communitarian criticism.) I should think it would be an awkward theme, for if the sociological argument of liberal theory is right, if society is actually decomposed, without residue, into the problematic coexistence of individuals, then we might well assume that liberal politics is the best way to deal with the problems of decomposition. If we have to create an artificial and ahistorical union out of a multitude of isolated selves, why not take the state of nature or the original position as our conceptual starting point? Why not accept, in standard liberal fashion, the priority of procedural justice over substantive conceptions of the good, since we can hardly expect, given our fragmentation, to agree about the good? Michael Sandel asks whether a community of those who put justice first can ever be more than a community of strangers.[6] The question is a good one, but its reverse form is more immediately relevant: If we really are a community of strangers, how can we do anything else but put justice first?

[3]

We are saved from this entirely plausible line of argument by the second communitarian critique of liberalism. The second critique holds that liberal theory radically misrepresents real life. The world is not like that nor could it be. Men and women cut loose from all social ties, literally unencumbered, each one the one and only inventor of his or her own life, with no criteria, no common standards, to guide the invention—these are mythical figures. How can any group of people be strangers to one another when each member of the group is born with parents, and when these parents have friends, relatives, neighbors, comrades at work, coreligionists, and fellow citizens—connections, in fact, which are not so much chosen as passed on and inherited? Liberalism may well enhance the significance of purely contractual ties, but it is obviously false to suggest, as Hobbes sometimes seemed to do, that all our connections are mere "market friendships," voluntarist and self-interested in character, which cannot outlast the advantages they bring.[7] It is in the very nature of a human society that individuals bred within it will find themselves caught up in patterns of relationship, networks of power, and communities of meaning. That quality of being caught up is what makes them persons of a certain sort. And only then can they make themselves persons of a (marginally) different sort by reflecting on what they are and by acting in more or less distinctive ways within the patterns, networks, and communities that are willy-nilly theirs.

The burden of the second critique is that the deep structure even of liberal society is in fact communitarian. Liberal theory distorts this reality and, insofar as we adopt the theory, deprives us of any ready access to our own experience of communal embeddedness. The rhetoric of liberalism—this is the argument of the authors of *Habits of the Heart*—limits our understanding of our own heart's habits, and gives us no way to formulate the convictions that hold us together as persons and that bind persons together into a community.[8] The assumption here is that we are in fact persons and that we are in fact bound together. The liberal ideology of separatism cannot take personhood and bondedness away from us. What it does take away is the *sense* of our personhood and bondedness, and this deprivation is then reflected in liberal politics. It explains our inability to form cohesive solidarities, stable movements and parties, that might make our deep convictions visible and effective in the world. It also explains our radical dependence (brilliantly foreshadowed in Hobbes' *Leviathan*) on the central state.

But how are we to understand this extraordinary disjunction between communal experience and liberal ideology, between personal conviction and public rhetoric, and between social bondedness and political isolation? That question is not addressed by communitarian critics of the second sort. If the first critique depends on a vulgar Marxist theory of reflection, the second critique requires an equally vulgar idealism. Liberal theory now seems to have a power over and against real life that has been granted to few theories in human history. Plainly, it has not been granted to communitarian theory, which cannot, on the first argument, overcome the reality of liberal separatism and cannot, on the second argument, evoke the already existing structures of social connection. In any case, the two critical arguments are mutually inconsistent; they cannot both be true. Liberal separatism either represents or misrepresents the conditions of everyday life. It might, of course, do a little of each—the usual muddle—but that is not a satisfactory conclusion from a communitarian standpoint. For if the account of dissociation and separatism is even partly right, then we have to raise questions about the depth, so to speak, of the deep structure. And if we are all to some degree communitarians under the skin, then the portrait of social incoherence loses its critical force.

[4]

But each of the two critical arguments is partly right. I will try to say what is right about each, and then ask if something plausible can be made of the parts. First, then, there cannot be much doubt that we (in the United States) live in a society where individuals are relatively dissociated and separated from one another, or better, where they are continually separating from one another—continually in motion, often in solitary and apparently random motion, as if in imitation of what physicists call Brownian movement. Hence we live in a profoundly unsettled society. We can best see the forms of unsettlement if we track the most important moves. So, consider (imitating the Chinese style) the Four Mobilities:

1. *Geographic mobility.* Americans apparently change their residence more often than any people in history, at least since the barbarian migrations, excluding only nomadic tribes and families caught up in civil or foreign wars. Moving people and their possessions from one city or town to another is a major industry in the United States, even though many people manage to move themselves. In another sense, of course, we are all self-moved, not refugees but voluntary migrants. The sense of place must be greatly weakened by this extensive geographic mobility, although I find it hard to say whether it is superseded by mere insensitivity or by a new sense of many places. Either way, communitarian feeling seems likely to decline in importance. Communities are more than just locations, but they are most often successful when they are permanently located.

2. *Social mobility.* This chapter will not address the arguments about how best to describe social standing or how to measure changes, whether by income, education, class membership, or rank in the status hierarchy. It is enough to say

that fewer Americans stand exactly where their parents stood or do what they did than in any society for which we have comparable knowledge. Americans may inherit many things from their parents, but the extent to which they make a different life, if only by making a different living, means that the inheritance of community, that is, the passing on of beliefs and customary ways, is uncertain at best. Whether or not children are thereby robbed of narrative capacity, they seem likely to tell different stories than their parents told.

3. *Marital mobility*. Rates of separation, divorce, and remarriage are higher today than they have ever been in our own society and probably higher than they have ever been in any other (except perhaps among Roman aristocrats, although I know of no statistics from that time, only anecdotes). The first two mobilities, geographic and social, also disrupt family life, so that siblings, for example, often live at great distances from one another, and later as uncles and aunts, they are far removed from nephews and nieces. But what we call "broken homes" are the product of marital breaks, of husbands or wives moving out—and then, commonly, moving on to new partners. Insofar as home is the first community and the first school of ethnic identity and religious conviction, this kind of breakage must have countercommunitarian consequences. It means that children often do not hear continuous or identical stories from the adults with whom they live. (Did the greater number of children ever hear such stories? The death of one spouse and the remarriage of the other may have once been as common as divorce and remarriage are today. But, then, other sorts of mobility have to be considered: Both men and women are more likely today to marry across class, ethnic, and religious lines; remarriage will therefore often produce extraordinarily complex and socially diverse families—which probably are without historical precedent.)

4. *Political mobility*. Loyalty to leaders, movements, parties, clubs, and urban machines seems to decline rapidly as place and social standing and family membership become less central in the shaping of personal identity. Liberal citizens stand outside all political organizations and then choose the one that best serves their ideals or interests. They are, ideally, independent voters, that is, people who move around; they choose for themselves rather than voting as their parents did, and they choose freshly each time rather than repeating themselves. As their numbers increase, they make for a volatile electorate and hence for institutional instability, particularly at the local level where political organization once served to reinforce communal ties.

The effects of the Four Mobilities are intensified in a variety of ways by other social developments which we are likely to talk about in the common metaphor of movement: the advance of knowledge, technological progress, and so on. But I am concerned here only with the actual movement of individuals. Liberalism is, most simply, the theoretical endorsement and justification of this movement.[9] In the liberal view, then, the Four Mobilities represent the enactment of liberty, and the pursuit of (private or personal) happiness. And it has to be said that, conceived in this way, liberalism is a genuinely popular creed. Any effort to curtail mobility in the four areas described here would require a massive and harsh application of state power. Nevertheless, this popularity has an under-side of sadness and discontent that are intermittently articulated, and commu-nitarianism is, most simply, the intermittent articulation of these feelings. It reflects a sense of loss, and the loss is real. People do not always leave their old neighborhoods or hometowns willingly or happily. Moving may be a personal adventure in our standard cultural mythologies, but it is as often a family trauma in real life. The same thing is true of social mobility, which carries people down as well as up and requires adjustments that are never easy to manage. Marital breaks may sometimes give rise to new and stronger unions, but they also pile up what we might think of as family fragments: single-parent households, sepa-rated and lonely men and women, and abandoned children. And independence in politics is often a not-so-splendid isolation: Individuals with opinions are cut loose from groups with programs. The result is a decline in "the sense of efficacy," with accompanying effects on commitment and morale.

All in all, we liberals probably know one another less well, and with less assurance, than people once did, although we may see more aspects of the other than they saw, and recognize in him or her a wider range of possibilities (includ-ing the possibility of moving on). We are more often alone than people once were, being without neighbors we can count on, relatives who live nearby or with whom we are close, or comrades at work or in the movement. That is the truth of the first communitarian argument. We must now fix the limits of this truth by seeking what is true of the second argument.

In its easiest version, the second argument—that we are really, at bottom, creatures of community—is certainly true but of uncertain significance. The ties of place, class or status, family, and even politics survive the Four Mobilities to a remarkable extent. To take just one example, from the last of the Four: It remains true, even today in this most liberal and mobile of societies, that the best predictor of how people will vote is our knowledge of how their parents voted.[10] All those dutifully imitative young Republicans and Democrats testify to the failure of liberalism to make independence or waywardness of mind the distinctive mark of its adherents. The predictive value of parental behavior holds even for independent voters: They are simply the heirs of independence. But we do not know to what extent inheritances of this sort are a dwindling communal resource; it may be that each generation passes on less than it received. The full liberalization of the social order, the production and reproduction of self-inventing individuals, may take a long time, much longer, indeed, than liberals themselves expected. There is not much comfort here for communitarian critics, however; while they can recognize and value the survival of older ways of life, they cannot count on, and they must have anxieties about, the vitality of those ways.

But there is another approach to the truth of the second critical argument. Whatever the extent of the Four Mobilities, they do not seem to move us so far apart that we can no longer talk with one another. We often disagree, of course, but we disagree in mutually comprehensible ways. I should think it fairly obvious that the philosophical controversies that MacIntyre laments are not in fact a mark of social incoherence. Where there are philosophers, there will be controversies, just as where there are knights, there will be tournaments. But these are highly ritualized activities, which bear witness to the connection, not the disconnection, of their protagonists. Even political conflict in liberal societies rarely takes forms so extreme as to set its protagonists beyond negotiation and compromise, procedural justice, and the very possibility of speech. The American civil rights struggle is a nice example of a conflict for which our moral/political language was and is entirely adequate. The fact that the struggle has had only partial success does not reflect linguistic inadequacy but rather political failures and defeats.

Martin Luther King's speeches evoked a palpable tradition, a set of common values such that public disagreement could focus only on how (or how quickly) they might best be realized.[11] But this is not, so to speak, a traditionalist tradition, a *Gemeinschaft* tradition, a survival of the preliberal past. It is a liberal tradition modified, no doubt, by survivals of different sorts. The modifications are most obviously Protestant and republican in character, though by no means exclusively so: The years of mass immigration have brought a great variety of ethnic and religious memories to bear on American politics. What all of them bear on, however, is liberalism. The language of individual rights—voluntary association, pluralism, toleration, separation, privacy, free speech, the career-open-to-talents, and so on—is simply inescapable. Who among us seriously attempts to escape? If we really are situated selves, as the second communitarian critique holds, then our situation is largely captured by that vocabulary. This is the truth of the second critique. Does it make any sense then to argue that liberalism prevents us from understanding or maintaining the ties that bind us together?

It makes some sense, because liberalism is a strange doctrine, which seems continually to undercut itself, to disdain its own traditions, and to produce in each generation renewed hopes for a more absolute freedom from history and society alike. Much of liberal political theory, from Locke to Rawls, is an effort to fix and stabilize the doctrine in order to end the endlessness of liberal liberation. But beyond every current version of liberalism, there is always a super liberalism, which, as Roberto Unger says of his own doctrine, "pushes the liberal premises about state and society, about freedom from dependence and governance of social relations by the will, to the point at which they merge into a large ambition: the building of a social world less alien to a self that can always violate the generative rules of its own mental or social constructs."[12] Although Unger was once identified as a communitarian, this ambition—large indeed!— seems designed to prevent not only any stabilization of liberal doctrine but also any recovery or creation of community. For there is no imaginable community that would not be alien to the eternally transgressive self. If the ties that bind us together do not *bind* us, there can be no such thing as community. If it is anything at all, communitarianism is antithetical to transgression. And the transgressive self is antithetical even to the liberal community which is its creator and sponsor.[13]

Liberalism is a self-subverting doctrine; for that reason, it really does require periodic communitarian correction. But it is not a particularly helpful form of correction to suggest that liberalism is literally incoherent or that it can be replaced by some preliberal or antiliberal community waiting somehow just beneath the surface or just beyond the horizon. Nothing is waiting; American communitarians have to recognize that there is no one out there but separated, rights-bearing, voluntarily associating, freely speaking, liberal selves. It would be a good thing, though, if we could teach those selves to know themselves as social beings, the historical products of, and in part the embodiments of, liberal values. For the communitarian correction of liberalism cannot be anything other than a selective reinforcement of those same values or, to appropriate the well-known phrase of Michael Oakeshott, a pursuit of the intimations of community within them.

[5]

The place to begin the pursuit is with the liberal idea of voluntary association, which is not well-understood, it seems to me, either among liberals or among their communitarian critics. In both its theory and its practice, liberalism expresses strong associative tendencies alongside its dissociative tendencies: Its protagonists form groups as well as split off from the groups they form; they join up and resign, marry and divorce. Nevertheless, it is a mistake, and a characteristically liberal mistake, to think that the existing patterns of association are entirely or even largely voluntary and contractual, that is, the product of will alone. In a liberal society, as in every other society, people are born into very important sorts of groups, born with identities, male or female, for example, working class, Catholic or Jewish, black, democrat, and so on. Many of their subsequent associations (like their subsequent careers) merely express these underlying identities, which, again, are not so much chosen as enacted.[14] Liberalism is distinguished less by the freedom to form groups on the basis of these identities than the freedom to leave the groups and sometimes even the identities behind. Association is always at risk in a liberal society. The boundaries of the group are not policed; people come and go, or they just fade into the distance without ever quite acknowledging that they have left. That is why liberalism is plagued by free-rider problems—by people who continue to enjoy the benefits of membership and identity while no longer participating in the activities that produce those benefits.[15] Communitarianism, by contrast, is the dream of a perfect free-riderlessness.

At its best, the liberal society is the social union of social unions that John Rawls described: a pluralism of groups bonded by shared ideas of toleration and democracy.[16] But if all the groups are precarious, continually on the brink of dissolution or abandonment, then the larger union must also be weak and vulnerable. Or, alternatively, its leaders and officials will be driven to compensate for the failures of association elsewhere by strengthening their own union, that is, the central state, beyond the limits that liberalism has established. These limits are best expressed in terms of individual rights and civil liberties, but they also include a prescription for state neutrality. The good life is pursued by individuals, sponsored by groups; the state presides over the pursuit and the sponsorship but does not participate in either. Presiding is singular in character; pursuing and sponsoring are plural. Hence it is a critical question for liberal theory and practice whether the associative passions and energies of ordinary people are likely over the long haul to survive the Four Mobilities and prove themselves sufficient to the requirements of pluralism. There is at least some evidence that they will not prove sufficient—without a little help. But, to repeat an old question, whence cometh our help? A few of the existing social unions live in the expectation of divine assistance. For the rest, we can only help one another, and the agency through which help of that sort comes most expeditiously is the state. But what kind of state is it that fosters associative activities? What kind of a social union is it that includes without incorporating a great and discordant variety of social unions?

Obviously, it is a liberal state and social union; any other kind is too dangerous for communities and individuals alike. It would be an odd enterprise to argue in the name of communitarianism for an alternative state, for that would be to argue against our own political traditions and to repudiate whatever community we already have. But the communitarian correction does require a liberal state of a certain sort, conceptually though not historically unusual: a state that is, at least over some part of the terrain of sovereignty, deliberately nonneutral. The standard liberal argument for neutrality is an induction from social fragmentation. Since dissociated individuals will never agree on the good life, the state must allow them to live as they think best, subject only to John Stuart Mill's harm principle, without endorsing or sponsoring any particular understanding of what "best" means. But there is a problem here: The more dissociated individuals are, the stronger the state is likely to be, since it will be the only or the most important social union. And then membership in the state, the only good that is shared by all individuals, may well come to seem the good that is "best."

There is only to repeat the first communitarian critique, and it invites a response like the second critique: that the state is not in fact the only or even, for ordinary people in their everyday lives, the most important social union. All sorts of other groups continue to exist and to give shape and purpose to the lives of their members, despite the triumph of individual rights, the Four Mobilities in which that triumph is manifest, and the free-riding that it makes possible. But these groups are continually at risk. And so the state, if it is to remain a liberal state, must endorse and sponsor some of them, namely, those that seem most likely to provide shapes and purposes congenial to the shared values of a liberal society.[17] No doubt, there are problems here too, and I do not mean to deny their difficulty. But I see no way to avoid some such formulation—and not only for theoretical reasons. The actual history of the best liberal states, as of the best social democratic states (and these tend increasingly to be the same states), suggest that they behave in exactly this way, although often very inadequately.

Let me give three relatively familiar examples of state behavior of this kind. First, the Wagner Act of the 1930s: This was not a standard liberal law, hindering the hindrances to union organization, for it actively fostered union organization, and it did so precisely by solving the free-rider problem. By requiring collective bargaining whenever there was majority support (but not necessarily unanimous support) for the union, and then by allowing union shops, the Wagner Act sponsored the creation of strong unions capable, at least to some degree, of determining the shape of industrial relations.[18] Of course, there could not be strong unions without working-class solidarity; unionization is parasitic on underlying communities of feeling and belief. But those underlying communities were already being eroded by the Four Mobilities when the Wagner Act was passed, and so the Act served to counter the dissociative tendencies of liberal society. It was nevertheless a liberal law, for the unions that it helped create enhanced the lives of individual workers and were subject to dissolution and abandonment in accordance with liberal principles should they ever cease to do that.

The second example is the use of tax exemptions and matching grants of tax money to enable different religious groups to run extensive systems of day-care centers, nursing homes, hospitals, and so on—welfare societies inside the welfare state. I do not pretend that these private and pluralist societies compensate for the shoddiness of the American welfare state. But they do improve the delivery of services by making it a more immediate function of communal solidarity. The state's role here, besides establishing minimal standards, is to abate, since in this case it cannot entirely solve, the free-rider problem. If some number of men and women end up in a Catholic nursing home, even though they never contributed to a Catholic charity, they will at least have paid their taxes. But why not nationalize the entire welfare system and end free-ridership? The liberal response is that the social union of social unions must always operate at two levels: A welfare system run entirely by private, nonprofit associations would be dangerously inadequate and inequitable in its coverage; and a totally nationalized system would deny expression to local and particularist solidarities.[19]

The third example is the passage of plant-closing laws designed to afford some protection to local communities of work and residence. Inhabitants are insulated, although only for a time, against market pressure to move out of their old neighborhoods and search for work elsewhere. Although the market "needs" a highly mobile work force, the state takes other needs into account, not only in a welfarist way (through unemployment insurance and job retraining programs) but also in a communitarian way. But the state is not similarly committed to the preservation of every neighborhood community. It is entirely neutral toward communities of ethnicity and residence, offering no protection against strangers who want to move in. Here, geographic mobility remains a positive value, one of the rights of citizens.

Unions, religious organizations, and neighborhoods each draw on feelings and beliefs that, in principle if not always in history, predate the emergence of the liberal state. How strong these feelings and beliefs are, and what their survival value is, I cannot say. Have the unions established such a grip on the imaginations of their members as to make for good stories? There are some good stories, first told, then retold, and sometimes even re-enacted. But the narrative line does not seem sufficiently compelling to younger workers to sustain anything like the old working-class solidarity. Nor is it sufficient for a religious organization to provide lifecycle services for its members if they are no longer interested in religious services. Nor are neighborhoods proof for long against market pressure. Still, communal feeling and belief seem considerably more stable than we once thought they would be, and the proliferation of secondary associations in liberal society is remarkable—even if many of them have short lives and transient memberships. One has a sense of people working together and trying to cope, and not, as the first communitarian critique suggests, just getting by on their own, by themselves, one by one.

[6]

A good liberal (or social democratic) state enhances the possibilities for cooperative coping. John Dewey provided a useful account of such a state in *The Public and Its Problems*. Published in 1927, the book is a commentary on and partial endorsement of an earlier round of communitarian criticism. Dewey shared with the critics of his time, who called themselves "pluralists," an uneasiness with the sovereign state, but he was not quite as uneasy as most of them were. He also shared an admiration for what he called "primary groupings" within the state, but he was more inclined than the pluralists were to qualify his admiration. Primary groupings, he wrote, are "good, bad, and indifferent," and they cannot by their mere existence fix the limits of state activity. The state is not "only an umpire to avert and remedy trespasses of one group upon another." It has a larger function: "It renders the desirable association solider and more coherent. . . . It places a discount upon injurious groupings and renders their tenure of life precarious . . . [and] it gives the individual members of valued associations greater liberty and security; it relieves them of hampering conditions. . . . It enables individual members to count with reasonable certainty upon what others will do."[20] These may seem like tasks too extensive for a *liberal* state, but they are constrained by the constitutional establishment of individual rights—which are themselves (on the pragmatic understanding) not so much recognitions of what individuals by nature are or have as expressions of hope about what they will be and do. Unless individuals act together in certain ways, state action of the sort that Dewey recommended cannot get started. When we recognize the "right of the citizens peacefully to assemble," for example, we are hoping for assemblies of citizens. If we then discriminate among such assemblies, we do so on limited grounds, fostering only those that really do express communities of feeling and belief and do not violate liberal principles of association.

It is often argued these days that the nonneutral state, whose activities I have made some attempt to justify, is best understood in republican terms. A revival of neoclassical republicanism provides much of the substance of contemporary communitarian politics. The revival, I have to say, is largely academic; unlike other versions of communitarianism in Dewey's time and ours, it has no external reference. There really are unions, churches, and neighborhoods in American society, but there are virtually no examples of republican association and no movement or party aimed at promoting such association. Dewey would probably not recognize his "public," nor Rawls his "social union," as versions of republicanism, if only because in both these cases, energy and commitment have been drained from the singular and narrowly political association to the more various associations of civil society. Republicanism by contrast is an integrated and unitary doctrine in which energy and commitment are focused primarily on the political realm. It is a doctrine adapted (in both its classical and neoclassical forms) to the needs of small, homogeneous communities, where civil society is radically undifferentiated. Perhaps the doctrine can be extended to account for a "republic of republics," a decentralized and participatory revision of liberal democracy. A considerable strengthening of local governments would then be required in the hope of encouraging the development and display of civic virtue in a pluralist variety of social settings. This indeed is a pursuit of the intimations of community *within* liberalism, for it has more to do with John Stuart Mill than with Rousseau. Now we are to imagine the nonneutral state empowering cities, towns, and boroughs; fostering neighborhood committees and review boards; and always on the look-out for bands of citizens ready to take responsibility for local affairs.[21]

None of this is any guarantee against the erosion of the underlying communities or the death of local loyalties. It is a matter of principle that communities must always be at risk. And the great paradox of a liberal society is that one cannot set oneself against this principle without also setting oneself against the traditional practices and shared understandings of the society. Here, respect for tradition requires the precariousness of traditionalism. If the first communitarian critique were true in its entirety, if there were no communities and no traditions, then we could just proceed to invent new ones. Insofar as the second critique is even partly true, and the work of communal invention is well begun and continually in progress, we must rest content with the kinds of corrections and enhancements—they would be, in fact, more radical than these terms suggest—that Dewey described.

[7]

I have avoided until now what is often taken to be the central issue between liberals and their communitarian critics—the constitution of the self.[22] Liberalism, it is commonly said, is founded on the idea of a presocial self, a solitary and sometimes heroic individual confronting society, who is fully formed before the confrontation begins. Communitarian critics then argue, first, that instability and dissociation are the actual and disheartening achievement of individuals of this sort and, second, that there really cannot be individuals of this sort. The critics are commonly said in turn to believe in a radically socialized self that can never "confront" society because it is, from the beginning, entangled in society, itself the embodiment of social values. The disagreement seems sharp enough, but in fact, in practice, it is not sharp at all—for neither of these views can be sustained for long by anyone who goes beyond staking out a position and tries to elaborate an argument.[23] Nor does liberal or communitarian theory require views of this sort. Contemporary liberals are not committed to a presocial self, but only to a self capable of reflecting critically on the values that have governed its socialization; and communitarian critics, who are doing exactly that, can hardly go on to claim that socialization is everything. The philosophical and psychological issues here go very deep, but so far as politics is concerned, there is little to be won on this battlefield; concessions from the other side come too easily to count as victories.

The central issue for political theory is not the constitution of the self but the connection of constituted selves, the pattern of social relations. Liberalism is best understood as a theory of relationship, which has voluntary association at its center and which understands voluntariness as the right of rupture or withdrawal. What makes a marriage voluntary is the permanent possibility of divorce. What makes any identity or affiliation voluntary is the easy availability of alternative identities and affiliations. But the easier this easiness is, the less stable all our relationships are likely to become. The Four Mobilities take hold and society seems to be in perpetual motion, so that the actual subject of liberal practice, it might be said, is not a presocial but a postsocial self, free at last from all but the most temporary and limited alliances. Now, the liberal self reflects the fragmentation of liberal society: It is radically undetermined and divided, forced to invent itself anew for every public occasion. Some liberals celebrate this freedom and self-invention; all communitarians lament its arrival, even while insisting that it is not a possible human condition.

I have argued that insofar as liberalism tends toward instability and dissociation, it requires periodic communitarian correction. Rawls' "social union of social unions" reflects and builds on an earlier correction of this kind, the work of American writers like Dewey, Randolph Bourne, and Horace Kallen. Rawls has given us a generalized version of Kallen's argument that America, after the great immigration, was and should remain a "nation of nationalities."[24] In fact, however, the erosion of nationality seems to be a feature of liberal social life, despite intermittent ethnic revivals like that of the late 1960s and 1970s. We can generalize from this to the more or less steady attenuation of all the underlying bonds that make social unions possible. There is no strong or permanent remedy for communal attenuation short of an antiliberal curtailment of the Four Mobilities and the rights of rupture and divorce on which they rest. Communitarians sometimes dream of such a curtailment, but they rarely advocate it. The only community that most of them actually know, after all, is just this liberal union of unions, always precarious and always at risk. They cannot triumph over this liberalism; they can only, sometimes, reinforce its internal associative capacities. The reinforcement is only temporary, because the capacity for dissociation is also strongly internalized and highly valued. That is why communitarianism criticism is doomed—it probably is not a terrible fate—to eternal recurrence.

NOTES

1. Karl Marx, "On the Jewish Question," in *Early Writings*, ed. T. B. Bottomore (London: C. A. Watts, 1963), 26.

2. Alasdair MacIntyre, *After Virtue* (Notre Dame: University of Notre Dame Press, 1981).

3. Thomas Hobbes, *The Elements of Law*, pt. 1, chap. 9, para. 21. I have noticed that the two favorite writers of communitarian critics of this first kind are Hobbes and Sartre. Is it possible that the essence of liberalism is best revealed by these two, who were not, in the usual sense of the term, liberals at all?

4. See Albert Hirschman's *Exit, Voice, and Loyalty* (Cambridge: Harvard University Press, 1970).

5. MacIntyre, *After Virtue*, chaps. 2, 17.

6. This is Richard Rorty's summary of Sandel's argument: "The Priority of Democracy to Philosophy," in *The Virginia Statue for Religious Freedom*, ed. Merrill D. Peterson and Robert C. Vaughan (Cambridge: Cambridge University Press, 1982).

7. Thomas Hobbes, *De Cive*, ed. Howard Warrender (Oxford: Oxford University Press, 1983), pt. 1, chap. 1.

8. Robert Bellah et al., *Habits of the Heart* (Berkeley: University of California Press, 1985), 21, 290; see Rorty's comment, "Priority," 275, n. 12.

9. And also its practical working out, in the career-open-to-talents, the right of free movement, legal divorce, and so on.

10. See Angus Campbell et al., *The American Voter* (New York: Wiley, 1960), 147–48.

11. See the evocation of King in *Habits of the Heart*, 249, 252.

12. Roberto Mangabeira Unger, *The Critical Legal Studies Movement* (Cambridge: Harvard University Press, 1986), 41.

13. Cf. Buff-Coat (Robert Everard) in the Putney debates: "Whatsoever . . . obligations I should be bound unto, if afterwards God should reveal himself, I would break it speedily, if it were a hundred a day." In *Puritanism and Liberty*, ed. A. S .P. Woodhouse (London: J. M. Dent, 1938), 34. Is Buff-Coat the first superliberal or Unger a latter-day Puritan saint?

14. I do not intend a determinist argument here. We mostly move around within inherited worlds because we find such worlds comfortable and even life-enhancing; but we also move out when we find them cramped—and liberalism makes the escape much easier than it was in preliberal societies.

15. I describe how free-ridership works in ethnic groups in "Pluralism: A Political Perspective," in the *Harvard Encyclopedia of American Ethnic Groups*, ed. Stephan Thernstrom (Cambridge: Harvard University Press, 1980), 781–87.

16. John Rawls, *A Theory of Justice* (Cambridge: Harvard University Press, 1971), 527ff.

17. See the argument for a modest "perfectionism" (rather than neutrality) in Joseph Raz, *The Morality of Freedom* (Oxford: Clarendon Press, 1986), chaps. 5, 6.

18. Irving Bernstein, *Turbulent Years: A History of the American Worker, 1933–1941* (Boston: Houghton Mifflin, 1970), chap. 7.

19. See my essay "Socializing the Welfare State" in *Democracy and the Welfare State*, ed. Amy Gutmann (Princeton: Princeton University Press, 1988), 13–26.

20. John Dewey, *The Public and Its Problems* (Athens, Ohio: Swallow Press, 1985), 71–72.

21. This kind of pluralist republicanism is also likely to advance the prospects of what I called "complex equality" in *Spheres of Justice* (New York: Basic Books, 1983). I cannot pursue this question here, but it is worth noting that both liberalism and communitarianism can take egalitarian and non- or anti-egalitarian forms. Similarly, the communitarian correction of liberalism can strengthen the old inequalities of traditionalist ways of life or it can counteract the new inequalities of the liberal market and the bureaucratic state. The "republic of republics" is likely, though by no means certain, to have effects of the second sort.

22. The issue is starkly posed in Michael Sandel, *Liberalism and the Limits of Justice* (Cambridge: Cambridge University Press, 1982); much of the recent discussion is a commentary on or argument with Sandel's book.

23. See Will Kymlicka, "Liberalism and Communitarianism," *Canadian Journal of Philosophy* 18:2 (June 1988), 181–204.

24. Horace Kallen, *Culture and Democracy in the United States* (New York: Boni and Liveright, 1924).

CHAPTER EIGHT

The Civil Society Argument

A Path to Social Reconstruction

[1]

My aim here is to defend a complex, imprecise, and at crucial points, uncertain account of society and politics. I have no hope of theoretical simplicity, not at this historical moment when so many stable oppositions of political and intellectual life have collapsed; but I also have no desire for simplicity, since a world that theory could fully grasp and neatly explain would not, I suspect, be a pleasant place. In the nature of things, then, my argument won't be elegant, and though I believe that arguments should march, the sentences following one another like soldiers on parade, the route of my march today will be twisting and roundabout. I shall begin with the idea of civil society, recently revived by Central and East European intellectuals, and go on to discuss the state, the economy, and the nation, and then civil society and the state again. These are the crucial social formations that we inhabit, but we do not at this moment live comfortably in any of them. Nor is it possible to imagine, in accordance with one or another of the great simplifying theories, a way to choose among them—as if we were destined to find, one day, the best social formation. I mean to argue against choosing, but I shall also claim that it is from within civil society that this argument is best understood.

The words "civil society" name the space of uncoerced human association and also the set of relational networks—formed for the sake of family, faith, interest, and ideology—that fill this space. Central and East European dissidence flourished within a highly restricted version of civil society, and the first task of the new democracies created by the dissidents, so we are told, is to rebuild the networks: unions, churches, political parties and movements, cooperatives, neighborhoods, schools of thought, societies for promoting or preventing this and that. In the West, by contrast, we have lived in civil society for many years without knowing it. Or, better, since the Scottish Enlightenment, or since Hegel, the words have been known to the knowers of such things, but they have rarely served to focus anyone else's attention. Now writers in Hungary, Czechoslovakia, and Poland invite us to think about how this social formation is secured and invigorated.

We have reasons of our own for accepting the invitation. Increasingly, associational life in the "advanced" capitalist and social democratic countries seems at risk. Publicists and preachers warn us of a steady attenuation of everyday cooperation and civic friendship. And this time it is possible that they are not, as they usually are, foolishly alarmist. Our cities really are noisier and nastier than they once were. Familial solidarity, mutual assistance, political like-mindedness —all these are less certain and less substantial than they once were. Other people, strangers on the street, seem less trustworthy than they once did. The Hobbesian account of society is more persuasive than it once was.

Perhaps this worrisome picture follows—in part, no more, but what else can a political theorist say?—from the fact that we have not thought enough about solidarity and trust or planned for their future. We have been thinking too much about social formations different from, in competition with, civil society. And so we have neglected the networks through which civility is produced and reproduced. Imagine that the following questions were posed, one or two centuries ago, to political theorists and moral philosophers: what is the preferred setting, the most supportive environment, for the good life? What sorts of institutions should we work for? Nineteenth- and twentieth-century social thought provides four different, by now familiar, answers to these questions. Think of them as four rival ideologies, each with its own claim to completeness and correctness. Each of them is importantly wrong. Each of them neglects the necessary pluralism of any *civil* society. Each of them is predicated on an assumption I mean to attack: that such questions must receive a singular answer.

[2]

I shall begin, since this is for me the best-known ground, with two leftist answers. The first of the two holds that the preferred setting for the good life is the political community, the democratic state, within which we can be citizens: freely engaged, fully committed, decision-making members. And a citizen, on this view, is much the best thing to be. To live well is to be politically active, working with our fellow citizens, collectively determining our common destiny —not for the sake of this or that determination but for the work itself, in which our highest capacities as rational and moral agents find expression. We know ourselves best as persons who propose, debate, and decide.

This argument goes back to the Greeks, but we are most likely to recognize its neo-classical versions. It is Rousseau's argument, or the standard leftist interpretation of Rousseau's argument. His understanding of citizenship as moral agency is one of the key sources of democratic idealism. We can see it at work in liberals like John Stuart Mill, in whose writings it produced an unexpected defense of syndicalism (what is today called "workers control") and, more generally, of social democracy. It appeared among nineteenth- and twentieth-century democratic radicals, often with a hard populist edge. It played a part in the reiterated demand for social inclusion by women, workers, blacks, and new immigrants, all of whom based their claims on their capacity as agents. And this same neo-classical idea of citizenship resurfaced in the 1960s in New Left theories of participation, where it was, however, like many latter-day revivals, highly theoretical and without local resonance.

Today, perhaps in response to the political disasters of the late 1960s, "communitarians" in the United States struggle to give Rousseauian idealism a historical reference, looking back to the early American republic and calling for a renewal of civic virtue. They prescribe citizenship as an antidote to the fragmentation of contemporary society—for these theorists, like Rousseau, are disinclined to value the fragments. In their hands, republicanism is still a simplifying creed. If politics is our highest calling, then we are called away from every other activity (or, every other activity is redefined in political terms); our energies are directed toward policy formation and decision-making in the democratic state.

I don't doubt that the active and engaged citizen is an attractive figure— even if some of the activists that we actually meet carrying placards and shouting slogans aren't all that attractive. The most penetrating criticism of this first answer to the question about the good life is not that the life isn't good but that it isn't the "real life" of very many people in the modern world. This is so in two senses. First, though the power of the democratic state has grown enormously, partly (and rightly) in response to the demands of engaged citizens, it cannot be said that the state is fully in the hands of its citizens. And the larger it gets, the more it takes over those smaller associations still subject to hands-on control. The rule of the demos is in significant ways illusory; the participation of ordinary men and women in the activities of the state (unless they are state employees) is largely vicarious; even party militants are more likely to argue and complain than actually to decide.

Second, despite the single-mindedness of republican ideology, politics rarely engages the full attention of the citizens who are supposed to be its chief protagonists. They have too many other things to worry about. Above all, they have to earn a living. They are more deeply engaged in the economy than in the political community. Republican theorists (like Hannah Arendt) recognize this engagement only as a threat to civic virtue. Economic activity belongs to the realm of necessity, they argue; politics to the realm of freedom. Ideally, citizens should not have to work; they should be served by machines, if not by slaves, so that they can flock to the assemblies and argue with their fellows about affairs of state. In practice, however, work, though it begins in necessity, takes on value of its own—expressed in commitment to a career, pride in a job well done, a sense of camaraderie in the workplace. All of these are competitive with the values of citizenship.

[3]

The second leftist position on the preferred setting for the good life involves a turning away from republican politics and a focus instead on economic activity. We can think of this as the socialist answer to the questions I began with; it can be found in Marx and also, though the arguments are somewhat different, among the utopians he hoped to supersede. For Marx, the preferred setting is the cooperative economy, where we can all be producers—artists (Marx was a romantic), inventors, and craftsmen. (Assembly line workers don't quite seem to fit.) This again is much the best thing to be. The picture Marx paints is of creative men and women making useful and beautiful objects, not for the sake of this or that object but for the sake of creativity itself, the highest expression of our "species-being" as *homo faber,* man-the-maker.

The state, in this view, ought to be managed in such a way as to set productivity free. It doesn't matter who the managers are so long as they are committed to this goal and rational in its pursuit. Their work is technically important but not substantively interesting. Once productivity is free, politics simply ceases to engage anyone's attention. Before that time, in the Marxist here and now, political conflict is taken to be the superstructural enactment of economic conflict, and democracy is valued mainly because it enables socialist movements and parties to organize for victory. The value is instrumental and historically specific. A democratic state is the preferred setting not for the good life but for the class struggle; the purpose of the struggle is to win, and victory brings an end to democratic instrumentality. There is no intrinsic value in democracy, no reason to think that politics has, for creatures like us, a permanent attractiveness. When we are all engaged in productive activity, social division and the conflicts it engenders will disappear, and the state, in the once-famous phrase, will wither away.

In fact, if this vision were ever realized, it is politics that would wither away. Some kind of administrative agency would still be necessary for economic coordination, and it is only a Marxist conceit to refuse to call this agency a state. "Society regulates the general production," Marx wrote in *The German Ideology*, "and thus makes it possible for me to do one thing today and another tomorrow . . . just as I have a mind."[1] Since this regulation is non-political, the individual producer is freed from the burdens of citizenship. He attends instead to the things he makes and to the cooperative relationships he establishes. Exactly how he can work with other people and still do whatever he pleases is unclear to me and probably to most other readers of Marx. The texts suggest an extraordinary faith in the virtuosity of the regulators. No one, I think, quite shares this faith today, but something like it helps to explain the tendency of some leftists to see even the liberal and democratic state as an obstacle that has to be, in the worst of recent jargons, "smashed."

The seriousness of Marxist antipolitics is nicely illustrated by Marx's own dislike of syndicalism. What the syndicalists proposed was a neat amalgam of the first and second answers to the question about the good life: for them, the preferred setting was the worker-controlled factory, where men and women were simultaneously citizens and producers, making decisions and making things. Marx seems to have regarded the combination as impossible; factories could not be both democratic and productive. This is the point of Engels's little essay on authority,[2] which I take to express Marx's view also. More generally, self-government on the job called into question the legitimacy of "social regulation" or state planning, which alone, Marx thought, could enable individual workers to devote themselves, without distraction, to their work.

But this vision of the cooperative economy is set against an unbelievable background—a nonpolitical state, regulation without conflict, "the administration of things." In every actual experience of socialist politics, the state has moved rapidly into the foreground, and most socialists, in the West at least, have been driven to make their own amalgam of the first and second answers. They call themselves *democratic* socialists, focusing on the state as well as (in fact, much more than) on the economy and doubling the preferred settings for the good life. Since I believe that two are better than one, I take this to be progress. But before I try to suggest what further progress might look like, I need to describe two more ideological answers to the question about the good life, one of them capitalist, the other nationalist. For there is no reason to think that only leftists love singularity.

[4]

The third answer holds that the preferred setting for the good life is the marketplace, where individual men and women, consumers rather than producers, choose among a maximum number of options. The autonomous individual confronting his, and now her, possibilities—this is much the best thing to be. To live well is not to make political decisions or beautiful objects; it is to make personal choices. Not any particular choices, for no choice is substantively the best: it is the activity of choosing that makes for autonomy. And the market within which choices are made, like the socialist economy, largely dispenses with politics; it requires at most a minimal state—not "social regulation," only the police.

Production, too, is free even if it isn't, as in the Marxist vision, freely creative. More important than the producers, however, are the entrepreneurs, heroes of autonomy, consumers of opportunity, who compete to supply whatever all the other consumers want or might be persuaded to want. Entrepreneurial activity tracks consumer preference. Though not without its own excitements, it is mostly instrumental: the aim of all entrepreneurs (and all producers) is to increase their market power, maximize their options. Competing with one another, they maximize everyone else's options too, filling the marketplace with desirable objects. The market is preferred (over the political community and the cooperative economy) because of its fullness. Freedom, in the capitalist view, is a function of plenitude. We can only choose when we have many choices.

It is also true, unhappily, that we can only make effective (rather than merely speculative or wistful) choices when we have resources to dispose of. But people come to the marketplace with radically unequal resources—some with virtually nothing at all. Not everyone can compete successfully in commodity production, and therefore not everyone has access to commodities. Autonomy turns out to be a high-risk value, which many men and women can only realize with help from their friends. The market, however, is not a good setting for mutual assistance, for I cannot help someone else without reducing (for the short term, at least) my own options. And I have no reason, as an autonomous individual, to accept any reductions of any sort for someone else's sake. My argument here is not that autonomy collapses into egotism, only that autonomy in the marketplace provides no support for social solidarity. Despite the successes of capitalist production, the good life of consumer choice is not universally available. Large numbers of people drop out of the market economy or live precariously on its margins.

Partly for this reason, capitalism, like socialism, is highly dependent on state action—not only to prevent theft and enforce contracts but also to regulate the economy and guarantee the minimal welfare of its participants. But these participants, insofar as they are market activists, are not active in the state: capitalism in its ideal form, like socialism again, does not make for citizenship. Or, its protagonists conceive of citizenship in economic terms, so that citizens are transformed into autonomous consumers, looking for the party or program that most persuasively promises to strengthen their market position. They need the state but have no moral relation to it, and they control its officials only as consumers control the producers of commodities, by buying or not buying what they make.

Since the market has no political boundaries, capitalist entrepreneurs also evade official control. They need the state but have no loyalty to it; the profit motive brings them into conflict with democratic regulation. So arms merchants sell the latest military technology to foreign powers and manufacturers move their factories overseas to escape safety codes or minimum wage laws. Multinational corporations stand outside (and to some extent against) every political community. They are known only by their brand names, which, unlike family names and country names, evoke preferences but not affections or solidarities.

[5]

The fourth answer to the question about the good life can be read as a response to market amorality and disloyalty, though it has, historically, other sources as well. According to the fourth answer, the preferred setting is the nation, within which we are loyal members, bound to one another by ties of blood and history. And a member, secure in his membership, literally part of an organic whole—this is much the best thing to be. To live well is to participate with other men and women in remembering, cultivating, and passing on a national heritage. This is so, on the nationalist view, without reference to the specific content of the heritage, so long as it is one's own, a matter of birth, not choice. Every nationalist will, of course, find value in his own heritage, but the highest value is not in the finding but in the willing: the firm identification of the individual with a people and a history.

Nationalism has often been a leftist ideology, historically linked to democracy and even to socialism. But it is most characteristically an ideology of the right, for its understanding of membership is ascriptive; it requires no political choices and no activity beyond ritual affirmation. When nations find themselves ruled by foreigners, however, ritual affirmation isn't enough. Then nationalism requires a more heroic loyalty: self-sacrifice in the struggle for national liberation. The capacity of the nation to elicit such sacrifices from its members is proof of the importance of this fourth answer. Individual members seek the good life by seeking autonomy not for themselves but for their people. Ideally, this attitude ought to survive the liberation struggle and provide a foundation for social solidarity and mutual assistance. Perhaps, to some extent, it does: certainly the welfare state has had its greatest successes in ethnically homogeneous countries. It is also true, however, that once liberation has been secured, nationalist men and women are commonly content with a vicarious rather than a practical participation in the community. There is nothing wrong with vicarious participation, on the nationalist view, since the good life is more a matter of identity than activity—faith, not works, so to speak, though both of these are understood in secular terms.

In the modern world, nations commonly seek statehood, for their autonomy will always be at risk if they lack sovereign power. But they don't seek states of any particular kind. No more do they seek economic arrangements of any particular kind. Unlike religious believers who are their close kin and (often) bitter rivals, nationalists are not bound by a body of authoritative law or a set of sacred texts. Beyond liberation, they have no program, only a vague commitment to continue a history, to sustain a "way of life." Their own lives, I suppose, are emotionally intense, but in relation to society and economy this is a dangerously free-floating intensity. In time of trouble, it can readily be turned against other nations, particularly against the internal others: minorities, aliens, strangers. Democratic citizenship, worker solidarity, free enterprise and consumer autonomy—all these are less exclusive than nationalism but not always resistant to its power. The ease with which citizens, workers, and consumers become fervent nationalists is a sign of the inadequacy of the first three answers to the question about the good life. The nature of nationalist fervor signals the inadequacy of the fourth.

[6]

All these answers are wrong-headed because of their singularity. They miss the complexity of human society, the inevitable conflicts of commitment and loyalty. Hence I am uneasy with the idea that there might be a fifth and finally correct answer to the question about the good life. Still, there is a fifth answer, the newest one (it draws upon less central themes of nineteenth- and twentieth-century social thought), which holds that the good life can only be lived in civil society, the realm of fragmentation and struggle but also of concrete and authentic solidarities, where we fulfill E. M. Forster's injunction, "only connect," and become sociable or communal men and women. And this is, of course, much the best thing to be. The picture here is of people freely associating and communicating with one another, forming and reforming groups of all sorts, not for the sake of any particular formation—family, tribe, nation, religion, commune, brotherhood or sisterhood, interest group or ideological movement—but for the sake of sociability itself. For we are by nature social, before we are political or economic, beings.

I would rather say that the civil society argument is a corrective to the four ideological accounts of the good life—part denial, part incorporation—rather than a fifth to stand alongside them. It challenges their singularity, but it has no singularity of its own. The phrase "social being" describes men and women who are citizens, producers, consumers, members of the nation, and much else besides—and none of these by nature or because it is the best thing to be. The associational life of civil society is the actual ground where all versions of the good are worked out and tested . . . and proven to be partial, incomplete, ultimately unsatisfying. It cannot be the case that living on this ground is good-in-itself; there isn't any other place to live. What is true is that the quality of our political and economic activity and of our national culture is intimately connected to the strength and vitality of our associations.

Ideally, civil society is a *setting of settings:* all are included, none is preferred. The argument is a liberal version of the four answers, accepting them all, insisting that each leave room for the others, therefore not finally accepting any of them. Liberalism appears here as an anti-ideology, and this is an attractive position in the contemporary world. I shall stress this attractiveness as I try to explain how civil society might actually incorporate and deny the four answers. Later on, however, I shall have to argue that this position too, so genial and benign, has its problems.

Let's begin with the political community and the cooperative economy, taken together. These two leftist versions of the good life systematically under-valued all associations except the demos and the working class. Their pro-tagonists could imagine conflicts between political communities and between classes, but not within either; they aimed at the abolition or transcendence of particularism and all its divisions. Theorists of civil society, by contrast, have a more realistic view of communities and economies. They are more accom-modating to conflict, that is, to political opposition and economic competition. Associational freedom serves for them to legitimate a set of market relations, though not necessarily the capitalist set. The market, when it is entangled in the network of associations, when the forms of ownership are pluralized, is without doubt the economic formation most consistent with the civil society argument. This same argument also serves to legitimate a kind of state, liberal and pluralist more than republican (not so radically dependent upon the virtue of its citi-zens). Indeed, a state of this sort, as we will see, is necessary if associations are to flourish.

Once incorporated into civil society, neither citizenship nor production can ever again be all-absorbing. They will have their votaries, but these people will not be models for the rest of us—or they will be partial models only, for some people at some time of their lives, not for other people, not at other times. This pluralist perspective follows in part, perhaps, from the lost romance of work, from our experience with the new productive technologies and the growth of the service economy. Service is more easily reconciled with a vision of man as a social animal than with *homo faber*. What can a hospital attendant or a school teacher or a marriage counselor or a social worker or a television repairman or a government official be said to *make?* The contemporary economy does not offer many people a chance for creativity in the Marxist sense. Nor does Marx (or any socialist thinker of the central tradition) have much to say about those men and women whose economic activity consists entirely in helping other people. The helpmate, like the housewife, was never assimilated to the class of workers.

In similar fashion, politics in the contemporary democratic state does not offer many people a chance for Rousseauian self-determination. Citizenship, taken by itself, is today mostly a passive role: citizens are spectators who vote. Between elections, they are served, well or badly, by the civil service. They are not at all like those heroes of republican mythology, the citizens of ancient Athens meeting in assembly and (foolishly, as it turned out) deciding to invade Sicily. But in the associational networks of civil society, in unions, parties, movements, interest groups, and so on, these same people make many smaller decisions and shape to some degree the more distant determinations of state and economy. And in a more densely organized, more egalitarian civil society, they might do both these things to greater effect.

These socially engaged men and women—part-time union officers, movement activists, party regulars, consumer advocates, welfare volunteers, church members, family heads—stand outside the republic of citizens as it is commonly conceived. They are only intermittently virtuous; they are too caught up in particularity. They look, most of them, for many partial fulfillments, no longer for the one clinching fulfillment. On the ground of actuality (unless the state usurps the ground), citizenship shades off into a great diversity of (sometimes divisive) decision-making roles; and, similarly, production shades off into a multitude of (sometimes competitive) socially useful activities. It is, then, a mistake to set politics and work in opposition to one another. There is no ideal fulfillment and no essential human capacity. We require many settings so that we can live different kinds of good lives.

All this is not to say, however, that we need to accept the capitalist version of competition and division. Theorists who regard the market as the preferred setting for the good life aim to make it the actual setting for as many aspects of life as possible. Their single-mindedness takes the form of market imperialism; confronting the democratic state, they are advocates of privatization and laissez-faire. Their ideal is a society in which all goods and services are provided by entrepreneurs to consumers. That some entrepreneurs would fail and many consumers find themselves helpless in the marketplace—this is the price of individual autonomy. It is, obviously, a price we already pay: in all capitalist societies, the market makes for inequality. The more successful its imperialism, the greater the inequality. But were the market to be set firmly within civil society, politically constrained, open to communal as well as private initiatives, limits might be fixed on its unequal outcomes. The exact nature of the limits would depend on the strength and density of the associational networks (including, now, the political community).

The problem with inequality is not merely that some individuals are more capable, others less capable, of making their consumer preferences effective. It's not that some individuals live in fancier apartments than others, or drive better-made cars, or take vacations in more exotic places. These are conceivably the just rewards of market success. The problem is that inequality commonly translates into domination and radical deprivation. But the verb "translates" here describes a socially mediated process, which is fostered or inhibited by the structure of its mediations. Dominated and deprived individuals are likely to be disorganized as well as impoverished, whereas poor people with strong families, churches, unions, political parties, and ethnic alliances are not likely to be dominated or deprived for long. Nor need these people stand alone even in the marketplace. The capitalist answer assumes that the good life of entrepreneurial initiative and consumer choice is a life led most importantly by individuals. But civil society encompasses or can encompass a variety of market agents: family businesses, publicly owned or municipal companies, worker communes, consumer cooperatives, nonprofit organizations of many different sorts. All these function in the market though they have their origins outside. And just as the experience of democracy is expanded and enhanced by groups that are in but not of the state, so consumer choice is expanded and enhanced by groups that are in but not of the market.

It is only necessary to add that among the groups in but not of the state are market organizations, and among the groups in but not of the market are state organizations. All social forms are relativized by the civil society argument—and on the actual ground too. This also means that all social forms are contestable; moreover, contests can't be won by invoking one or another account of the preferred setting—as if it were enough to say that market organizations, insofar as they are efficient, do not have to be democratic or that state firms, insofar as they are democratically controlled, don't have to operate within the constraints of the market. The exact character of our associational life is something that has to be argued about, and it is in the course of these arguments that we also decide about the forms of democracy, the nature of work, the extent and effects of market inequalities, and much else.

The quality of nationalism is also determined within civil society, where national groups co-exist and overlap with families and religious communities (two social formations largely neglected in modernist answers to the question about the good life) and where nationalism is expressed in schools and movements, organizations for mutual aid, cultural and historical societies. It is because groups like these are entangled with other groups, similar in kind but different in aim, that civil society holds out the hope of a domesticated nationalism. In states dominated by a single nation, the multiplicity of the groups pluralizes nationalist politics and culture; in states with more than one nation, the density of the networks prevents radical polarization.

Civil society as we know it has its origin in the struggle for religious freedom. Though often violent, the struggle held open the possibility of peace. "The establishment of this one thing," John Locke wrote about toleration, "would take away all ground of complaints and tumults upon account of conscience."[3] One can easily imagine groundless complaints and tumults, but Locke believed (and he was largely right) that tolerance would dull the edge of religious conflict. People would be less ready to take risks once the stakes were lowered. Civil society simply is that place where the stakes are lower, where, in principle, at least, coercion is used only to keep the peace and all associations are equal under the law. In the market, this formal equality often has no substance, but in the world of faith and identity, it is real enough. Though nations don't compete for members in the same way as religions (sometimes) do, the argument for granting them the associational freedom of civil society is similar. When they are free to celebrate their histories, remember their dead, and shape (in part) the education of their children, they are more likely to be harmless than when they are unfree. Locke may have put the claim too strongly when he wrote that "There is only one thing which gathers people into seditious commotions, and that is oppression,"⁴ but he was close enough to the truth to warrant the experiment of radical tolerance.

But if oppression is the cause of seditious commotion, what is the cause of oppression? I don't doubt that there is a materialist story to tell here, but I want to stress the central role played by ideological single-mindedness: the intolerant universalism of (most) religions, the exclusivity of (most) nations. The actual experience of civil society, when it can be had, seems to work against these two. Indeed, it works so well, some observers think, that neither religious faith nor national identity is likely to survive for long in the network of free associations. But we really don't know to what extent faith and identity depend upon coercion or whether they can reproduce themselves under conditions of freedom. I suspect that they both respond to such deep human needs that they will outlast their current organizational forms. It seems, in any case, worthwhile to wait and see.

[7]

But there is no escape from power and coercion, no possibility of choosing, like the old anarchists, civil society alone. A few years ago, in a book called *Anti-Politics*, the Hungarian dissident George Konrad described a way of living alongside the totalitarian state but, so to speak, with one's back turned toward it. He urged his fellow dissidents to reject the very idea of seizing or sharing power and to devote their energies to religious, cultural, economic, and professional associations. Civil society appears in his book as an alternative to the state, which he assumes to be unchangeable and irredeemably hostile. His argument seemed right to me when I first read his book. Looking back, after the collapse of the communist regimes in Hungary and elsewhere, it is easy to see how much it was a product of its time—and how short that time was! No state can survive for long if it is wholly alienated from civil society. It cannot outlast its own coercive machinery; it is lost, literally, without its firepower. The production and reproduction of loyalty, civility, political competence, and trust in authority are never the work of the state alone, and the effort to go it alone—one meaning of totalitarianism—is doomed to failure.

The failure, however, has carried with it terrible costs, and so one can understand the appeal of contemporary antipolitics. Even as Central and East European dissidents take power, they remain, and should remain, cautious and apprehensive about its uses. The totalitarian project has left behind an abiding sense of bureaucratic brutality. Here was the ultimate form of political single-mindedness, and though the "democratic" (and, for that matter, the "communist") ideology on which it rested was false, the intrusions even of a more genuine democracy are rendered suspect by the memory. Post-totalitarian politicians and writers have, in addition, learned the older antipolitics of free enterprise—so that the laissez-faire market is defended in the East today as one of the necessary institutions of civil society, or, more strongly, as the dominant social formation. This second view takes on plausibility from the extraordinary havoc wrought by totalitarian economic planning. But it rests, exactly like political single-mindedness, on a failure to recognize the pluralism of associational life. The first view leads, often, to a more interesting and more genuinely liberal mistake: it suggests that pluralism is self-sufficient and self-sustaining.

This is, indeed, the experience of the dissidents: the state could not destroy their unions, churches, free universities, illegal markets, *samizdat* publications. Nonetheless, I want to warn against the antipolitical tendencies that commonly accompany the celebration of civil society. The network of associations incorporates, but it cannot dispense with the agencies of state power; neither can socialist cooperation or capitalist competition dispense with the state. That's why so many dissidents are ministers now. It is indeed true that the new social movements in the East and the West—concerned with ecology, feminism, the rights of immigrants and national minorities, workplace and product safety, and so on—do not aim, as the democratic and labor movements once aimed, at taking power. This represents an important change, in sensibility as much as in ideology, reflecting a new valuation of parts over wholes and a new willingness to settle for something less than total victory. But there can be no victory at all that doesn't involve some control over, or use of, the state apparatus. The collapse of totalitarianism is empowering for the members of civil society precisely because it renders the state accessible.

Here is the paradox of the civil society argument. Citizenship is one of many roles that members play, but the state itself is unlike all the other associations. It both frames civil society and occupies space within it. It fixes the boundary conditions and the basic rules of all associational activity (including political activity). It compels association members to think about a common good, beyond their own conceptions of the good life. Even the failed totalitarianism of, say, the Polish communist state had this much impact upon the Solidarity union: it determined that Solidarity was a Polish union, focused on economic arrangements and labor policy within the borders of Poland. A democratic state, which is continuous with the other associations, has at the same time a greater say about their quality and vitality. It serves, or it doesn't serve, the needs of the associational networks as these are worked out by men and women who are simultaneously members and citizens. I will give only a few obvious examples, drawn from American experience.

Families with working parents need state help in the form of publicly funded day-care and effective public schools. National minorities need help in organizing and sustaining their own educational programs. Worker-owned companies and consumer cooperatives need state loans or loan guarantees; so (even more often) do capitalist entrepreneurs and firms. Philanthropy and mutual aid, churches and private universities, depend upon tax exemptions. Labor unions need legal recognition and guarantees against "unfair labor practices." Professional associations need state support for their licensing procedures. And across the entire range of association, individual men and women need to be protected against the power of officials, employers, experts, party bosses, factory supervisors, directors, priests, parents, patrons; and small and weak groups need to be protected against large and powerful ones. For civil society, left to itself, generates radically unequal power relationships, which only state power can challenge.

Civil society also challenges state power, most importantly when associations have resources or supporters abroad: world religions, pan-national movements, the new environmental groups, multinational corporations. We are likely to feel differently about these challenges, especially after we recognize the real but relative importance of the state. Multinational corporations, for example, need to be constrained, much like states with imperial ambitions; and the best constraint probably lies in collective security, that is, in alliances with other states that give economic regulation some international effect. The same mechanism may turn out to be useful to the new environmental groups. In the first case, the state pressures the corporation; in the second it responds to environmentalist pressure. The two cases suggest, again, that civil society requires political agency. And the state is an indispensable agent—even if the associational networks also, always, resist the organizing impulses of state bureaucrats.

Only a democratic state can create a democratic civil society; only a democratic civil society can sustain a democratic state. The civility that makes democratic politics possible can only be learned in the associational networks; the roughly equal and widely dispersed capabilities that sustain the networks have to be fostered by the democratic state. Confronted with an overbearing state, citizens, who are also members, will struggle to make room for autonomous associations and market relationships (and also for local governments and decentralized bureaucracies). But the state can never be what it appears to be in liberal theory, a mere framework for civil society. It is also the instrument of the struggle, used to give a particular shape to the common life. Hence citizenship has a certain practical pre-eminence among all our actual and possible memberships. That's not to say that we must be citizens all the time, finding in politics, as Rousseau urged, the greater part of our happiness. Most of us will be happier elsewhere, involved only sometimes in affairs of state. But we must have a state open to our sometime involvement.

Nor need we be involved all the time in our associations. A democratic civil society is one controlled by its members, not through a single process of self-determination but through a large number of different and uncoordinated processes. These need not all be democratic, for we are likely to be members of many associations, and we will want some of them to be managed in our interests, but also in our absence. Civil society is sufficiently democratic when in some, at least, of its parts we are able to recognize ourselves as authoritative and responsible participants. States are tested by their capacity to sustain this kind of participation—which is very different from the heroic intensity of Rousseauian citizenship. And civil society is tested by its capacity to produce citizens whose interests, at least sometimes, reach farther than themselves and their comrades, who look after the political community that fosters and protects the associational networks.

[8]

I mean to defend a perspective that might be called, awkwardly, "critical associationalism." I want to join, but I am somewhat uneasy with, the civil society argument. It can't be said that nothing is lost when we give up the single-mindedness of democratic citizenship or socialist cooperation or individual autonomy or national identity. There was a kind of heroism in those projects—a concentration of energy, a clear sense of direction, an unblinking recognition of friends and enemies. To make one of them one's own was a serious commitment. The defense of civil society doesn't quite seem comparable. Associational engagement is conceivably as important a project as any of the others, but its greatest virtue lies in its inclusiveness, and inclusiveness does not make for heroism. "Join the associations of your choice" is not a slogan to rally political militants. And yet that is what civil society requires: men and women actively engaged—in state, economy, and nation, and also in churches, neighborhoods, and families, and in many other settings too. To reach this goal is not as easy as it sounds; many people, perhaps most people, live very loosely within the networks; a growing number of people seem to be radically disengaged—passive clients of the state, market drop-outs, resentful and posturing nationalists. And the civil society project doesn't confront an energizing hostility, as all the others do; its protagonists are more likely to meet sullen indifference, fear, despair, apathy, and withdrawal.

In Central and Eastern Europe, civil society is still a battle cry, for it requires a dismantling of the totalitarian state and it brings with it the exhilarating experience of associational independence. Among ourselves what is required is nothing so grand; nor does it lend itself to a singular description (but this is what lies ahead in the East too). The civil society project can only be described in terms of all the other projects, against their singularity. Hence my account here, which suggests the need 1) to decentralize the state, so that there are more opportunities for citizens to take responsibility for (some of) its activities; 2) to socialize the economy so that there is a greater diversity of market agents, communal as well as private; and 3) to pluralize and domesticate nationalism, on the religious model, so that there are different ways to realize and sustain historical identities.

None of this can be accomplished without using political power to redistribute resources and to underwrite and subsidize the most desirable associational activities. But political power alone cannot accomplish any of it. The kinds of "action" discussed by theorists of the state need to be supplemented (not, however, replaced) by something radically different: more like union organizing than political mobilization, more like teaching in a school than arguing in the assembly, more like volunteering in a hospital than joining a political party, more like working in an ethnic alliance or a feminist support group than canvassing in an election, more like shaping a co-op budget than deciding on national fiscal policy. But can any of these local and small-scale activities ever carry with them the honor of citizenship? Sometimes, certainly, they are narrowly conceived, partial and particularist; they need political correction. The greater problem, however, is that they seem so ordinary. Living in civil society, one might think, is like speaking in prose.

But just as speaking in prose implies an understanding of syntax, so these forms of action (when they are pluralized) imply an understanding of civility. And that is not an understanding about which we can be entirely confident these days. There is something to be said for the neoconservative argument that in the modern world we need to recapture the density of associational life and relearn the activities and understandings that go with it. And if this is the case, then a more strenuous argument is called for from the Left: we have to reconstruct that same density under new conditions of freedom and equality. It would appear to be an elementary requirement of social democracy that there exist a *society* of lively, engaged, and effective men and women—where the honor of "action" belongs to the many and not to the few.

Against a background of growing disorganization—violence, homelessness, divorce, abandonment, alienation, and addiction—a society of this sort looks more like a necessary achievement than a comfortable reality. In truth, however, it was never a comfortable reality, except for the few. Most men and women have been trapped in one or another subordinate relationship, where the "civility" they learned was deferential rather than independent and active. That is why democratic citizenship, socialist production, free enterprise, and nationalism were all of them liberating projects. But none of them has yet produced a general, coherent, or sustainable liberation. And their more single-minded adherents, who have exaggerated the effectiveness of the state or the market or the nation and neglected the networks, have probably contributed to the disorder of contemporary life. The projects have to be relativized and brought together, and the place to do that is in civil society, the setting of settings, where each can find the partial fulfillment that is all it deserves.

Civil society itself is sustained by groups much smaller than the demos or the working class or the mass of consumers or the nation. All these are necessarily pluralized as they are incorporated. They become part of the world of family, friends, comrades, and colleagues, where people are connected to one another and made responsible for one another. Connected and responsible: without that, "free and equal" is less attractive than we once thought it would be. I have no magic formula for making connections or strengthening the sense of responsibility. These aren't aims that can be underwritten with historical guarantees or achieved through a single unified struggle. Civil society is a project of projects; it requires many organizing strategies and new forms of state action. It requires a new sensitivity for what is local, specific, contingent—and, above all, a new recognition (to paraphrase a famous sentence) that the good life is in the details.

NOTES

1. Karl Marx, *The German Ideology* (1845), pt. 1, A, section 4.
2. Friedrich Engels, *On Authority* (1872).
3. John Locke, A Letter Concerning Toleration (1689).
4. Ibid.

CHAPTER NINE

Deliberation, and What Else?

The recent outpouring of books and articles on deliberative democracy is very impressive, and many of the arguments are persuasive. But there has been so little disagreement about deliberation—and no effort at all to consider its contexts and complements—that the idea is in danger of becoming commonplace and sterile.[1] So I intend to indulge a contrarian impulse and try to make a list of all the nondeliberative activities that democratic politics legitimately, and perhaps even necessarily, involves. I doubt that the list is exhaustive, though I have not knowingly left anything out. As will quickly become obvious, I have not made deliberation synonymous with thinking; mine is not a list of thoughtless activities. Deliberation here describes a particular way of thinking: quiet, reflective, open to a wide range of evidence, respectful of different views. It is a rational process of weighing the available data, considering alternative possibilities, arguing about relevance and worthiness, and then choosing the best policy or person. Now, what else do we do? What is going on in the political world besides deliberation?

The point of these questions is not to deny the importance of deliberation or to criticize theoretical accounts of what it requires, like that provided by Amy Gutmann and Dennis Thompson in *Democracy and Disagreement*.[2] Nor do I mean to suggest that those two, or any other theorists of deliberation, would deny the importance of the activities that I shall list in my answer—though they might describe them somewhat differently than I do. For I do mean to offer, in almost all the cases, a strongly sympathetic description. But my main purpose here is to figure out how deliberation fits into a democratic political process that is, as my list makes clear, pervasively nondeliberative. So let's assume, but for the moment set aside, the value of "reasoning together" as Gutmann and Thompson describe it, where reason is qualified by reciprocity, publicity, and accountability. Politics has other values in addition to, and often in tension with, reason: passion, commitment, solidarity, courage, and competitiveness (all of which also require qualification). These values are exemplified in a wide range of activities in the course of which men and women sometimes find occasion to "reason together" but which are better described in other terms.

   1. *Political education.* People have to learn how to be political. Some of what they learn they are taught in school: a rough outline of the history of democratic politics, the crucial events and actors; basic information about the federal system, the three branches of government, the structure and timing of elections; perhaps also an account of the leading ideologies, at least in caricature; and so on. But parties, movements, unions, and interest groups are also schools of a sort, teaching their members the ideas that the groups are organized to advance. What the old communist parties called "agitprop" is a form of political education. Theorists committed to deliberation will say that this is a bad form of education, really indoctrination; and it is literally true that parties and movements seek to indoctrinate their members, that is, to bring them to accept a doctrine—and, whenever possible, to represent it, to repeat its central tenets (even when it is unpopular to do that), so that each indoctrinated member becomes an agent of doctrinal transmission. Whether this sort of thing is good or bad, it is enormously important in political life, because the political identity of most people, or, better, of most of the people who are engaged by politics, is shaped in this way. This is how they become agents with opinions. Of course, political identities are also shaped by familial life: Agents with opinions marry agents with similar opinions and raise children to whom they try, most often successfully, to pass on those opinions. Socialization in the family, the earliest form of political education, is just agitprop with love. But the opinions that are transmitted reflect doctrines developed outside the family and inculcated in public settings through a great variety of public media.

   2. *Organization.* One of the aims of political education, or, at least, of agitprop and indoctrination, is to induce people to identify with and work for particular organizations. But organizing itself is a highly specific activity, which involves getting people actually to sign up, carry a card, accept a discipline, pay their dues, and learn to act in accordance with a script that they don't write themselves. "The union makes us strong!" is a democratic maxim, even if it is also true in nondemocratic settings; it reflects democracy's majoritarianism, which puts a premium on association and combination. But unions, like armies,

are not strong if their members stop to deliberate about every action that the leadership commands. The leaders deliberate on behalf of everyone else, and this process is more or less public, so that the members can speculate about what the deliberations of the leaders will come to. But organizers try to persuade people to act in unison, rather than as speculating or deliberating individuals.

3. *Mobilization.* Large-scale political action requires more than organization. Individual men and women have to be stimulated, provoked, energized, excited, called to arms. The military metaphor is appropriate: An army can be an inert organization, held in reserve, the soldiers sitting in camps, cleaning their weapons, occasionally exercising. If they are to fight a war, they have to be mobilized. Something similar is true in political life. Ordinary members must be turned into militants, at least for the duration of a particular activity. An especially intense sort of agitprop is necessary here, to capture their interest, focus their energies, draw them tightly together—so that they actually read the party's manifesto, say, and argue on its behalf, and march, carry banners, and shout slogans in the party's parades. I know that the image of masses of people shouting slogans will suggest to deliberative democrats an antidemocratic politics. But the character of the politics depends on the slogans, and these have often been prodemocratic. Indeed, what might be called the struggle for deliberative democracy—that is, for political equality, a free press, the right of association, civil rights for minorities, and so on—has required a lot of slogan shouting. It is not easy to imagine a democratic politics to which popular mobilization has become superfluous. (Whether that should be our ideal is a question I will come to only at the end of my list.)

4. *Demonstration.* The point of a democratic mobilization is not to storm government offices and literally seize state power but rather to demonstrate personal intensity, numerical strength, and doctrinal conviction—all of which are critical to popular power. Hence the march or parade, the party rally, the placards and banners, the shouting of the participants, the oratory of the leaders, and the fierce applause it is meant to elicit. There is no room here for quiet deliberation, for that would not show to the world the force of these people's concern, their passionate commitment and solidarity, their determination to achieve a particular political object. Once again, the aim is demonstrative: to deliver a message—sometimes more generally to one's fellow citizens, sometimes more narrowly to an entrenched elite. The message goes like this: Here we stand; this is what we believe must be done; and we don't believe it casually, it isn't an "opinion" of the sort that might be captured by an opinion poll, it's not what we think today and might or might not think tomorrow; we will keep

coming back until we have won; and if you want to get on with the ordinary business of politics, you had better accommodate us on this point (or on this series of seventeen points). Of course, all this can be said in a fanatical way, reflecting ideological or religious absolutism rather than political determination. But demonstrating intensity and conviction now doesn't necessarily preclude negotiating later on, and this combination can be used, and has been, in defense of democratic rights—to vote, or strike, or associate freely—as well as in defense of substantive but contested reforms like prohibition, or gun control, or the minimum wage.

5. *Statement.* "Making a statement" is the aim of the demonstration, but it can also take a more literal form. I have already mentioned the party manifesto, which the militants endorse and repeat. Sometimes it is politically useful to reduce the manifesto to a credo or declaration, affirming this or that ideological conviction (something like the profession of faith of a religious community), or staking out a position on some more immediate issue, and then ask people to sign on. The publication of the credo, with names attached, signals to the world the commitment of these people, their readiness to take a stand in a public way. The authors of the credo may have deliberated about what to say, more likely about how to say it; the people asked to sign presumably deliberate about whether to sign or not. But the credo itself has the form of an assertion, which is not likely to be modified as a result of counterassertions. At moments of intense political conflict, newspapers and magazines will be filled with statements of this sort—declarations for and against this or that policy, say; but all of them taken together do not constitute a democratic deliberation, since the different sets of authors and signatories don't always make arguments, and when they do, they rarely read each other's arguments.

6. *Debate.* Statement and counterstatement make for something like a debate, though we usually expect debaters to speak directly to one another, arguing back and forth in a quicker, more spontaneous, more heated way than is possible in the formal exchange of credos and declarations. Debaters do have to listen to one another, but listening in this case does not produce anything like a deliberative process: Their object is not to reach an agreement among themselves but to win the debate, that is, to persuade the audience that this position, rather than any of the alternatives, is the best one. (Some members of the audience may then deliberate among themselves or within themselves—going over the different positions in their own minds.) A debate is a contest between verbal athletes, and the aim is victory. The means are the exercise of rhetorical skill, the mustering of favorable evidence (and the suppression of unfavorable

evidence), the discrediting of the other debaters, the appeal to authority or celebrity, and so on. All these are plain to see in party debates in parliaments and assemblies and in debates between or among candidates at election time. But they are also standard on the lecture circuit and in newspapers and magazines, whenever representatives of different positions are challenged to engage each other's arguments. The others are rivals, not fellow participants; they are already committed, not persuadable; the objects of the exercise, again, are the people in the audience—though many of them have come just to cheer for their own side, which can also be a useful political activity.

7. *Bargaining.* Sometimes the positions defended in this or that demonstration or manifesto or debate have been deliberated on, but very often they are the products of long and complicated negotiations among interested as well as opinionated individuals. That means that they don't represent anyone's idea of the best position; they are compromises with which no one is entirely satisfied; they reflect the balance of forces, not the weight of arguments. Commonly, bargaining doesn't begin until the relative strength of the different parties has been tested; sometimes its purpose is to avoid further costly or bloody tests. So the parties agree to split the differences between them, the precise split depending on the previous tests of strength. "Balanced tickets" are worked out in the same way. And government policy in a democracy is more often the result of a negotiating process of this sort than of any deliberative process. The best policy is the one that accommodates the largest number of interests or, better, that accommodates precisely those interests that are able to assert themselves politically (hence the importance of organization and mobilization). I can imagine people arguing about how to serve the common good, above and beyond all the particular interests, given the constraint that the particular interests must also be served. But that is a pretty severe constraint, and the result is surely closer to give-and-take than to deliberation. Gutmann and Thompson argue for a distinction between "self-interested" bargaining and mutual accommodation—the latter representing a properly deliberative process.[3] But I suspect that mutuality in political life is always qualified by interest and tested by conflict. What marks off deliberation is better seen if we consider the example of the jury. We don't want the jurors in a criminal case bargaining with one another or even accommodating one another: "I'll vote your way on the first count if you vote my way on the second and third counts." We want them to weigh the evidence as best they can and come up with a verdict, that is, a true statement about guilt or innocence. But politicians can legitimately act in exactly the way jurors are barred from acting; indeed, a bargain is often the better part of political wisdom.

8. *Lobbying.* The cultivation of public officials by private parties is pervasive in politics, in both democratic and nondemocratic settings. It may well be the case that in democracies the private parties are more likely to argue with the officials (rather than bargain with them) or at least to provide them with arguments, since democratically responsible officials will have to defend their positions in one or another open forum. Still, lobbying at its most effective involves the forging of close personal relations; it depends on social networks and individual friendships. A good lobbyist makes up in charm, access, and insider knowledge whatever he lacks in arguments. And the arguments he makes will probably have less to do with the issue at hand than with the political future of the official he is lobbying.

9. *Campaigning.* Sometimes this military metaphor is used to refer to any coordinated program of organizing, mobilizing, demonstrating, and so on, for a particular cause. But I mean here to describe only electoral campaigns, the democratic search for voter support. This obviously involves most of the activities that I have listed so far, but it also has its own specific character—in part because it is focused, even when political parties are strong, on specific characters, on leaders with names and faces and life histories as well as programs. It is these leaders who bear the brunt of the campaigning, actively soliciting the votes of their fellow citizens, making promises, trying to look trustworthy, and trying to suggest the untrustworthiness of their opponents. We can imagine them working within a set of limits, legal or moral rules, say, defining "fair campaign practices"—though in fact virtually no effective limits exist today except those enforced by public opinion. What would the rules of a fair campaign be like? They would certainly bear little resemblance to the rules about what can and can't be said in a courtroom, and the reason for that, again, is that we don't believe that voters, any more than politicians, are like jurors.

10. *Voting.* What should citizens do when they vote? Clearly, they should attend to the arguments being made by the different candidates and to the platforms of the parties. They should think about the consequences of this or that candidate's victory, not only for themselves but for the various groups to which they belong, and for the country as a whole. Nonetheless, the body of citizens is not a search committee, deliberating on the most qualified candidate for the Senate, say, or the presidency. The members of a search committee are like jurors in that they are assumed (sometimes wrongly) to have a common understanding of the relevant qualifications and to deliberate impartially among the candidates. But neither of those assumptions is justified in the case of citizens. Some of them may believe that it is toughness and commitment on this

or that issue that qualifies someone for the presidency, while others believe that the capacity to produce compromises on all the issues is the best qualification. Some of them may identify with candidate X because she has defended their interests or their values in the past or with candidate Y because he is a member of their ethnic or religious community, or of their union or interest group, or because he has a political history similar to their own. Certainly, again, we want voters to consider the available evidence carefully and to reflect long and hard on the arguments of the contending candidates and parties. But they don't have to disqualify themselves if, because of their current interests or previous commitments, they can't or won't pay equal attention to each of the contenders. Nor are they barred from choosing the issues on which they focus their considerations and reflections for nondeliberative reasons. Indeed, voters have a right to choose issues and candidates alike with reference to their interests, or their passions, or their ideological commitments, and most of them do just that. Perhaps it is a general truth that the issues on which citizens deliberate (or do not) arise through a political process that is largely nondeliberative. It is through the mobilization of passions and interests that we are forced to address what is (only now) the "question" of poverty, or corruption, or exploitation.

11. *Fund-raising.* Not much can be done in politics without money. Even before the age of television, money had to be raised to pay for salaries and offices; leaflets, newsletters, advertisements, and mass mailings; travel, meeting halls, and party conferences. Nothing is more common in political life than the varied activities that come under the rubric of fund-raising. Historically, in the United States, these activities have probably provided the best examples of participatory democracy—precisely because they don't involve studying the issues, arguing in public, making speeches, or sitting on deliberative committees. Of course, asking rich individuals for their money isn't the work of the demos, but fund-raising on a smaller scale—raffles, rummage sales, bake sales, dinners and dances, "passing the hat"—is in fact a mass activity; one that involves thousands of men and women. And there can't be any doubt that money raised in this way is a bond: People who have given it, and people who have helped to get it, are more loyal to the cause, or loyal longer, than those who merely have reason to think that the cause is just.

12. *Corruption.* This powerful censorious term describes a set of activities, outright bribery and extortion the most obvious and probably the most common, that ought to be excluded from democratic politics. These activities, taken together, constitute my only negative example, and what I am interested in is the argument for their exclusion. Bribery is a nondeliberative activity like many

others (though its protagonists might well reason together about whom to bribe and how much to offer); more important, it is an activity that interferes with deliberation. That's why it is barred from some social and governmental settings, but not why it is barred from the primary political setting, the arena of electoral politics. Bribing judges and jurors is wrong precisely because it produces a result that doesn't reflect an impartial deliberative process. Bribing government officials who dispense licenses and grants is wrong because it produces a result that doesn't reflect an honest search for qualified people and worthy projects. But bribing voters is wrong only because it interferes with the democratic representation of the voters themselves, not with any activity required of them: we don't get an accurate picture of their interests, concerns, or opinions. The result lacks democratic legitimacy, but it isn't illegitimate because impartial reason and reflection have played no part in its production. A candidate who promises to reduce unemployment is appealing, let's say, to the unreflective interests of the unemployed (and all their friends and relatives), yet her appeal doesn't corrupt the political process. In fact, it is an important and entirely legitimate result of her appeal that we find out how many people share those particular interests and give them high priority. But she can't hire the unemployed to vote for her.

13. *Scut work.* A lot of what passes for political participation, a lot of the activity that is critical to the success of organizations and campaigns, is simply boring and repetitive work that has no intrinsically political character at all—like stuffing envelopes, setting up chairs, preparing placards, handing out leaflets, making phone calls (to ask for signatures or money, or to get people to go to meetings or to vote on election day), knocking on doors (for the same purposes), sitting at the literature table at party conferences, and so on. None of this requires much thought, though it often takes a lot of thought, and even some ingenuity, to motivate oneself to do it. Since scut work is necessary—"someone has to do it"—it's worth dwelling for a moment on how it gets done. Obviously, commitment plays a major part, but I think it is important that this commitment exists within a competitive system. The excitement of the competition, the sense of possible victory, the fear of defeat—all these things press people to take on tasks they would otherwise be reluctant to perform. Even when politics begins to get dangerous, there isn't much difficulty recruiting people to do scut work: Danger has its own excitements. Properly deliberative men and women, of course, might be reluctant to stuff envelopes even if no one was threatening to beat up all the envelope stuffers. They might be too busy reading position papers; they might be unmoved by competitive emotions. That scut work

regularly gets done may well be the clearest example of the appeal of non-deliberative political activity.

14. *Ruling.* If scut work is the low end of politics, ruling is the high end. Aristotle defined citizenship in a democracy as "ruling and being ruled in turn." But it is the first of these that is commonly valued; the acceptance of "being ruled" is an accommodation to democratic doctrine. If everyone is to have the experience of ruling, we have to take turns. In practice, of course, some people rule for long periods of time; others are ruled all the time. What distinguishes democratic ruling from undemocratic domination is the legitimation of the former through consent. But whatever its legitimacy (and there is domination even in democracies), ruling is for most rulers a pleasurable activity. Aristotle probably believed that some part of the pleasure derived from the exercise of reason on a large scale, over the whole agenda, so to speak, of public issues. In this sense, ruling is a deliberative activity. But the pleasures of command are by no means wholly rational, else people would not seek to rule with such passion. And we sometimes want rulers who are not likely to deliberate too much—whose "native hue of resolution" is not, like Hamlet's, "sicklied o'er with the pale cast of thought."[4]

That is my list, and it is a hard question whether, if I had not started by asking What else?, deliberation would have a place on it. Does deliberation belong in the same series that includes "organization," "mobilization," "demonstration," and so on? If we take what jurors do as the model of a deliberative process, it probably doesn't. Of course, courts are political institutions insofar as they exist within constitutional structures and sometimes find themselves in conflict with officials exercising legislative and executive authority. But political considerations are supposed to be ruled out when a civil or criminal trial is in progress. The reason for ruling them out is our standard assumption that there is a single just outcome of the trial, which the jury is or should be united in pursuing. No such assumption is possible in political life, which is not merely adversarial but inherently and permanently conflictual. Very few political decisions are "verdicts" in the literal sense of that term. I don't mean that we can't, sometimes, insist that it is morally right and perhaps imperative to do X; but even the people who agree on what X is and on the necessity of doing it are likely to disagree about how to do it, or how soon, or at whose expense.

It isn't necessary to adopt Carl Schmitt's view of politics to recognize that different interests and ideological commitments are often irreconcilable. Of course, parties in conflict negotiate, and settle, and then reconcile themselves to the settlement, but they are likely to feel that something has been lost in the negotiating process and to reserve the right to reopen the discussion whenever conditions seem more propitious. We protect criminals against second prosecutions for the same crime, but we don't protect politicians against repeated challenges on the same issue. Permanent settlements are rare in political life precisely because we have no way of reaching anything like a verdict on contested issues. Passions fade; men and women disengage from particular commitments; interest groups form new alignments; the world turns. But certain deep disagreements, like those between Left and Right, are remarkably persistent, and local forms of religious or ethnic conflict are often so embedded in a political culture as to seem natural to the participants. So politics is the endless return of these disagreements and conflicts, the struggle to manage and contain them, and, at the same time, to win whatever temporary victories are available. The democratic way to win is to educate, organize, mobilize . . . more people than the other side has. "More" is what makes the victory legitimate, and while legitimacy is strengthened if good arguments can be made about the substantive issues at stake, the victory is rarely won by making good arguments.

But it isn't only the permanence of conflict that accounts for the omission of deliberation from my list but also, more particularly, the prevalence of inequality. Political history, when it doesn't take an ideological form, is mostly the story of the slow creation or consolidation of hierarchies of wealth and power. People fight their way to the top of these hierarchies and then contrive as best they can to maintain their position. The "ruling class" may be much less coherent than Marxist theory suggests; nonetheless, something like it exists, with more or less self-awareness, and aims to sustain itself. Popular organizations and mobilizations are the only ways to oppose this aim. Their effect is not—at least it never has been—to level the hierarchies, but only to shake them up, bring new people in, and perhaps set limits to the differentiations they define and entrench. So democratic politics makes possible an amended version of political history: Now it is the story of the establishment *and partial disestablishment* of inequality. I don't see any way to avoid the endless repetition of this story, any way to replace the struggles it involves with a deliberative process. Who would deliberate? On what issues? With reference to what facts and theories? And why would dissatisfied citizens accept the outcome of the deliberations? Couldn't they always claim that the best thinking of the best thinkers, deliberating under the best conditions, reflects nothing more than the interests of the powers-that-be? Of course, one can design a deliberative process that excludes those interests altogether—by requiring the participants to deliberate behind a veil of ignorance, say, and strictly controlling the facts and theories to which they have access. But that is a utopian design, not realizable in any extant political world.

Should we aim at realizing it? Is this our utopia, the dream of committed democrats—a world where political conflict, class struggle, and ethnic and religious differences are all replaced by pure deliberation? As Joseph Schwartz has recently argued, left-wing political theorists have often written as if this were their ultimate goal.[5] But theories of this sort, as Schwartz correctly claims, reflect an antipolitical bias, and they are unlikely to be realized except by the repression of conflict. No doubt, repression would be undertaken only in defense of policies that the theorists and their friends had thought about long and hard, in imperfect but nor implausible deliberative settings, like academic seminars, or communities of exiled intellectuals, or the committees of vanguard parties far from political power. Still, committed democrats can hardly endorse the repression.

Deliberation does have a place, in fact an important place, in democratic politics, but I don't think it has an independent place—a place, so to speak, of its own. There is no setting in the political world quite like the jury room, in which we don't want people to do anything *except* deliberate. Similarly, though politics is often said to involve more committee work than anything else, there are no political committees quite like a search committee looking to appoint a professor or a prize committee trying to identify the best novel of the year. The work of searching out candidates and awarding prizes is often politicized, of course, but when it is, the results are likely to be called into question. By contrast, one expects political considerations to prevail in the committees of a party or movement and even in legislative and administrative committees—at least, such considerations are legitimately invoked; something would be wrong with the democratic process if they had no role at all. Imagine a group of bureaucrats deliberating with great seriousness for many hours, and then doing what they have concluded is the right thing to do—without taking into account the recorded preferences of a majority of the people or the interests of whatever coalition of groups currently constitutes the majority (which is exactly what juries are supposed to do). The chosen policy of the deliberating bureaucrats might well be the "best" one, but it would not be the right policy for a democratic government.

Deliberation's proper place is dependent on other activities that it doesn't constitute or control. We make room for it, and should do that, in the larger space that we provide for more properly political activities. We try to introduce a certain measure of calm reflection and reasoned argument into, say, the work of political education. Even agitprop can be better or worse, and it is clearly better if its arguments are honestly informed and addressed to the hardest questions, the most difficult challenges that the parry or movement confronts. Similarly, we can imagine the party platform drawn up by a group of people who are not only good negotiators but reflective men and women aiming at proposals that are morally justified and economically realistic as well as politically appealing. We can imagine a negotiating process in which people try to understand and accommodate the interests of the other side (while still defending their own) rather than just driving the hardest possible bargain. We can imagine parliamentary debates where the rival speakers listen to one another and are prepared to modify their positions. And finally, we can imagine citizens who actually think about the common good when they evaluate candidates or party programs, the deals their representatives strike or the arguments they make.

It is an interesting question, one that has been addressed most inventively by James Fishkin,[6] what practical arrangements might help citizens think about the common good. But I don't believe that these arrangements, whatever they are, can or should replace the settings and activities that I have listed. Fishkin's argument for citizens' juries, where scientific sampling substitutes for electoral politics, suggests the central problem of deliberative democracy: Deliberation is not an activity for the demos. I don't mean that ordinary men and women don't have the capacity to reason, only that 100 million of them, or even 1 million or 100,000 can't plausibly "reason together." And it would be a great mistake to turn them away from the things they can do together. For then there would be no effective, organized opposition to the powers-that-be. The political outcome of such a move is readily predictable: The citizens who were turned away would lose the fights they probably wanted, and may well have needed, to win.

NOTES

1. The continental analogue and possible source of the American arguments, Habermas's communication theory, has been the subject of a vast critical literature, most of it focused on the technical philosophical aspects of the theory. American writers, who mostly avoid technical argument, have escaped the criticism. But see Lynn Sanders, "Against Deliberation," *Political Theory* 25:3 (June 1997), and my own "Critique of Philosophical Conversation," this volume, chap. 2.

2. Amy Gutmann and Dennis Thompson, *Democracy and Disagreement* (Cambridge: Belknap Press of Harvard University Press, 1996).

3. Ibid., 352–53.

4. William Shakespeare, *Hamlet*, 3.1.

5. Joseph M. Schwartz, *The Permanence of the Political: A Democratic Critique of the Radical Impulse to Transcend Politics* (Princeton: Princeton University Press, 1995).

6. James Fishkin, *Democracy and Deliberation: New Directions for Democratic Reform* (New Haven: Yale University Press, 1991). If the purpose of the juries is simply to add their own conclusions to the mix of ideas and proposals that are already being debated in the political arena, then they are useful in the same way that think tanks and presidential commissions are useful. If any sort of democratic authority is claimed for them, if the sample displaces the sampled, they are dangerous.

CHAPTER TEN

Drawing the Line

Religion and Politics

[I]

Once upon a time, Americans were taught that religion was a private matter. But increasingly, around the world, and here too, it is a political matter. Religious believers have become political activists, seeking to shape public policy or to seize state power, sometimes within, sometimes outside democratic and constitutional structures. It is obviously time to ask again: can there, should there, be a radical separation between religion and politics?

Once upon a time, people on the left or, at least, the secular left, defenders of liberal enlightenment, believed that religion would soon fade away even as a private matter, disappearing along with other irrationalities as ordinary men and women took control of their society and economy. But it hasn't faded away (we haven't taken control . . .); it not only endures but is subject to periodic revival, and at this moment its militants have rather more enthusiasm for and confidence in their project than do their liberal and secular counterparts. Can they be kept out of politics? Should they be?

Liberal and left secularists may once have hoped for total exclusion: not only the religiously motivated militants but also the sentiments and doctrines that motivate them would play no part in political decision making. But no such exclusion is possible in a democratic society. Men and women with religious convictions can't be expected to leave them behind at the entrance to the political arena. Nor has the left consistently asked its own religious friends and comrades to do that. Think of the abolitionists, many of whom were religiously inspired; or of Christian socialists like R. H. Tawney, who had such a powerful influence on the British Labor Party; or of civil rights activists in the United States in the 1960s, rooted in the black churches, led by Baptist preachers, supported by liberal priests and rabbis; or of Catholic liberation theologians in Latin America; or of the American bishops, writing pastoral letters against nuclear deterrence and in defense of economic justice.

And if one accepts this sort of thing, one has to expect interventions of other sorts too: like the participation of the Women's Christian Temperance Union in the fight for prohibition; or the campaigns of contemporary evangelical churches in the United States against abortion, pornography, and assisted suicide; or the role of the Irish bishops in opposing legalized divorce; or the influence of Jewish messianists in the Greater Israel movement. A democratic society cannot inquire into how or where the political views of its citizens are shaped, and it cannot censor the doctrinal or rhetorical forms in which those views are expressed.

Even so, the separation of religion and politics is an important democratic value, with policy implications that need to be mapped in detail.[1] I can offer only a brief description here, focusing on three standard requirements for a successful separation. In drawing the line, I follow the contours and conventions of American political geography and hew as closely as I can to the conventional understanding of the "wall of separation between church and state."[2] At the same time, I shall try to give this understanding its strongest possible form— and I will write in the same way in Section 2 of this chapter, when I present two critical perspectives on the standard separationist position and try to make these as persuasive as possible. Though I will be guided by my own sense of strength and persuasiveness in these first two Sections, it is only in Section 3 that I will speak entirely in my own voice.

These are the three separationist requirements:

1) Separation requires a sharp institutional divide. This means simply that the state must have an effective monopoly of coercive power and that religious associations must have no coercive power at all—except what they can muster in the form of social pressure—and no ability to call on the coercive power of the state to advance their religious purposes. Religious associations have the character of voluntary associations (even if their members believe themselves to live under divine command), and no one of them is entitled, nor are all of them together entitled, to state support.[3] The state must be neutral among the different religions and neutral also between religious and nonreligious groups. This rules out ecclesiastical courts with official jurisdiction, allows no role to state bureaucrats in church affairs, bans any sort of favored treatment even for majority religions and any discrimination against religious or irreligious minorities, and forbids the use of tax money for the promotion of religious projects—

including, most importantly, the schooling of children in accordance with a particular religious creed.

2) Separation requires that the public ceremonies and celebrations of the state be distinct from those of any religious group. The "civil religion"[4] must be genuinely civil. Its holidays, like the Fourth of July, must have their source in political history. Its ceremonies, however much they echo those of (different) religious groups, must be open to a purely political interpretation. Consider the inauguration of an American president, which has sometimes been taken as an example of the Christian colonization of our public culture.[5] But the presidential oath derives from feudal, not Christian, practice and is familiar from many parts of the world. Reciting poetry on such occasions is an ancient custom, of which there are many examples—from ancient Greece, for example, as well as biblical Israel (some psalms are commonly taken to be coronation poems). The "address from the throne" is copied from monarchic regimes, where it is pretty much universal. Only the hand-on-the-Bible is specifically Christian, and American law permits alternatives to that, if any president-elect ever wants to make a secularist point.

Civil religion aims at religiosity without a positive religion.[6] The state is not or, at least, it shouldn't be, an object of worship; nor are its laws or its constitution worshipped, even when they are treated almost like sacred texts. But we do hope to inspire a kind of reverence for the political community and its history and institutions and also a strong fellow feeling, a sense of mutual engagement among the citizens, something like the bond that joins the members of a religious community. I want to stress those qualifying phrases: "almost like," "a kind of," "something like." Political ties are not the same as religious ties. They don't bind men and women into a mystical body or a holy congregation. Politics makes for a cooler fellowship, whose character, organization, and purposes are not conceived to be divinely ordained or eternal; they are constructed by human beings in human time and always subject to reconstruction. An American Supreme Court justice once described the voting booth as the "temple" of the democratic state.[7] Maybe so, but we often go there to vote against the High Priest.

3) Separation requires an acceptance of the open, pragmatic, contingent, uncertain, inconclusive, and tolerant character of all arguments, positions, and alliances on the political side of the line. This is the hardest requirement of the three, since it can never (and should never) be made a matter for legal enforcement. It has to do with political culture and public education. The language of religion is absolutist in character, at least some of the time. It is also,

obviously, discursive, speculative, and argumentative, but absolutism—in the form of faith, mystery, dogma, and orthodoxy—is not alien to religion, whereas it is, or ought to be, alien to politics. "Whoever doesn't believe in the true revelation will have no place in the millennial kingdom" is the sort of statement that has no place in campaign rhetoric—not its content, clearly, and not its tone either. Political language, even when it is spoken fiercely and loudly, should always be open to questioning, disagreement, and revision.

When politics goes bad, we use religious language to describe it: the cult of personality, sectarian dogmas, the ritual incantation of the party line, the search for heretics, messianic pretension, and so on. A healthy political competition invites different descriptive terms. Even the language of war—fight a campaign, adopt a strategy, outflank your opponents (on the right or left)—is better suited to politics than the language of religion, since in war it is at least possible to respect one's opponents, whereas infidels and apostates haven't been respected in the history of most of the world's religions.[8] Jozef Cardinal Glemp was not offering an appropriately political account of the 1995 Polish election when he said that it was a contest between "Christian" and "neo-pagan" values.[9] On Glemp's view, how were victorious Christians supposed to treat their pagan foe? How would they be able to acknowledge the legitimacy of their defeat, if they lost (as they did)?

So it is very important that people whose views have had a religious formation learn to politicize them. They don't need to leave them behind when they enter the political arena, but they do need to surrender their absolutism. Henceforth, these views will have to be defended with evidence and arguments (rather than, say, with assertions of divine authority) and, since even the best arguments will be challenged, and won't bring total victory, their defenders will have to compromise with people who hold different views. Thus, the American bishops participate in the democratic process when they invoke Catholic just war theory in criticism of nuclear deterrence—so long as they treat the theory as an argument, not a dogma, and recognize the legitimacy of democratic decisions that only partially reflect their criticism or that don't reflect it at all.[10]

Religious militants and, more recently, their neo-conservative allies, have criticized each of these requirements. They claim that the moral level of our public life can't be, and isn't being, sustained by the (triumphant) secular advocates of separation. It's not that the secularists have no morality, but rather that they don't have, so to speak, a firm grip on their own moral ideas—which are mostly carry-overs from the religious traditions they have abandoned. Only religion provides morality with a foundation. "Secular humanists," who have broken loose from this foundation, now float freely, buoyed by good intentions, but without a compass or steering mechanism, blown by the winds of relativism. State policy, society and culture more generally, reflect the secularists' confusion, which is the cause of, or at least fails to prevent, crime, drug use, welfare fraud, tax evasion, family breakup, teenage pregnancy, child abuse, pornography, and random violence. And the only remedy is to bring God back into the public square (and, of course, into the public schools).[11]

There are plausible arguments against separation, but this, it seems to me, isn't one of them. It is certainly true that secular philosophers and social and political theorists disagree about the ultimate ground of morality. Some of them, for example, insist that there is no ultimate ground (which doesn't prevent them from making strong moral claims). But these disagreements are more than matched by disagreements among the theologians and preachers of the different religions about how that ultimate ground is best described and what actual moral codes rest upon it. People making the anti-secularist argument seem to have in mind some mock-up of a singular, generalized, all-purpose Religion. They are obviously not thinking about the many actual religions that have to coexist in pluralist societies, and they are not remembering the persecutions and religious wars that originally gave rise to the idea of separation.

Men and women disagree about morality, just as they disagree about politics. Even believers in one God don't have one view of what God wants of them; nor does belief have one universal effect. Religion, according to conservative writers, makes for civic responsibility and high levels of moral performance in everyday life. Well, some religions do, some of the time. Other religions (or the same ones at different times) make for political withdrawal and personal passivity, and still others make for obsession and fanaticism. Religion is a mixed bag, exactly like secular ideology.

So the critical question is: How should the inevitable disagreements, insofar as they affect the uses of state power, be worked out? The standard claim of separationists is that they have to be worked out politically—that is, through argument, deliberation, bargaining, and compromise. Where the arguments come from doesn't matter. If believers are convinced that the best arguments come from God, or his prophets, or his authorized texts, they should say so; they still have to persuade their fellow citizens. But if they agree to this last requirement, haven't they effectively accepted the separationist view and so given up the battle? Aren't they forced to compete, henceforth, on the alien ground of public reason?[12] To some degree, that must be right: the authority structures of most of the world's religions are antithetical to those of liberal democracy, and so when we require believers to adhere to the rules of the political arena, we are requiring them to speak and act in unfamiliar ways. Nonetheless, all the major religions have traditions of argument that can be adapted to democratic use—as American Catholic bishops, black Baptist preachers, and liberal rabbis in their different fashions have shown. (Religious groups that refuse to adapt their arguments and join the democratic debate can opt for a sectarian existence— outside the arena but still protected by its rules.)

But politics isn't only a matter of argument, and it's not always the case, perhaps it's only rarely the case, that the best arguments win. Passion and power are also determinative. And the greatest fear of liberal separationists is not that religious men and women will carry their ideas into the political arena, but that they will pursue power with religious zeal and rule zealously as soon as they get the chance.[13] The standard view of separation doesn't preclude zeal in politics, but it does generate a disposition to avoid it, even a prejudice against it (like the distaste for "enthusiasm" among eighteenth-century English Whigs).[14] Of course, zeal doesn't always bear a religious label; the twentieth century has seen many examples of secular zealousness, including a burning anti-religious absolutism. These are the risks of the mixed bag. Separationists have to accept the risks—but they will also struggle to reduce them, to limit the political effectiveness of zealotry by strengthening the intellectual and institutional bulwarks of a democratic culture.

The separationist ideal is a political world where God's word carries no special authority. But citizens are free to proclaim the word, if they think they know it, and the rest of us ought to listen exactly as we listen to any of our fellow citizens (so long as they don't threaten us with damnation and hellfire). I doubt that salvation lies in our attentiveness. All the social pathologies that plague us today have existed in societies where religion was far more dominant than it is among us. Radical inequality and its frequent concomitant, the arrogance, corruption, and unscrupulousness of the upper classes, have been especially prevalent in (some) religious societies. At the same time, and perhaps for that reason, some of the strongest denunciations of inequality and corruption have been delivered in a religious idiom, by prophets and preachers of many different faiths, from the time of Amos, say, to that of Martin Luther King. The liberal left has had, and will have, its own religious legions. Separationist doctrine doesn't require liberals to abandon this kind of support, but if they accept it (as they do), they must then defend separation *politically*, without absolutist pretension, without hostility toward believers, and without (too much) fear of their faith.

[2]

So far, I have given an account of the standard argument for the separation of religion and politics—but in a political rather than a moral or legal form, since it is this political form that seems to me most persuasive. "Political" means that the dividing line has no absolute or singular location. It has to be negotiated; it is always subject to renegotiation. Still, the argument so far is a defense of a clear and systematic separation; its bias is that organized religion, especially in its more dogmatic forms, is not good for politics and, however the line between religion and politics is drawn, should be kept at a certain distance from politics. But the only counter-argument I have considered is the neo-conservative claim that secularism will bring (is actually bringing) the end of civilization as we know it: without God, there is only decadence and mayhem. That just doesn't look to me like a serious argument, for reasons that I have already said enough about. But serious arguments can be made against the separationist position, and I want to consider two of them now, the first a populist argument against liberal secularism, the second communitarian or pluralist in character. Once again, I will make them as strong as I can, but I don't mean to make them my own.

1) Once separation is established, politics on the "political" side of the line is likely to become worldly and sophisticated, cautious and pragmatic in its style. It will be marked increasingly by the rule of professional politicians, assisted by academic experts, lobbied by interest groups, endorsed by "the people" only at fixed intervals. Separation is best understood as the ideology of these professionals, for whom political debate is mostly a technical, prosaic, spiritless affair. Significant and sustained popular participation, by contrast, requires a larger story than such people are prepared to tell—a story that evokes a vision of the good life and the good society, that invites actual belief rather than merely experimental acceptance, and that generates excitement and enthusiasm.[15] And stories of this kind tend to be teleological or providential in character, that is, they tend to be religious or near-religious stories; they derive from theological accounts of world history or from ideological accounts that mimic theology. They begin, for example, with a description of oppression, danger, and despair, meant to describe our present condition, and they end in the promised land or the millennial age of peace, prosperity, and justice. It is because of the power of such stories that republican or popular politics so often has its origin in religious revival—as in Savonarola's Florence or Puritan England or colonial America; or starts so often with a secular imitation of religion—as in the confessional

exercises of the Jacobin clubs during the French revolution (which Crane Brinton usefully compared to Protestant "experience meetings")[16], or the political messianism of the Marxists,[17] or the founding oath of so many national liberation movements: to remember the nation's martyrs and defend its sacred soil.

This sort of thing is not politics gone bad—only its enemies describe it that way. It is just politics or, better, it is popular politics. Religious or near-religious promises are necessary, on this view, to turn ordinary men and women into political activists. These promises can never, of course, receive a political fulfillment, but that's not to say that the activism they inspire has no effects; it is the only possible source of political excitement, popular participation, and forward movement, which is to say, of movement in a "left" direction. It can also move people in a "right" direction, which is the wrong direction, but that is the really unavoidable risk of the mixed bag.

What does religion bring to popular politics?[18] First, it brings a sense of radical hope, the belief that large-scale transformations and reversals are possible. It destabilizes the conventional patterns. "Many that are first shall be last; and the last shall be first."[19] Second, it brings a narrative of liberation or redemption guaranteed by God (or Reason or Spirit or History), an extended story with its own internal dramas, heroes, crises—all of which invite popular as well as academic interpretation. Third, it brings a picture of the end of days, the distant goal of the political movement, wonderfully comforting even if many believers don't quite believe in it. Fourth, it brings a discipline for the long march: this-worldly asceticism, methodical work for the cause, determination, endurance, and obedience. Pragmatic engagement, by contrast, is likely to leave the movement short of all these useful qualities. Fifth, and finally (and dangerously too), it brings a clear view of the enemies of the cause: oppressors, infidels, heretics, apostates, renegades, and traitors. There is nothing like enmity to fire the spirit. Insofar as we succeed in bringing our enemies into the system, insofar as we negotiate and compromise with them, share power in coalition governments or alternate in power as we win and lose elections, popular enthusiasm is sure to fade. When politicians make deals, ordinary men and women withdraw from the political arena.

According to this first critique, popular mobilization is simply impossible without all, or most of, these five elements. They are provided for purely secular governments, as Hegel suggests, only by the experience of war.[20] For only the urgency, enmity, and discipline that war requires can pull people out of their private and familial absorptions (which liberal secularism is designed to accommodate). The use of military language to describe political competition (to which I referred earlier) is a minor matter; *real war is the life of the state.*

Hannah Arendt's argument about democracy has a somewhat similar form. The exhilarating sense of freedom and responsibility that comes with citizenship cannot be sustained, she argues, by debates about "housekeeping"— economic policy or welfare matters.[21] Popular participation requires what we might think of as a "higher" agenda.[22] When the citizens of Athens met in the assembly and argued about whether or not to destroy Melos or invade Sicily— that was a paradigmatic moment for democratic politics.[23]

Populist critics of separation need not, however, take quite so strong a position; they are likely to prefer the more local excitements of domestic debates, which they have their own way of elevating above mere housekeeping. The advantage of class war or culture war or even religious war is that each of these, at least sometimes, is merely metaphorical, whereas Athens and Sicily is almost always the real thing.

Short of the real thing, we can still fight the Lord's battles, joining the struggles between good and recurrent evil, and it is from these struggles, according to this first critique, that domestic politics acquires its necessary heat. Hence separation is a profound mistake. Not only can the line between politics and religion never be drawn with finality, but religion is itself one of the main sources of democratic energy as well as one of the main subjects of democratic debate—and always will be, and should be, because religious and near-religious commitments and enthusiasms are crucial features of political life. So the debates about prayer in the schools, the content of the curriculum, the celebration of religious holidays, the display of religious symbols, or the public condemnation of blasphemy and vice, are not transgressive boundary crossings. Nor, when American Catholics argue against abortion with a fervor and absolutism that they never displayed in their opposition to nuclear deterrence, are they expressing politically illegitimate concerns. Religious absolutism is one possible democratic political language.

On this view, a tough anti-secular politics, even a politics claiming, say, that the United States is or ought to be a "Christian republic," can't be ruled out on constitutional grounds or with the argument that *this* side of the dividing line is neutral ground, where adjectives like "Christian" have no application.[24] There is no neutral ground, as the protagonists of the Christian republic know, having experienced the secular state as a hostile force for many years. And these too are fellow citizens; their concerns matter; their mobilization is a democratic event.

They have to be engaged (I would want to say, opposed) openly. Democratic politics is constituted by engagements of this kind, which inevitably produce division: friends and enemies, winners and losers. What the ideology of separation expresses is an intense dislike for all this, a kind of antiseptic liberalism: a disdain for religious enthusiasm and a fear of popular mobilization.

This first critique of separation stresses the capacity of religion and its secular surrogates, such as Marxism and nationalism, to engage people in a politics of large causes. This is contrasted with the merely technical or bureaucratic universality of the neutral state, which indeed serves all its citizens but gives them no reason to serve themselves, to participate in the political process. Only religious or near-religious conviction can provide effective reasons. But some critics of separation pursue an entirely different line of argument. They would probably say that this first critique is focused too much on historical melodrama: ultimate questions, political crises, and moral crusades. In any case, its radicalism is unappealing to them. It misses the role that religion plays in everyday life; it mistakes the real contrast with state neutrality; and it misrepresents the fear that motivates separation.[25] Hence the second critique.

2) Religion is above all a particularist force, perhaps the most important expression of the human need for meaning, enclosure, and intensity. It creates very strong communal bonds, and separation is best understood as an effort to weaken those bonds and so to prevent them from distorting the more distant but also more inclusive "friendship" of citizens. Like the ban on nepotism and other forms of familial favoritism, separation aims to ensure that all citizens are treated equally as individuals: judged by what they do, not by who they are. The motivating fear is that the faithful will enter politics only in order to prefer one another and support particularist projects, using state power to enhance their own presence in the larger community. And so they will come into conflict with other religious groups trying to do the same thing, and public space will be contaminated by parochial displays and sectarian hostilities. Or they will come into conflict with non-religious groups and individuals, whom they are likely, so it is said, to persecute and exclude.

The second critique holds that this is, again, an antiseptic view of political life—though now the infection to be avoided is not populist militancy but the politics of identity and difference. Secularists insist upon a sharp distinction between the private sphere where difference is allowed to produce its characteristic forms of passion and parochialism and the public sphere where deliberation is supposed to be perfectly dispassionate. They are driven by a deep anxiety about difference itself: on the political side of the line, they believe, all citizens should look and act alike. But difference, so the critics say, can't be erased on either side of the line, and it has to be allowed some public expression if the different groups are to feel at home in the state.[26]

Liberal secularism, according to this second critique, produces an alienated world, a society of strangers. Religion, by contrast, is not only or primarily a mobilizing force, it is also an associative force that can serve, and has served historically, to strengthen moral solidarity and political attachment. That's why communities of faith have been able—in many different countries with different cultures and regimes—to create strong welfare institutions and inspire high levels of popular participation in everyday forms of mutual aid. Modern states rely on this capacity; none of the secular associations of civil society can rival it. (Left-wing parties and movements once provided support for a wide range of welfare services, building on the solidarity of working-class culture. But the integration of the working class and the decline of its cultural independence have undercut this achievement.[27]) So it is an appropriate recognition of the moral realities of contemporary life if the civil religion incorporates features of the local positive religions, if religious symbols are displayed in public places, if prayers are offered at state ceremonies, if church bells ring on days of national mourning, and so on. God-in-the-public-square can be a benign and helpful figure—so long as we can manage some degree of pluralism in his representations, and so long as the rights of minorities are protected.

According to this second critique, religious toleration is more important than the separation of religion and politics—and to some degree in conflict with it. For the religions that we tolerate aim to determine the way people act in public as well as in private; one of their chief purposes is to shape identities, interests, anxieties, and aspirations. None of these can be excluded from political debate or, indeed, from political life generally, however uncomfortable they make liberal secularists—and however uncomfortable the secularists try to make anyone who brings religious feelings and opinions into the open. But if these feelings and opinions can't be excluded, they ought to be accommodated: why should everyone be uncomfortable?

The accommodation can follow democratic lines. If a single religious faith is shared by the great majority of the people, there can even be an established church (though without church attendance laws or heresy trials)—as in Great Britain, an example that suggests that this gross violation of secular principles is compatible with liberal democracy. The overlap of religion and politics that "establishmentarianism" permits in the British case has been ratified, but also modified, by history. It obviously doesn't mean (though it once did) that nonbelievers are second-class citizens. In countries where no religion has majority support, more pluralistic and complicated arrangements are necessary, which might reach to large-scale budgetary support for religious institutions, not only those that are welfarist in character but also those that are educational.

No doubt, all such accommodations with religion will produce conflict; curiously, however, conflict itself is not the greatest worry of their opponents. Today, the most common secularist argument against the accommodation of religion advocated in the second critique is that, however far the accommodation goes, someone is bound to be left out and then to feel threatened or diminished or dishonored by the exclusion.[28] There is only room for so many clerical performances at the Memorial Day ceremonies. And what are atheists to think, listening to the parade of ministers, priests, and rabbis? What are their children to think when prayers are recited in the public schools? But when public life is naked of religious expression and symbolism, believers feel left out. The claim that they can always cultivate their faith in private is unpersuasive to them: atheists, they respond, can cultivate their lack of faith in private too.

[3]

Both these critiques are valuable; neither is entirely right. It seems to me impossible to deny the claims that are made on behalf of passion-in-politics, mass mobilization, and Grand Causes. It is equally impossible to deny the claims made on behalf of community and solidarity. But it is necessary at the same time to set limits on these claims, so that people committed to different Grand Causes and different communities can live together and join in a common democratic politics. We still need to draw a separationist line. The two critiques help us to understand separation in a better way; they don't, however, give us reasons to reject it. Indeed, I am inclined to say that they give us reasons to extend its reach.

Once again, my restatement of the separationist argument relates only to the contemporary United States; the line that I mean to defend can be, and probably should be, differently drawn in different times and places.

Still, I want to start with a general argument: even in a democracy, it is possible to concede too much to popular excitement and enthusiasm. Mass mobilization is often, in fact, antidemocratic; it can make for a very bad politics— sometimes religious in character, sometimes ideological, sometimes nationalist —which we should have no difficulty recognizing. When religious zealots forcibly convert the infidels, or persecute them, or exclude them from public life;

when murder is committed in God's name (or in the name of the nation or the cause); when ethnic militants "cleanse" their territory of foreign or minority residents; when triumphant revolutionaries send the "class enemy" to reeducation camps: *that* is politics gone bad. We should never deny the reality of the "badness" or make ourselves into its apologists. In the United States, we have so far avoided badness of this kind, and the separation of religion from politics has been a critically important means of avoidance.

It is in fact an exemplary means: the argument about mass mobilization helps us to see clearly that the denial of coercive power to religious groups has to be repeated in the case of racial and ethnic groups, cultural communities, social movements, and even political parties. The U.S. Constitution singles out religion, but this is presumably because the American colonists had vivid memories of religious wars and persecutions. At the end of the twentieth century, we have related but more extended memories—of ideological and communalist, as well as religious, wars and persecutions, and so it is entirely plausible to expand the argument to groups like those I have just listed.

All of them are voluntary associations (at least in the minimal sense that there is no bar to exit); they operate in the open space that the state creates and frames. Of course, this space is not neutral ground: we should think of it as civil or even as secular ground. That doesn't mean that religious arguments can't be made there or even that religious ceremonies can't be enacted there. It only means—but this is very important—that religion can't be grounded there; no church can be established there; no holy commonwealth, Islamic republic, or Torah state can be organized there; God's kingdom cannot be realized there. The end of history has to take place somewhere else. Civil space in a democratic society is hostile to finality. And similarly, no ethnic or racial community can be established there and, if communist society is anything like the millennial age, no communist society can be established there either. There can't be a *last* revolution or a messianic kingdom within the democratic framework. The separation of religion and politics, and all the parallel separations, are guarantees of temporality and also of temporariness.[29]

But it doesn't follow from these guarantees that we can't actively pursue this or that idea of the good society. What follows is simply that, so long as there are different ideas, no realization can be definitive. On the religious or ideological side of the line, the good society can have an absolute form; on the political side, it is always provisional. State power can never be wholly engaged on behalf of its stability or permanence; power must always be potentially available to men and women defending competing conceptions of goodness. It doesn't matter whether the conceptions are religious or secular; their protagonists have exactly the same right to join the competition, to mobilize their followers, to appeal to their passions and convictions. If an antiseptic liberalism treats this sort of thing with disdain or fear, the antisepsis needs to be reconsidered: this isn't infection but normal democratic engagement. All that separation requires is that the engaged citizens, religious and secular, be prevented *in exactly the same way* from achieving anything like total victory.

The state should be neutral, then, in this specific sense: though it is committed to the idea of civil space and actively on guard against finality, it must not interfere in the competition among religious or other groups; it must not prefer one religious or ethnic or racial community over another—or one ideological party or movement over another. Even this limited neutrality, however, will always be incomplete, its exact meaning always disputed. Popular insurgencies, like the civil rights movement of the 1960s or the evangelical campaigns of the 1990s, commonly make claims on the state for what might be called "favored group" status, hence for a suspension of strict neutrality: affirmative action, school prayer, creationism in the curriculum are all (American) examples of this. Some of these claims should be supported, some opposed.

Sometimes justice comes into conflict with the practice of separation and takes precedence over it—as in the affirmative action cases, where the long history of racial discrimination seems to call for a policy of racial preference, the refusal of neutrality so long as the races are radically unequal (the adverb is important: the state cannot enforce perfect equality but it can and should act against radical inequality among its citizens). Sometimes justice and separation stand together, as I believe they do in the school prayer cases, where the authority of teachers over students makes religious practice coercive in a way that it might not be in the community at large (but the limits on Christian teachers are no different from the limits on, say, communist teachers). It is absurd, however, to deny groups of students the right to organize extracurricular activities of a religious (or ideological) character: activities of that sort are not coercive. Similarly, putting a crèche on the village common or a menorah in Manhattan's Herald Square is not a coercive act (a cross placed on the common by the Ku Klux Klan has a different significance). I suppose that Americans will disagree about such cases, but these are disagreements about how to draw the separationist line: there is no avoiding that activity.

Separation creates a regime of toleration, where the singular state tolerates a multiplicity of religious groups and forces the groups to tolerate (or to act as if they tolerate) one another. The extension of this regime establishes a similar toleration among ethnic groups, political parties, and so on. But toleration doesn't rule out competition among these groups, nor is it meant to curtail the popular mobilization and the passionate political engagement that competition (sometimes) produces. There is this seeming difference: we imagine a political party winning the electoral competition and enacting its program. Religious and ethnic groups presumably cannot do this.

In fact, however, parties and churches are more similar than different with regard to the practice of separation—and an account of the similarity can help us understand what separation really means. Victorious political parties can only act within political or constitutional limits of a liberal, democratic sort. They can't, for example, use state power to guarantee the permanence of their electoral victory; they can't require the daily recitation of the party platform in the public schools; they can't make the study of party history a required subject.[30] Note the difference: a party can turn its program into law but not into a school catechism. Anything that gives the party an air of establishment, anything that makes its authority final—a matter not of revisable legislation but of creedal orthodoxy—is ruled out. It is as if the Constitution said that "Congress shall make no law regarding the establishment of a political party."

In the same way, there are things that religious groups can rightly do in the political arena: they can defend the welfare state or oppose nuclear deterrence in the name of natural law, as the Catholic bishops have done; they can argue for civil rights and affirmative action in the name of prophetic justice, as liberal rabbis have done; they can join debates about family law, the school curriculum, the censorship of pornography, as evangelical Christians have done, and so on. And in the course of activities of this sort, they can appeal to religious ideas; under democratic conditions, the desire to win should lead them to make that appeal as wide as they can.

But there are also things they can't rightly do; they can't, for example, impose a religious catechism on the public schools. The limits are set not by the abstract principle of separation but by the concrete needs of the regime of toleration. No religious program can be enacted into law if it threatens the other religions, or undercuts the legal equality of all citizens, or calls into question the civil character of political space. So what is separated is probably not best described as religion and politics. We separate religion from state power, and also ethnicity from state power, and even politics from state power.

It follows, then, that the first of the three requirements of separation must be maintained and extended: coercion belongs only to the state and has to be denied to ecclesiastical authorities and charismatic religious leaders—and also to ethnic activists, party chiefs, and the master teachers of this or that ideology. But the state can defer to the habits of its citizens, or the greater number of its citizens, as it does, for example, when it closes its offices on Sunday. Here common sense overrides separationist purity; it isn't necessary to find some randomizing procedure for fixing a weekly day of rest; deference of this sort doesn't count as coercion. (To require work on all or any of the other days would count.) But it would be wrong to make Easter a state holiday,[31] and it would be wrong in exactly the same way, in any country where people are seriously engaged in the class struggle, to make May Day a state holiday. Labor Day, by contrast, is fine—a characteristically pragmatic American compromise. It is a nonpartisan version of May Day, celebrating the role of labor in national life without endorsing the political goals of the labor movement. A day of rest or nonpartisan celebration is broadly beneficial, even if it retains some specifically religious or political significance.

Similarly, many actual activities of religious and political organizations are broadly beneficial, even if they also serve particular religious and political purposes. Hence the first requirement can also be modified—interpreted to allow public financial support for welfare institutions, like day care centers, hospitals, and nursing homes (to take the easy examples first), that are also funded by, and then run by, religious groups.[32] It is only necessary that similar financing be available more widely, not only to communities of faith, but to any communities that succeed in organizing similar services. The fact that the program of this or that nursing home follows a religious calendar isn't an objection. If Easter is celebrated at this home and Passover at that one, and May Day somewhere else, residents are only getting what they should get—a familiar place and a customary routine in their old age—and taxpayers can legitimately be asked to help provide that.

Education poses much harder questions, since children have still to acquire a place and routine, and they are peculiarly vulnerable to coercive pressures. Insofar as private or parochial schools provide specifically religious training, they have been, and probably should be, denied state money;[33] the case would be the same with schools that aimed to cultivate a specific ethnic or political identity—to reproduce committed Italians or Hungarians, say, or libertarians or socialists. But schools seem much like welfare institutions when they teach secular subjects (mandated by the state), help disabled children, enforce public health measures, or offer career counseling. Whether to support activities of this kind, and how to support them, and what conditions to impose, and how much support to give: these are political questions, which can legitimately be decided in different ways. The argument against providing any state aid at all to parochial schools isn't a principled but only a prudential argument. It resembles the recommendation in Jewish law that one should "build a fence around the Torah"; one draws a line, takes a stand, before principles are endangered in order to make sure that principles are never endangered. But exactly how and where to draw that line is not itself a matter of principle.[34] I should stress that the principle at stake here is not that religion and politics should be separated (that is a means to an end), but that political space must have a civil character; the state should be a state for all its citizens.

The second two requirements of separation are open to modifications of a similar sort, recognizing in a similar way the value of religious (and other) associations and the central role they play in the lives of so many citizens. The civil religion should indeed be distinctively civil and therefore inclusive of the greatest possible number of citizens, but mixing and matching elements from the practices of different religions and from the histories of different ethnic groups can be a legitimate method of inclusion—legitimate even if the inclusion isn't total, which, in any given instance, it cannot be. And while the style of political debate should be as pragmatic and open as we (separationists) can make it, there is in fact no way of excluding absolutist convictions and passions without excluding the people who hold them. So it is better to welcome their expression and hope that the pressure of democratic argument will ensure that absolutism is not the last word. Within constitutional limits, religious and ideological movements can mobilize whatever passion they can mobilize: democratic politics can and should be permissive in this regard.

But the constitutional limits do serve to lower the stakes of political competition. That's what they are there for. Whether God or Satan will rule is not what's at stake in an American election, and that makes politics less "interesting," less dangerous; hence less exciting than it might otherwise be. Denying God's authority in political life is a shorthand phrase for making politics safe for human beings doomed to unending disagreement and conflict. We might say that it makes politics safe for politics itself, since religious and near-religious mobilizations are often profoundly anti-political. The dream of a millennial age, the contempt for parliamentary compromise, the all-too-clear identification of enemies, the frighteningly rigid discipline: together these represent a kind of political escapism, where what is being escaped is the day-in, day-out negotiation of difference.

Civic ceremonies in the public square and civics courses in the public schools (and in private schools too) should teach, whatever else they teach, the values that underlie this negotiation and make it possible: political equality and mutual respect. These are anti-millennial values (because infidels, heretics, apostates, and renegades are included in their compass), and so they may well make for tension between politics and religion—also between politics and political messianism and between politics and every sort of sectarian or communalist absolutism. Most of the time, this tension is a good thing, natural to any democratic society many of whose citizens are religious believers or political militants. But when it erupts into religious or ideological conflict, when the separationist line is directly challenged, we shouldn't hesitate to engage ourselves (passionately) in its defense and aim to win the battle if we can, even if this would be nothing more than a victory for ordinary life, co-existence, peace-for-the-moment. Indeed, the victory is so important that we might allow ourselves to describe it in more exciting ways.

Is it really true that people can only be mobilized for political activity by anti-political visions of Armageddon, the final struggle against the forces of evil, the last revolution—and, just beyond that, eternal peace, perfect harmony? If so, it might be better if the people were not mobilized. But in fact the history of liberal and democratic regimes is full of examples of more partial and short-term mobilizations, driven by religious or near-religious faith.[35] Democratic politics, when it is working well, has effects on the other side of the line, modifying the force of religious (and ethnic, communal, sectarian, and party) commitments and so opening the way for a politics that begins in passion but ends in compromise.

Politics separated from religion in this extended and qualified sense—that all the crusaders, religious and secular alike, are denied the sword (but allowed to fly their banners)—is an open-ended conflict over interests and values among people who understand that they have to co-exist with one another. Both the conflict and the co-existence are permanent conditions, which need to be protected from the temptations of eternity. We have to set ourselves against the closure that God's name, again and again, has licensed—but also against every other kind of closure, licensed by any of the secular substitutes for God's name. Only someone who has never experienced, or who can't imagine experiencing, the dangers of politics gone bad could possibly complain about that.

NOTES

This paper was originally delivered as the Leary Lecture at the University of Utah College of Law in November 1998.

1. For a strong statement of the standard view, written in a rather embattled tone, see Isaac Kramnick and R. Laurence Moore, *The Godless Constitution: The Case Against Religious Correctness* (New York: W. W. Norton, 1996).

2. Ibid., 14.

3. They receive their tax exemptions as nonprofit and philanthropic, not as religious, organizations; if they were the only nonprofit organizations, the exemption would presumably be problematic under the standard separationist view.

4. Robert Bellah, *The Broken Covenant: American Civil Religion in Time of Trial* (New York: Seabury, 1975), 142.

5. Elizabeth M. Bounds criticizes my account of American political culture. See Elizabeth M. Bounds, "Conflicting Harmonies: Michael Walzer's Vision of Community," *Journal of Religious Ethics* 22:2 (Fall 1994), 370: "But U.S. public culture or civil religion . . . is completely congruent with Christian Western culture—something readily apparent at any presidential inauguration."

6. For a discussion of civil religion, see Jean-Jacques Rousseau, *The Social Contract*, bk. 4, chap. 8. The application of this term to contemporary American practices is the work of Bellah, *The Broken Covenant*.

7. David J. Brewer, *American Citizenship* (New York: Scribner's, 1902), 79.

8. For a discussion of the language of war, see Neal Wood's Introduction to Machiavelli's *The Art of War* (Indianapolis: Library of Liberal Arts, 1996), describing the role of military imagery in a Machiavellian political discourse (esp. section 5)—but the images are more widely used and more generally useful.

9. Jane Perlez, "Ex-Communist Appears to Best Walesa for President of Poland," *The New York Times* (November 20, 1995), A1.

10. For a very strong statement of the exclusionist argument—no religious discourse in the political arena—see Robert Audi, "The Separation of Church and State and the Obligations of Citizenship," *Philosophy and Public Affairs* 18:3 (Summer 1989), 259–96. For the text of the Bishop's pastoral letter on deterrence, see Jim Castelli, *The Bishops and the Bomb: Waging Peace in the a Nuclear Age* (Garden City, N.Y.: Image Books, 1983), 185–276.

11. For a discussion of this argument, see Richard John Neuhaus, *The Naked Public Square: Religion and Democracy in America* (Grand Rapids: Eerdmans, 1984), though I have described it in caricature. See also any issue of the magazine *First Things*, of which Neuhaus is editor-in-chief. For an argument that can't be caricatured, see Pat Robertson, *The Turning Tide: The Fall of Liberalism and the Rise of Common Sense* (Dallas: W. Pub. Group, 1993).

12. For a philosophical account of this alien ground, see John Rawls, *Political Liberalism*, (New York: Columbia University Press, 1993).

13. This is the fear that motivates Kramnick and Moore. See especially *Godless Constitution*, chap. 8 ("What is unacceptable to us in light of the godless Constitution is for religious certainty ever to trump politics and for government policy in any way to privilege or codify religious beliefs in ways that preempt a pluralist democratic process").

14. See, for example, David Hume, *An Enquiry Concerning the Principles of Morals*, sec. 3, pt. ii ("That there were *religious* fanatics of this kind in England, during the civil wars, we learn from history; though it is probable, that the obvious *tendency* of these principles excited such horror in mankind, as soon obliged the dangerous enthusiasts to renounce, or at least conceal their tenets").

15. The idea that liberal politics is vitiated by its refusal to bring questions of the Good into the political arena is a common theme of American communitarianism, probably most

clearly expressed by Alasdair MacIntyre, *After Virtue: A Study in Moral Theory* (Notre Dame, Ind.: University of Notre Dame Press, 1981).

16. Clarence Crane Brinton, *The Jacobins: An Essay in the New History* (New York: Russell and Russell, 1961).

17. See Jacob L. Talmon, *Myth of the Nation and Vision of Revolution: Ideological Polarization in the Twentieth Century* (London: Secker and Warburg, 1980), suggesting that Marx and Engels developed "messianic expectations" for the socialist movement.

18. For a general account, see Guenter Lewy, *Religion and Revolution* (New York: Oxford University Press, 1974), discussing the political implications and consequences of religion for politics. For a discussion of the connection between religion and radical politics, see Michael Walzer, *The Revolution of the Saints* (Cambridge: Harvard University Press, 1965), and *Exodus and Revolution* (New York: Basic Books, 1985).

19. Matthew 19:30

20. See G. W. F. Hegel, *Philosophy of Right,* trans. T. M. Knox (Oxford: Oxford University Press, 1942), 209–10.

21. For the clearest and most complete statement of Arendt's view of the *polis* and the household, of labor, work, and "the disclosure of the agent in speech and action" (which is what happens in the assembly), see Hannah Arendt, *The Human Condition* (Chicago: University of Chicago Press, 1958).

22. Ibid.

23. Ibid.

24. See Kramnick and Moore, *Godless Constitution,* chap. 1 ("Is America a Christian Nation?").

25. The second critique is pluralist and multi-culturalist: for an example, which I do not, however, follow closely in my own exposition, see Michael W. McConnell, "Religious Freedom at a Crossroads," *University of Chicago Law Review* 59:1 (Winter 1992), esp. pt. 3 ("A Religious Clause Jurisprudence for a Pluralistic Nation").

26. For versions of this view, see Neuhaus, *Naked Public Square,* 20–38, and Stephen L. Carter, *The Culture of Disbelief: How American Law and Politics Trivialize Religious Devotion* (New York: Basic Books, 1993), 105–24. For a liberal account of deliberation, see Amy Gutmann and Dennis Thompson, *Democracy and Disagreement* (Cambridge: Harvard University Press, 1997), 55–68.

27. See, for example, Carl E. Schorske, *German Social Democracy, 1905–1917: The Development of the Great Schism* (Cambridge: Harvard University Press, 1983), discussing the schism within the labor movement in pre–World War I Germany.

28. This argument will be familiar to anyone who has helped to plan a civic event where some sort of religious blessing seems—to at least some of the participants—to be necessary or appropriate.

29. It should be clear now that I am talking specifically of the United States. Nation-states like Norway (to take an easy example) do involve an establishment of ethnicity; the state is an engine for cultural reproduction, and separationist doctrine, if it applies at all, must apply in a more limited way than in the United States.

30. This is, of course, exactly what parties do in totalitarian states, which provide an exact analogue for religious republics like, say, Iran today. But I don't want to suggest that

there can't be required courses in democratic schools. A party that advocated the teaching of civics in high school could, after winning an election, require the establishment of courses on civics. But these courses would have to recognize the existence and legitimacy of other parties.

31. I take Easter as a clearer example than Christmas, a Christian holiday that Christians have been complicit in transforming into, so to speak, a holiday for general consumption. Even so, the presidential lighting of the national Christmas tree does seem to violate separationist principles.

32. For an account of this kind of funding, with numbers attached, see Milt Freudenheim, "Charities Aiding Poor Fear Loss of Government Subsidies," *New York Times* (February 5, 1996), B8.

33. I say "probably" because I can imagine arrangements in the United States modeled on those in some European countries—where the state pays for religious instruction in the public schools, allowing representatives of the different religions to come in at fixed times. Given the fissiparous tendencies of American religion, however, this might prove terribly divisive, or it might require state decisions as to which so-called religions were serious or genuine—not impossible, perhaps, but also not desirable.

34. A useful survey of the relevant court cases, as of twenty years ago, can be found in Frank J. Sorauf, *The Wall of Separation: The Constitutional Politics of Church and State* (Princeton: Princeton University Press, 1976). My own view is that many of these cases are not best decided by the courts at all. On "building a fence around the Torah," see Joel Roth, *The Halakhic Process: A Systematic Analysis* (New York: Jewish Theological Seminary, 1986), 189ff.

35. Contemporary evangelical politics in the United States provides a useful example of this. See Carter, *Culture of Disbelief,* 265–66, for a sympathetic account or at least an account that makes the Christian Right seem something less than an ultimate danger to democracy. I can think of no good democratic reason to tell these Christian activists that they should withdraw from political life, though I regard them as opponents and hope for their defeat.

CHAPTER ELEVEN

The Politics of Difference

Statehood and Toleration in a Multicultural World

[1]

I will begin, like a good professor, by making a couple of distinctions. I am not going to focus in this chapter (except at the very end) on the toleration of eccentric or dissident individuals in civil society or even in the state. Individual rights may well lie at the root of every sort of toleration, but I am interested in those rights primarily when they are exercised in common (in the course of voluntary association or religious worship or cultural expression) or when they are claimed by groups on behalf of their members. The eccentric individuals, solitary in their differences, are fairly easy to tolerate, and at the same time social repugnance for and resistance to eccentricity, while certainly unattractive, are not terribly dangerous. The stakes are much higher when we turn to eccentric and dissident groups.

I am also not going to focus here on the political toleration of oppositional movements and parties. These are competitors for political power, necessary in democratic regimes, which quite literally require that there be alternative leaders (with alternative programs), even if they never actually win an election. They are fellow participants, like the members of the opposing team in a basketball game, without whom there couldn't be a game and who therefore have a right to score baskets and win if they can. Problems arise only in the case of people who want to disrupt the game while still claiming the rights of players and the protection of the rules. These problems are often hard, but they don't have much to do with the toleration of difference, which is intrinsic to democratic politics, but rather with the toleration of disruption (or the risk of disruption)—another matter entirely.

My concern here is with toleration when the differences at stake are cul-

tural, religious, way-of-life differences—when the others are not fellow participants and there is no common game and no intrinsic need for difference. Even a
liberal society doesn't require a multiplicity of ethnic groups or religious communities; nor do any of the groups require any or all of the others. The groups
will often be competitive with one another, seeking converts or supporters
among uncommitted or loosely committed individuals, but their primary aim is
to sustain a way of life among their own members, reproducing their culture or
faith in successive generations. They are in the first instance inwardly focused,
which is exactly what political parties cannot be. At the same time, they require
some kind of extended social space (outside the household) for the sake of
assembly, worship, argument, celebration, mutual aid, schooling, and so on.

Now, what does it mean to tolerate groups of this sort? Understood as an
attitude or state of mind (from which characteristic practices follow), toleration
describes a number of possibilities. The first of these, which reflects the origins
of religious toleration in the sixteenth and seventeenth centuries, is simply a
resigned acceptance of difference for the sake of peace. People kill one another
for years and years, and then, mercifully, exhaustion sets in, and we call this
toleration. But we can trace a continuum of more substantive acceptances. A
second possible attitude is passive, relaxed, benignly indifferent: "It takes all
kinds to make a world." A third expresses openness to the others, curiosity,
respect, a willingness to listen and learn. And furthest along the continuum,
there is the enthusiastic endorsement of difference: an aesthetic endorsement, if
difference is taken to represent in cultural form the largeness and diversity of
God's creation or of the natural world or a functional endorsement if difference
is viewed as a necessary condition of human flourishing, offering to individual
men and women the choices that make their autonomy meaningful.

But perhaps this last attitude falls outside my subject: how can I be said to
tolerate what I in fact endorse? If I want the others to be *here,* in this society,
among us, then I don't tolerate otherness; I support it. I don't, however, necessarily support this or that version of otherness; I might well prefer another
other, culturally or religiously closer to my own practices and beliefs (or, perhaps, more distant, exotic, posing no competitive threat). So it seems right to
say that though I support the idea of difference, I tolerate the instantiated
differences. And there will always be people, in any democratic society and
however well entrenched the commitment to pluralism is, for whom some
particular difference—this or that form of worship, family arrangement, dietary
rule, or dress code—is very hard to tolerate. I shall say of all people who actually accept differences of this sort, without regard to their standing on the

continuum of resignation, indifference, curiosity, and enthusiasm, that they possess the virtue of tolerance.

Similarly, I shall treat all the social arrangements through which we incorporate difference, coexist with it, allow it a share of social space, as the institutionalized forms of this same virtue. Historically, there have been four different sorts of arrangements that make for toleration, four models of a tolerant society. I want now to describe these briefly and roughly, and then to say something about the self-understanding of the men and women who make them work today (insofar as they actually work—toleration is always a precarious achievement). What exactly do we do when we tolerate difference?

[2]

The oldest arrangements are those of the great multinational empires—beginning, for our purposes, with Persia and Rome. Here the various groups are constituted as autonomous communities, political/legal as well as cultural/religious in character, ruling themselves across a considerable range of their activities. The groups have no choice but to co-exist with one another, for their interactions are governed by imperial bureaucrats in accordance with an imperial code, like the Roman *jus gentium*, designed to maintain some minimal fairness, as fairness is understood in the imperial center. Ordinarily, however, the bureaucrats don't interfere in the internal life of the autonomous communities for the sake of fairness or anything else—so long as taxes are paid and peace maintained. Hence they can be said to tolerate the different ways of life, and the imperial regime can be called a regime of toleration, whether or not the members of the different communities are tolerant of one another. Under imperial rule, they willy-nilly manifest tolerance in their everyday interactions, and some of them perhaps learn to accept difference, standing somewhere on the continuum that I have described. But the survival of the different communities doesn't depend on this acceptance. It depends only on bureaucratic toleration, sustained, mostly, for the sake of peace (though individual bureaucrats have been variously motivated, a few of them famously curious about difference or even enthusiastic in its defense).

This is probably the most successful way of incorporating difference and facilitating (requiring is more accurate) peaceful coexistence. But it isn't, or at least it never has been, a democratic way. Whatever the character of the different "autonomies," the incorporating regime is autocratic. I don't want to idealize this autocracy; it can be brutally repressive, for the sake of maintaining its conquests, as the history of Assyria and Israel, Rome and Carthage, Spain and the Aztecs, Russia and the Tatars, amply demonstrates. But settled imperial rule is often tolerant—and tolerant precisely because it is everywhere autocratic, which is to say, not bound by the interests or prejudices of any of the conquered groups, equally distant from all of them. Roman proconsuls in Egypt or British regents in India ruled more evenhandedly than any local prince or tyrant was likely to do, more evenhandedly than local majorities today are likely to do.

Imperial autonomy tends to lock individuals into their communities and therefore into a singular ethnic or religious identity. It tolerates groups and their authority structures and customary practices, not (except in a few cosmopolitan centers and capital cities) free-floating men and women. Lonely dissidents or heretics, cultural vagabonds, and intermarried couples and their children will flee to the imperial capital, which is likely to become as a result a fairly tolerant place (think of Rome, Baghdad, and Vienna)—and the only place where social space is measured to an individual fit. Everyone else will live in homogeneous neighborhoods or districts, tolerated there but not likely to be welcome or even safe across whatever line separates them from the others; they can mix comfortably only in neutral space—the market, say, or the imperial courts and prisons. Still, they live, most of the time, in peace alongside one another, respectful of cultural as well as geographic boundaries.

Today, all this is gone (the Soviet Union was the last of the empires): the autonomous institutions, the carefully preserved boundaries, the ethnically marked identity cards, the far-flung bureaucracies. Autonomy did not mean much at the end (which is one reason, perhaps, for imperial decline); its scope was greatly reduced by the impact of modern ideas about sovereignty and by totalizing ideologies uncongenial to the accommodation of difference. But ethnic and religious differences survived, and wherever they were territorially based, local agencies, more or less representative, retained some minimal functions and some symbolic authority. These they were able to convert very quickly once the empires fell into a kind of state machinery, driven by nationalist ideology, aiming at sovereign power. With sovereignty, of course, comes membership in international society, the most tolerant of all societies but until very recently not so easy to get into. I shall not consider international society at any length in this paper, but it is important to recognize that this is where and how most groups would prefer to be tolerated: as nation-states (or religious republics) with governments, armies, and borders, coexisting with other nation-states in mutual respect or, at least, under the rule of a common (even if rarely enforced) set of laws.

[3]

Before I consider the nation-state as a possibly tolerant society, I want to turn briefly to a morally similar but not politically more likely heir to the multi-national empire—the consociational or bi- or tri-national state. Examples like Belgium, Switzerland, Cyprus, Lebanon, and the still-born Bosnia suggest the range of possibility here and also the imminence of disaster. Consociationalism is a heroic program since it aims to maintain imperial coexistence without the imperial bureaucrats and without the distance that made those bureaucrats more or less impartial rulers. Now the different groups are not tolerated by a single transcendent power; they have to tolerate one another and work out among themselves the terms of their coexistence.

This isn't impossible. Success is most likely where there are only two groups roughly equal either in size or political power—and where the equality is stable over time. Then the proportionate allocation of resources and offices in the civil service is relatively easy, and neither group need fear the dominance of the other. Each pursues its own customs, perhaps even enforces its own customary law, undisturbed. It's the fear of disturbance, even more, of domination by the other group, that breaks up consociations. Mutual toleration depends on trust, not so much in each other's good will as in the institutional arrangements that guard against the effects of ill will. I can't live tolerantly alongside a dangerous other. What is the danger that I fear? It is that the consociation will collapse into an ordinary nation-state where I will be a member of the minority, seeking to be tolerated by my former associates, who no longer require my toleration.

[4]

Most of the states that make up international society are nation-states. To call them that doesn't mean that they have nationally (or ethnically or religiously) homogeneous populations. Homogeneity is rare, if not non-existent, in the world today. It means only that a single dominant group organizes the common life in a way that reflects its own history and culture and, if things go as intended, carries the history forward and sustains the culture. It is these intentions that determine the character of public education, the symbols and cere-monies of public life, the state calendar and the holidays it enjoins. Among histories and cultures, the nation-state is not neutral; its state apparatus is an engine for national reproduction. At the same time, nonetheless, it can, as liberal and democratic nation-states commonly do, tolerate minorities. This toleration takes different forms, though it rarely reaches to the full autonomy of the old empires. Regional autonomy is especially unlikely, for then members of the dominant nation living in the region would be subjected to "alien" rule in their own country.

Toleration in nation-states is commonly focused not on groups but on members of groups, minorities, generally conceived stereotypically, *qua* members, and allowed (or expected) to form voluntary associations, organizations for mutual aid, private schools, cultural societies, publishing houses, and so on. They are not allowed to sustain a corporate existence or exercise legal jurisdiction over their fellows. Minority religion, culture, and history are matters for what might be called the private collective—about which the public collective, the nation-state, is always suspicious. Any claim to act out minority culture in public is likely to produce anxiety among the majority (hence the controversy in France over the wearing of Muslim headdress in state schools). In principle, there is no coercion of individuals, but pressure to assimilate to the dominant nation, at least with regard to public practices, has been fairly common and, until recent times, fairly successful. When nineteenth-century German Jews described themselves as German in the street, Jewish at home, they were aspiring to a nation-state norm that made privacy a condition of toleration.

The politics of language is one key area where this norm is both enforced and challenged. The majority insists that all minorities learn and use the language of the dominant nation, at least in their public transactions. Minorities, if they are strong enough, and especially if they are territorially based, will seek the legitimization of their own languages in schools, state documents, public signage, and so on. Sometimes one of the minority languages is recognized as a second official language; more often, the dominant nation watches its own language being transformed by minority use (which is also, I suppose, a test of toleration).

There is less room for difference in nation-states than in multinational empires or consociations. Since the tolerated members of the minority group are also citizens, with rights and obligations, the practices of the group are more likely than in multinational empires to be subject to majority scrutiny. Nonetheless, a variety of differences, especially religious differences, have been successfully sustained in liberal and democratic nation-states. Minorities often, in fact, do fairly well in sustaining a common culture precisely because they are under pressure from the national majority. Individuals may drift away, pass themselves off as members of the majority, or slowly assimilate to majority lifestyles. But for most people these self-transformations are too difficult or too humiliating; they cling to their own identities and to similarly identified men and women.

National minorities are the groups most likely to find themselves at risk. If they are territorially concentrated, they will be suspected, perhaps rightly, of hoping for a state of their own or for incorporation into a neighboring state where their ethnic relatives hold sovereign power. In time of war (whether they are territorially concentrated or not), their loyalty to the nation-state will readily be called into doubt—even against all available evidence, as in the case of anti-Nazi German refugees in France during the first months of World War II. Once again, toleration fails when minorities look, or when nationalist demagogues can make them look, dangerous. The fate of Japanese-Americans a few years later makes the same point—their fellow Americans imitating, as it were, conventional nation-statehood. In fact, the Japanese were not, and are not, a national minority in the United States, at least not in the usual sense. Where is the majority nation? American majorities are temporary in character, differently constituted for different purposes and occasions, whereas a crucial feature of the nation-state is its permanent majority. Toleration in nation-states has only one source, moves or doesn't move in only one direction. The case of the United States suggests a very different set of arrangements.

[5]

The fourth model of coexistence and possible toleration is the immigrant society. Now the members of the different groups have left their territorial base, their homeland, behind them, come individually or in families, one by one, to a new land and then dispersed across it. They cluster for comfort only in relatively small numbers, always intermixed with other, similar groups in cities, states, and regions. Hence no sort of territorial autonomy is possible. (Quebec is the crucial exception here—and another exception must be made for conquered native peoples; I will focus primarily on the immigrants.) If ethnic and religious groups are to sustain themselves, they must do so as voluntary associations— which means that they are more at risk from the indifference of their own members than from the intolerance of the others. The state, once it is pried loose from the grip of the first immigrants (who imagined in every case that they were forming a nation-state of their own), is committed to none of the groups that make it up. It is, in the current phrase, neutral among them, tolerant of all of them, autonomous in its purposes.

The state claims exclusive jurisdictional rights, regarding all its citizens as individuals rather than as members of groups. Hence, the objects of toleration, strictly speaking, are individual choices and performances: acts of adhesion, participation in rituals of membership and worship, enactments of cultural difference, and so on. Individual men and women are encouraged to tolerate one another as individuals, difference being understood in each case as a personalized (rather than stereotypical) version of group culture—which also means that the members of each group, if they are to display the virtue of tolerance, must accept each other's different versions. Everyone has to tolerate everyone else. No group is allowed to organize itself coercively, to seize control of public space, or to monopolize public resources. In principle, the public schools teach the history and "civics" of the state, which is conceived to have no national but only a political identity. The history and culture of the different groups is either not taught at all or it is taught, as in the United States in recent times (and in some places), in equal doses, "multiculturally." Similarly, the state provides no help to any group or it is equally supportive of all of them—encouraging, for example, a kind of general religiosity as in subway and bus advertisements of the 1950s that urged Americans to "attend the church of your choice."

As this last maxim suggests, neutrality is always a matter of degree. Some groups are, in fact, favored over others—in this case, groups with "churches." But the others are still tolerated; nor is church attendance or any other culturally specific practice turned into a condition of citizenship. It is relatively easy, then, and not at all humiliating, to escape one's own group and take on the reigning political identity ("American"). But many people in an immigrant society prefer a hyphenated or dual identity, differentiated along cultural/ political lines as in, say, Italian-American. The hyphen joining the two symbolizes the acceptance of "Italianness" by other Americans, the recognition that "American" is a political identity without strong or specific cultural claims. The consequence, of course, is that "Italian" represents a cultural identity without political claims. That is the only form in which Italianness is tolerated, and then it must sustain itself, if it can or as long as it can, privately, through the voluntary efforts and contributions of committed Italians. And this is the case, in principle, with every cultural and religious group, not only with minorities (but, again, there is no permanent majority).

Whether groups can sustain themselves under these conditions—without autonomy, without access to state power or official recognition, without a territorial base or the fixed opposition of a permanent majority—is a question still to be answered. Religious communities, of both sectarian and "churchly" sorts, have not done badly in the United States up until now. But one reason for their relative success, it might be thought, is the considerable intolerance that many of them have, in fact, encountered—which often has, as I have already suggested, group-sustaining effects. The form of toleration characteristic of immigrant societies is still emergent, not yet fully realized. We might think of it—the toleration of individual choices and personalized versions of culture and religion—as the maximal (or the most intensive) kind of toleration. And, again, it is still radically unclear whether the long-term effect of this maximalism will be the fostering or the dissolving of group life.

The fear that soon the only objects of toleration will be eccentric individuals leads some groups (or their most committed members) to seek positive support from the state—in the form, say, of quota systems or subsidies. Given the logic of multiculturalism, however, state support must be provided equally to every social group. Since quotas and subsidies cannot be provided equally on that scale, hard choices would have to be made if policies like these were ever adopted. Toleration is, at least potentially, infinite in its extent; but the state can underwrite group life only within some set of political and financial limits.

[6]

Let me summarize the argument so far by considering these four regimes first in terms of the power relations they involve and then in terms of the range of (morally problematic) practices they tolerate. It is often said that toleration is necessarily a relationship of inequality, where the tolerated groups or individuals are cast in an inferior position. Therefore, we should aim at something better, beyond toleration, like mutual respect. Once we have mapped out the four regimes, however, the story looks more complicated; mutual respect is one of the forms toleration can take—the most attractive form, perhaps, but not necessarily the most stable.

In multinational empires, power rests with the central bureaucrats. All of the incorporated groups are encouraged to regard themselves as equally powerless, hence incapable of coercing or persecuting their neighbors. Any local attempt at coercion will produce an appeal to the center. So Greeks and Turks, for example, lived peacefully side by side under Ottoman rule. Were they mutually respectful? Some of them probably were; some were not. But the character of their relationship did not depend on their mutual respect; it depended on their mutual subjection. Consociation, by contrast, requires mutual respect at least among the leaders of the different groups—for the groups must not only co-exist but negotiate among themselves the terms of their co-existence. Cyprus, before its partition into Greek and Turkish states, represents a failed example.

In nation-states, power rests with the majority nation, which uses the state, as we have seen, for its own purposes. This is no necessary bar to mutuality among individuals, which is, in fact, likely to flourish in democratic states. But minority groups are unequal by virtue of their numbers and will be democratically over-ruled on most matters of public culture. The case is similar early on in the history of immigrant societies, when the first immigrants aspire to nation-statehood. Successive waves of immigration produce what is, in principle again, a neutral state, the democratic version of imperial bureaucracy. But this state addresses itself to individuals rather than groups, and so creates an open society in which everyone is required to tolerate everyone else. The much heralded move "beyond toleration" is, presumably, now possible. As I have argued, however, it remains unclear how much of group difference will remain to be respected once this move is made.

[7]

Toleration is no doubt widest in the case not considered here: international society, where no one is authorized to decide whether or not to tolerate this or that group or practice. International law legitimates "humanitarian intervention" by any capable state in cases of massacre, radical persecution, or mass deportation. Hence we can say, I suppose, that these practices, in principle at least, are not tolerated, and whenever there is an actual intervention (relatively rare in the history of states), we can say that they are, in fact, not tolerated. But in general the agents of international society—political leaders and diplomats— and perhaps also the people they claim to represent are remarkably tolerant of what goes on across their borders. They are resigned, indifferent, curious, or enthusiastic (it hardly matters) and so disinclined to interfere. It may also be the case, of course, that they are hostile to their neighbors' culture and customs but, given the conditions of international society, are unprepared to pay the costs of interference. Or, though culturally intolerant, they may accept the logic of sovereignty, which decrees a kind of institutional toleration.

Among the political regimes with which I am directly concerned, the multinational empire comes closest to accepting a similar logic. Each autonomous community has its own legal system, and until its members interact with the members of other communities—in commerce, for example—it is likely to be allowed to enforce its own shared understandings of lawful behavior. Strange commercial customs won't be tolerated in the common markets, but there will not be much interference in the work of local courts dealing, say, with domestic affairs.

Consider the extraordinary reluctance with which the British finally, in 1829, banned suttee (the self-immolation of a Hindu widow on her husband's funeral pyre) in their Indian states. For many years first the East India Company and then the British government tolerated the practice because of what a twentieth-century historian calls their "declared intention of respecting both Hindu and Muslim beliefs and allowing the free exercise of religious rights." Even Muslim rulers, who had, according to this same historian, no respect whatsoever for Hindu beliefs, made only sporadic and halfhearted efforts to suppress the practice. Imperial toleration extends, then, as far as suttee, which—given British accounts of what the practice actually involved—is pretty far.

It is at least conceivable that consociational arrangements might produce a similar toleration if the power of the joined communities was in near balance and the leaders of one of them were strongly committed to this or that customary practice. A nation-state, however, where power is by definition unbalanced, would not tolerate customs like suttee among a national or religious minority. Nor is toleration at that reach likely in an immigrant society, where each of the groups is a minority relative to all the others. The case of the Mormons in the United States suggests that deviant practices won't be tolerated even when they are wholly internal, involving "only" domestic life. In these last two cases, the state grants equal citizenship to all its members and enforces a single law. There are no communal courts; the whole country is one jurisdiction within which state officials are bound, say, to stop a suttee in progress in exactly the same way that they are bound to stop a suicide attempt if they possibly can. And if the suttee is coercively assisted, as it often was, in fact, they have to treat the coercion as murder; there are no religious or cultural excuses.

In other sorts of cases, where the moral values of the larger community—the national majority or the coalition of minorities—are not so directly challenged, religious or cultural excuses may be accepted and non-standard, even illegal, practices tolerated. This is the case with narrowly constituted or sectarian minorities like the American Amish or the Hasidim, to whom state authorities are sometimes ready to offer (or the courts to mediate) one or another compromise arrangement. But similar concessions won't be offered to larger, more powerful groups—and even the standing compromises can always be challenged by any sect member who claims his or her citizen rights. Imagine that an arrangement is worked out allowing Muslim girls in French public schools to wear their customary headdress. (What stands in the way of any such arrangement is the fact that the Muslims in France are not a narrowly constituted minority, but let's leave that aside for the sake of the example.) This would be a compromise with the *laïciste* traditions of French education, which would continue, however, to govern the school calendar and curriculum. At some point, let's say, a number of Muslim girls claim that they are being coerced by their families to wear the headdress and that the compromise arrangement facilitates this coercion. Then, perhaps, the compromise would have to be renegotiated. In the nation-state and in the immigrant society, though not in the multinational empire, the right to be protected against coercion of this kind would take precedence over the values of the minority religion or culture.

[8]

I have talked about some of the limits of toleration, but I haven't said anything yet about regimes of intolerance, which is what many empires and nation-states actually are. These sometimes succeed in obliterating difference but sometimes (when they stop short of genocide and mass deportation or "ethnic cleansing") serve in fact to reinforce it. They mark off the members of minority groups, persecute them because of their membership, compel them to rely on one another, forge intense solidarities. Nonetheless, neither the leaders of such groups nor their most committed members would choose a regime of intolerance. Given the opportunity, they usually seek some form of individual or collective toleration: assimilation into the body of citizens or recognition of their standing in domestic or international society, with this or that degree of self-rule—autonomy, consociation, or sovereign statehood.

We might think of these two as the central projects of modern democratic politics. They are standardly conceived in mutually exclusive terms; either individuals or groups will be liberated from persecution and invisibility—and individuals only insofar as they abandon their groups. Thus Jean-Paul Sartre's description of the prototypical democrat's view of the Jewish question: "He wants to separate the Jew from his religion, from his family, from his ethnic community, in order to plunge him into the democratic crucible whence he will emerge naked and alone, an individual and solitary particle like all the other particles."[1] (This project can obviously be described in a more positive way; since it is not my subject here, I don't need to say anything more about it.) The alternative is to provide the group as a whole with a voice, a place, and a politics of its own. For many people on the political left, this was once thought to require a struggle for inclusion, on the model of the working class and socialist movements, storming and breaching the walls of the bourgeois city. But the groups with which I am concerned here require a struggle for boundaries.

The crucial slogan of this struggle is "self-determination," which implies the need for a piece of territory or, at least, a set of independent institutions—hence decentralization, devolution, autonomy, partition, sovereignty. Getting the boundaries right, not only in geographic but also in functional terms, is enormously difficult, but it is necessary if the different groups are to exercise significant control over their own lives and to do so with some security.

The work goes on today, adapting the old imperial arrangements, extending the modern international system, proliferating nation-states, self-governing regions, local authorities, and so on. Note what is being recognized and tolerated here: always groups and their members, men and women with singular or primary identities, ethnic or religious in character. The work obviously depends upon the mobilization of these people, but it is only their leaders who are actually engaged with one another, across boundaries, one-on-one (except when the engagement is military in nature). Autonomy confirms the authority of traditional elites; consociation is a kind of power-sharing arrangement among those same elites; nation-states interact through their diplomatic corps and political leaderships. For the mass of group members, toleration is maintained by separation, on the assumption that these people understand themselves *as members* and want to associate mostly with one another. Like a character from Robert Frost's "Mending Wall," they believe that "good fences make good neighbors."

The last of my toleration models, however, suggests a different pattern and, perhaps, a postmodern project. In immigrant societies (and also now in nation-states under immigrant pressure), people experience what we might think of as a life without boundaries and without secure or singular identities. Difference is, as it were, dispersed, so that it is encountered everywhere, everyday. Individuals mix but don't necessarily assimilate to a common identity. The hold of groups on their members is looser than it has ever been, though it is by no means broken entirely. And the result is a constant commingling of ambiguously identified individuals, intermarriage among them, and hence a literal multiculturalism, instantiated not only in the society as a whole but in each and every family, even in each and every individual. Now tolerance begins at home, where we often have to make ethnic, religious, and cultural peace with our spouses, in-laws, and children—and with our own hyphenated or divided selves. Religious fundamentalism must be understood in part as a rejection of any such peace, an attack on ambiguity.

The Bulgarian-French writer Julie Kristeva has been the most important theoretical defender of this postmodern project, urging us to recognize a world of strangers and acknowledge the stranger in ourselves. In addition to a psychological argument, which I must pass by here, she restates a very old moral argument, whose first version is the biblical injunction: do not oppress the stranger, for you were strangers in the land of Egypt. Kristeva changes the verb tense and the geography for the sake of a contemporary reiteration: do not oppress the stranger, for you *are* strangers in *this* very land. Surely it is easier to tolerate otherness if we acknowledge the other in ourselves. I doubt, however, that this acknowledgment is sufficient by itself or in a merely moral form. We don't live in the world of strangers all of the time; nor do we encounter each other's strangeness only one on one but also, still, collectively, in situations where morality must be seconded by politics.

It is not the case that the postmodern project simply supersedes modernism, as in some grand metanarrative of historical stages. The one is superimposed on the other, without in any way obliterating it. There still are boundaries, but they are blurred by all the crossings. We still know ourselves to be this or that, but the knowledge is uncertain, for we are also this *and* that. Strong identity groups exist and assert themselves politically, but the allegiance of their members is measured by degrees, along a broad continuum, with greater and greater numbers clustered at the further end (which is why the militants at the near end are so strident these days).

This dualism of the modern and the postmodern requires that difference be doubly accommodated, first in its singular individual and collective versions and then in its pluralist, dispersed, and divided versions (or the other way around; I am not committed to a sequential argument, though the order as I have just stated it is the more likely). We need to be tolerated and protected as citizens and members and also as strangers. Self-determination has to be both political and personal—the two are related, but they are not the same. The old understanding of difference, which tied individuals to their autonomous or sovereign groups, will be resisted by dissident and ambivalent individuals. But any new understanding, focused solely on the dissidents, will be resisted by men and women struggling to enact, elaborate, revise, and pass on a common religious or cultural tradition. So difference must be twice tolerated, with whatever mix—it doesn't have to be the same mix in both cases—of resignation, indifference, curiosity, and enthusiasm.

Even those of us who are enthusiasts are bound to come up against differences, cultural and personal, that give us trouble. For we don't want to tolerate hatred and cruelty; nor does our respect for difference extend to oppressive practices within groups (which were commonly tolerated by imperial bureaucrats). The more closely we live together, the more the limits of toleration become everyday issues. And closeness is one of the aims of the postmodern project. So the solid lines on the old cultural and political maps are turned into dotted lines, but co-existence along and across those lines is still a problem.

NOTES

1. Jean-Paul Sartre, *Anti-Semite and Jew*, trans. George J. Becker (New York: Grove Press, 1962), 56–57.

CHAPTER TWELVE

Nation and Universe

PART I. Two Kinds of Universalism

[I]

Much has been written in recent years about moral absolutism and moral relativism, foundationalism and contextualism, monism and pluralism, universalism and particularism—all the fervent *isms*—and yet our understanding of these simple polarities does not seem to advance. Advocates of liberal enlightenment confront advocates of communal tradition; those who aspire to global reach confront those who yearn for local intensity. We all know one another's lines. In every argument, we anticipate the opening gambits; we have memorized the standard replies and the follow-up moves; no one's closing flourish is at all surprising. The different positions can be defended well or badly; it is still possible to win a debate, much as one might win a game of chess, with superior skill or the quickness to seize upon an opponent's mistakes. But victories of this kind have no larger resonance. So I have looked for a way of being persuasive without trying to be victorious, a way of escaping the conventional oppositions or, at least, of redescribing them in less contentious terms. I want to argue from within what I, and many others, have taken to be the opposing camp; I want to take my stand among the universalists and suggest that there is another universalism, a non-standard variety, which encompasses and perhaps even helps to explain the appeal of moral particularism.

I shall begin my argument with the historical example of Judaism, which has often been criticized (not without reason) as a tribal religion, the very emblem of a particularist creed. And yet Judaism is one of the chief sources of the two universalisms, the first of which became standard when it was adopted within Christianity. It probably would have become standard even if Judaism rather than Christianity had triumphed in the ancient world—not only because of its strength among the Jews but also because of a certain connection, which will become apparent as I go along, between the first universalism and the idea or the experience of triumph.

The first universalism holds that as there is one God, so there is one law, one justice, one correct understanding of the good life or the good society or the good regime, one salvation, one messiah, one millennium for all humanity. I will call this the "covering-law" version of universalism, though in Christian doctrine it is not law so much as the sacrifice of the son of God that "covers" all men and women everywhere—so that the line "Christ died for your sins" can be addressed to any person in any time or place and will always be true, the pronoun having an indefinite and infinite reference. However many sinners there are, and whoever they are, Christ died for *them*. But I mean to defer here to Jewish "legalism" (and to later natural law arguments), where the aim is to provide an account of what it means not to sin, to live well or, at least, rightly. Covering-law universalism has been called an "alternative" doctrine within Judaism, but by prophetic times it was a very well established alternative, and perhaps even the dominant doctrine, at least in the written literature of the Jews.[1] Jewish tribalism had by then been reinterpreted and reconstructed in a way that made it instrumental to a universal end. The Jews were chosen for a purpose, which had to do not only with their own history but also with the history of the human race. That is the meaning of Isaiah's description of Israel as "a light unto the nations."[2] One light for all the nations, who will eventually be uniformly enlightened: though, the light being somewhat dim and the nations recalcitrant, this may take a long time. It may take until the end of time.

The end can be described in militant and triumphalist terms as the victory of the universalizing tribe; or it can be described more modestly as the "coming in" or the "going up" of the nations. "And many people shall go and say Come ye, and let us go up to the mountain of the Lord."[3] Whatever its form, the result is an identical triumph of religious and moral singularity—many people will climb one mountain. The hope for a triumph of this sort has been incorporated into the daily prayers: "On that day the Lord shall be one and his name shall be one."[4] Until that day, this first universalism can take on the character of a mission, as it often did in the history of Christianity and, later on, in the imperialism of nations that called themselves Christian. You will all remember these lines from Kipling's "Song of the English":

> Keep ye the law—be swift in all obedience—
> Clear the land of evil, drive the road and
>   bridge the ford.

Make ye sure to each his own
That he reap where he hath sown.
By the peace among our peoples, let men know
    we serve the Lord.[5]

Eventually, roads and bridges built and peace secured, "our peoples," all the subject nations, will learn to serve the Lord on their own; for now, "we" must rule over them. The experience of nations that do not keep the law is radically devalued. This is a common feature of covering-law universalism. The Lord's servants stand in the center of history, constitute its main current, while the histories of the others are so many chronicles of ignorance and meaningless strife. Indeed, there is a sense in which they have no history at all—as in the Hegelian/Marxist conception—since nothing of world-historical significance has happened to them. Nothing of world-historical significance will ever happen to them except insofar as they move toward and merge with the main current. The Christian version of this sort of thing, the inspiration of much missionizing activity, is well-known, as are its secular analogues. But there is a Jewish version too, according to which the exile and dispersion of the Jews, though in one sense a punishment for their sins, was in another sense central to God's own world-historical design. It served to ensure that the true monotheistic faith would have local adherents and exemplars everywhere in the world—a dispersed light, but a light still.[6] The exile is hard on its particulars but good for the generality. Monotheism on this view is the burden of the Jews, much as civilization is the burden of Kipling's English and communism of Marx's working class.

Since at any given moment, some people know the law and some people do not, some people keep it and some people do not, this first universalism makes for a certain pride among the knowers and keepers—the chosen, the elect, the true believers, the vanguard. Of course, the rejection of pride is commonly one of the covering laws and, as I have already suggested, the triumph of God can come in ways that do not invite the triumphalism of his servants. Still, it is always the case that these men and women (we can disagree over who they are) live right now in a fashion that all men and women will one day imitate. They possess right now a body of knowledge and a legal code that one day will be universally accepted. What is the state of mind and feeling appropriate to such people? If not pride, then certainly confidence: we can recognize covering-law universalism by the confidence it inspires.

The second universalism is the true alternative doctrine in Jewish history; we have to recover it from its biblical fragments. Once Judaism is in full-scale conflict with Christianity, it is repressed; it reappears in secular form in eighteenth and nineteenth-century romanticism. The crucial fragment comes from the prophet Amos, who has God ask:

> Are ye not as children of the
>   Ethiopians unto me, O children
>   of Israel? . . .
> Have I not brought Israel out of the
>   land of Egypt,
> And the Philistines from Caphtor,
> And the Syrians from Kir?[7]

These questions suggest that there is not one exodus, one divine redemption, one moment of liberation, for all mankind, the way there is, according to Christian doctrine, one redeeming sacrifice. Liberation is a particular experience, repeated for each oppressed people. At the same time, it is in every case a good experience, for God is the common liberator. Each people has *its own* liberation at the hands of a single God, the same God in every case, who presumably finds oppression universally hateful. I propose to call this argument reiterative universalism. What makes it different from covering-law universalism is its particularist focus and its pluralizing tendency. We have no reason to think that the exodus of the Philistines or the Syrians is identical with the exodus of Israel, or that it culminates in a similar covenant, or even that the laws of the three peoples are or ought to be the same.

There are two very different ways of elaborating on a historical event like the exodus of Israel from Egypt. It can be made pivotal in a universal history, as if all humanity, though not present at the sea or the mountain, had at least been represented there. Then the experience of Israel's liberation belongs to everyone. Or it can be made exemplary, pivotal only in a particular history, which other people can repeat—*must* repeat if the experience is ever to belong to them—in their own fashion. The exodus from Egypt liberates only Israel, only the people whose exodus it was, but other liberations are always possible. In this second view, there is no universal history, but rather a series of histories (which probably don't converge or only converge at the mythical end of time—like the many national roads to communism) in each of which value can be found. I assume that Amos would not have said "equal value," nor do I want to insist that equality of that sort follows from the idea of reiteration. Nevertheless, the purpose of Amos's questions is to rebuke the pride of the Israelites. They are not the only chosen or the only liberated people; the God of Israel attends to other nations as well. Isaiah makes the same point, presumably for the same purpose, in an even more dramatic way: "For [the Egyptians] shall cry unto the Lord because of the oppressors. And he shall send them a savior, and a great one, and he shall deliver them. And the Lord shall be known to Egypt, and the Egyptians shall know the Lord in that day. . . . In that day shall Israel be the third with Egypt and with Assyria, even a blessing in the midst of the land: Whom the Lord of hosts shall bless, saying, Blessed be Egypt my people, and Assyria the work of my hands, and Israel mine inheritance."[8] Instead of many people, one mountain, what we have here is one God, many blessings. And as the blessings are distinct, so the histories of the three nations do not converge toward a single history.

Reiterative universalism can always be given a covering-law form. We can claim, for example, that oppression is always wrong, or that we ought to respond morally and politically to the cry of every oppressed people (as God is sometimes said to do), or that we should value every liberation. But these are covering laws of a special sort: first, they are learned from experience, through an historical engagement with otherness—Israel, the Philistines, the Syrians; second, because they are learned in this way, they impose upon us a respect for particularity, for different experiences of bondage and pain, by different people, whose liberation takes different forms; and finally, because they are qualified by difference, they are less likely to inspire confidence in those who know them. Indeed, it is always possible that covering laws of this sort will produce mental and moral outcomes that contradict their likely intention: that we will be overwhelmed by the sheer heterogeneity of human life and surrender all belief in the relevance of our own history for anyone else. And if our history is irrelevant to them, so will theirs be to us. We retreat to inwardness and disinterest. Acknowledging difference makes for indifference. Though we grant the value of Egyptian liberation, we have no reason to promote it. It is God's business, or it is the business of the Egyptians. We are not engaged; we have no world-historical mission; we are, if only by default, advocates of nonintervention. But not only by default, for reiterative universalism derives in part from a certain view of what it means to have a history of one's own. So non-intervention can claim a positive foundation: the state of mind and feeling most appropriate to this second universalism is tolerance and mutual respect.[9]

[2]

Given the "burden" of a monotheistic faith, reiterative universalism could never be anything more than a possibility within Judaism. But a God conceived to be active in history, engaged in the world, makes it always a lively possibility.

There is no reason to confine such a God—who is, moreover, omnipotent and omnipresent—to Jewish history or even to the Jewish version of world history. Isn't the strength of his hand everywhere in evidence? And isn't he, with regard to all the nations, even-handed? Consider these lines from Jeremiah (once again, it is God who is talking): "At what instant I shall speak concerning a nation, and concerning a kingdom, to pluck up and to pull down, and to destroy it; If that nation, against whom I have pronounced, turn from their evil, I will repent of the evil that I thought to do unto them. And at what instant I shall speak concerning a nation, and concerning a kingdom, to build and to plant it; If it do evil in my sight, that it obey not my voice, then I will repent of the good wherewith I said I would benefit them."[10] Clearly the reference here is to all the nations, though each one is considered independently of the others, at its own "instant." We might suppose that God judges them all by the same standard; the phrase "evil in my sight" refers always to the same set of evil acts. But this isn't necessarily the case. If God covenants separately with each nation or if he blesses each nation differently, then it would make sense to suggest that he holds each of them to its own standard. There is a set of evil acts for each nation, though the different sets certainly overlap. Or, if there is only one set of evil acts (fixed by the overlap: murder, betrayal, oppression, and so on), it might still be the case that the good is produced in multiple sets—for goodness is not (I come back to this point in my second lecture) the simple opposite of evil. It is because there are multiple sets, different kinds of goods, that there must also be multiple blessings. In either of these views, God is himself a reiterative universalist, governing and constraining but not overruling the diversity of human-kind.

It might nonetheless be argued that this second universalism works best if one makes a kind of peace with the idea that divinity itself is diverse and plural. Of this there is scarcely a hint in the Jewish bible, though the prophet Micah comes close to such an argument in the following verses (the first of which is more often quoted than the second): "And they shall sit every man under his vine and under his fig-tree; and none shall make them afraid. . . . For all peoples will walk every one in the name of his God, and we will walk in the name of the Lord our God for ever and ever."[11] The second verse is commonly taken to be a survival of some earlier belief which held that each people has its own god, the god of Israel but one among many. But to take it this way doesn't explain the survival. Why did successive editors preserve and include the second verse? In any case, the two verses fit together; they have a parallel form and are joined by the conjunction "for" (Hebrew: *ki*), as if the happy "sitting" described in the first is a consequence of the plural "walking" described in the second. Perhaps that is Micah's meaning; it is certainly one of the arguments most often made on behalf of reiterative universalism—that the tolerance it inspires makes for peace. How many of us will sit quietly under our vines and fig trees once the agents of the first universalism go to work, making sure that everyone is properly covered by the covering law?

But perhaps pluralism under the vines and fig trees doesn't require pluralism in the heavens above but only a plurality of divine names here on earth: "for all peoples will walk everyone in the name of his god." And that plurality may be consistent, at least in principle, with the single, omnipotent God of Israel who creates men and women in his own image—hence as creative men and women. For then God himself must make some kind of peace with their plurality and creativity.[12] The artists among them won't all paint the same picture; the playwrights won't write the same play; the philosophers won't produce the same account of the good; and the theologians won't call God by the same name. What human beings have in common is just this creative power, which is not the power to do the same thing in the same way but the power to do many different things in different ways: divine omnipotence (dimly) reflected, distributed, and particularized. Here is a creation story—it is not, I concede, the dominant version—that supports the doctrine of reiterative universalism.[13]

[3]

But however things are with divine creativity, the values and virtues of human creativity can best be understood in the reiterative mode. Independence, inner-direction, individualism, self-determination, self-government, freedom, autonomy: all these can be regarded as universal values, but they all have particularist implications. (The case is the same, though the particularism is greatly heightened, with the chief virtues of romanticism: originality, authenticity, nonconformity, and so on). We can readily imagine a covering law something like "Self-determination is the right of every people / nation." But this is a law that quickly runs out; it cannot specify its own substantive outcomes. For we value the outcomes only insofar as they are self-determined, and determinations vary with selves. Reiterated acts of self-determination produce a world of difference. New covering laws may come into effect, of course, as the production continues. But it is hard to see what value self-determination could have if it were entirely "covered," legally controlled at every point. When Moses (speaking, once again, for God) tells the Israelites, "I have set before you life and death . . . therefore choose life that both thou and thy seed may live," we may agree that the choice is in some sense free, but the life that is chosen is surely not self-determined.[14] On the other hand, when we watch the Jews, later on, arguing over the interpretation of God's laws and creating thereby a *way of life*—then we see what can properly be called a process of self-determination.

Self-determination is a value that I have to defend, if I defend it at all, even if I believe that unworthy or wrongful choices will often be made. (I may oppose self-determination in a particular case, however, if the agent's choices in that case are sure or virtually sure to violate critically important moral principles; but I would still count myself as a defender of self-determination.) People have to choose for themselves, each people for itself. Hence, we determine our way of life, and they do, and they do, up to the nth they—and each determination will differ in significant ways from preceding and concurrent determinations. Obviously, we can criticize each other's work, urge that it be made more like our own, for example, but unless our lives and liberties (or those of other presumptively innocent men and women) are injured or threatened by it, we cannot forcibly interfere. We cannot play the part of the police, enforcing the law, for (serious injury aside) the law runs out before it can be enforced. There is no covering law or set of laws that provides a sufficiently complete blueprint for our work or theirs. Nor is it the case that the laws agreed to by one people "cover" all the others, so that substantive imitation can replace procedural reiteration. There can't be a replacement of that sort if the values and virtues of autonomy are real values and virtues.

The same argument holds for the individual as for the people / nation. If we value autonomy, we will want individual men and women to have their own lives. But if all lives are radically covered by a single set of covering laws, the idea of "own-ness" has no scope. Individual autonomy can be and undoubtedly is constrained in a variety of ways, but it cannot be and is not entirely controlled. There is no single mode of "having" a life of one's own. We are inclined to think that such a life must be made before it can be had, that is, we think of an individual life as a project, a career, an undertaking, something that we plan and then enact according to the plan. But this is simply our (collective) understanding of individuality; it does not get at the thing-in-itself; it does not suggest the only legitimate or authentic way of being an individual. In fact, it is entirely possible to inherit a life and still possess it as one's own; and it is also possible to find a life, literally light upon it, with no forethought at all. In any account of autonomy, there has to be room not only for different self-determinations but also for different kinds of self-possession.

Reiterative universalism is not concerned only with the varieties of selfhood. The values and virtues of attachment are also best understood in the reiterative mode. Love, loyalty, faithfulness, friendship, devotion, commitment, patriotism: any or all of these can be universally enjoined, but the injunction is necessarily abstract; it does not govern the substantive experience. "Love thy neighbor" is a familiar covering law; every particular love relationship that it covers, however, is unique. The case is the same with group attachments, including those that constitute the family, the primary group. Tolstoy was wrong to claim that "all happy families resemble one another."[15] Novelists have, I suppose, good and sufficient reasons to focus on familial unhappiness, but if happy families are ones whose members are (among other things) mutually attached, we can be sure that the attachments are complex and diverse, varying within families as well as among them—and varying even more obviously across the range of cultures, where the very idea of familial attachment is differently understood. One can specify how lovers or family members should treat one another only in the most general ways—and these are not the ways that give the relationships their specificity and value.

Every lover must love for himself; it must be *his own* love, not some universal love, that he offers to the other person. To be sure, there is an argument within Christianity according to which the only love that we can offer to others is the overflowing love with which God loves us.[16] But I think that it is a misunderstanding of the Christian God, certainly of the Jewish God, a failure to grasp the meaning of his omnipotence, to suggest that his love is always the same. We should assume, instead, that divine love is differentiated every time it is focused on a particular human being—else it would not be his love *for me* (or you). But even if divine love is not differentiated in this way, human love certainly is. When it is communicated to others, it takes on different intensities, it is expressed in different ways, and it carries different emotional and moral entailments. The differences are sometimes personal, sometimes cultural, but they are in any case crucial to the experience. We know love in its differences and would not recognize it as love if it were ever wholly conventionalized, submitted to the rule of a covering law.

Patriotism or the love of country is similarly known in its differences: how would it be possible to love one's country if it were indistinguishable from all the others? Different countries command different kinds and degrees of loyalty. These are the attachments through which the "self" in the phrase "national self-determination" is constituted, and as determinations vary with selves, so national selves vary with kinds of attachment. In political life, the values of autonomy and loyalty work together to produce diversity—men and women differently associated, whose mutual attachments are differently expressed, enacted, and celebrated. If people are to love their country, Edmund Burke wrote, their country must be lovely.[17] Yes; and perhaps we can find some minimal standards of loveliness that everyone will acknowledge (or, more likely, some widely recognized, because widely experienced, forms of ugliness), but for the most part what is lovely is determined in the eyes of the beholder. There is no universal aesthetic for countries.

Is there a universal ethic? Justice is certainly the chief of the values and virtues that are claimed for the covering law account. "But let judgment run down as waters," says Amos, "and righteousness as a mighty stream."[18] In the geography of ethics, as it is commonly understood, there is only one mighty stream, one Nile or Mississippi that floods and fertilizes the whole world. There is only one just social order, and all the negative injunctions of the theory of righteousness—against killing, torturing, oppressing, lying, cheating, and so on—invite covering-law expression: the general and absolute "Thou shalt not!" Similarly, any exceptions to such laws must be exceptions for everyone, everywhere, as in the standard example of killing in self-defense.

Justice seems to be universal in character for the same reason that autonomy and attachment are reiterative—out of recognition of and respect for the human agents who create the moral world and who come, by virtue of that creativity, to have lives and countries of their own. Their creations are greatly diverse and always particular, but there is something singular and universal about their creativity, some brute fact of agency captured, as I have already suggested, by the claim that all human agents have been created in the image of a creator God. Justice is the tribute we have learned to pay to the brute fact and the divine image. The principles and rules of justice have been worked out, over many centuries, so as to protect human agents and set them free for their creative (reiterative) tasks: one set of principles for one set of agents. But there is a problem here. It is certainly possible to build an account of justice on the foundation of agency. Start with equal respect for the agents (and every man and woman equally an agent), and there is probably no clear stopping point short of a fully elaborated description of a just society. Looking at the elaborated description, however, we may well feel that we have made too much of agency—for the more we make of it, the less there is for it to make. Why should we value human agency if we are unwilling to give it any room for maneuver and invention?

If we think of justice as a social invention, variously made, one more product of human creativity, then its making does not seem all that different from the practical working out of autonomy and attachment. What reasons do we have to expect a singular and universal justice? Is that not like protecting the plurality of playwrights while insisting that they all write the same play? But do not all the playwrights require the same protection—not, to be sure, against unfriendly audiences or bad reviews, but against censorship and persecution? How are we to draw the line between covering laws and reiterative moralities?

[4]

I want now to look at an attempt by a contemporary philosopher to draw this critical line—Stuart Hampshire's essay "Morality and Convention."[19] Hampshire provides an especially useful argument because he is equally sensitive to the claims of particular ways of life rooted in "local memories and local attachments" and to the claims of a universal morality "arising from a shared humanity and an entirely general norm of reasonableness." The first set of claims are strongest, he thinks, in those parts of morality that have to do with "the prohibitions and prescriptions that govern sexual morality and family relationships and the duties of friendship."[20] "Govern" here is one of the verbs of particularity: in these areas, at least, we are to determine our own prohibitions and prescriptions. The second set of claims finds its proper place in the principles of right and the rules of distribution. "Principles" and "rules" here are nouns with global reach; their content is supplied by a reason that belongs to no one in particular.

This is to mark off autonomy and attachment from justice in a way that seems to fit nicely with the distinction between reiterative and covering-law universalism. With regard to kinship and friendship, Hampshire recognizes a "license for distinctiveness." With regard to distribution, he recognizes a "requirement of convergence." His "license" allows for many different histories; his "requirement" suggests a steady (and familiar) pressure toward singularity.[21] The values and virtues of autonomy and attachment are matters of custom, feeling, and habit; and there is no reason why they should be the same in different societies (hence the "license" is itself universal). The values and virtues of justice are a matter for rational argument; in principle, they should be similar, if not identical, everywhere.

It is not easy, however, to make practical sense of this distinction. Consider for a moment the question of family relationships, that is, the kinship system. In most of the societies that anthropologists study (and still, to some extent, in our own), the rules of kinship are also the rules of distributive justice. They determine who lives with whom, who sleeps with whom, who defers to whom, who has power over whom, who gives dowries to whom, and who inherits from whom—and once all this has been determined not much room is left for the imposition of a rational and universal distributive code. Now the license for distinctiveness and the requirement of convergence come starkly into conflict, for they both seem to govern the same terrain.

Hampshire deals with this conflict by suggesting that justice serves as a kind of negative constraint on autonomy and attachment. What rationality requires, he writes, is "that the rules and conventions [in this case, of sexual morality] should not cause evident and avoidable unhappiness or offend accepted principles of fairness." This is a proposal for cultural diversity within the limits of reason alone (or of common sense: what does "accepted" mean?), and the proposal will seem more or less attractive depending on how limiting the limits are. For Hampshire, the model of cultural diversity is the diversity of natural languages, with their radically distinct and seemingly arbitrary grammars and "rules of propriety," and the model of the rational limits is the "presumed deep structure in all languages."[22]

But this linguistic analogy is also a puzzle, for the deep structure of language, which is indeed reiterated in all natural languages, constitutes rather than regulates the various grammars. Were we ever to find a language with an alternative deep structure we would have to surrender the universality presumption; we would not set about "correcting" the deviant language. But covering laws in morality—the "accepted principles" of justice, for example—are precisely regulative in character: were Hampshire to find a morality without them, he would want, presumably, to criticize and correct it.

It is entirely possible that our reiterated moralities and ways of life have a common deep structure. But the more important question for us is whether they have a common substance. Is there in fact a single set of principles located somewhere in the core of every morality, regulating all the workings-out of autonomy and attachment? Put this way, the question invites a negative answer; we have only to consult the anthropological literature. Reiteration makes for difference. We will find, however, an overlapping plurality of sets, each of which bears a family resemblance to the others. Hence we will know them (all) to be principles of justice, and we may well be led, by the interactions of states and peoples, say, to interpret them in ways that emphasize their common features. But our interpretations can do no more than suggest the *differentiated commonalities* of justice—for these common features are always incorporated within a particular cultural system and elaborated in highly specific ways. We abstract from the differences to a universal code, something like H. L. A. Hart's "minimum natural law."[23] But there can never be a single correct statement of the code, any more than there can be a single set of positive laws that gets the natural law right once and for all. Every statement is also an interpretation, carrying, let us say, philosophical freight; and it is likely to take on, additionally, the cultural freight of the language in which it is stated.

In any case, the same search for commonality and the same abstraction is possible, as the world grows smaller, in the realms of sexuality and kinship. So if the abstracted code sets some limits on social practice, it does so across the full range of moral life, and not only with regard to justice. And the possibility of differentiation also exists across the range: there is no distinction of areas here, no separable social space where covering-law universalism can play a dominant part. When we draw the critical line, there is nothing on the other side. Either the covering law covers everything—or better, only trivialities are reiterated: each people has its own folk dances—or everything is reiterated, and (partially) differentiated in the course of reiteration, including justice itself.[24]

[5]

Reiterative universalism, however, is still a form of universalism. I have already suggested the ways in which it invites covering law expression: the warrant for reiteration (like Hampshire's license for distinctiveness) is itself universal. I don't mean that the warrant pre-exists every reiterative effort—though it might do that if we took it to be a divine warrant—but only that every claim to moral making, every claim to shape a way of life, justifies the claims that come later. And the experience of reiteration makes it possible, at least, for people to acknowledge the diversity of claims. Just as we are capable of recognizing a particular history as our own and another history as someone else's, and both of them as human histories, so we are capable of recognizing a particular understanding of autonomy and attachment as our own and another understanding as someone else's, and both of them as moral understandings. We can see the family resemblances and acknowledge at the same time the particular character of each member of the family. The acknowledgment is additive and inductive, as I suggested earlier, and so it doesn't require an external standpoint or a universal perspective (from which we might leap immediately to a covering law). We stand where we are and learn from our encounters with other people. What we learn is that we have no special standing; the claims that we make they make too, the children of Israel and the children of the Ethiopians. But it is a moral act to recognize otherness in this way. If reiteration is, as I believe, a true story, then it carries in its telling the sorts of moral limits that are usually said to come only from covering-law universalism.

Reiteration is also universal in its occasions. We may make our own moralities, but we don't make them randomly or any which way. The autonomous and attached agents are persons of a certain sort, morally creative human beings, and the moralities they create must fit the experiences they have.[25] The experiences that make for moral making have to do most often with lordship and bondage, that is, with oppression, vulnerability, and fear, and, pervasively, the exercise of power—experiences that require us to justify ourselves and to appeal for help to one another. We respond to the requirement creatively, which is to say, differently, though most often, perhaps, with the misplaced confidence that ours is the only legitimate response. What the historical record suggests, however, is that there is a wide range of possible responses and a significant number of actual responses that are legitimate in at least this sense, that they fit the experiences; they meet the requirements of their occasions.

These requirements can be inadequately or dishonestly met, but it is hard to see how they might be missed entirely. It is a common and often accurate criticism of existing moralities, for example, that they conceal the fact of oppression and so serve the interests of the oppressors. But no morality made by human beings, in the face of human experience, can serve the interests of oppressors alone. For no particular human interest can be served without opening the way to a wider service. Consider again the exodus story, which has as its apparent moral starting point Israel's consciousness of oppression. "And the children of Israel sighed by reason of the bondage, and they cried, and their cry came up to God by reason of the bondage."[26] The bondage was the reason for the cry, and this suggests an already established understanding of what a free human life is or might be like. However such lives are socially assigned, they can be claimed by anyone. We can be sure that the Philistines and the Syrians made similar (but not identical) claims: they also "cried"—though their cries were thematically as well as idiomatically different from those of the Israelites. Moral making encompasses and enables these cries, always providing (or sooner or later providing) principles of justice in terms of which they make sense.

Every response to a moral occasion can be criticized from the standpoint of other, earlier or concurrent, responses. We can learn from each other, even when the lesson learned isn't exactly what the other intended to teach. The value of the gift is not fixed by the giver. Nevertheless, there is a value in gifts: one nation can in fact be a "light" to another. Moral makers (legislators and prophets and also ordinary men and women) are like artists or writers who pick up elements of one another's style, or even borrow plots, not for the sake of imitation but in order to strengthen their own work. So we make ourselves better without making ourselves the same. Indeed, we cannot make ourselves the same without denying or repressing our creative power. But denial and repression are themselves creative, if perverse, uses of that same power and are always followed by other uses.

Consider now a more concrete illustration of our different responses to similar moral occasions. I begin with the strongest contemporary candidate for covering law status: the principle that human beings are entitled to equal respect and concern.[27] The relevant moral occasion is the experience of humiliation or degradation—conquest, slavery, ostracism, pariah status. Some of the men and women who are conquered, enslaved, ostracized, or declassed will respond with arguments about respect—drawing on the resources of the existing morality. But because this response has to be repeated again and again in different circumstances, with different resources, the idea of respect is itself differentiated and its names are multiplied: honor, dignity, worth, standing, recognition, esteem, and so on. These are all the same thing, perhaps, under a sufficiently abstract description; in practice, in everyday life, they are very different things. We can hardly treat everyone in accordance with all of them; nor is it clear, in fact, despite the covering law, that we can treat everyone equally in accordance with any one of them. The injunction of the covering law presupposes the universality that it is intended to create. Only God can show equal respect and concern for each of the creatures created in his image. This does not preclude particularly fashioned relationships with individual men and women, but it does preclude the sort of favoritism that the biblical God regularly displays— as, for example, when he prefers Abel's sacrifice to Cain's. The fact that even God is imagined to play favorites suggests how hard it is for us to imagine ourselves behaving differently.

In practice, again, we show equal respect and concern only when our roles require it and then only over the population relevant to the roles. Today, the injunction is most often directed to state officials: they must exemplify this sort of egalitarianism in all their dealings with citizens of the state (but not with anyone else). The citizens are, so to speak, collectively their favorites, but among citizens no further favoritism is allowed. And then the same injunction is reiterated for other officials and other sets of citizens. The effective covering law is that all officials should treat their *fellow* citizens with equal respect and concern. But this is another one of those covering laws that immediately makes for difference. Neither the same fellowship nor the same idea of respect will be universally shared—and then what demands respect is only indirectly the individual himself; it is more immediately the way of life, the culture of respect and concern, that he shares with his fellows. Hence, the law has this form: people should be treated in accordance with their own ideas about how they should be treated (or, to guard against arrogance and presumption and to protect people with inferiority complexes or what Marxists call "false consciousness," according to the ideal standards of their own way of life). That isn't an unimportant moral rule, but it is probably best understood in the reiterative rather than the covering-law mode.

We respect the different outcomes of the rule insofar as we recognize them as reiterations of our own moral effort, undertaken on similar occasions but in different historical circumstances and under the influence of different beliefs about the world. Respecting the outcomes does not preclude criticizing them, nor need it prevent us from calling into question the beliefs on which they rest. But the most common occasion for criticism is the failure of practical outcomes to match conceptual ones: performances falling short of promises. Thus we might express a special concern for our own children and recognize that another set of parents were doing the same thing—even though what they were actually doing, the concrete behavior through which their concern was expressed, was significantly different from our own. And then, since we know what it means to express concern, we will also be able to recognize cases where there was no genuine concern at all but rather abuse or neglect (or no equal concern but rather favoritism and discrimination). Similarly with states and officials: we have little difficulty in recognizing situations where, whatever is being said, the required moral effort is not in fact being made—as in the case, for example, of British officials and Irish peasants in the years 1845–1849.[28] But that is not to say that when the effort is made it must always be made in the same way.

So I have a special concern for my own children, my friends, my comrades, and my fellow citizens. And so do you. What reiterative universalism requires is that we recognize the legitimacy of these repeated acts of moral specialization. I make some people special, but that only means that they are special for me; and I am capable of acknowledging *and ought to acknowledge* that other people are special for you. What we might then think of as restricted or particularized covering laws extend across each field of specialization. But there is no cover across all the fields except for the cover provided by mutual recognition and then by our (different) accounts of the differentiated commonalities of reiteration. Perhaps there is a general rule that all the fields must be covered; we must meet the requirements of our moral occasions. We must explain and defend ourselves, ground our complaints, justify our claims, situate ourselves within the moral world, and contribute as best we can to its construction and reconstruction. But we do all these things among ourselves, in some particular here-and-now, working with a local set of concepts and values. This is only to say again that reiteration is a true story.

Reiterative universalism operates mostly within the limits of ours and theirs —not of Reason with a capital "R" but of our reason and their reason. It requires respect for the others, who are just as much moral makers as we are. That doesn't mean that the moralities we and they make are of equal value (or disvalue). There is no single uniform or eternal standard of value; standards get reiterated too. But at any moment in time, a given morality may prove inadequate to its occasions, or its practice may fail to measure up to its own standards or to a newly developed or dimly made out set of alternative standards—for reiteration is a continuous and contentious activity. The largest requirement of morality, then, the core principle of any universalism, is that we find some way of engaging in that activity while living in peace with the other actors.

PART 2. The National Question Revisited

[6]

In the second part of this chapter, I want to try to make the argument developed in the first do some serious work—to use the ideas of covering-law and reiterative universalism in a discussion of the national question. I will begin by restating the two ideas, dwelling for a moment on the second, which is less familiar. Covering-law universalism describes the standard philosophical effort to bring all human activities, all social arrangements, all political practices, under a single set of principles or a single conception of the right or the good. The idea of reiteration, by contrast, reflects an understanding that morality is made again and again; hence there can't be a single stable covering law. Moral creativity is plural in its incidence and differentiated in its outcomes—and yet, it is not wholly differentiated, as if the agents and subjects of all moralities had no common kinship. In fact, they can recognize themselves and one another as moral makers, and from this recognition there follows the minimalist universalism of reiteration.

A rough analogy may serve to illustrate my argument. Think of a hundred architects, from different times and places, each one engaged in designing the same sort of building, a home, say, or a temple or a school. They are each trying as best they can to get the building right, a goal they have in common with moral makers. But they are not trying to design the same building—the one perfect building, which, if any of them did get it right, would make all future designs unnecessary (we would just go on building that one building over and over again). In principle, they could all get it right, even if all their buildings were radically different from one another. For though their efforts are similarly occasioned by the need for a place to live or pray or study, their circumstances and conceptions are dissimilar; they understand places differently, and also living, praying, and studying. In practice, of course, they won't get it right; all their buildings will be controversial, subject to criticism and improvement, serving eventually as the background of new designs and new understandings of design. At the same time, since they are all designing buildings for human beings, there will be certain features common to all the buildings, and reiterated theories about these features will always be one source of architectural criticism.

In a similar way, morally creative men and women produce many different moralities, none of them the one perfect morality that would render their creativity superfluous. From the differentiated commonalities of these creations, we can recognize all of them as the work of human hands, and our accounts of what is common and why provide us with a set (itself never perfectly understood or articulated) of universal constraints. But one can make too much of these constraints, so that they overwhelm the creative effort, pressing us all to live in accordance with a single ideal, a practical orthodoxy of one sort or another. I have argued that this is the usual thrust of the covering-law view—and that it is better, in morality as in architecture, to leave room for the reiteration of difference. But what if the things we make (buildings, codes, countries) turn out to be ugly?

[7]

It is not only morality but also immorality that gets reiterated in the course of human history. There are, however, important differences between the two reiterations. We would not talk of "making" immoralities, only of acting immorally; for when we act immorally we do not act in accordance with a theory of immorality and we don't conceptualize our activity or elaborate it into a series of injunctions and rules. We usually lie about what we are doing, sometimes to other people, sometimes to ourselves. We do evil, thinking or pretending that we are doing good. There are contradictions, then, between what is said and what is done whenever what is done is wrong. But the contradiction between theory and practice, pervasive in morality, is entirely missing in immorality. No theoretical construction of evil, no "doctrine of ill-doing" exists that can be betrayed in practice.

This point is not a logical one. We can easily enough imagine a theorist of evil who was also a timid soul—a hypocrite, therefore, who failed to live down to the standards he defended. Perhaps the Marquis de Sade, despite a few tawdry adventures, was a person of this sort. But there have not been many such people. The positive doctrinal creation, the making of immorality, is as uncommon as the practice of immorality is common. People do evil in the same repetitive way in which they do good, but they don't think about evil in the same way. It may be that there is less to think about, at least in this sense: that goodness is more readily elaborated and differentiated, while evil has a more singular and uniform character.[29] I don't mean to deny the imaginativeness that can be invested in cruelty, say, but cruelty is imaginative in practice, not in theory. It would be a waste of creative energy to develop an account, let alone a series of accounts, of the bad life. We understand the bad life in negative or oppositional terms. But it is not the case that every version of the good life has an opposite that is a version of the bad life. Rather, the standard form of badness is an opposition to or denial of the principles and rules that make all the versions of goodness possible—and then evil is an overt, active, and inventive opposition.

We act immorally whenever we deny to other people the warrant for or what I will now call the rights of reiteration, that is, the right to act autonomously and the right to form attachments in accordance with a particular understanding of the good life. Or, immorality is commonly expressed in a refusal to recognize in others the moral agency and the creative powers that we claim for ourselves. And immorality passes into evil when the refusal is willful and violent, turning the others, against their will, into beings "less than human" (or, less human than we are). Conduct of this sort will usually be accompanied by theoretical justifications, but these will not take the form of creative immoralities. Justification is always moral in character, and the justification of evil is no exception. The central problem of moral creativity is that it encompasses and justifies evil actions. My purpose in the second part of this chapter is to address this problem, looking in some detail at one of the most commonly reiterated theories of autonomy and attachment, the theory of nationalism.

Certainly, there is evil enough in our domestic societies, among ourselves, in families, schools, markets, corporations, and states. But it is probably true that the greatest evils in human history have occurred and continue to occur between nations, and a certain sort of nationalism has been the political carrier of these evils, as well as their theoretical justification. To see our own nation in a certain way is also to will evil toward some or all of the others. At the same time, however, nationalism is one of the most direct expressions of collective autonomy and attachment. That is why, in Part 1, I took national self-determination as the paradigmatic form of moral reiteration: first one nation, and then another. The paradigm, to be sure, is conceptually limited and historically contingent. The nation is by no means the most important of the collectivities within which moral ideas and ways of life have been elaborated. The experience of ancient Israel in this regard is distinctly unusual. Even with reference to self-determination, the national entity, itself differently constituted and understood in different historical periods, could as easily be replaced by the clan or the tribe or the city-state or the community of faith.[30] The argument, for better and worse, would be the same. Any collectivity can provide the institutional structures and the patterns of agency necessary for working out a version of the good life. And any collectivity can display the egoism, arrogance, and general nastiness that we associate today with the rogue nation. In any case, it is this association that I want to investigate.

[8]

The nation is for us the chief representative of particularity. And on one standard philosophical view, particularity makes for nastiness; groups like the nation, as soon as they are politically organized, eagerly take up the business of self-aggrandizement, seizing, dominating, destroying rival groups (which act in exactly the same way whenever they can). Edmund Wilson, in his book on the American Civil War, expresses this view in biological terms: "In a recent . . . film showing life at the bottom of the sea, a primitive organism called a sea slug is seen gobbling up small organisms through a large orifice at one end of its body; confronted with another sea slug of an only slightly lesser size, it ingurgitates that, too. . . . The wars fought by human beings are stimulated as a rule . . . by the same instincts as the voracity of the sea slug."[31]

But it would be difficult to construct a plausible account of international society on this model. And if we replace instincts with interests and interests with conceptions of interest (or ideologies), we won't get anything like a uniform voraciousness. Nations, even nation-states, behave very differently according to their (reiterated and differentiated) understandings of themselves and of their place in the world. Writing about individuals in domestic society,

Machiavelli suggests a class basis for such understandings: "If we consider the objects of the nobles and of the people, we must see that the first have a great desire to dominate, while the latter have only the wish not to be dominated . . . to live in the enjoyment of liberty."[32] Conceivably, there are "noble" and "plebeian" nations, the first always a threat, the second always threatened. It is not only a question of instinct and size, as with Wilson's sea slugs, but also of ambition and honor. And then the classic solution to the problem of domination is this: the less ambitious or smaller and weaker individuals/nations, whose only wish is not to be dominated, band together, invent something like covering-law universalism, and create a political agency—the state—to enforce the law. In international society, covering-law universalism, were it ever to be fully effective, would require a universal state.

But the classic solution works best in domestic society, where the nobles are indeed defeated, though usually not, as Machiavelli advised, exterminated, and a state is fashioned which, sometimes at least, protects its members from domination. What lies behind this success, when and where it occurs, is the common culture of the two classes. Though their material life is very different, and though they develop somewhat different moral understandings and an often antagonistic politics, they are likely to share a wide range of cultural artifacts: language, religion, historical memory, the calendar and its holidays, the sense of place, a specific experience of art and music—and as a result of some or all of these, what we call "nationality." The emergent nation-state, then, can be viewed by its members as an appropriate and already familiar framework for the exercise of autonomy and the formation of attachments. The strongest evidence that they do in fact view it this way came in 1914, with the collapse of Marxist internationalism. The international proletariat, apparently, had no common culture; nor is there much commonality in what is sometimes called, with more hope than insight, the community of nations. Hence the plebeian nations are unlikely to imagine a universal state (as individual plebeians might well imagine the nation-state) as a framework within which *their own* culture could find expression. Perhaps no existing culture would find expression in such a frame; perhaps the language of the universal state would be Esperanto and its morality an Esperanto-like code. But the more plausible expectation of the plebeian nations is that universalism would take shape as a "noble" imposition.

So it appears, indeed, to the noble nations as well. And it is at this point that their national ambition becomes morally interesting. If ambition is merely appetite, if it is satisfactorily explained as a will to power, a desire to dominate for the sheer pleasure (or for any of the other advantages) of domination, then the nobility of the noble nations has only psychological interest. We have to understand it in order to repress or contain it. But national leaders and the intellectuals they enlist commonly give reasons for their pursuit of domination. They need to justify themselves; hence their reasons are moral reasons, which take the form—I am not sure that any other is available—of covering-law universalism. They seek to extend their power, so the leaders and intellectuals say, only in order to enforce the law:

> Make ye sure to each his own
> That he reap where he hath sown.

Kipling, of course, is a poet of imperialism, and we are likely to think of nationalism as the ideology of anti-imperial revolt. But empires in the modern world are acquired and sustained by nations, and the ideology of imperialism is also nationalist in character, inviting us to recognize (and approve of) a nation-with-a-mission. Freedom is the primary goal of the anti-imperial revolt; the imperial nation aims higher—at civilization, enlightenment, modernity, democracy, communism, and so on. In a brilliant book on the nation as an "imagined community," Benedict Anderson has argued that nationalism necessarily involves an acceptance of limits: "The nation is imagined as *limited* because even the largest of them . . . has finite, if elastic boundaries, beyond which lie other nations. No nation imagines itself coterminous with mankind. The most messianic nationalists do not dream of a day when all the members of the human race will join their nation in the way that it was possible, in certain epochs, for, say, Christians to dream of a wholly Christian planet."[33] That is true enough, and helps to explain why reiterative universalism has long been a favorite doctrine of nationalist intellectuals. But it has never been the only doctrine; there have always been other intellectuals who, if they did not dream of a wholly naturalized humanity, no foreigners left in the world, dreamt nonetheless of a humanity whose life would be shaped by the values of one of the nations that composed it—the whole world, say, made safe for democracy.

This is covering-law universalism; it is different, no doubt, from the religious version of the same thing but not entirely different. Indeed, to imagine a nation-with-a-mission is to come very close to Jewish, if not to Christian, understandings of universalism. It is appropriate, then, that one of the strongest defenses of the idea of a national mission comes from a contemporary Jewish philosopher. "No nation in the world," writes Martin Buber, "has [self-preservation and self-assertion] as its only task, for just as an individual who wishes only to preserve and assert himself leads an unjustified and meaningless existence, so a nation with no other aim deserves to pass away." Every nation, Buber says, has (or should quickly find!) a "mission" of its own—a claim that sets up the central problem of his political thought: how to draw the "line of demarcation" between different and possibly conflicting national missions so that all of them can be (reiteratively) pursued. But though it is his word, "mission" does not seem to me the word that best expresses Buber's meaning— for it belongs to the world of the covering law, and that is not his world. He is arguing for a commitment to the kind of belief or value that might inspire and sustain a common life and lift it out of mere existence. No doubt he has views about the most appropriate beliefs and values, at least for his own people. At the same time, however, he denies that there is any "scale of values" with which national commitments can be ranked and ordered.[34] Among missionaries, such denials are uncommon, if not impossible. Nor are national missions, especially noble ones, at all easy to mark off from one another. They have global reach; they reflect the highest aspirations; and they require a kind of triumph that is incompatible with Buber's commitment to reiteration. If one believes in the covering law, how is it possible to avoid the further belief that some missions are more urgent, more valuable to a suffering or benighted humanity, than others?

In fact, what I have been calling "covering-law universalism" often takes more modest forms: the civilizing mission of this or that nation may extend only to a few neighboring tribes; the correct ideological position may be imposed only on the country next door; immoral and unnatural practices may be stamped out only in the scattered provinces of a minor empire. One does what one can. All such efforts, however, are universalist in spirit—first, because they are governed by a "law" whose coverage is not limited to the people among whom it was first enforced; and second, because they are aimed at the good of other people. We are inclined today to doubt the legitimacy of the coverage and the sincerity of the aim—except in our own case, when doubt is commonly repressed. But I suspect that the legitimacy and sincerity have always been doubted, except in the local case. Covering-law universalism is a jealous God, and all the other gods but mine are idols.

Of course, the covering law is always a cover for expansion and exploitation. But it would be wrong to assume that that is all it is. There has probably never been a case of national aggrandizement that did not draw on, that did not have to draw on, the idealism of (some of) the members of the nation. And idealism here means their belief in this or that version of covering-law universalism and in themselves as agents of the law. They carry to foreign lands a culture to which other people ought to be assimilated or a doctrine by which they ought to be ruled. They teach the others a way of life that more closely expresses natural law or divine command or historical development. Might such beliefs ever be true? In his articles on India, Marx argued that a particular set of them was true, while at the same time denying the idealism of their agents. The more advanced nations, as if moved by an invisible hand, did good for the people they conquered and oppressed. "England it is true, in causing a social revolution in Hindustan, was actuated only by the vilest interests. . . . But that is not the question. The question is, can mankind fulfill its destiny without a fundamental revolution in the social state of Asia? If not, whatever may have been the crimes of England, she was the unconscious tool of history in bringing about the revolution."[35] In the next historical stage, socialist governments in the advanced nations would play the same revolutionary role with greater self-awareness and, presumably, less violence. But Marx's argument depends, like all other covering-law universalisms, on the further belief that mankind has a single destiny, which all its members must alike "fulfill." We have no way of knowing our destiny, however, and there is probably more historical warrant for expectations of difference—even in the local uses, say, of new and universal technologies. For now, at least, every attempt to enforce singularity is an act of faith, exactly as such attempts were at the time of the Islamic conquests or the crusades of Christendom.

Marx was also wrong to insist that the English in India were "actuated *only* by the vilest interests." No doubt, their interests were mixed, as human interests always are. We would probably not be inclined to say of John Stuart Mill, working in the London offices of the East India Company, that he was doing something vile, moved only by personal or national selfishness.[36] But we do judge imperial expansion and colonial domination harshly, and for good reason. Expansion and domination deny to their victims the rights of reiteration: autonomous development and freely chosen attachment. The denial is immediately effective even if its intention is, as it surely would have been had Marx or Mill been in charge, to vindicate those same rights in the long run. For what underlies this benevolent intention is the morally dangerous belief that the victims have somehow lost their powers of agency, their cultural and moral creativity, their capacity to shape their own lives. They are dim, unenlightened, barbarian, ignorant, and passive—trapped in a stagnant traditionalism, cut off from history itself, helplessly waiting to be rescued by the more advanced nations.

[9]

The victim nations, plebeians all, prove this belief to be false whenever they resist the power that dominates them—as the Indians did in 1857, in the Sepoy Rebellion, long before they had reaped the benefits of the English social revolution. Indeed, the resistance falsifies not only the imperial nation's view of its subjects but also, soon enough, its view of itself. To sustain their empire, the agents of enlightenment must adopt the manner and methods of the barbarians. A harsh cruelty is necessary to enforce the covering laws of civilization and to further the cause of progress. And when the resistance is renewed, the cruelty is increased. Nationalism, in its best-known version, is the creed of the resistance, especially of the resistance in its second phase, when self-consciousness has been heightened by repression. It is "the ideology," as Tom Nairn has written, "of weaker, less developed countries struggling to free themselves from alien oppression."[37] Each nationalist movement produces its own variant of this ideology. I shall make no attempt to catalogue the actual and possible varieties; they are best understood as the products of reiteration: similar struggles (or at least struggles to which we give the same name) with different ideological and practical outcomes. But these are now reactive reiterations, and they involve certain distortions in what we might imagine as the normal processes of cultural production—when production is free from both the constraints of imperial power and the imperatives of resistance. Perhaps normality of this sort is utopian: normal nowhere. Distortion is still the right word to describe the pressures that push (some) new nations toward an imperialism of their own.

Nationalist ideology in the "less developed countries" often has a forced or hothouse quality. The making of cultures and moralities is a process within which, at any particular moment, many elements are in play. But the effort to generate a coherent nationalism, driven by political urgencies, has highly artificial results; its protagonists are less interested in sustaining the process than in inventing a homogeneous and unilinear "tradition." And then the nationalist movement or the state that it creates will try to suppress whatever doesn't fit the invention. It is indeed a problem of reiterative processes that they can themselves be reiterated; there is no patent, as Anderson has written, on the idea of liberation. If the global reach of imperial covering laws is challenged by nationalism, so the local reach of nationalism can be challenged by still more localized and parochial communities—Greater India, for example, by Pakistan, Kashmir, Dravidistan, and so on—each one claiming its right to enact its own culture. The leaders and intellectuals of nationalist movements commonly demand a full stop, absolute loyalty to the nation as they conceive it. But that conception, designed to serve an immediate political purpose, is necessarily subject to further development and differentiation.[38] The test of every nationalism, then, is the "nation" that comes next. I will come back to this point later on.

The "forcing" of nationalism has a second result; it helps to account for the regressive character of many nationalist ideologies. I hasten to add that "regressive" is a misleading term if it suggests that the processes of cultural creativity move in a single direction, toward a goal that is uniformly affirmed. But they do *move*, and just as the need to generate a coherent ideology may cut off the movement, so the need to oppose the "civilizing" or progressive ends of covering-law universalism may reverse it. Then the new ideology is likely to proclaim the sacredness of everything old and archaic in the national heritage and to assign a higher value than was ever assigned before to religious fundamentalism and cultural integrity. Gandhi's spinning wheel is the sort of symbol that many nationalists seek, evocative of a cherished, if mostly mythical, past.[39]

Normally, the ancient and honorable usages of the nation are subject to a continuous (and also continuously contested) revision. Now the agents of revision are likely to be called disloyal and its products inauthentic. And though authenticity is, one would think, always relative to a particular national history (and dubious even in its relativity, given the actual variousness and the internal contradictions of all such histories), nationalist intellectuals often reach for a stronger argument: that their culture, morality, and politics is authentic *tout court*—real, historical, orthodox, organic, faithful, uncorrupted, pure, and enduring—and so superior to all the synthetic, unnatural, and hybrid creations of other peoples. Here they imitate the universalists they oppose, insisting that national cultures can be ranked on a single scale. They adopt new criteria and reverse the old order, but they retain the ranking. In this sense, though not in many others, nationalist perversity resembles enlightenment virtue.

But this response to imperial enlightenment and its covering laws, this invention of a "superior" traditionalism, is often inadequate to its occasion—and it suggests very nicely what such inadequacy means and how it can be recognized. The occasion is a history of oppressive and degrading rule; the response is both ideological and practical; and it is inadequate insofar as it reproduces, rather than resolves, the occasion. Nations with "superior" traditions are quick to impose themselves on smaller and weaker nations in their midst or on their borders, quick to repeat what Isaiah Berlin, in his essay on Herder, describes as "the barbarous disregard of . . . spontaneous, natural forms of human self-expression."[40] The disregard is only made easier by the new oppressors' claim that they stand at the very top of the scale of naturalness and spontaneity.

[10]

The rank ordering of cultures always threatens the men and women whose culture it devalues. There is no innocent ranking, as if we could give grades that were merely hortatory and not invidious. Low grades are invitations to, and potential justifications for, "barbarous disregard," and that last phrase translates often enough into a politics of conquest and repression. But have I not just given a low grade to certain national cultures? Have I not set up a rank ordering according to which nations committed to rank ordering rank low? Yes, I have done exactly that: following the minimalist universalism that governs reiteration, I have proposed a very limited ranking, which is compatible with recognizing rather than disregarding (most of) the "spontaneous, natural forms of human self-expression." But I want to leave open the possibility that "barbarous disregard" is also, sometimes, spontaneous and natural. If it is, then it needs theoretical devaluation and political control. This is only to acknowledge that while there are (as the prophet Isaiah proclaimed) blessings available to every nation, not every nationalism is blessed.

The point of a limited ranking of this sort is to protect the commonality of nations from the "noble" nations—and also from plebeian nations aspiring to join the ranks of the noble. The point is to devalue nobility whenever it aims, as Machiavelli thought it always would, at domination. I have argued that covering-law universalism, in its different versions, is the most important of the doctrines that justify (I do not say bring about) this "noble" nationalism. I want to argue now that the theory of reiterative universalism provides the best account of nationalism in general and the most adequate constraint on its various immoralities. The adequacy, of course, is conceptual, not practical; I shall not have much to say about practical constraints. But then, why isn't the standard of adequacy met perfectly well by a single covering law that prohibits conquest and oppression? Do not most versions of covering-law universalism include a law of that sort? The problem lies with the other laws, which commonly require national cultures to conform to a single standard and which devalue those that fall short. A doctrine is not conceptually adequate by virtue of one of it concepts, so long as this one is undermined by all the others. Marxism (or Marxism-Leninism) once again provides a useful example, when it simultaneously upholds the right of national self-determination and defends revolutionary wars against nations that resist the forces of historical advance. The Marxist concept of developmental stages, even when it is conceived in predictive rather than normative terms, stands uneasily alongside the concept of self-determination.[41]

Reiterative universalism, by contrast, makes no predictions at all. Or, at least, it makes no predictions about the substance of the successive reiterations. There is a general prediction, suggested by those deviant lines from Micah that I quoted in Part 1: if each of us walks with his own god, then all of us will sit at peace under our vines and fig trees. In his defense of religious toleration, John Locke makes a similar prediction: "The establishment of this one thing," he wrote, "would take away all ground of complaints and tumults upon account of conscience." I suppose that it is a piece of extraordinary optimism to suggest that there won't be ungrounded complaints and tumults, but that was Locke's claim: "There is only one thing which gathers people into seditious commotions, and that is oppression."[42] The parallel argument for international society would hold that oppression is the sole cause of all the wars of national liberation and national unification that have plagued the modern world. The peace of vines and fig trees will finally arrive when consciences are no longer constrained and nations are set free.

I have in the past defended a weakened and chastened version of this argument.[43] It does appear, however, that peace is a more immediate outcome of religious toleration than of national liberation. The most obvious reason for this is that churches do not come attached to territories, and so the reiterative processes that split and divide churches do not often provoke territorial disputes. The control of holy places is disputed, of course, but mostly it is otherworldly territory that is at issue. Nationalism, by contrast, is much more significantly an ideology of place. New nationalisms make for contested places, either because populations are intermixed or because borders are uncertain; and these contests are readily enacted in blood. But whatever nationalist leaders and intellectuals say about the places for which they fight, no body of land is like the body of the baby brought before King Solomon: it does not die if it is divided. Partition is almost always an available (though rarely a neat) solution in territorial disputes.

New nationalisms are probably more dangerous when they take on universalist missions than when they make localized claims to territory. Now they are like the old religions, before religion was domesticated by toleration, and they often assume a religious character. Advocates of enlightenment universalism are then surprised to find themselves no longer alone in the field—secular modernizers, for example, suddenly confronted by religious fundamentalists, men and women complacent about the future overtaken by men and women passionate about the past. Theorists of reiteration, who are equally incapable of predicting the next version of cultural or political nationalism, at least expect to be surprised. They are prepared for a succession of nationalist claims, and they are also prepared to make some (modest) judgments about the successive nations.

[11]

The critical test of any nationalism comes when it has to cope with the surprise of a new nation or, more accurately, of a new liberation movement laying claim to nationhood. The experience is common enough, and the test, I suppose, is commonly failed. There are many examples: Turkey and the Armenians, Nigeria and the Ibos, Iraq and the Kurds, Israel and the Palestinians—though in the last two of these, the story is not yet over. In the first two, the number of dead Armenians and Ibos suggests the extent of the evil that failure involves and helps to explain the harsh judgment that is so often passed on nationalism as an ideology. But it is important to stress that nationalism in these cases was also the ideology of the victims, and though it is always possible to condemn both sides—the victors for the murders they have actually committed and the victims for the murders they would have committed—I think it more seemly at least to consider the possibility that the defeated nation, had it encountered a less harsh opposition, would have opted for peace. Sometimes it would, and sometimes it would not: no singular judgment is possible, as if all nationalists, everywhere, stood in defiance of some universal covering law. Eric Hobsbawm argued for something like this wholesale condemnation when he wrote that "nationalism by definition subordinates all other interests to those of its specific 'nation.' "[44] This is to understand nationalism as a form of collective egoism. It is better understood, however, as a form of collective individualism—which is to say that nationalist movements and nation-states, like individual men and women, behave both well and badly and must be judged accordingly.[45]

There is nothing that we should feel bound to condemn in the nationalist politics defended, for example, by Giuseppe Mazzini, who founded Young Italy and then went on to help in the founding of Young Switzerland and Young Germany. Like the man who wanted to dance at every wedding, Mazzini was eager to endorse every reiteration of Italy's national struggle—but he remained throughout his life an Italian nationalist. His liberal nationalism, at least as he lived it, is a classic example of reiterative universalism. When he wrote about it, however, he did not always capture the full force of reiteration. Consider his famous image of the universal orchestra. In this orchestra, each nation plays its own instrument, but apparently not its own music, for the result, Mazzini seems to suggest, is a single harmonious symphony.[46] It is useful to compare this supposedly happy picture with Marx's reference to the orchestra, in the third volume of *Capital*, as a model for cooperative work in a socialist factory.[47] This is also odd given what we know about the dictatorial behavior of directors in most great orchestras, but the reference is appropriate in this sense: that the workers in a factory cooperate in the production of a single product. There is no similar cooperation in international society, where the different national players are likely to produce a cacophony rather than a symphony—music only to the modernist (or perhaps the postmodernist) ear. In fact, there isn't one performance but a series of performances, and nationalist intellectuals like Mazzini are to be praised when they acknowledge the right of the other players to play what they please. They are to be praised even more highly if they are also prepared to listen to what the others play.

Don't some of the others play well and some badly? It will certainly seem so to those of us who are accustomed to our own music and (even more) to those of us who take our own music to be mandated by a universal aesthetics. But all that we can say with any assurance is that they play *what they play* well or badly—and no doubt have their own critics who tell them so. This kind of criticism can also be morally important, and I don't mean to underestimate it. Nor do I mean to underestimate our own less assured judgments about the internal harmonies and disharmonies, so to speak, of particular national cultures. But these are not judgments about nationalism in general or in particular. The proper judgment of nationalism has to do with the attitudes and practices it adopts toward other nations.

There is no universal model for a national culture, no covering law or set of laws that controls the development of a nation. But there is a universal model for the behavior of one nation toward the others—a model that Herder thought natural to all nations: "He [did] not see," writes Berlin, "why one community, absorbed in the development of its own native talent, should not respect a similar activity on the part of others."[48] This is indeed the core principle of reiterative universalism, but nothing in recent history suggests that the respect it enjoins comes naturally, not to old nations and not even to new ones, despite their own recent experience of oppression and liberation. Often enough, as I have already suggested, new nations are new oppressors, because of the mono-lithic character of their nationalist ideology or because of the claims they make to cultural authenticity or to a "nobility" of their own, and then to a universalizing mission. Sometimes they are genuinely insecure in their newness, uncertain of their own political unity and physical safety, threatened by (but also, often, more fearful than they need be of) the national minorities in their midst. In all such cases, reiterative universalism operates as a constraint, ruling out policies that are inconsistent with the further "development of native talent" and local cultures. But it also happens that new nationalisms, "absorbed" in their own development, literally fail to see the nation that is standing next in line. They are self-absorbed and blind. Now the necessary moral task is admonition, a kind of moral pointing toward the other. Martin Buber provides a nice example, very much in the reiterative mode. In 1929, responding to those of his fellow-Zionists who thought Arab nationalism an "artificial" (that is, an imperial) creation, he wrote: "We know that . . . we have genuine national unity and a real nationalist movement; why should we assume that these do not exist among the Arabs?"[49]

[12]

The advantage of the reiterative mode is that it recognizes the value of what it admonishes. Confronting nationalist blindness, it is not itself blind to the strength and meaning of nationalism (Buber remained a Zionist). Here the contrast with covering-law universalists is especially clear, and I should like to make this contrast the conclusion of my argument. Defenders of one or another version of the covering law have sometimes also defended the cause of the nation that comes next. We may take Jean-Paul Sartre's commitment to Algerian national liberation as a classic case. (Though France was not itself a new nation, it had only just emerged from a period of occupation and resistance.) Sartre's politics in the 1950s was very brave, but it was also blind with a blindness that is as characteristic of universalism as self-absorption is characteristic of nationalism. For the foundation of his politics was the firm belief that Algerian nationalists were morally and politically identical to French leftists (like himself) and would create a just society in accordance with the universal principles acknowledged on the French left.[50] The FLN, Sartre believed (setting himself up to be surprised), was the historic agent of his own covering-law universalism. This was a radically false view of the FLN, but it was held with such confidence that it is difficult even to imagine what Sartre would have said had he understood its falseness: the possibility, so far as we can tell from his writings, was never considered. What would his general position have been had he recognized that reiterated liberations produce in each case a new and different, and often morally problematic, outcome?

When it is combined with covering-law universalism, this recognition can give rise to a purely instrumental view of national liberation. According to Eric Hobsbawm, this is the proper Marxist view: "The fundamental criterion of Marxist pragmatic judgment has always been whether nationalism as such, or any specific case of it, advances the cause of socialism."[51] Only those liberation movements that get things right, that hold the correct ideological position, deserve support. (Not quite true: there may be Marxist reasons for supporting a particular movement that have nothing to do with ideology but only with the international balance of power. This is an even more radical instrumentalism, and I won't take it up here.) Sartrean blindness makes it virtually impossible to criticize liberation movements; Hobsbawm's pragmatic Marxism provides a clearcut critical standard. But this doesn't seem to me the right standard, for it can't be the case that socialism is the one and only legitimate nationalist goal. It is, indeed, a misunderstanding of the phrase "national liberation" to insist that the process it describes can have only one endpoint, for this denies to the adjective any qualifying power over the noun. Liberation properly depends upon its subject, that is, upon the history of the nation, the autonomous processes of cultural creativity, the pattern of mutual attachment, and so on. When we criticize nationalist movements, we must look, as I have already argued, at the attitude they adopt toward other nations, not at the quality of their internal life. That is not to say, again, that we can't also criticize their internal life. But reiterative rights don't wait upon ideological correctness.

A nation is a historic community, connected to a meaningful place, enacting and revising a way of life, aiming at political or cultural self-determination. I have waited until my last breath to offer this definition, since I do not want to suggest too strong a link between nation and community. Communities can take other forms, as they have in the past and no doubt will in the future. But all the forms have pluralism in common—if communities are real, they are also different—and nations are probably the best current examples of this pluralism. When we think of the nation we are led to think of boundaries (as Anderson argues) and then we are led to think of other nations: this is a useful intellectual progress.

Reiterative universalism offers a way of understanding and justifying those boundaries. There is no sure way, given the circumstances of national life, to get them right. Nor is it any part of my argument that these boundaries should always be state boundaries. Political sovereignty is one outcome of national liberation, not the only one, not always the best possible one. If reiteration makes for a world of nations, it also makes for what the American political theorist Horace Kallen called a "nation of nationalities."[52] It is compatible with any political framework that permits cultural pluralism and diverse ways of life. Multinational empires, though they are inconsistent with democratic principles, are not inconsistent with the principles of reiterative universalism, so long as the different nations are allowed to live in accordance with their own ways, free from czarist "russification," for example, or any of its historical equivalents.

"Russification" provides a nice illustration of the wasteful and no doubt unjust war of state officials against cultural creativity and pluralism. Politics aims at unity: from many, one. But this is a unity that can be achieved in very different ways: by accommodating difference (as in the case of religious toleration) as well as by repressing it, by inclusion as well as forced assimilation, negotiation as well as coercion, federal or corporate arrangements as well as centralized states. Reiterative universalism favors the first alternative in each of these pairs. Given the first alternative, it is not incompatible with a common citizenship embracing a plurality of nations.[53]

Covering-law universalism, by contrast, offers a way of explaining and justifying assimilation, integration, and unification, within and across states and empires; it looks to a time when all nations converge on the same moral and political regime or to a time when nationalism itself has been definitively superceded and all boundaries erased. These ends can be described in more evocative terms: global democracy, international communism, world government, the rule of the messiah. I mean to disparage all of these, though not because I find the laws or ways of life they propose entirely unattractive. I mean to disparage them because they would require us to disregard or repress processes of cultural creativity and patterns of mutual attachment that we ought to value. Nor could we sustain the disregard or the repression without violating the most important of the covering laws—without acting immorally, though always, of course, with "noble" intentions.

NOTES

1. Paul D. Hanson, *The People Called: The Growth of Community in the Bible* (San Francisco: Harper and Row, 1986), 312–24.
2. Isaiah 49:6; cf. 42:6. All biblical quotations are from the King James Version.
3. Isaiah 2:3.

4. *Daily Prayer Book: Ha-Siddur Ha-Shalem,* trans. Philip Birnbaum (New York: Hebrew Publishing Co., 1977), 138. See the discussion of this line in George Foot Moore, *Judaism in the First Centuries of the Christian Era: The Age of the Tannaim* (Cambridge: Harvard University Press, 1962), 1:228–31, 2:371–74.

5. Rudyard Kipling, "A Song of the English," in *Rudyard Kipling's Verse: Inclusive Edition, 1885–1926* (New York: Doubleday, Page, 1927), 194–95.

6. Judah Halevi, *The Kuzari: An Argument for the Faith of Israel,* trans. Hartwig Hirschfeld (New York: Schocken Books, 1964), 226–27; Samson Raphael Hirsch, *Horeb: A Philosophy of Jewish Laws and Observances,* trans. I. Grunfeld (London: Soncino Press, 1962), 1:143–44.

7. Amos 9:7.

8. Isaiah 19:20–25.

9. See the discussion of tolerance in David B. Wong, *Moral Relativity* (Berkeley: University of California Press, 1984), chap. 12.

10. Jeremiah 18:7–10.

11. Micah 4:4–5.

12. According to the rabbis of the Talmud, human difference, if not quite human creativity, is the special feature of divine creation: "If a man strikes many coins from one mold, they all resemble one another, but the Supreme King of Kings . . . fashioned every man in the stamp of the first man, and yet not one of them resembles his fellow" (Babylonian Talmud, Sanhedrin 37a).

13. I have been helped here by David Hartman's account of the moral meaning of creation in *A Living Covenant: The Innovative Spirit in Traditional Judaism* (New York: Free Press, 1985), esp. 22–24, 265–66.

14. Deuteronomy 30:19.

15. Leo Tolstoy, *Anna Karenina,* pt. 1, chap. 1.

16. Anders Nygren, *Agape and Eros,* trans. Philip Watson (Chicago: University of Chicago Press, 1982).

17. Edmund Burke, *Reflections on the Revolution in France* (London: J. M. Dent [Everyman's Library], 1910), 75.

18. Amos 5:24.

19. Stuart Hampshire, *Morality and Conflict* (Cambridge: Harvard University Press, 1983), chap. 6.

20. Ibid., 134–35.

21. Ibid., 139.

22. Ibid., 136

23. H. L. A. Hart, *The Concept of Law* (Oxford: Clarendon Press, 1961), 189–95.

24. An argument somewhat similar to Hampshire's is suggested in Aurel Kolnai's essay "Erroneous Conscience." Kolnai has a fine sensitivity to the thickness and diversity of moral experience. He argues, nonetheless, against the claim that there are "different moralities." Morality is necessarily singular in character, but it is diversified by our "affiliations." For moral experience is always the experience of particular people, located in a time and place, and attached to particular other people. "Thus the social entities to which we naturally

belong or which we join by free choice embody, among other things, certain distinctive moral features, performances, and accents . . . our loyalty toward them conforms to a general moral demand [i.e., a "covering law"], and in its turn begets certain derived moral obligations: from our familial, national, religious, political, etc., affiliations will arise for each of us a set of moral bylaws." A distinct set, not just because the bylaws have as their "incidental point of application" different families and nations, but also because the affiliations they reflect constitute in each case a distinct "framework of life" or "sphere of duties" with its own "features, performances, and accents." Morality is particularized through the operation of what Kolnai calls "non-moral facts" (our associational inclinations, our passionate attachments). But the processes set in motion by these "facts" would seem to go very far toward producing, if not different moralities, then different understandings and experiences of morality—hence, different ways of life. The "moral obligation of honesty" would doubtless survive these processes with only minor variation, but it is hard to believe that the rules of distributive justice would not be significantly differentiated in their course. (*Ethics, Value and Reality: Selected Papers of Aurel Kolnai,* introduction by Bernard Williams and David Wiggins [Indianapolis: Hackett, 1978], 21–22.)

25. Anthony Smith, *The Ethnic Origins of Nations* (New York: Basil Blackwell, 1988).

26. Exodus 2:23.

27. See Ronald Dworkin, *Taking Rights Seriously* (Cambridge: Harvard University Press, 1977), 180–83.

28. C. B. Woodham-Smith, *The Great Hunger: Ireland 1845–1849* (London: Harper and Row, 1962).

29. This argument was suggested to me by Adi Ophir. Compare Barrington Moore on "the unity of misery and the diversity of happiness," in *Reflections on the Causes of Human Misery and upon Certain Proposals to Eliminate Them* (Boston: Beacon Press, 1972), chap. 1.

30. But see Anthony Smith, *The Ethnic Origins of Nations* (New York: Basil Blackwell, 1988), which suggests that our national communities, though not our nationalist ideologies, are very old.

31. Edmund Wilson, *Patriotic Gore: Studies in the Literature of the American Civil War* (New York: Oxford University Press, 1962), xi.

32. Niccolò Machiavelli, *The Discourses,* bk. 1, chap. 5, trans. Christian Detmold (New York: Modern Library, 1940), 122.

33. Benedict Anderson, *Imagined Communities: Reflections on the Origin and Spread of Nationalism* (London: Verso, 1983), 16.

34. Martin Buber, *Israel and the World: Essays in a Time of Crisis* (New York: Schocken, 1963), 221, 248.

35. Karl Marx, "The British Rule in India," in *Karl Marx on Colonialism and Modernization,* ed. Shlomo Avineri (Garden City, N.Y.: Anchor, 1969), 94.

36. See Mill's defense of his role, which is not entirely different from Marx's defense: *On Liberty,* chap. 2, in *The Philosophy of John Stuart Mill,* ed. Marshall Cohen (New York: Modern Library, 1961), 197–98.

37. Tom Nairn, *The Break-up of Britain: Crisis and Neo-Nationalism* (London: NLB, 1977), 331.

38. See Clifford Geertz, "The Integrative Revolution: Primordial Sentiments and Civil Politics in the New States," in Geertz, *The Interpretation of Cultures* (New York: Basic Books, 1973), 255–310.

39. See Francis Hutchins, *Spontaneous Revolution: The Quit India Movement* (Delhi: Manohar Book Service, 1971), chaps. 3, 4, 5.

40. Isaiah Berlin, *Vico and Herder: Two Studies in the History of Ideas* (New York: Vintage, 1977), 159.

41. For a complete account of the Marxist argument, see Walker Connor, *The National Question in Marxist-Leninist Theory and Strategy* (Princeton: Princeton University Press, 1984).

42. John Locke, *A Letter Concerning Toleration*, ed. Patrick Romanell (Indianapolis: Bobbs-Merrill, 1950), 52, 54.

43. Michael Walzer, "The Reform of the International System," in *Studies of War and Peace* (Oslo: Norwegian University Press, 1986), 227–40.

44. Eric Hobsbawm, "Some Reflections on *The Break-Up of Britain*," in *New Left Review* 105 (September–October 1977), 9.

45. "Egoism" ranks the self ahead of all other selves; "individualism" has no such connotation. In a roughly analogous way, "racism," "sexism," and "chauvinism" imply a rank ordering of races, sexes, and states, but "nationalism" works differently: it is entirely compatible with a theory of incommensurability (like Buber's) or with a simple agnosticism about ranks and orders. Nationalists are more like patriots, in that they can respect and value commitments similar to their own in other people—and they can do so, unlike egoists, without viewing the others as competitors and antagonists. (This is not to say that there aren't many nationalists who adopt both a collective version of egoism and a political version of racism.)

46. So the "harmony" and "mission" metaphors get mixed: "From the harmonious interplay of [each people's] mission will derive the general mission of all peoples." *The Living Thoughts of Mazzini*, ed. Ignazio Silone (Westport, Conn.: Greenwood Press, 1972), 55.

47. Karl Marx, *Capital: A Critique of Political Economy*, ed. Frederick Engels (New York: International Publishers, 1967), 3:383.

48. Berlin, *Vico and Herder*, 164.

49. Martin Buber, *A Land of Two Peoples: Martin Buber on Jews and Arabs*, ed. Paul R. Mendes-Flohr (Oxford: Oxford University Press, 1983), 91.

50. See Sartre's preface to Franz Fanon, *The Wretched of the Earth*, trans. Constance Farrington (New York: Grove Press, 1963), 7–26.

51. Hobsbawm, "Some Reflections," 10.

52. Horace Kallen, *Culture and Democracy in the United States* (New York: Boni and Liveright, 1924).

53. For a defense of this "civil" commonality, see Geertz, "The Integrative Revolution," esp. 309–10.

CHAPTER THIRTEEN

The Moral Standing of States

A Response to Four Critics

[I]

The argument of *Just and Unjust Wars* has been criticized in a number of ways, most of them overtly political in character, as if in paraphrase of Clausewitz's famous maxim: writing about war is a continuation of writing about politics. . . . [1] That is not an entirely false maxim; indeed, it contains, as will be apparent below, unavoidable truth. And yet it is the purpose of a *theory* of just war to produce principles that, however they apply in this or that case, cannot be conscripted permanently into the service of any particular political creed or of any state or party. They are critical principles, and they open all states and parties to moral criticism. The principles I have put forward are of this sort, and I am less concerned—at least here—to defend the casuistic judgments through which they were worked out than the overall structure of the argument.

But there is one set of criticisms to which I want to respond here because it does raise deep questions about the overall structure. Four writers, in substantial reviews or articles, have adopted the same position, developed it in somewhat different ways, arrived at a common conclusion: that *Just and Unjust Wars*, despite its putative foundation in a theory of individual rights, is ultimately "statist" in character. "The rights of states, and not the rights of individuals," says Wasserstrom, "come in the end to enjoy an exalted, primary status within the moral critique of aggression."[2] The book, says Doppelt, "furnishes a rhetoric of morality in international relations which places the rights of de facto states above those of individuals."[3] Beitz and Luban, while trying to suggest what an alternative morality might look like, make similar arguments.[4] The criticism of these writers rests in places upon a misreading of my own position, but it rests more largely upon significant philosophical disagreements about the nature of political life. And so it is worth pursuing.

The immediate issue is the doctrine of non-intervention, a feature of *jus ad bellum*, the part of the theory that explains the criminality of aggressive war. Wasserstrom, Doppelt, Beitz, and Luban all argue that the theory as I have formulated it (1) protects states that should not be protected against foreign intervention and (2) does so on grounds that are either inadequate or incoherent. The theory has, on their view, conservative implications, and what it conserves is the authority or sovereignty of illegitimate, that is tyrannical, regimes. They, on the other hand, are more open, given certain qualifications about proportionality, to an activist and interventionist politics aimed at overthrowing such regimes and maximizing the enjoyment of individual rights. This is not a line of criticism that I anticipated with any clarity. My own worries had a different focus: I thought the theory might be too permissive with regard to secessionist movements and foreign support for such movements. Hence, in responding now, I shall have to enlarge upon the argument of the book, and at one or two points, indicated below, I shall have to amend or qualify the argument. But the basic position remains intact. The state is presumptively, though by no means always in practice, the arena within which self-determination is worked out and from which, therefore, foreign armies have to be excluded.

[2]

The real subject of my argument is not the state at all but the political community that (usually) underlies it. And I will compound my putative conservatism by saying at the outset that that community rests most deeply on a contract, Burkeian in character, among "the living, the dead, and those who are yet to be born." It is hard, therefore, to imagine the assembly at which it was ratified. Contract, as I wrote in the book, is a metaphor. The moral understanding on which the community is founded takes shape over a long period of time. But the idea of communal integrity derives its moral and political force from the rights of contemporary men and women to live as members of a historic community and to express their inherited culture through political forms worked out among themselves (the forms are never entirely worked out in a single generation). I shall describe later on, with several examples, how these individual rights are violated when communal integrity is denied, even if the denial is benevolent in intention.

The members of the community are bound to one another. That is Luban's "horizontal" contract, and it constitutes the only form of political obligation.[5] There is no "vertical" or governmental contract—at least, not one that is mutually binding. Though the community requires a government, it is not the case that the citizens are bound to the government to defend it against foreigners. Rather, the government is bound to the citizens to defend them against foreigners. That is what it is for, or one of the things it is for. The citizens defend one another and their common life; the government is merely their instrument. But sometimes this instrument is turned against the citizens: perhaps it still defends them against foreigners, but it also constrains and represses their common life; it denies their civil liberties; it imposes religious uniformity; it blocks attempts at self-help against political or economic oppression. It is a tyrannical government. Now it is the claim of my four critics, if I understand them correctly, that such a government, because it has no standing with its own people (no moral claim upon their allegiance), has no standing in international society either. It is an outlaw government, without rights, or it is simply an ugly government, with something less than the usual complement of rights, subject to attack by anyone capable of attacking it and altering (for the better) the conditions of its rule. That is a large claim, for countries with tyrannical governments make up the greater part of international society. But it is a false claim—false not only in the law, as the law currently stands, but false morally too, for reasons I shall come to below. The international standing of governments derives only indirectly from their standing with their own citizens. The derivation is complex because it is mediated by foreigners and because foreigners are not confronted (as citizens are) by a naked government, but by a state.

The state is constituted by the union of people and government, and it is the state that claims against all other states the twin rights of territorial integrity and political sovereignty. Foreigners are in no position to deny the reality of that union, or rather, they are in no position to attempt anything more than speculative denials. They don't know enough about its history, and they have no direct experience, and can form no concrete judgments, of the conflicts and harmonies, the historical choices and cultural affinities, the loyalties and resentments, that underlie it. Hence their conduct, in the first instance at least, cannot be determined by either knowledge or judgment. It is, or it ought to be, determined instead by a morally necessary presumption: that there exists a certain "fit" between the community and its government and that the state is "legitimate." It is not a gang of rulers acting in its own interests, but a people governed in accordance with its own traditions. This presumption is simply the respect that foreigners owe to a historic community and to its internal life. Like other presumptions in morality and law, it can be rebutted and disregarded, and what I have called "the rules of disregard" are as important as the presumption itself. So long as it stands, however, the boundaries of international society stand with it. This first presumption entails a second: that if a particular state were attacked, its citizens would think themselves bound to resist, and would in fact resist, because they value their own community in the same way that we value ours or in the same way that we value communities in general. The general valuation is, of course, crucial to the argument, but I won't stop to defend it until I am in a position to consider alternatives. In any case, it is the expectation of resistance that establishes the ban on invasion.

The obligation of citizens to fight for the state is something very different from the expectation that they will in fact fight. The expectation arises, or ought to arise, from the mere existence of a state, any state—with important exceptions to which I will come later. The obligation arises from the existence of a state of a certain sort, shaped to the requirements of moral and political philosophy. Now, this particular state is of that sort, or not; the obligation is real, or it isn't. These are questions open to argument, and foreigners, even foreign officials, are free to argue that the citizens of a particular state have no such obligations, and then to make further arguments about consent, freedom, participation, and so on. But they are not free to act on such arguments and go to war against a state whose citizens are not (so the foreigners think) bound to fight. They cannot claim that such states are literally indefensible. For as long as substantial numbers of citizens believe themselves bound and are prepared, for whatever reasons, to fight, an attack upon their state would constitute aggression. And again, foreigners are required (with exceptions . . .) to assume the belief and the preparedness, whether the obligation is real or not.

In a footnote in *Just and Unjust Wars*, I wrote that "the question of when territory and sovereignty can rightly be defended is closely connected to the question of when individual citizens have an obligation to join the defense." Doppelt takes this sentence to say that the citizens of a sovereign state, whatever its character and whatever their convictions about its character, are bound to fight on its behalf.[6] I meant only to suggest, as I went on to say, that both questions "hang on issues in social contract theory" (and to point readers to the arguments that I put forward in *Obligations*). But the sentence is misleading. In fact, a state whose citizens are not bound to fight may still find citizens ready to fight against an invading army, and it can hardly be doubted that these citizens (with exceptions . . .) have a right to fight and that the invaders are guilty of aggressive war. If no citizens come forward, or if they immediately surrender, then the state simply isn't defended. And then the invasion is a lesser crime than the crime we commonly call aggression, or it isn't a crime at all.[7] Nothing in my book was meant to suggest that citizens are bound to one another to defend tyrannical states (and they certainly are not bound to their tyrants). They are as free not to fight as they are free to rebel. But that freedom does not easily transfer to foreign states or armies and become a right of invasion or intervention; above all, it does not transfer at the initiative of the foreigners.

Hence states can be presumptively legitimate in international society and actually illegitimate at home. The doctrine of legitimacy has a dual reference. It is this dualism to which I referred when I wrote in *Just and Unjust Wars* that intervention is not justified whenever revolution is.[8] The two justifications do not coincide because they are addressed to different audiences. First, then, a state is legitimate or not depending upon the "fit" of government and community, that is, the degree to which the government actually represents the political life of its people. When it doesn't do that, the people have a right to rebel. But if they are free to rebel, then they are also free not to rebel—because they (or the greater number of them) judge rebellion to be imprudent or uncertain of success or because they feel that "slowness and aversion . . . to quit their old Constitutions," which Locke noted in his *Second Treatise.* That is, they still believe the government to be tolerable, or they are accustomed to it, or they are personally loyal to its leaders. And so arguments about legitimacy in this first sense of the word must be addressed to the people who make up a particular community. Anyone can make such arguments, but only subjects or citizens can act on them.

The second set of arguments concerns the presumptive legitimacy of states in international society. These arguments too can be made by anyone, including subjects and citizens, but they are properly addressed to foreigners, for it is foreigners who must decide whether to intervene or not. They are not to intervene unless the absence of "fit" between the government and community is radically apparent. Intervention in any other case usurps the rights of subjects and citizens. Wasserstrom asks: If the established government already deprives subjects and citizens of their rights, how can an attack narrowly aimed at that government add to the deprivation?[9] But the tyranny of established governments gives rise to a right of revolution, held individually by each subject or citizen, rightly exercised by any group of them, of which they cannot be deprived. When invasions are launched by foreign armies, even armies with revolutionary intentions, and even when revolution is justified, it is entirely plausible to say that the rights of subjects and citizens have been violated. Their "slowness" has been artificially speeded up, their "aversion" has been repudiated, their loyalties have been ignored, their prudential calculations have been rejected—all in favor of someone else's conceptions of political justice and political prudence. But this argument, Wasserstrom and Doppelt claim, suggests a Hobbesian theory of legitimacy: any Leviathan state that is stable, that manages successfully to control its own people, is therefore legitimate.[10] In a sense, that is right. In international society, Leviathan states, and many other sorts of states too, enjoy the rights of territorial integrity and political sovereignty. It has to be said, however, that Hobbes' argument is directed to the subjects of Leviathan, and it is not my intention, not by any means, to recommend its acceptance by that audience.

The first kind of legitimacy is or is likely to be singular in character. The judgments we make reflect our democratic values and suggest that there is only one kind of legitimate state or only a narrow range of legitimacy. Given an illiberal or undemocratic government, citizens are always free to rebel, whether they act on that right or not, and whether they believe themselves to have it or not. Their opinions are not relevant, for whatever they think, we can argue that such a government does not and cannot represent the political community.[11] But the second kind of legitimacy is pluralist in character. Here the judgments we make reflect our recognition of diversity and our respect for communal integrity and for different patterns of cultural and political development. And now the opinions of the people, and also their habits, feelings, religious convictions, political culture, and so on, do matter, for all these are likely to be bound up with, and partly explanatory of, the form and character of their state. That's why states objectively illegitimate are able, again and again, to rally subjects and citizens against invaders. In all such cases, though the "fit" between government and community is not of a democratic sort, there is still a "fit" of some sort, which foreigners are bound to respect.

The confusion of these two kinds of legitimacy, or the denial of the distinction between them, is the fundamental error of these four writers. They insist that the theory of *Just and Unjust Wars* requires me to call tyrannical states legitimate. My actual claim is that foreign officials must act as if they were legitimate, that is, must not make war against them. My critics are uneasy with the politics of *as if*, more uneasy with the presumption that underlies it, and most uneasy, I think, with the pluralism that that presumption mandates. They are committed to the view that the first kind of legitimacy is the only kind, and they are prepared to press international society toward a kind of reiterated singularity—the same government or roughly the same sort of government for every political community. But I won't try to address their positive arguments until I have worked through the cases where I am prepared to allow intervention and until I have indicated the far greater extent of their own allowance.

[3]

Though the concept of state sovereignty is, as Luban says, "insensitive" to legitimacy in its first sense, it is not insensitive to "the entire dimension of legitimacy," for there is such a thing as an illegitimate state even in international society, and there are cases when sovereignty can be disregarded.[12] These are the rules of disregard as I describe them in *Just and Unjust Wars*.[13] First, when a particular state includes more than one political community, when it is an empire or a multinational state, and when one of its communities or nations is in active revolt, foreign powers can come to the assistance of the rebels. Struggles for secession or national liberation justify or may justify intervention because in such cases there is no fit at all between government and community, and the state cannot claim, once the rebellion has reached certain proportions, even a presumptive legitimacy. While some citizens will probably feel bound to resist an intervention, it can be assumed that the citizens of the rebellious nation won't resist, and hence military action on their behalf does not count as aggression.

Second, when a single community is disrupted by civil war, and when one foreign power intervenes in support of this or that party, other powers can rightfully intervene in support of the other party. Counter-interventions of this sort can be defended without reference to the moral character of the parties. Hence it may be the case that a foreign state has a right to intervene even when, given certain political principles, that would not be the right thing to do (similarly, the right may exist where intervention isn't the wise or prudent thing to do). Some of my critics object to the neutrality of the rule, but that kind of neutrality is a feature of all the rules of war; without it there could be no rules at all but only permissions addressed to the Forces of Good entitling them to do whatever is necessary (though only what is *necessary*) to overcome their enemies.

Third, interventions can be justified whenever a government is engaged in the massacre or enslavement of its own citizens or subjects.[14] In such cases, the usual presumption is reversed, and we ought to assume either that there is no "fit" between the government and the community or that there is no community. I think that I would now add to massacre and enslavement the expulsion of very large numbers of people (not simply the retreat of political opponents after a revolution or the transfer of populations that sometimes follows upon national liberation struggles—though these can be brutal enough). The example of Bangladesh which I used in the book to suggest the meaning of massacre may also be used to suggest the meaning of expulsion. The Indian intervention might as easily have been justified by reference to the millions of refugees as by the reference to the tens of thousands of murdered men and women. The purpose of stressing these extreme forms of oppression is, of course, to rule out intervention in cases of "ordinary" oppression. By democratic standards, most states throughout human history have been oppressive (and illegitimate), but those are not necessarily or usually the standards by which they are judged among their own people. On the other hand, we can always assume that murder, slavery, and mass expulsion are condemned, at least by their victims.

I will consider now some examples suggested by my critics—and first, the example of South Africa, referred to briefly by Wasserstrom and more extensively by Doppelt.[15] It is important to both these writers to assimilate the treatment of blacks in South Africa to the category of ordinary oppression so that they can challenge the limits set by the three exceptions. But politically active blacks do not, in fact, talk about their own situation in this manner. Their arguments fall readily into the structure of the theory I have presented; they claim that South Africa is an exceptional case in two different ways.[16] (1) They describe black South Africans as near-slaves, virtual slaves, in-effect-slaves, and true (for the moment at least) to the logic of that description, they call for measures short of military intervention—economic boycott, for example. But it would not, I think, be an unreasonable extension of the argument to hold that, from a moral standpoint, in-effect-slaves (if that description is accurate) and legal slaves count in the same way and that foreign intervention on behalf of either is justifiable.[17] (2) They describe the struggle of black South Africans as a struggle for national liberation. This is especially plausible since it parallels the official position of the South African government: that blacks are a separate nation and that they are not entitled to full citizenship in the Republic of South Africa. The policy of apartheid turns internal revolution into national liberation, even though the actual separation of the races is not such as to make possible a black secession. And so it opens the possibility of external support for the subject people. I would guess that if such support ever takes military forms, it will be defended in one or another of these two ways.

But South Africa is a stalking horse for a larger argument which is better examined in a case where my critics would permit intervention and the theory of *Just and Unjust Wars* would prohibit it. Consider secondly, then, the recent revolution in Nicaragua, which Luban treats in some detail.[18] The Sandinista struggle in Nicaragua extended over many years and culminated in two periods of civil war, the first of which (in August and September of 1978) resulted in a defeat for the rebels. The fighting was resumed in the summer of 1979, and the Somoza government was overthrown. What happened in the months between the two military campaigns usefully illustrates the meaning of self-determination under conditions of political oppression. During that time, the rebels regrouped, re-armed (with some outside help) and, what is most important for us, negotiated a significant broadening of the revolutionary "front." In the course of those negotiations, they were required to commit themselves in fairly explicit ways as to the character of the regime they hoped to establish. Now, had there been a foreign intervention at the time of the first campaign, aimed at rescuing the rebels from defeat, as Luban believes there should have been, this internal process of bargaining and commitment would have been cut short. And then the character of the new regime would have been determined by the intervening state together with whatever faction of rebels it chose to support. It is my claim that such an intervention would have violated the right of Nicaraguans as a group to shape their own political institutions and the right of individual Nicaraguans to live under institutions so shaped. Wasserstrom is wrong, then, to say that this individual right comes to nothing more than the right to live in "a civil society of almost any sort."[19] It is, in this case, the right to live in a civil society of a Nicaraguan sort.

But what if the Sandinistas, facing defeat in September 1978 had asked for foreign military intervention? Can the right of revolution transfer at the initiative of the revolutionaries? It does exactly that in the case of a national liberation struggle, when the revolutionaries are themselves, in a sense, at war with foreigners and are assumed to have the support of their own people. But in the case of revolution and civil war, no such assumption is possible. In principle, revolutionaries who enjoy the active and visible support of a clear majority of their own people can invite foreign armies to intervene on their behalf. But I do not believe that revolutionaries are ever in that position until they are well beyond the point where they need foreign help. All that they need then is that there be no help for the government. The case that Mill envisioned in his essay on nonintervention is more realistic: a group of rebels fighting for the freedom of the people and claiming their passive support, hard-pressed militarily, asks for the help of some foreign state. The rebels, Mill argued, must mobilize their own (putative) supporters, not some alien army.[20] Only a popular mobilization will pave the way for the establishment of a free government. I would add that only such a mobilization, which makes foreign assistance superfluous, could also make it justifiable.

In practice, the request for foreign help is an admission of domestic weakness. It is probably for that reason that the Sandinistas never asked for help (except for equipment to match what the government was receiving or had received). They thought themselves to have, or they thought themselves capable of achieving, majority support. And they were "unrealistic" in the same way I am, according to Wasserstrom. "It is surprisingly unrealistic to suppose that a modern state cannot control its citizens effectively without their genuine consent."[21] The Sandinistas believed, at the least, that the Somoza government could not control its citizens against their active opposition. They wanted their own victory to build upon and reflect that opposition, that is, to be a popular victory. And that is what foreigners should want too, if they are committed to Nicaraguan self-determination.

In most civil wars, it just isn't possible to determine whether the government or the rebels (or which faction among the rebels) has majority support. Most citizens hide if they can, or profess to support whatever forces control the territory in which they live, or try to guess who will win and join the winners as early as possible. And then, the right of revolution can't and doesn't transfer to foreigners, whatever invitations are offered. Foreign states can't join a civil war, when no other states have joined, simply because they admire the principles of the party that has invited them in or even because they believe that that party would, under ideal conditions, win a free election. If they intervene successfully, the party on whose behalf they have intervened will certainly win the elections, but the conditions will not be ideal. In any case, they have no right to make their own principles or their own beliefs definitive for other people.

But if the eventual outcome, writes Doppelt, "reflects nothing but the balance of internal military might, I see no more reason for calling this process one of 'self-determination' . . . than I do for denying that it is self-determination on the mere basis that foreign troops have played some role in it."[22] In fact, however, there is no such thing as a bare "balance of internal military might." Armies and police forces are social institutions; soldiers and policemen come from families, villages, neighborhoods, classes. They will not fight cohesively, with discipline, or at length unless the regime for which they are fighting has some degree of social support. A civil war is the sign of a divided society. As an extended insurrection indicates popular support for the rebels (that's why the Viet Cong, despite the claims of the United States Government, could not have been sustained entirely from North Vietnam), so an extended resistance to insurrection indicates popular support for the government. That support may be ignorant, passive, bewildered; it may reflect nothing more than the people's "slowness and aversion" to change. Still, no foreigner can rightly override it. Of course, the actual outcome of a particular struggle will also reflect factors "irrelevant from a moral point of view." There is no way to guarantee the "right" result. But foreign troops are more irrelevant than any local factor, for their strength depends upon the character of their own government and community, their historical traditions, loyalties, and so on, and bears no relation at all to the history and culture of the people whose fate they are determining.

I am inclined to doubt that the issues raised in the last few paragraphs are, in any simple sense, empirical issues. At any rate, they are not susceptible to empirical resolution. We have no reliable indices of popular sentiment in time of civil war. For more or less similar reasons, it is virtually impossible to judge the strength or likely endurance of some established tyranny. There is no point at which foreigners can point to a tyrannical regime and say, "Self-determination has clearly failed; there is nothing to do but intervene." For revolution often comes unexpectedly, as it came to the Iran of the Shah, a sudden upsurge of previously invisible political currents. Intervention denies the political significance of such currents or it denies their moral significance. These are not denials that can be empirically justified. They are instead principled denials of self-determination itself—because it is too slow or too costly, or because its outcome is not foreknown, or because the likely outcome is thought to be unattractive. Underlying all such reasons, however, there must be some alternative principle. The alternative figures only implicitly in Doppelt's article; it is called "reform intervention" by Beitz;[23] Luban provides its formulas; and Wasserstrom gives it an appropriate theoretical label: "the utilitarianism of rights."[24] This principle poses a radical challenge to communal integrity, and I want now to consider it in some detail.

[4]

It is easiest to begin with Luban's formulas, the most important of which is simply this: "A just war is (1) a war in defense of socially basic human rights (subject to proportionality). . . ."[25] Socially basic rights include security rights, against tyrannical governments as well as against foreign invaders, and subsistence rights. Luban would not justify a war fought for the sake of democracy or social justice, though Doppelt and Beitz apparently would.[26] Still, this is a far-reaching license. Or something more than a license: since socially basic rights "are the demands of all of humanity on all of humanity," it might be Luban's view that we are bound to fight all the just wars we are able to fight—up to the point of exhaustion and incapacity. Then "the utilitarianism of rights" would have the same consequence as ordinary utilitarianism, leaving us no time to ourselves. But I won't pursue this line of argument.

If rights don't require us to intervene, however, then it is difficult to see why they should be called rights (in Luban's sense) or why Luban should object to my own argument, which would also permit interventions against governments that murdered or starved their own people. I suspect that he is reaching for a wider permissiveness—as the others certainly are—not only against governments that violate his list of rights, narrowly conceived, but against all repressive governments and against all governments that are or seem to be indifferent to the poverty of their people. Hence, the phrase "in defense of rights," though technically correct, is politically misleading. Since these are rights that people don't, in the relevant cases, enjoy and may not know themselves to have, the actual purpose of just wars might be better described: to establish or enforce rights, or to maximize their effectiveness, or to enlarge the population for which they are effective. Maximizing rights is very much like maximizing well-being—hence "the utilitarianism of rights"—though with the important proviso that the maximization can be pursued only up to a certain point by military force. But any extra enjoyment of rights, like any extra well-being, probably wouldn't balance the costs of the fighting anyway.

To whom is this far-reaching license granted? Who is to make the crucial calculations? In principle, I suppose, the license is extended to any and all foreigners; in practice, today, to the officials of foreign states; tomorrow, perhaps, to some set of global bureaucrats acting by themselves or as advisers to and agents of a Universal Assembly. Now, why them? And here a more serious sort of rights argument properly begins. Rights are in an important sense distributive principles. They distribute decision-making authority. When we describe individual rights, we are assigning to individuals a certain authority to shape their own lives, and we are denying that officials, even well-meaning officials, are authorized to interfere. The description of communal rights makes a similar assertion and a similar denial. In the individual case, we fix a certain area for personal choice; in the communal case, we fix a certain area for political choice. Unless these areas are clearly marked out and protected, both sorts of choices are likely to become problematic.

But unless they are democratically made, my critics might argue, political choices are already problematic and can't plausibly count as the free choices of the community. The area within which tyrants, oligarchs, ruling classes, priestly castes, and military cliques make their choices isn't worth protecting. Only liberal or democratic states have rights against external intervention. This claim plays on a (pretended) domestic equivalent: that only the uncoerced choices of minimally rational individuals are protected against intervention. But it is not the sign of some collective derangement or radical incapacity for a political community to produce an authoritarian regime. Indeed, the history, culture, and religion of the community may be such that authoritarian regimes come, as it were, naturally, reflecting a widely shared worldview or way of life. Such views and ways may be wrong or badly conceived; they are not necessarily insane. The authoritarian regime is not, to be sure, freely chosen, but then no set of political institutions is ever freely chosen from the full range of alternatives by a single set of people at a single moment in time. Institutions have histories; they are the products of protracted struggles. And it can't be the case that communities are protected against intervention only if those struggles have a single philosophically correct or universally approved outcome (or one of a small number of correct or approved outcomes). That would not be the same thing as protecting only free individuals; it would be more like protecting only individuals who had arrived at certain opinions, life styles, and so on.

The difference between my own views and those of my critics may be sharpened if we consider a hypothetical case designed to neutralize the proportionality qualification and all the other issues raised by the use of force and to focus exclusively on the question of communal integrity. Imagine, then, a country called Algeria in which a group of revolutionaries come to power pledged to create a democratic and secular state, with equal rights for all citizens. The regime they actually create, or which is created as a result of their struggles with one another, is very different: a military dictatorship and a religious "republic," without civil and political liberties, and brutally repressive, not only because a new political elite has established itself and resists all challenges but also because women have been returned to their traditional religious subordination to patriarchal authority. It is clear, however, that this regime (in contrast to the one the revolutionaries originally had in mind) has deep roots in Algerian history and draws importantly upon Algerian political and religious culture. It is not a democratic regime; its popularity has never been tested in a democratic way; but there can be no doubt that it is an Algerian regime. Now, imagine further that the Swedish government had in its possession a wondrous chemical which, if introduced into the water supply of Algeria, would turn all Algerians, elites and masses, into Swedish-style social democrats. It would wipe out of their minds their own political and religious culture (though it would leave them with no sense of loss). And it would provide them instead with the knowledge, capacity, and will to create a new regime in which basic security rights, political and civil liberties too, would be respected, women would be treated as equals, and so on. Should they use the chemical? Do they have a right to use it? The force of the argument depends upon the reader's readiness to value Swedish social-democracy far above Algerian "socialism." I assume that valuation, and yet I am certain that the Swedes should not use the chemical. They should not use it because the historical religion and politics of the Algerian people are values for the Algerian people (even though individual Algerians have not chosen their religion and politics from among a range of alternatives) which our valuation cannot override. It may seem paradoxical to hold that the Algerian people have a right to a state within which their rights are violated. But that is, given the case as I have described it, the only kind of state that they are likely to call their own.

Nor would the case be different if there were a democratic political movement or a feminist movement within Algeria. For foreigners cannot judge the relative strength of such movements or allow them to substitute themselves for the people as a whole, not until they have won sufficient support to transform Algerian politics on their own. That may be a long process; it will certainly involve compromises of different sorts; and the movements if and when they win will be different from what they were when they began. All that is Algerian self-determination, a political process that also has value, even if it isn't always pretty, and even if its outcome doesn't conform to philosophical standards of political and social justice.

Individual rights may well derive, as I am inclined to think, from our ideas about personality and moral agency, without reference to political processes and social circumstances. But the enforcement of rights is another matter. It is not the case that one can simply proclaim a list of rights and then look around for armed men to enforce it. Rights are only enforceable within political communities where they have been collectively recognized, and the process by which they come to be recognized is a political process which requires a political arena. The globe is not, or not yet, such an arena. Or rather, the only global community is pluralist in character, a community of nations, not of humanity, and the rights recognized within it have been minimal and largely negative, designed to protect the integrity of nations and to regulate their commercial and military transactions.

Beitz seems to believe that this pluralist world order has already been transcended and that communal integrity is a thing of the past. In a world of increasing interdependence, he argues, it is an "evident falsity" to claim "that states are relatively self-enclosed arenas of political development."[27] Just as no man is an island, so no state is an island—not even Britain, Japan, or Singapore. We are all involved in one another's politics, responsible for one another, and open (it seems) to one another's interventions. I don't know what evidence might be presented for this view, what sorts of comparisons might be drawn with what previous historical periods. Perfect self-enclosure has probably never existed. Relative self-enclosure seems to me an evident truth. Anyone doubting it would have to account on psychological grounds for the enormous importance colonial peoples attach to their recently won independence and the enormous importance revolutionary groups attach to the seizure of power in their own political communities. In fact, psychological explanations are quite unnecessary. Political power within a particular community remains the critical factor in shaping the fate of the members. Of course, that fate (like all fates) is shaped within political and economic limits, and these can be more or less narrow; there are some states with relatively little room for maneuver. And yet, even economically dependent states, locked into international markets they can't control, can dramatically alter the conditions of their dependence and the character of their domestic life. Surely the histories of Yugoslavia since World War II, of Cuba since 1960, and of Iran over the last two years, suggest strongly that what actually happens within a country is a function, above all, of local political processes. An internal decision (or an internal revolution) can turn a country around in a way no decision by another country, short of a decision to invade, can possibly do.

So the political community with its government, that is, the state, is still the critical arena of political life. It has not been transcended, and there are two important reasons, I think, for hesitating a long time before attempting the transcendence. The first reason is prudential. If the outcome of political processes in particular communal arenas is often brutal, then it ought to be assumed that outcomes in the global arena will often be brutal too. And this will be a far more effective and therefore a far more dangerous brutality, for there will be no place left for political refuge and no examples left of political alternatives.

The second reason has to do with the very nature of political life. Politics (as distinct from mere coercion and bureaucratic manipulation) depends upon shared history, communal sentiment, accepted conventions—upon some extended version of Aristotle's "friendship." All this is problematic enough in the modern state; it is hardly conceivable on a global scale. Communal life and liberty requires the existence of "relatively self-enclosed arenas of political development." Break into the enclosures and you destroy the communities. And that destruction is a loss to the individual members (unless it rescues them from massacre, enslavement, or expulsion), a loss of something valuable, which they clearly value, and to which they have a right, namely, their participation in the "development" that goes on and can only go on within the enclosure. Hence the distinction of state rights and individual rights is simplistic and wrongheaded. Against foreigners, individuals have a right to a state of their own. Against state officials, they have a right to political and civil liberty. Without the first of these rights, the second is meaningless: as individuals need a home, so rights require a location.

[5]

My own argument is perhaps best understood as a defense of politics, while that of my critics reiterates what I take to be the traditional philosophical dislike for politics. This dislike is most readily recognized in utilitarian argument, commonly addressed to real or imaginary bureaucrats. But it is also apparent among rights theorists, whenever the enforcement of rights is assigned to authorities who stand outside the political arena or who are allowed (or required) to act even in the absence of prior consent. Some such assignment, I don't doubt, is necessary even to my own argument, as the three exceptions suggest, and so it might be said that the question is only where to draw the line between external (bureaucratic or military) enforcement, on the one hand, and political decision-making, on the other. But I suspect that the disagreement goes deeper than that formulation allows. It has to do with the respect we are prepared to accord and the room we are prepared to yield to the political process itself, with all its messiness and uncertainty, its inevitable compromises, and its frequent brutality. It has to do with the range of outcomes we are prepared to tolerate, to accept as presumptively legitimate, though not necessarily to endorse. "For Walzer," writes Doppelt, states that possess the collective right of sovereignty "may violate the individual rights of all or some group of [their] citizens."[28] No, I do not give out permissions of that sort; obviously, I oppose all such violations. But I don't believe that the opposition of philosophers is a sufficient ground for military invasion. Perhaps, indeed, like Prince Hamlet, we are born to set things right, but we do that, or try to do it, by making arguments, not by summoning up armies.

NOTES

1. Michael Walzer, *Just and Unjust Wars* (New York, 1977).

2. Richard Wasserstrom, "Review of Michael Walzer's *Just and Unjust Wars: A Moral Argument with Historical Illustrations,*" *Harvard Law Review* 92:2 (December 1978), 544.

3. Gerald Doppelt, "Walzer's Theory of Morality in International Relations," *Philosophy and Public Affairs* 8:1 (Autumn 1978), 26.

4. Charles R. Beitz, "Bounded Morality: Justice and the State in World Politics," *International Organization* 33:3 (Summer 1979), 405–24; David Luban, "Just War and Human Rights," *Philosophy and Public Affairs* 9:2 (Winter 1980), 161–81.

5. Luban, "Just War," 167.

6. Doppelt, "Walzer's Theory," 14.

7. This claim parallels the argument in *Just and Unjust Wars* (330) about non-violence. If citizens choose civil rather than military resistance, then the criminality of the aggressor is diminished, for he has evidently not forced them to fight, risk their lives, and die for their rights. If the invaders are welcomed by a clear majority of the people, then it would be odd to accuse them of any crime at all. But it is almost certain that such a welcome will be extended only in circumstances that make for the three exceptions that I take up below. And then the invasion will be blameless even before it is welcomed.

8. Walzer, *Just and Unjust Wars,* 89.

9. Wasserstrom, "Review," 540.

10. Ibid., 542; Doppelt, "Walzer's Theory," 16.

11. Hence the Italian nationalist Mazzini was wrong to say (in his opening address to Young Europe in 1847), "There is no international question as to forms of government, but only a national question." Instead, a simple distinction holds. The philosophical question is indeed international (or transnational or universal), but the political question can only rightly be answered by some national process of decision making.

12. Luban, "Just War," 166.

13. The following paragraphs summarize the argument of *Just and Unjust Wars,* 89–108.

14. For reasons I cannot understand, Doppelt takes me to mean by "enslavement" the "forced resettlement of masses of people" (7), referring to a discussion of Spanish policy in Cuba in 1898. But all that I say about Spanish policy is that it was carried out "with so little regard for the health of the people involved that thousands of them suffered and died" (*Just and Unjust Wars,* 102). No, by "enslavement" I mean enslavement: the dictionary definition will do well enough. I offer no examples because, so far as I know, enslavement has never been made the occasion for (even the pretext for) a military intervention. Hence Doppelt's reference to the American South (20) is otiose. Slaves are not to be conceived of as participants in any social or political process of self-determination.

15. Wasserstrom, "Review," 544; Doppelt, "Walzer's Theory," 20, 23–25.

16. I can't refer authoritatively here to any body of South African literature; my reference is to arguments made in leaflets and at political meetings in the United States.

17. It is a problem, of course, that even ordinary oppression can be and commonly is described in the language of enslavement—as in the Marxist phrase "wage slavery." But that

only suggests the importance of drawing a line that protects internal political and social processes (not against philosophical criticism or domestic resistance and revolution but only) against military intervention.

18. Luban, "Just War," 170–71

19. Wasserstrom, "Review," 542.

20. See the discussion of Mill's argument, *Just and Unjust Wars*, 87–91.

21. Wasserstrom, "Review," 542.

22. Doppelt, "Walzer's Theory," 13

23. Beitz, "Bounded Morality," 413.

24. The notion of a "utilitarianism of rights" was first formulated by Robert Nozick in *Anarchy, State, and Utopia* (New York, 1974), 28. Nozick goes on to argue, on Kantian grounds, that rights must be understood as constraints on action rather than as goals of a maximizing politics. Though I don't share his views as to the substance of a rights theory, the same conception of its structure underlies my own position in *Just and Unjust Wars*.

25. Luban, "Just War," 175.

26. I am not sure, however, that Beitz means to defend *military* intervention. Reviewing a book on war, he certainly seems to do so. But in his own book, he introduces a similar argument by saying that he wishes "to bracket the case of military intervention" and talk only of "policies of interference that . . . fall short of the actual use of violence" (*Political Theory and International Relations* [Princeton, 1979], 72). For myself, I was concerned in *Just and Unjust Wars* only with military intervention, but the arguments I constructed do rule out any external determination of domestic constitutional arrangements (as an example below will suggest). I don't, however, mean to rule out every effort by one state to influence another or every use of diplomatic and economic pressure. Drawing the line is sure to be difficult, but the precise location of the line is not at issue here, for all my critics, with only the possible exception of Beitz, are ready for "the actual use of violence" in other people's countries, in order to do them good.

27. Beitz, "Bounded Morality," 422–23.

28. Doppelt, "Walzer's Theory," 25.

CHAPTER FOURTEEN

The Argument about
Humanitarian Intervention

There is nothing new about human disasters caused by human beings. We have always been, if not our own, certainly each other's worst enemies. From the Assyrians in ancient Israel and the Romans in Carthage to the Belgians in the Congo and the Turks in Armenia, history is a bloody and barbaric tale. Still, in this regard, the twentieth century was an age of innovation, first—and most important—in the way disasters were planned and organized and then, more recently, in the way they were publicized. I want to begin with the second of these innovations—the product of an extraordinary speedup in both travel and communication. It may be possible to kill people on a very large scale more efficiently than ever before, but it is much harder to kill them in secret. In the contemporary world there is very little that happens far away, out of sight, or behind the scenes; the camera crews arrive faster than rigor mortis. We are instant spectators of every atrocity; we sit in our living rooms and see the murdered children, the desperate refugees. Perhaps horrific crimes are still committed in dark places, but not many; contemporary horrors are well-lit. And so a question is posed that has never been posed before—at least never with such immediacy, never so inescapably: What is our responsibility? What should we do?

In the old days, "humanitarian intervention" was a lawyer's doctrine, a way of justifying a very limited set of exceptions to the principles of national sovereignty and territorial integrity. It is a good doctrine, because exceptions are always necessary, principles are never absolute. But we need to rethink it today, as the exceptions become less and less exceptional. The "acts that shock the conscience of humankind"—and, according to the nineteenth-century law books, justify humanitarian intervention—are probably no more frequent these days than they were in the past, but they are more shocking, because we are more intimately engaged by them and with them. Cases multiply in the world and in the media: Somalia, Bosnia, Rwanda, East Timor, Liberia, Sierra Leone, and Kosovo in only the past decade. The last of these has dominated recent political debates, but it isn't the most illuminating case. I want to step back a bit, reach for a wider range of examples, and try to answer four questions about humanitarian intervention: First, what are its occasions? Second, who are its preferred agents? Third, how should the agents act to meet the occasions? And fourth, when is it time to end the intervention?

[1]

The occasions have to be extreme if they are to justify, perhaps even require, the use of force across an international boundary. Every violation of human rights isn't a justification. The common brutalities of authoritarian politics, the daily oppressiveness of traditional social practices—these are not occasions for intervention; they have to be dealt with locally, by the people who know the politics, who enact or resist the practices. The fact that these people can't easily or quickly reduce the incidence of brutality and oppression isn't a sufficient reason for foreigners to invade their country. Foreign politicians and soldiers are too likely to misread the situation, or to underestimate the force required to change it, or to stimulate a "patriotic" reaction in defense of the brutal politics and the oppressive practices. Social change is best achieved from within.

I want to insist on this point; I don't mean to describe a continuum that begins with common nastiness and ends with genocide, but rather a radical break, a chasm, with nastiness on one side and genocide on the other. We should not allow ourselves to approach genocide by degrees. Still, on this side of the chasm, we can mark out a continuum of brutality and oppression, and somewhere along this continuum an international response (short of military force) is necessary. Diplomatic pressure and economic sanctions, for example, are useful means of engagement with tyrannical regimes. The sanctions might be imposed by some free-form coalition of interested states. Or perhaps we should work toward a more established regional or global authority that could regulate the imposition, carefully matching the severity of the sanctions to the severity of the oppression. But these are still external acts; they are efforts to prompt *but not to preempt* an internal response. They still assume the value, and hold open the possibility, of domestic politics. The interested states or the regional or global authorities bring pressure to bear, so to speak, at the border; and then they wait for something to happen on the other side.

But when what is going on is the "ethnic cleansing" of a province or country or the systematic massacre of a religious or national community, it doesn't seem possible to wait for a local response. Now we are on the other side of the chasm. The stakes are too high, the suffering already too great. Perhaps there is no capacity to respond among the people directly at risk and no will to respond among their fellow citizens. The victims are weak and vulnerable; their enemies are cruel; their neighbors indifferent. The rest of us watch and are shocked. This is the occasion for intervention.

We will need to argue, of course, about each case, but the list I've already provided seems a fairly obvious one. These days the intervening army will claim to be enforcing human rights, and that was a plausible and fully comprehensible claim in each of the cases on my list (or would have been, since interventions weren't attempted in all of them). We are best served, I think, by a stark and minimalist version of human rights here: it is life and liberty that are at stake. With regard to these two, the language of rights is readily available and sufficiently understood across the globe. Still, we could as easily say that what is being enforced, and what should be enforced, is simple decency.

In practice, even with a minimalist understanding of human rights, even with a commitment to nothing more than decency, there are more occasions for intervention than there are actual interventions. When the oppressors are too powerful, they are rarely challenged, however shocking the oppression. This obvious truth about international society is often used as an argument against the interventions that do take place. It is hypocritical, critics say to the "humanitarian" politicians or soldiers, to intervene in this case when you didn't intervene in that one—as if, having declined to challenge China in Tibet, say, the United Nations should have stayed out of East Timor for the sake of moral consistency. But consistency isn't an issue here. We can't meet all our occasions; we rightly calculate the risks in each one. We need to ask what the costs of intervention will be for the people being rescued, for the rescuers, and for everyone else. And then, we can only do what we can do.

The standard cases have a standard form: a government, an army, a police force, tyrannically controlled, attacks its own people or some subset of its own people, a vulnerable minority, say, territorially based or dispersed throughout the country. (We might think of these attacks as examples of state terrorism and then consider forceful humanitarian responses, such as the NATO campaign in Kosovo, as instances of the "war against terrorism," *avant la lettre*. But I won't pursue this line of argument here.) The attack takes place within the country's borders; it doesn't require any boundary crossings; it is an exercise of sovereign power. There is no aggression, no invading army to resist and beat back. Instead, the rescuing forces are the invaders; they are the ones who, in the strict sense of international law, begin the war. But they come into a situation where the moral stakes are clear: the oppressors or, better, the state agents of oppression are readily identifiable; their victims are plain to see.

Even in the list with which I started, however, there are some nonstandard cases—Sierra Leone is the clearest example—where the state apparatus isn't the villain, where what we might think of as the administration of brutality is decentralized, anarchic, almost random. It isn't the power of the oppressors that interventionists have to worry about, but the amorphousness of the oppression. I won't have much to say about cases like this. Intervention is clearly justifiable but, right now at least, it's radically unclear how it should be undertaken. Perhaps there is not much to do beyond what the Nigerians did in Sierra Leone: they reduced the number of killings, the scope of the barbarism.

[2]

"We can only do what we can do." Who is this "we"? The Kosovo debate focused on the United States, NATO, and the UN as agents of military intervention. These are indeed three political collectives capable of agency, but by no means the only three. The United States and NATO generate suspicion among the sorts of people who are called "idealists" because of their readiness to act unilaterally and their presumed imperial ambitions; the UN generates skepticism among the sorts of people who are called "realists" because of its political weakness and military ineffectiveness. The arguments here are overdetermined; I am not going to join them. We are more likely to understand the problem of agency if we start with other agents. The most successful interventions in the last thirty years have been acts of war by neighboring states: Vietnam in Cambodia, India in East Pakistan (now Bangladesh), Tanzania in Uganda. These are useful examples for testing our ideas about intervention because they don't involve extraneous issues such as the new (or old) world order; they don't require us to consult Lenin's, or anyone else's, theory of imperialism. In each of these cases, there were horrifying acts that should have been stopped and agents who succeeded, more or less, in stopping them. So let's use these cases to address the two questions most commonly posed by critics of the Kosovo war:

Does it matter that the agents acted alone? Does it matter that their motives were not wholly (or even chiefly) altruistic?

In the history of humanitarian intervention, unilateralism is far more common than its opposite. One reason for this is obvious: the great reluctance of most states to cede the direction of their armed forces to an organization they don't control. But unilateralism may also follow from the need for an immediate response to "acts that shock." Imagine a case where the shock doesn't have anything to do with human evildoing: a fire in a neighbor's house in a new town where there is no fire department. It wouldn't make much sense to call a meeting of the block association, while the house is burning, and vote on whether or not to help (and it would make even less sense to give a veto on helping to the three richest families on the block). I don't think that the case would be all that different if, instead of a fire, there was a brutal husband, no police department, and screams for help in the night. Here too, the block association is of little use; neighborly unilateralism seems entirely justified. In cases like these, anyone who can help should help. And that sounds like a plausible maxim for humanitarian intervention also: who can, should.

But now let's imagine a block association or an international organization that planned in advance for the fire, or the scream in the night, or the mass murder. Then there would be particular people or specially recruited military forces delegated to act in a crisis, and the definition of "crisis" could be determined—as best it can be—in advance, in exactly the kind of meeting that seems so implausible, so morally inappropriate, at the moment when immediate action is necessary. The person who rushes into a neighbor's house in my domestic example and the political or military commanders of the invading forces in the international cases would still have to act on their own understanding of the events unfolding in front of them and on their own interpretation of the responsibility they have been given. But now they act under specified constraints, and they can call on the help of those in whose name they are acting. This is the form that multilateral intervention is most likely to take, if the UN, say, were ever to authorize it in advance of a particular crisis. It seems preferable to the different unilateral alternatives, because it involves some kind of prior warning, an agreed-upon description of the occasions for intervention, and the prospect of overwhelming force.

But is it preferable in fact, right now, given the UN as it actually is? What makes police forces effective in domestic society, when they are effective, is their commitment to the entire body of citizens from which they are drawn and the (relative) trust of the citizens in that commitment. But the UN's General Assembly and Security Council, so far, give very little evidence of being so committed, and there can't be many people in the world today who would willingly entrust their lives to UN police. So if, in any of my examples, the UN's authorized agents or their domestic equivalents decide not to intervene, and the fire is still burning, the screams can still be heard, the murders go on—then unilateralist rights and obligations are instantly restored. Collective decisions to act may well exclude unilateral action, but collective decisions not to act don't have the same effect. In this sense, unilateralism is the dominant response when the common conscience is shocked. If there is no collective response, anyone can respond. If no one is acting, act.

In the Cambodia, East Pakistan, and Uganda cases, there were no prior arrangements and no authorized agents. Had the UN's Security Council or General Assembly been called into session, it would almost certainly have decided against intervention, probably by majority vote, in any case because of great-power opposition. So, anyone acting to shut down the Khmer Rouge killing fields or to stem the tide of Bengalese refugees or to stop Idi Amin's butchery would have to act unilaterally. Everything depended on the political decision of a single state.

Do these singular agents have a right to act or do they have an obligation? I have been using both words, but they don't always go together: there can be rights where there are no obligations. In "good Samaritan" cases in domestic society, we commonly say that passersby are bound to respond (to the injured stranger by the side of the road, to the cry of a child drowning in the lake); they are not, however, bound to risk their lives. If the risks are clear, they have a right to respond; responding is certainly a good thing and possibly the right thing to do; still, they are not morally bound to do it. But military interventions across international boundaries always impose risks on the intervening forces. So perhaps there is no obligation here either; perhaps there is a right to intervene but also a right to refuse the risks, to maintain a kind of neutrality—even between murderers and their victims. Or perhaps humanitarian intervention is an example of what philosophers call an "imperfect" duty: someone should stop the awfulness, but it isn't possible to give that someone a proper name, to point a finger, say, at a particular country. The problem of imperfect duty yields best to multilateral solutions; we simply assign responsibility in advance through some commonly accepted decision procedure.

But perhaps, again, these descriptions are too weak: I am inclined to say that intervention is more than a right and more than an imperfect duty. After all, the survival of the intervening state is not at risk. And then why shouldn't the obligation simply fall on the most capable state, the nearest or the strongest, as in the maxim I have already suggested: Who can, should? Nonintervention in the face of mass murder or ethnic cleansing is not the same as neutrality in time of war. The moral urgencies are different; we are usually unsure of the consequences of a war, but we know very well the consequences of a massacre. Still, if we follow the logic of the argument so far, it will be necessary to recruit volunteers for humanitarian interventions; the "who" who can and should is only the state, not any particular man or woman; for individuals the duty remains imperfect. Deciding whether to volunteer, they may choose to apply the same test to themselves—who can, should—but the choice is theirs.

The dominance that I have ascribed to unilateralism might be questioned—commonly is questioned—because of a fear of the motives of single states acting alone. Won't they act in their own interests rather than in the interests of humanity? Yes, they probably will or, better, they will act in their own interests as well as in the interests of humanity; I don't think that it is particularly insightful, merely cynical, to suggest that those larger interests have no hold at all (surely the balance of interest and morality among interventionists is no different than it is among noninterventionists). In any case, how would humanity be better served by multilateral decision-making? Wouldn't each state involved in the decision process also act in its own interests? And then the outcome would be determined by bargaining among the interested parties—and humanity, obviously, would not be one of the parties. We might hope that particular interests would cancel each other out, leaving some kind of general interest (this is in fact Rousseau's account, or one of his accounts, of how citizens arrive at a "general will"). But it is equally possible that the bargain will reflect only a mix of particular interests, which may or may not be better for humanity than the interests of a single party. Anyway, political motivations are always mixed, whether the actors are one or many. A pure moral will doesn't exist in political life, and it shouldn't be necessary to pretend to that kind of purity. The leaders of states have a right, indeed, they have an obligation, to consider the interests of their own people, even when they are acting to help other people. We should assume, then, that the Indians acted in their national interest when they assisted the secession of East Pakistan, and that Tanzania acted in its own interests when it moved troops into Idi Amin's Uganda. But these interventions also served humanitarian purposes, and presumably they were intended to do that too. The victims of massacre or "ethnic cleansing" are very lucky if a neighboring state, or a coalition of states, has more than one reason to rescue them. It would be foolish to declare the multiplicity morally disabling. If the intervention is expanded beyond its necessary bounds because of some "ulterior" motive, then it should be criticized; within those bounds, mixed motives are a practical advantage.

[3]

When the agents act, how should they act? Humanitarian intervention involves the use of force, and it is crucial to its success that it be pursued forcefully; the aim is the defeat of the people, whoever they are, who are carrying out the massacres or the ethnic cleansing. If what is going on is awful enough to justify going in, then it is awful enough to justify the pursuit of military victory. But this simple proposition hasn't found ready acceptance in international society. Most clearly in the Bosnian case, repeated efforts were made to deal with the disaster without fighting against its perpetrators. Force was taken, indeed, to be a "last" resort, but in an ongoing political conflict "lastness" never arrives; there is always something to be done before doing whatever it is that comes last. So military observers were sent into Bosnia to report on what was happening; and then UN forces brought humanitarian relief to the victims, and then they provided some degree of military protection for relief workers, and then they sought (unsuccessfully) to create a few "safe zones" for the Bosnians. But if soldiers do nothing more than these things, they are hardly an impediment to further killing; they may even be said to provide a kind of background support for it. They guard roads, defend doctors and nurses, deliver medical supplies and food to a growing number of victims and refugees—and the number keeps growing. Sometimes it is helpful to interpose soldiers as "peacekeepers" between the killers and their victims. But though that may work for a time, it doesn't reduce the power of the killers, and so it is a formula for trouble later on. Peacekeeping is an honorable activity, but not if there is no peace. Sometimes, unhappily, it is better to make war.

In Cambodia, East Pakistan, and Uganda, the interventions were carried out on the ground; this was old-fashioned war-making. The Kosovo war provides an alternative model: a war fought from the air, with technologies designed to reduce (almost to zero!) the risk of casualties to the intervening army. I won't stop here to consider at any length the reasons for the alternative model, which have to do with the increasing inability of modern democracies to use the armies they recruit in ways that put soldiers at risk. There are no "lower orders," no invisible, expendable citizens in democratic states today. And in the absence of a clear threat to the community itself, there is little willingness even among political elites to sacrifice for the sake of global law and order or, more particularly, for the sake of Rwandans or Kosovars. But the inability and the unwillingness, whatever their sources, make for moral problems. A war fought entirely from the air, and from far away, probably can't be won without attacking civilian targets. These can be bridges and television stations, electric generators and water purification plants, rather than residential areas, but the attacks will endanger the lives of innocent men, women, and children nonetheless. The aim is to bring pressure to bear on a government acting barbarically toward a minority of its citizens by threatening to harm, or actually harming, the majority to which, presumably, the government is still committed. Obviously this isn't a strategy that would have worked against the Khmer Rouge in Cambodia, but it's probably not legitimate even where it might work—so long as there is the possibility of a more precise intervention against the forces actually engaged in the barbarous acts. The same rules apply here as in war generally: noncombatants are immune from direct attack and have to be protected as far as possible from "collateral damage"; soldiers have to accept risks to themselves in order to avoid imposing risks on the civilian population.

Any country considering military intervention would obviously embrace technologies that were said to be risk-free for its own soldiers, and the embrace would be entirely justified so long as the same technologies were also risk-free for civilians on the other side. This is precisely the claim made on behalf of "smart bombs": they can be delivered from great distances (safely), and they never miss. But the claim is, for the moment at least, greatly exaggerated. There is no technological fix currently available, and therefore no way of avoiding this simple truth: from the standpoint of justice, you cannot invade a foreign country, with all the consequences that has for other people, while insisting that your own soldiers can never be put at risk. Once the intervention has begun, it may become morally, even if it is not yet militarily, necessary to fight on the ground—in order to win more quickly and save many lives, for example, or to stop some particularly barbarous response to the intervention.

That's the moral argument against no-risk interventions, but there is also a prudential argument. Interventions will rarely be successful unless there is a visible willingness to fight and to take casualties. In the Kosovo case, if a NATO army had been in sight, so to speak, before the bombing of Serbia began, it is unlikely that the bombing would have been necessary; nor would there ever have been the tide of desperate and embittered refugees. Postwar Kosovo would look very different; the tasks of policing and reconstruction would be easier than they have been; the odds on success much better.

[4]

Imagine the intervening army fully engaged. How should it understand the victory that it is aiming at? When is it time to go home? Should the army aim only at stopping the killings, or at destroying the military or paramilitary forces carrying them out, or at replacing the regime that employs these forces, or at punishing the leaders of the regime? Is intervention only a war or also an occupation? These are hard questions, and I want to begin my own response by acknowledging that I have answered them differently at different times.

The answer that best fits the original legal doctrine of humanitarian intervention, and that I defended in *Just and Unjust Wars* (1977), is that the aim of the intervening army is simply to stop the killing. Its leaders prove that their motives are primarily humanitarian, that they are not driven by imperial ambition, by moving in as quickly as possible to defeat the killers and rescue their victims and then by leaving as quickly as possible. Sorting things out afterward, dealing with the consequences of the awfulness, deciding what to do with its agents—that is not properly the work of foreigners. The people who have always lived there, wherever "there" is, have to be given a chance to reconstruct their common life. The crisis that they have just been through should not become an occasion for foreign domination. The principles of political sovereignty and territorial integrity require the "in and quickly out" rule.

But there are three sorts of occasions when this rule seems impossible to apply. The first is perhaps best exemplified by the Cambodian killing fields, which were so extensive as to leave, at the end, no institutional base, and perhaps no human base, for reconstruction. I don't say this to justify the Vietnamese establishment of a satellite regime, but rather to explain the need, years later, for the UN's effort to create, from the outside, a locally legitimate political system. The UN couldn't or wouldn't stop the killing when it was actually taking place, but had it done so, the "in and quickly out" test would not have provided a plausible measure of its success; it would have had to deal, somehow, with the aftermath of the killing.

The second occasion is exemplified by all those countries—Uganda, Rwanda, Kosovo, and others—where the extent and depth of the ethnic divisions make it likely that the killings will resume as soon as the intervening forces withdraw. If the original killers don't return to their work, then the revenge of their victims will prove equally deadly. Now "in and quickly out" is a kind of bad faith, a choice of legal virtue at the expense of political and moral effectiveness. If one accepts the risks of intervention in countries like these, one had better accept also the risks of occupation.

The third occasion is the one I called nonstandard earlier on: where the state has simply disintegrated. It's not that its army or police have been defeated; they simply don't exist. The country is in the hands of paramilitary forces and warlords—gangs, really—who have been, let's say, temporarily subdued. What is necessary now is to create a state, and the creation will have to be virtually *ex nihilo*. And that is not work for the short term.

In 1995, in an article called "The Politics of Rescue," published in *Dissent*, I argued that leftist critics of protectorates and trusteeships needed to rethink their position, for arrangements of this sort might sometimes be the best outcome of a humanitarian intervention. The historical record makes it clear enough that protectors and trustees, under the old League of Nations, for example, again and again failed to fulfill their obligations; nor have these arrangements been as temporary as they were supposed to be. Still, their purpose can sometimes be a legitimate one: to open a span of time and to authorize a kind of political work between the "in" and the "out" of a humanitarian intervention. This purpose doesn't cancel the requirement that the intervening forces get out. We need to think about better ways of making sure that the purpose is actually realized and the requirement finally met. Perhaps this is a place where multilateralism can play a more central role than it does, or has done, in the original interventions. For multilateral occupations are unlikely to serve the interests of any single state and so are unlikely to be sustained any longer than necessary. The greater danger is that they won't be sustained long enough: each participating state will look for an excuse to pull its own forces out. An independent UN force, not bound or hindered by the political decisions of individual states, might be the most reliable protector and trustee— if we could be sure that it would protect the right people, in a timely way. Whenever that assurance doesn't exist, unilateralism returns, again, as a justifiable option.

Either way, we still need an equivalent of the "in and out" rule, a way of recognizing when these longstanding interventions reach their endpoint. The appropriate rule is best expressed by a phrase that I have already used: "local legitimacy." The intervening forces should aim at finding or establishing a form of authority that fits or at least accommodates the local political culture, and a set of authorities, independent of themselves, who are capable of governing the country and who command sufficient popular support so that their government won't be massively coercive. Once such authorities are in place, the intervening forces should withdraw: "in and finally out."

But this formula may be as quixotic as "in and quickly out." Perhaps foreign forces can't do the work that I've just described; they will only be dragged deeper and deeper into a conflict they will never be able to control, gradually becoming indistinguishable from the other parties. That prospect is surely a great disincentive to intervention; it will often override not only the benign intentions but even the imperial ambitions of potential interveners. In fact, most of the countries whose inhabitants (or some of them) desperately need to be rescued offer precious little political or economic reward to the states that attempt the rescue. One almost wishes that the impure motivations of such states had more plausible objects, the pursuit of which might hold them to their task. At the same time, however, it's important to insist that the task is limited: once the massacres and ethnic cleansing are really over and the people in command are committed to avoiding their return, the intervention is finished. The new regime doesn't have to be democratic or liberal or pluralist or (even) capitalist. It doesn't have to be anything, except non-murderous. When intervention is understood in this minimalist fashion, it may be a little easier to see it through.

As in the argument about occasions, minimalism in endings suggests that we should be careful in our use of human rights language. For if we pursue the legal logic of rights (at least as that logic is understood in the United States), it will be very difficult for the intervening forces to get out before they have brought the people who organized the massacres or the ethnic cleansing to trial and established a new regime committed to enforcing the full set of human rights. If those goals are actually within reach, then, of course, it is right to reach for them. But intervention is a political and military process, not a legal one, and it is subject to the compromises and tactical shifts that politics and war require. So we will often need to accept more minimal goals, in order to minimize the use of force and the time span over which it is used. I want to stress, however, that we need, and haven't yet come close to, a clear understanding of what "minimum" really means. The intervening forces have to be prepared to use the weapons they carry, and they have to be prepared to stay what may be a long course. The international community needs to find ways of supporting these forces—and also, since what they are doing is dangerous and won't always be done well, of supervising, regulating, and criticizing them.

[5]

I have tried to answer possible objections to my argument as I went along, but there are a couple of common criticisms of the contemporary practice of humanitarian intervention that I want to single out and address more explicitly, even at the cost of repeating myself. A few repetitions, on key points, will make my conclusion. I am going to take Edward Luttwak's critical review of Michael Ignatieff's *Virtual War*[1] as a useful summary of the arguments to which I need to respond, since it is short, sharp, cogent, and typical. Ignatieff offers a stronger human rights justification of humanitarian warfare than I have provided, though he would certainly agree that not every rights violation "shocks the conscience of humankind" and justifies military intervention. In any case, Luttwak's objections apply (or fail to apply) across the board—that is, to the arguments I've made here as well as to Ignatieff's book.

First objection: the "prescription that X should fight Y whenever Y egregiously violates X's moral and juridical norms would legitimize eternal war." This claim seems somewhat inconsistent with Luttwak's further claim (see below) that the necessity of fighting not only forever but everywhere follows from the fact that there are so many violations of commonly recognized norms. But leave that aside for now. If we intervene only in extremity, only in order to stop mass murder and mass deportation, the idea that we are defending X's norms and not Y's is simply wrong. Possessive nouns don't modify morality in such cases, and there isn't a series of different moralities—the proof of this is the standard and singular lie told by all the killers and "cleansers": they deny what they are doing; they don't try to justify it by reference to a set of private norms.

Second objection: "Even without civil wars, massacres, or mutilations, the perfectly normal, everyday functioning of armies, police forces, and bureaucracies entails constant extortion, frequent robbery and rape, and pervasive oppression"—all of which, Luttwak claims, is ignored by the humanitarian interveners. So it is, and should be, or else we would indeed be fighting all the time and everywhere. But note that Luttwak assumes now that the wrongness of the extortion, robbery, rape, and oppression is not a matter of X's or Y's private norms but can be recognized by anyone. Maybe he goes too far here, because bureaucratic extortion, at least, has different meaning and valence in different times and places. But the main actions on his list are indeed awful, and commonly known to be awful; they just aren't awful enough to justify a military invasion. I don't think the point is all that difficult, even if we disagree about exactly where the line should be drawn. Pol Pot's killing fields had to be shut down—and by a foreign army if necessary. The prisons of all the more ordinary dictators in the modern world should also be shut down—emptied and closed. But that is properly the work of their own subjects.

Third objection: "What does it mean," Luttwak asks, "for the morality of a supposedly moral rule when it is applied arbitrarily, against some but not others?" The answer to this question depends on what the word "arbitrarily" means here. Consider a domestic example. The police can't stop every speeding car. If they go after only the ones they think they will be able to catch without endangering themselves or anyone else, their arrests will be "determined by choice or discretion," which is one of the meanings of "arbitrary," but surely that determination doesn't undermine the justice of enforcing the speeding laws. On the other hand, if they only go after cars that have bumper stickers they don't like, if they treat traffic control as nothing more than an opportunity to harass political "enemies," then their actions "arise from will or caprice," another definition of "arbitrary," and are indeed unjust. It's the first kind of "arbitrariness" that ought to qualify humanitarian interventions (and often does). They are indeed discretionary, and we have to hope that prudential calculations shape the decision to intervene or not. Hence, as I have already acknowledged, there won't be an actual intervention every time the justifying conditions for it exist. But, to answer Luttwak's question, that acknowledgment doesn't do anything to the morality of the justifying rule. It's not immoral to act, or decline to act, for prudential reasons.

These three objections relate to the occasions for intervention, and rightly so. If no coherent account of the occasions is possible, then it isn't necessary to answer the other questions that I have addressed. My own answers to those other questions can certainly be contested. But the main point that I want to make is that the questions themselves cannot be avoided. Since there are in fact legitimate occasions for humanitarian intervention, since we know, roughly, what ought to be done, we have to argue about how to do it; we have to argue about agents, means, and endings. There are a lot of people around today who want to avoid these arguments and postpone indefinitely the kinds of action they might require. These people have all sorts of reasons, but none of them, it seems to me, are good or moral reasons.

NOTES

A slightly different version of this article was given as the Theodore Mitan Lecture at Macalester College, St. Paul, Minnesota.

1. Edward Luttwak, "No Score War," *Times Literary Supplement* (July 14, 2000), 11.

CHAPTER FIFTEEN

Beyond Humanitarian Intervention

Human Rights in Global Society

I want to begin in the middle of things so that I can move back and forth and not pretend that my argument is a march toward a necessary conclusion. It isn't that; maybe some later version of the argument will start at the beginning, if I can figure out where the beginning is. So let's agree that mass murder, ethnic cleansing, and the establishment of slave labor camps are not just barbarous and inhuman acts but violations of human rights, and that these violations should be dealt with, if they can be, all else having failed, through military intervention by neighboring states or coalitions of states or by an international force. And let's also agree that the perpetrators of mass murder, etc. should be removed from power and, if possible, brought to justice before an international court: call it the ICC. So we have a minimal conception of rights (extending to life and liberty but not much beyond that), a rough description of the agents responsible for enforcement and punishment, and a readiness to use force as a means of enforcement in extreme cases.

The agreement that I've just stipulated is, I believe, more or less actual in many parts of the world, though people differ widely about its meaning. We might think of humanitarian intervention as the first example of the global enforcement of human rights—contested, incomplete, uncertain, but still an example of something that has not existed until now. The question that I want to pose today is: How far can we or should we move beyond this example? What expansion (or revision) of these three ideas—rights, agency, and enforcement—is necessary if we are to create or, more modestly, imagine a better international society than the one we have?

There is a more standard way of opening the same discussion. Consider the extended and interconnected ideas of rights, agency, and enforcement that prevail in a stable democratic state—and then ask: What parts of this system should we introduce into international society? That last question assumes that we are not aiming at a global state, for then the answer would be easy: we would have to introduce the whole thing. But if international society remains a society of putatively sovereign or, better, semi-sovereign states, then the answer isn't easy at all.

I will make it a little easier by avoiding, as I go along, all the hard philosophical questions about the meaning and grounding of human rights. The questions will recur, and I will push them away each time. Of course, I could escape from the hard questions by avoiding the "rights-talk" with which I began. And there are philosophical reasons for doing that—namely, the argument that rights have neither meaning nor grounding. Remember Jeremy Bentham's quip that talk about rights is "nonsense on stilts."[1] He may be right, but I am going to manage my stilts as best I can and let my readers decide about the nonsense question. There are also political reasons for giving up on rights, propounded chiefly these days by writers on the postmodern left. Jean Baudrillard claims, for example, that "human rights have already been subsumed by the process of globalization and function [only] as an alibi. They belong to the juridical and moral superstructure—in short, they are *advertising*."[2] And Michael Hardt and Antonio Negri argue in their book *Empire* that the "moral intervention" of human rights NGOs in places like Bosnia "has become a frontline force of imperial intervention."[3] I don't doubt that rights-talk can function as an alibi for imperialism; still, imperialism predates rights-talk by at least four thousand years, so it can't be a necessary alibi; there have been and will be many others. In our own time, rights-talk is more often critical than ideological; it plays a large part in the arguments we make against murderous or tyrannical states and ultranationalist movements. In both domestic and international society, rights-talk has become the ordinary language with which we think about the protection we owe one another, at least in extreme cases. It is most useful, then, to powerless and vulnerable people who desperately need protection. And the organizations and activists trying to meet that need commonly talk that talk. So the rest of us should not give it up.

[1]

I mean to argue for the necessary interconnection of rights, agents, and (some sort of) enforcement, but I will begin with rights simply, which are standardly divided into negative and positive.[4] There are rights *against* certain sorts of aggressive or invasive acts, and there are rights *to* certain sorts of resources and services. We have already agreed on, or I have stipulated, the existence of a right not to be murdered or enslaved and also of a right to be rescued from mass murder and enslavement, and we have agreed that this applies internationally as well as domestically. Would the first of these rights have any value without the second? You and I and all our friends and relatives certainly have this negative right, and therefore no one should murder us. But suppose someone tries to do that or actually begins to do it: what then? Some second party is acting wrongly; do we have a right to third-party protection? A right to be protected is a positive right: someone has to allocate the money, recruit the necessary people, and provide the protective services. How can the right to life exist in the world at large if there is no provider, no agent in international society obligated to move forcefully across political boundaries to stop mass murder? I suppose that it can exist in its purely negative form; having declared its existence (or acknowledged or invented it), we can recognize when the right has been violated; we can protest against particular violations; we can organize associations for the moral or political defense of life and liberty. That's not nothing. Still, without a provider of protection, without an enforcer, it isn't much help to the people whose rights are at stake. Hence the need to talk concretely about enforcement and its agents.

In domestic society, we can say that this is what the state is for; the state is our enforcement agency. But we can't say, this is what the global state is for (since there is no global state). Is this what the UN is for? The UN does organize rescue and relief in some humanitarian crises, but do individual men and women around the world have a right to UN rescue and relief? If they do, the UN is in gross violation of human rights wherever people are being murdered. That doesn't seem the most useful description of the many recent examples, and yet my starting assumption was that someone is bound to act in such cases, and if no one acts, then it isn't only the actual murderers who are violating human rights. Can that be right? We haven't yet established (or recognized) a UN obligation to stop massacre and ethnic cleansing, though we may be in the process of doing that, and I think there is a strong case that that's what we should be doing. But should we be doing more than that? Something wrong is going on when people are massacred, transported, or enslaved, and the world's states are close to agreement on how to describe the wrongness—even if they don't yet agree on what to do about it. They also don't agree on how to describe all the other wrongs in international society. Is rights-talk always the right way?

Well, why not? Why not just declare that all human beings have a right to life and liberty (as I have done), and then look around for ways of enforcing that right? And why not add food and shelter, education and health care, to the list, and even some minimum of leisure time? If we are just "declaring" human rights, it is tempting to come up with a long list—as the UN did in 1948, in its own Declaration.[5] But that seems too easy. We don't have rights just because we would like to have them. Wanting them isn't enough. The most common argument among philosophers holds that we can derive the rights we need from our understanding of what it means to be a human being—rational, vulnerable, capable of agency, autonomous, and so on. But surely nothing is implied by the existence of a single rational or vulnerable agent. Rights require numbers greater than one; they are necessarily relational. Hence they are social creations or (since I am not committing myself on the philosophical questions) they require social recognition. My rights depend for their existence or their effectiveness on your obligations—or on somebody's obligations. So we can't just spin them out in accordance with what we want or what we think we essentially are; we have to specify the social structures without which, whatever rights mean, they don't mean much.

[2]

Agency comes next: I need to identify more precisely the reference of the pronoun in the phrase "your obligations." In the case of purely negative rights, the identification is easy: if I have a right not to be killed, you and everyone else in the world have an obligation not to kill me. But you don't have an obligation to protect me from being killed by someone else. For that second kind of obligation, we have to create a collective agent, which is, as I've said, exactly what a state is. The state is obligated to protect me against being killed by any person or organized group of persons, for whatever reason—except for reasons that the state itself establishes and by persons that it appoints. Once there is a state, we can ask what obligations it has to its citizens to act or refrain from acting, and these obligations define the actual or effective rights of the citizens (and, given some limits, of aliens too). We still have to argue about whether state officials properly understand their obligations and actually enforce the entailed rights. In these arguments, rights-talk is obviously necessary, and it is mostly critics on the right, not the left, who worry about its (over)use.

But before we join the arguments about what states should do to meet or recognize the rights of their citizens, I want to suggest a prior right: namely, the right to have a state, or some other collective agency, that is obligated to its citizens in specific ways. If we have rights, then we have a right to have effective rights. Where is the correlative obligation? Presumably it falls first on our friends and neighbors: any group of people who because of affinity or proximity are capable of setting up a collective agency to protect themselves and one another ought to do so. This is how, according to one well-known political theory, legitimate states come into the world—and arrive with their purposes fixed, though theorists disagree about the chronology of statehood and purposiveness. Does the right to be protected against murder pre-exist the state, or does the aspiration to have such a right motivate the state's formation, or do people create the right in the course of creating the state? I have no views about such questions; in any case, what actually happens when states are created is more complicated and less singularly purposeful than the questions suggest. States serve many purposes. But some states protect some rights some of the time, and no other political agency does that much.

What can we say, then, when people find themselves in a state that doesn't do what it is supposed to do? It fails to protect their rights to life and liberty, or it actively violates their rights. There are too many examples of states like that. Leaving aside the failures to protect, and thinking only of the last 35 years, the governments of Argentina, Cambodia, Chile, Iraq, Pakistan, Indonesia, Uganda, North Korea, Sudan, Serbia, Russia, and China have all been guilty of large-scale violations of the right to life of (some of) their own citizens—and that's not an exhaustive list. The right doesn't disappear in such cases, or else we wouldn't be able to say (what I just said) that it has been violated. The victims still live in a moral world in which rights exist or in which they are widely recognized and in which we can name the violations. Once again, I am not going to speculate on the character of this world and certainly not on its foundations. I only want to ask whether people living in it have a further right to a super-state, which would be obligated to step in and protect them from the violence of their own state. And since there is no super-state, and since the UN, which could fill this role, at least in extreme cases, doesn't yet do so, does this obligation-to-protect still exist? If it does, where does it find a home in international society?

With regard to murder, ethnic cleansing, and slave labor, we have a possible answer to that question—the answer with which I began. States that can intervene should intervene, militarily if all else fails. I will say something about the history of this obligation in a moment. That it exists is the implicit meaning of, for example, President Clinton's expression of regret for American inaction at the time of the Rwandan massacre. If a massacre is in progress, someone should stop it, and given the distribution of capabilities in the world, we can sometimes give that "someone" a proper name. Perhaps there is an even more specific responsibility: a particular state, let's say, has in the past armed or supported the murderers and now it has a special obligation to stop the killing. But the obligation is also general. At least in extreme cases, we all have a right to be rescued by anyone capable of rescuing us.

I should note that the collective agency of the state solves what we might call the "Good Samaritan" problem.[6] Good Samaritans acknowledge that they are bound to help people in desperate trouble—but not if helping puts their own lives at risk. For states this is not a possible excuse; they can help in humanitarian crises without risking their "lives," that is, their sovereignty and territorial integrity. Individual citizens may die; obviously they often do; I don't mean to make light of that, but they are acting in the name and at the behest of their state, which doesn't die. Perhaps they should be volunteers recruited specifically for humanitarian risk-taking. Still, at the critical moment, they act under orders. If I am drowning in a lake, I don't have a right to be rescued (though I will be very grateful if you jump in). But because states can direct such operations, it is possible to imagine that people at risk of massacre or enslavement do have a right to be rescued.

Where did this right come from? We have watched its creation (or its growing recognition), and so we should be able to say something about it. Nineteenth- and early twentieth-century law books describe a "right" of humanitarian intervention, which means that military action to stop mass murder was taken to be optional; there was no obligation to intervene and therefore no right to be rescued. That latter right is a very recent, and incomplete, creation (or, we have only recently, and partially, recognized it). Its background, I suppose, is the growing entanglement of a global society. But its most immediate source is the Holocaust, and the commitment expressed so widely in 1945 and '46 that nothing like that would ever happen again, and then the failure in these last decades to honor the commitment. One possible explanation of the right to be rescued is shame for all the rescues that haven't happened—culminating, I think, in the moral disasters of the former Yugoslavia and of Rwanda. So the right has been created, or it has been acknowledged, though the process of creation/acknowledgment is ongoing and unfinished. What the British theorist Norman Geras calls "the contract of mutual indifference," a kind of silent agreement to look away from people in trouble, is still in effect, but we are writing over it, so to speak, a new "duty to bring help."[7]

In domestic society, as I have argued, the right to be helped exists because of the obligations of states (or states are created to make rights like this effective).

In international society, the duty to bring help is imperfect because there is no global state. Someone should intervene, and sometimes we know who should do that, but sometimes we don't. Suppose a number of states are capable of stopping the massacre in country X: which one should act? Each would prefer that one of the others goes first. If we were more certain about how to assign responsibility, the right to be rescued would be stronger. On the other hand, we try to get particular states or the UN to take responsibility by pointing to the already existing strength of the right. These people are in desperate trouble, we say, and they have a right to be rescued—so rescue them!

My question again: Can we extend this rights-and-responsibility story beyond massacre, ethnic cleansing, and slave labor? I want to suggest that we should do that and that there are, perhaps, faint signs that we are doing it, though in the same informal and haphazard way I have already described: we are beginning to move from those three to famine and malnutrition, which cause even greater numbers of deaths each year—and also, though I won't say much about this, to pandemic disease. This would commonly be described as a move from negative to positive rights, but I believe that that's wrong. All rights are or must become positive if they are to be effective in the world. So, do we have a right to be protected against famine and malnutrition, a right to be provided with food or, better, helped to provide ourselves with food?

The strongest reason for an affirmative response is the claim that famine, exactly like massacre, is caused by malevolent or (probably more often) by negligent human agents. That is the argument the US government made when it sent troops into Somalia in 1990: the local warlords were, literally and deliberately, causing the famine. It seems to be a feature of our moral thinking that we are, or believe we are, more clearly obligated to deal with human wickedness or immoral indifference than with natural disaster. "The focal issue," as Amartya Sen says, "concerns the role of human agency in causing and sustaining famines."[8] Of course, both governments and individuals rush to send help after an earthquake, flood, or hurricane in a foreign country. But most of them think of this as philanthropy; they are acting under the aegis of humane sentiment. It's not that these people have a right to be helped, but rather that helping them is the right thing to do. We are moved by their need, not by their entitlement. And we are commonly moved only to relieve their suffering, not to invest in the prevention of future disasters.

But if we are responsible for the famine or if we know that someone else is responsible, if this famine has been caused by the tyranny, greed, or negligence of governments or corporations, then the case looks different. The argument that famines have political causes, made first by Sen and now by many others, has a two-fold purpose: to persuade us that it is possible to respond politically and also to persuade us that it is morally necessary to respond. If famine is not a natural phenomenon, if human agents "cause" famines by what they do or don't do, then the fundamental right to life has been violated, and we ought to act in its defense. I am not sure that I understand this intuitive sense that agency matters, but it has one very useful consequence: it presses us to look for the patterns of human action and inaction that cause or contribute to human suffering in the world.[9] And we commonly find that tyranny, greed, and negligence figure significantly in those patterns.

Even so, the story that we can tell about famines is not the same as the story that makes humanitarian intervention morally necessary. It is similar in this sense: that these people have a right to be rescued not only from the famine or malnutrition that other people have "caused" but also from the "causes"—just as the victims of a massacre have a right not only that the killing be stopped but that the killers be deprived of the capacity to kill again. In the case of famine, however, I have to put "caused" in scare quotes because I have learned from Sen and also from Iris Young's recent work on "political responsibility" not to insist on a straightforward liability model here. We may be intervening to stop a crime and punish government officials or warlords who are literally causing a famine, and then the intervention may plausibly take a military form: we will literally be "enforcing" human rights—and we may want to bring the guilty officials or warlords to justice. But that's not the usual case. Rather we can discern a complicated set of arrangements and activities of which the famine is one result and in which many different men and women are implicated. If we follow the humanitarian intervention model, we can say that the people suffering from the famine have rights not only against those implicated men and women, but also against any of us who are capable of stopping them from doing what they are doing or of altering the arrangements within which they are doing it. But can these rights be "enforced" in the strict sense? Though force may play a role, the relevant international obligations might better be described in terms of enablement and implementation.

If there are such obligations, they fall on states and NGOs that have the capacity to act effectively; they fall on the UN as the association of responsible states; they fall on the international agencies that control or shape the global economy. In international society today, economic regulation is more effective than political rule (that is, the IMF and the WTO are more effective than the Security Council) and so, faced with a famine, we can turn to the regulators in almost the same way as we might turn to the state in a domestic crisis. Their obligation is not to provide instant relief—that is someone else's task—but to alter the conditions that produced the famine. A corrupt, indifferent, or incompetent government may be the primary producer. "Bluntly stated," says a UN report on world hunger, "the problem is not so much a lack of food as a lack of political will"[10]—or, alternatively (the UN report isn't quite blunt enough), it is the presence of a malign political will. But governments of both these sorts, that don't act and that act badly, are themselves produced or supported, very often, by external forces. So the obligation to help is global in its extent.

That is a strong claim, but it still applies only to crises. I have moved from massacre to famine, which is some distance but not a great distance. Most defenders of human rights hope to go much farther than that. But I want to stop here and insist on the value of the move. Remember that my aim is to imagine a better, not a perfect, international society, and a society whose individual members were protected as a matter of right from massacre and famine, and also from events and conditions associated with each of these, like ethnic cleansing and pandemic disease, would be far better than anything we know today. Indeed, to make the rights meaningful and effective by specifying the correlative obligations would be a major achievement.

[3]

What ought to be done for the sake of this achievement? What kind of enforcement or implementation is morally necessary? Notice that in domestic society, police and public health officials don't intervene only when a crime is in progress, or people are actually starving to death, or a disease is rapidly spreading. They anticipate the danger and act to prevent its occurrence. We need that kind of anticipation in international society, and one version of it would involve giving some practical meaning to "the right to have rights," which is also the right to have an effective state. I described the correlative obligation as falling first on friends and neighbors, which is a whimsical idea, but now we should extend the obligation's reach to more organized agents. Failed and failing states are a key cause of many of the disasters of recent history (examples like Sierra Leone and Liberia suggest that it is Hobbes who got anarchy right, not the Anarchists). Once the failure is fully manifest and the war of all against all has begun, there may be no way of dealing with it—or no way except through military intervention. But before that happens, there are other and better ways. Imagine that successful states, acting, perhaps, through the UN or some other

international agency, were prepared to provide material assistance to governments struggling against failure: to alter the terms of trade, to assist in agricul-
tural development, to lower the cost of medicines, to send in doctors and nurses,
to train police, and so on. Imagine that they broke off political and commercial
relations with the predatory governments of failing states. Imagine that they
refused to recognize the validity of contracts signed with rulers who trade
their country's resources for personal profit. Imagine that they supported political movements and governments-in-exile committed to respect human rights.
These and other, related policies don't quite constitute the enforcement of
rights, but they would help to establish the conditions within which rights could
be enforced. And they would make disasters less frequent and less disastrous.[11]
Do people who live in failing states have a right to this kind of help? I suggest
that they do, but I am content with a more modest argument: if they have a right
to be helped later on, when the killing begins or the famine is taking its toll, then
it is certainly prudent to act *as if* they have rights in anticipation of the killing
and the famine.

Right now, states are the critical agents of rights enforcement. When they
have the power to enforce rights, of course, they also have the power to violate
rights. But that is equally true of all other imaginable agents, including a world
government. What is unique to the state is the description of rights enforcement
as its central purpose (even when that's not its actual purpose). When a state
fails its own citizens, no other entity exists whose central purpose it is to rescue
them. We can argue, as I have done, that the US had an obligation to stop, or
help stop, the Rwandan massacre. But we can't argue that the purpose of the
American state is to protect the people of Rwanda. Nor is that the purpose of the
UN or, at least, it is not a purpose that the UN effectively serves (though one
day it might); nor is it the purpose of any of the organizations that function in
international civil society. Human Rights Watch watches violations of human
rights, and reports on them, which is a very useful thing to do, but it doesn't
actively protect the victims. So the Rwandans need a protector of their own, and
since they live in a society of states, where this political formation is recognized,
where its sovereignty and territorial integrity are legally protected, and where
individual men and women commonly have no other recourse, it seems plausible to say that they have a right to a state—I mean, a decent state that protects
their rights. And the other members of international society are obligated, or
they should act as if they are obligated, to foster that kind of statehood, as best
they can, for the Rwandans and for any other people whose rights are at risk.

But states don't protect their citizens only against massacre, famine, and other associated evils. At their best, they provide a much wider range of protection and provision, which corresponds roughly to the wider agenda of human rights activists. The agenda isn't infinitely wide. These activists don't necessarily claim that everyone in the world has a right, say, to a vacation with pay—the most frequently mocked of the UN's declared rights. But they will certainly claim that everyone has a right to religious freedom; and to a number of further freedoms, of association and political speech, for example; and also to education and employment and collective bargaining with employers; and also to security and dignity in old age. All these rights are, or sometimes are, or can be, served by the state and, in democratic states, citizens can organize to ensure the service. I doubt, however, that there are agents beyond the state who are obligated to enforce or implement these rights if states default. And if there are no such agents, do the rights have any meaningful existence in international society? Whether they exist at all is the philosophical question that I am determined not to answer. Perhaps we should think of them as constituting a political agenda or party program—or we should think of them as claims waiting for a response. How should we respond?

Should we seek, for example, the creation of a global School Board empowered to make sure that "no child is left behind" (the Bush administration's promise to American children) anywhere in the world? Or should we send an army into country X, where the Ministry of Education is hopelessly corrupt and the schools in shambles? What if the Minister of Education refuses to allow the teaching of modern science? Should we rescue the students from (what will be called) "medieval superstition"? Or, more relevant to current human rights concerns, what if the minister insists that only boys should be educated? Should a foreign legion of Teachers with Swords forcibly open the schools to boys and girls alike? If we are not morally bound to do that, or to see that it is done, can we say that the children in country X have a right to an education? We might even ask whether they have a right against their own state, if gender discrimination is a feature of the dominant culture in the state. But I am not going to join the human rights versus local culture debate, since I believe that an argument for equal protection and provision can almost always be made from within the local culture. Amartya Sen has made just this kind of argument against the claim that "Asian values" exclude its possibility.[12] And in North Africa and the Middle East, a group called Women Living Under Muslim Law (WLUML) has waged an extensive campaign for equality, basing itself on texts and traditions from many parts of the Islamic world.[13]

Suppose that a feminist movement develops in country X, as such movements have developed in parts of Asia and the Middle East: it will almost certainly claim in its first manifesto that girls have a right to the same education as boys. Many of us would want to help vindicate that right—with money, with publicity, maybe even with tourist and trade boycotts. But only the citizens of the country, the parents of the children, could seek the coercive enforcement of this right by their state. And it clearly isn't a right against other states, requiring them to use military force or any other means of coercion. The right of children in country X to an education has no correlative obligation in international society; at least, it has no full-scale correlative. We may want the American state to work through UNESCO, say, to foster educational equality around the world, and we may also want our government to work for a stronger UNESCO. But this work, if we were ready to do it, would be more reflective of our commitments than of our obligations.

The absence of correlative obligations (except in extreme cases) makes what I have called the right to have rights, to have a state that enforces rights, all the more important. And this is so however we imagine the extension of those "rights," since the state provides, or a decent state provides, an opportunity for citizens to put together their own lists. The state isn't the only arena for doing that, as the work of multinational organizations like WLUML suggests. But it is right now the only agent of coercive enforcement—short of an invading army (and we should never be in a hurry to summon an invading army).

Meanwhile, the short list of global rights that I have defended still requires a lot of work. If men and women around the world are to be protected against all the man-made disasters of collective life, the killing and dying in which states and corporations and individuals are implicated, we need to name all the agents—those who should not have done what they did, those who should have done what they didn't, and those who must act now because of what the others did and didn't do. And we have to try to describe as concretely as we can what acting now means: what is the range of available and legitimate actions? That has been my strategy in this essay: not to multiply rights but to specify agents and enforcement mechanisms for the short list. I might well support an international campaign for multiplication, but that would be a cause, a political battle, and it would not depend on a philosophical or legal analysis of the concept of "rights." Meanwhile, however, we have to take care of the short list. If we do that, it is far more likely than it is today that the longer list will be taken care of by the people most directly concerned, who are also most capable of saying what goods should be protected and provided as a matter of right and how that might best be done.

NOTES

1. Jeremy Bentham, "Anarchical Fallacies: Being an Examination of the Declaration of Rights Issued during the French Revolution" (1796), in *The Works of Jeremy Bentham*, vol. 2, ed. John Bowring (Edinburgh: William Tait, 1843), 491–534. Reprinted (New York: Russell and Russell, 1962), 501.

2. Richard Wolin, "Kant at Ground Zero," *The New Republic* (February 9, 2004), 25–32. Quoted from "This Is the Fourth World War: The *Der Spiegel* Interview with Jean Baudrillard," *International Journal of Baudrillard Studies* 1:1 (January 2004). Interview translated by Samir Gandesha.

3. Michael Hardt and Antonio Negri, *Empire* (Cambridge: Harvard University Press, 2000), 36.

4. For a useful general account, see Jack Donnelly, *The Concept of Human Rights* (London: Croom Helm, 1985).

5. Maurice Cranston, *What Are Human Rights?* (New York: Taplinger, 1973), appendix A and comments in the preceding text.

6. See *The Good Samaritan and the Law: The Morality—and the Problems—of Aiding Those in Peril*, ed. James M. Ratcliffe (New York: Anchor Books, 1966).

7. Norman Geras, *The Contract of Mutual Indifference: Political Philosophy After the Holocaust* (London: Verso, 1998), 49ff.

8. Amartya Sen, *Development as Freedom* (New York: Knopf, 1999), 171.

9. See Iris Young, "From Guilt to Solidarity: Sweatshops and Political Responsibility," *Dissent* (Spring 2003), 39–44.

10. Somini Sengupta, "World Hunger Increasing, New U.N. Report Finds." *New York Times* (November 25, 2003): A10. Quoted from "The State of Food Insecurity in the World 2003" (Rome: Food and Agriculture Organization of the United Nations, 2003).

11. Thomas W. Pogge canvasses proposals of this sort in his chapter, "Priorities of Global Justice," in *Global Justice*, ed. Thomas W. Pogge (Oxford: Blackwell, 2001), 6–23.

12. See Amartya Sen, "Human Rights and Asian Values," *Sixteenth Morgenthau Memorial Lecture on Ethics and Foreign Policy* (New York: Carnegie Council on Ethics and International Affairs, 1997).

13. Madhavi Sunder, "Piercing the Veil," *Yale Law Journal* 112:6 (April 2003), 1433–57.

CHAPTER SIXTEEN

Terrorism and Just War

[1]

I will begin by arguing that just war theory helps us understand the wrong-
fulness of terrorism, and then I will do two things with this argument—
first, consider the choice of terror as a political strategy, and then worry
about some of the problems of combating it. What can go wrong in the "war"
against terrorism, and is just war theory equally helpful in thinking about this
"war"—where the scare quotes are always necessary?

Terrorism is the random killing of innocent people, in the hope of creating
pervasive fear. The fear can serve different political purposes, one of which, as I
will argue later on, might well figure in the definition or, at least, in our moral
understanding of the phenomenon. Nonetheless, it's easy to imagine a terrorist
organization, as it might be portrayed by Franz Kafka, say, that has no purpose
at all. Randomness and innocence are the crucial elements in the definition. The
critique of this kind of killing hangs especially on the idea of innocence, which is
borrowed from just war theory—and often misunderstood. "Innocence" functions in the theory as a term of art; it describes the group of noncombatants,
civilians, men and women who are not materially engaged in the war effort.
These people are "innocent" whatever their government and country are doing
and whether or not they are in favor of what is being done. The opposite of
"innocent" is not "guilty," but "engaged." Disengaged civilians are innocent
without regard to their personal morality or politics.

But why are all civilians immune from attack, while soldiers are collectively
at risk? According to the rules of *jus in bello*, once the fighting has begun, it is
entirely legitimate to kill soldiers at random, as they come within range, so to
speak, and it is legitimate to try to terrorize the ones who never come within

range. And yet, a lot of soldiers are not actual combatants; they serve behind the lines; they are involved in transportation, the provision of food, the storing of supplies; they work in offices; they rarely carry weapons. And no soldiers are always combatants; they rest and play, eat and sleep, read newspapers, write letters. Some of them are in the army by choice, but some of them are there unwillingly; if they had been given a choice, they would be doing something else. How can they all be subject to attack simply because they bear the name and wear the uniform of a soldier? Why doesn't innocence, as a term of art, describe some of them, some of the time? On the other hand, if soldiers are rightly subject to attack, all of them, all the time, if they are collectively at risk, then why can't civilians, as a class, also be legitimate targets? These civilians are members of a political community; by a clear majority, let's say, they elected a government that is waging an unjust war or is committed to a policy of oppression, and so they share responsibility for immoral, possibly criminal, acts. Why aren't the terrorists right when they say that membership and responsibility make civilians collectively vulnerable to attack?

I am going to take this question seriously despite my skepticism about the seriousness of some of the people who ask it. The answer has to do with the meaning of membership in an army and in civilian society. The army is an organized, disciplined, trained, and highly purposeful collective, and all its members contribute to the achievement of its ends. Even soldiers who don't carry weapons have been taught how to use them, and they are tightly connected, by way of the services they provide, to the actual users. It doesn't matter whether they are volunteers or conscripts; their individual moral preferences are not at issue; they have been mobilized for a singular purpose, and what they do advances that purpose. For its sake, they are isolated from the general public, housed in camps and bases, all their needs provided for by the state. In time of war they pose a unified threat.

The society of civilians is not at all like that; civilians have many different purposes; they have been trained in many different pursuits and professions; they participate in a highly differentiated set of organizations and associations, whose internal discipline, compared to that of an army, is commonly very loose. They don't live in barracks but in their own houses and apartments; they don't live with other soldiers but with parents, spouses, and children; they are not all of an age but include the very old and the very young; they are not provided for by the government but provide for themselves and one another. As citizens, they belong to different political parties; they have different views on public issues; many of them take no part at all in political life; and, again, some of them are children. Even a *levée en masse* cannot transform this group of people into anything like an organized military collective.

But they are a collective of another kind: they are, together with their sons and daughters in the army, a people. Whether their peoplehood is ethnic or national in character or wholly political, constituted only by their citizenship, doesn't matter here. They identify themselves as French, or Irish, or Bulgarian; they commonly share a language and a history and, in some prosaic sense of the term, a destiny. Their individual futures are closely linked, and this linkage is especially tight when their country is at war.

Implicit in the theory of just war is a theory of just peace: whatever happens to these two armies, whichever one wins or loses, whatever the nature of the battles or the extent of the casualties, the "peoples" on both sides must be accommodated at the end. The central principle of *jus in bello*, that civilians can't be targeted or deliberately killed, means that they will be—morally speaking, they have to be—present at the conclusion. This is the deepest meaning of noncombatant immunity: it doesn't only protect individual noncombatants; it also protects the group to which they belong. Just as the destruction of the group cannot be a legitimate purpose of war, so it cannot be a legitimate practice in war. Civilians are immune as ordinary men and women, disengaged from the business of warfare; they are also immune as members of a human community that is not a military organization.

There is one partial exception to this immunity rule that also suggests its general strength. If a country fights an unjust war, and is defeated, it can be forced to pay reparations to its victims, and this burden will be distributed through the tax system to all its citizens, whatever their role in the war or their views about the war. But this collective financial burden is the only one we allow; we would not impose forced labor on the citizens of the defeated state; and we would certainly not kill them simply because of their citizenship. Only individuals charged with specific war crimes can be brought to trial and, possibly, executed. All the others retain their individual and group immunities: it is both right and good that their lives continue and that their political or national community survives.

Terrorists attack both these immunities. They devalue not only the individuals they kill but also the group to which the individuals belong. They signal a political intention to destroy or remove or radically subordinate these people individually and this "people" collectively. That is the long-term purpose of the fear they inspire. Hence, while all terrorists are murderers, all murderers are not terrorists. Most murderers intend to kill specific people; terrorists kill at random within a specific group of people. The message they deliver is directed at the group: *we don't want you here.* We will not accept you or make our peace with you as fellow-citizens or partners in any political project. You are not candidates for equality or even co-existence.

This is most obviously the message of nationalist terror, aimed at a rival nation, and of religious terror, aimed at infidels or heretics. State terror is also most often focused on a collective that is thought to be oppositional or potentially so—sometimes an ethnic group, sometimes a socio-economic class: the Tatars, the Kurds, the kulaks, the urban middle class, anyone with a college education, and so on. But sometimes state agencies use random killing, "disappearances," arrests, and torture to terrorize the whole population of their country. Now it's not massacre or removal that is being signaled, but tyranny, that is, radical subordination. In fact, tyranny and terror are always closely connected. Tyrants rule by terror, as Aristotle first pointed out.[1] And when terrorists-out-of-power seize power, they are likely to rule in the same way; intimidation, not deliberation, is their modus operandi. Edmund Burke was not right about the French Revolution as a whole or about the political doctrines that inspired it, but he was certainly right about some of the revolutionaries—the ones who launched the Terror: "In the groves of *their* academy, at the end of every vista, you see nothing but the gallows."[2]

But isn't terror sometimes a more modest strategy, aimed only at changing the policy of a government? The innocent people targeted are the people this government is supposed to protect, and the message is that they will be at risk until the government surrenders or withdraws or concedes some set of demands. Once that happens, the killing will stop—so the terrorists say—and the innocent people, those of them who are still alive, won't be forced to abandon their homes or submit to a tyrannical regime. Consider the American use of nuclear weapons against Japan in 1945: this was surely an act of terrorism; innocent men and women were killed in order to spread fear across a nation and force the surrender of its government. And this action went along with a demand for unconditional surrender, which is one of the forms that tyranny takes in wartime. In the end, the US did not insist on unconditional surrender, and the occupation of Japan was not a permanent subordination of the Japanese people to American power. But this only means that the message terrorists send is not always acted out later on. There can't be any doubt that the destruction of Hiroshima and Nagasaki implied, at the moment the bombs were dropped, a radical devaluation of Japanese lives and a generalized threat to the Japanese people.

Sometimes, perhaps, terrorists do have limited purposes (and sometimes, perhaps, political militants with limited purposes are called terrorists but don't quite fit the definition). Consider the case of the Irish Republican Army as it once was. The aim of its members was to reunite Ulster with Eire, and they were prepared, officially at least, to accept Ulster Protestants as a minority in a unified Ireland. Perhaps for that reason, much of their violence involved attempts to kill political leaders, punish particular individuals for "collaboration" with the British, and bomb buildings that symbolized the power structure—giving notice in advance of their attacks, so as to allow people to get out of the way. But there were also random killings, bombs in pubs, for example, which were sometimes attributed to rogue elements within the organization, but probably also represented IRA policy.[3] Assume, though, that the policy had been different, that all violent acts were aimed at particular people. Even then, I would not want to justify IRA violence, only to suggest that when we condemn it, "terrorism" would not be the right word to use. It isn't, after all, the only negative term in our moral vocabulary.

In all those cases where violence is random, directed against innocent men and women, its victims have good reason to be skeptical about claims that the terrorists have a limited agenda. From the perspective of the victims, which is morally very important, terror is a totalizing practice. Random murder implies universal vulnerability, and the implication is often realized in practice. Stalinist terror, to take an obvious example, was not designed "to win the class struggle in the countryside" by threatening the kulaks; it was designed to get rid of the kulaks. Algerian terrorists probably intended what they achieved—the removal of Europeans from Algerian soil (they had considerable help from the Europeans). Palestinian terrorists have been remarkably honest about their intentions; they don't claim to have limited purposes, though the claim is sometimes made on their behalf. Perhaps Basque terrorists would settle for a state of their own; they don't intend the destruction of Spain. But they may well intend the ethnic (and ideological) cleansing of the Basque country. Similarly, revolutionary terrorists like the various "Red Armies" of the 1970s presumably would have stopped killing capitalists once the capitalist system had fallen. On the other hand, they might have tried to purge their country of its corrupt and now counter-revolutionary bourgeoisie. It seems best to take seriously the signal that terrorists send.

Of course, most terrorists don't want to be identified and judged by the signal they send but rather by the goals they announce—not the destruction, removal, or radical subordination of a nation or a community of faith or a social class but victory in a just war, national liberation, or the triumph of their religion. And why shouldn't we identify them first of all by reference to their stated ends rather than to the means they employ? I have often heard it said that a war against terrorism makes no sense, since terror is an instrument, not a full-scale politics like, say, communism or Islamic radicalism. But surely one of the most important reasons for opposing communism and Islamic radicalism is that these ideologies have served, in the real world, to inspire and justify terrorism. The instruments one chooses are often morally defining—as in the case of the members of Murder, Incorporated, say, or the Mafia, whose long-term end, making a lot of money, is shared with many other people and entirely acceptable in a capitalist society. No doubt, the goals of criminal gangs fail to justify the means they choose, but, what is equally important, the goals don't serve to identify the actors. Members of the Mafia may think of themselves as business-men, but we rightly call them gangsters. Similarly, men and women who bomb urban residential areas, or organize massacres, or make people "disappear," or blow themselves up in crowded cafes may think of themselves as political or religious militants or as public officials and civil servants, but we rightly call them terrorists. And we oppose them, or we should oppose them, *because* they are terrorists.

If we name terrorists by their actions rather than their supposed goals, we are then free to support the goals—if we think them just—and even actively to pursue them in non-terrorist ways. We can support the US war effort against Japan even while we oppose the bombing of Hiroshima and Nagasaki. We can work for Algerian independence even while we oppose FLN terrorism. We can call for Palestinian statehood, while condemning the groups that target Israeli civilians. A decent politics often requires a two front campaign—against op-pression and occupation, as in the last two cases, and also, simultaneously, against murder.

I don't believe that terrorism can ever be justified. But I also don't want to defend an absolute ban. "Do justice even if the heavens fall" has never seemed to me a plausible moral position. In rare and narrowly circumscribed cases, it may be possible, not to justify, but to find excuses for terrorism. I can imagine myself doing that in the hypothetical case of a terrorist campaign by Jewish militants against German civilians in the 1940s—if attacks on civilians had been likely (in fact they would have been highly unlikely) to stop the mass murder of the Jews. The argument from extremity might work in truly extreme circum-stances, but we have to be very careful here, for terrorism, as I have been insisting, threatens mass murder even when it doesn't reach that far. In fact, I don't know of any actual terrorist campaign that can be excused in this way, despite the common claim of desperation. The standard excuses—that terrorism is the weapon of the weak, used only as a last resort, in response to looming catastrophe—don't work.[4] Actual terrorists threaten mass murder in order to oppose or, better, with a pretense of opposing, something less. And most often they have the totalizing intentions that their actions signal.

This is the wrong of terrorism: the murder of the innocent and the creation of a devalued collective, a group of men and women who have been deprived of the right to life or, alternatively, of the right to live where they are living. They have been denied what may well be the most important of the Four Freedoms proclaimed by Roosevelt and Churchill in 1943: freedom from fear. It is the extension of violence or the threat of violence from individuals to groups that is the special feature of terrorism: men and women are targeted because of their ethnic, religious, or class membership—because they are Japanese, or Protestants in Northern Ireland, or Muslims in Gujarat, or kulaks in the Ukraine, or Jews in Israel. It is who you are, not what you are doing, that makes you vulnerable; identity is liability. And that's a connection that we are morally bound to resist.

[2]

Terror is a strategy that has to be chosen from a fairly wide range of possible strategies. It is always a choice. For many years, I have been urging that when we think about terrorism we have to imagine a group of people sitting around a table, arguing about what ought to be done. We don't have minutes of those meetings, but we have descriptions of them, and we know that they have taken place in all the cases of terrorist activity. We also know that some people around the table have argued against the choice of terror. Terrorism is not the general will of Irish Catholics or Algerians or Palestinians or Americans (there were leading figures in the US government and army who opposed the use of the atomic bomb in 1945[5]); it isn't the necessary product of a religious or political culture. Just as "Asian values," as Amartya Sen has insisted, don't mandate opposition to human rights, so Irish or Algerian or Palestinian or American values don't require the acceptance of terrorism. That is a decision supported by some, opposed by others.

I suppose that the arguments are more often prudential than moral, but I don't believe that the people sitting around the table are "realists" who simply seize political opportunities or are driven by military necessities. That is the standard view in political science and perhaps in politics generally, and on this view moral justification is nothing but a façade, hastily erected after the crucial choices have been made. Sometimes, perhaps, "realism" is an accurate description of what happens in the "real world," but I want to suggest—provocatively, I hope, but also realistically—that sometimes just the opposite is true: strategic arguments are a façade behind which militants and officials act out their deepest political/moral convictions. Sometimes strategy is a disguise for morality (or immorality).

Consider the British decision to bomb German cities. In the early 1940s, British politicians and generals, sitting around a table, debated strategic bombing policy. Should the goal of the RAF be to kill as many German civilians as possible, so as to terrorize the enemy and shut down the economy, or should the pilots aim only at military targets? The debate was conducted, as far as I can tell from the available memoirs and histories, entirely in the language of strategy; the principle of noncombatant immunity was never mentioned.[6] What were the probabilities of hitting military targets, given the navigational and aiming devices then available? What losses would the air force suffer if it flew by day so as to aim (a little) more precisely? What were the likely effects of bombing urban residential areas on civilian morale and then on the production and delivery of military supplies? Outside the government, a few people raised moral questions about bombing policy; inside, it was as if there was a ban on moral talk: there's no-one here but us realists! But if you look at the years after the war, it turns out that the people who favored bombing residential areas in, say, 1943 were, later on, advisors and office-holders in Tory governments where they continued to defend tough and "realistic" decision-making, and the people who opposed it were on the left, working for Labor governments or the Campaign for Nuclear Disarmament and, often, making the moral arguments they didn't make during the war. Surely their strategic arguments in the 1940s were driven in part by their repressed political/moral convictions—not only by their views on the "necessity" of killing civilians, but also by their views on the rightness or wrongness of such killing. After all, strategists commonly work from inadequate and uncertain information; their predictions are cast in very rough probabilities; they can easily go either way, and they seem to go, or often to go, the way the people making them (or the people for whom they are made) want them to go.

So, when terrorists tell us that they had no choice, there was nothing else to do, terror was their last resort, we have to remind ourselves that there were people around the table arguing against each of those propositions. And we also have to recognize that strategic considerations are not the sole, possibly not the most important, factor shaping these arguments. The overall politics and morality, the worldview, of the participants is also a factor. They are in fact answering questions like these: Do they acknowledge the human value of their enemies? Are they prepared for a compromise peace? Can they imagine a future state in which they share power but do not rule? This is what is actually at stake around the table, and we can see the wrong of terrorism reiterated in the negative answers that come from its advocates.

[3]

Once the decision is made, and terrorists are doing their work, how should we fight against them? I am going to assume the value of doing that, and I am not going to consider here efforts to do something else under cover of the "war" against terrorism (like fight a war in Iraq). There isn't any worthy political cause that can't be exploited for unworthy and unrelated purposes, but my subject here is the cause, not the exploitation. I am also not going to try to describe the necessary political response to terror. I take it for granted that a political response is necessary, but "fighting" is also necessary. The first answer to the question about how to fight is simple in principle, though often difficult in practice: not terroristically. That means, without targeting innocent men and women. I will focus on that principle, which derives from the theory of just war—though the "war" against terrorism is closer, as we will see, to police work than to actual combat. And so there is a second answer to the question about how to fight: we must operate within the constraints of constitutional democracy, just as the police are supposed to do. But constitutionalism, like politics more generally, is a subject for another occasion.

In order to fight, you have to identify the enemy, so it is very important to say at the outset that the people the terrorists claim to represent are not themselves complicit in the terror. Whatever their emotional connection or disconnection (and we know that they are often strongly connected), they are not material supporters; they fit my description of the civilian collective. The terrorists do have material support, but their supporters are particular men and women, not the people generally. At the end of the "war" against terrorism, as at the end of any other war, the people generally will have to be accommodated. The terrorists collectivize the guilt of the other side, insisting that every single person is implicated in the war or the oppression. The anti-terrorists must collectivize in the opposite way, insisting on the innocence of the people generally. Like the police, again, they have to look for the particular individuals who are planning, providing material support for, or actually carrying out terrorist operations. That search is more difficult than the search for legitimate targets in "ordinary" warfare. There are indeed terrorist organizations; sometimes they look like criminal gangs, sometimes like enemy armies, but most often they are different from both of these. In any case, however they are organized, they are not the same as "the people."

It is a moral and political mistake, then, to engage in collective punishments —destroying the family home where a suicide bomber lived, for example, as the Israelis have done, on the assumption that the family supported the bomber or could have prevented the bombing. That might sometimes be true, but it is often untrue (despite the statements family members are forced to issue after the event). In domestic society, the police are not allowed to act like that, demolishing the homes of Mafia relatives, say, because they live off the family business; nor should armies or "special forces" be allowed to do that either. If a particular relative is complicit in the crime, then the anti-terrorists have to find some way to apprehend and punish that person—not the family, the village, or the urban neighborhood. Collective punishment treats people as enemies who may be as different from one another (in their politics, for example) as were the people in the café or on the bus that the suicide bomber attacked. And it is to the advantage of the anti-terrorists that those (political) differences be brought into the open, not suppressed.

The terrorists hold that there is no such thing as "collateral" or, as the dictionary says, secondary damage. All damage for them is primary, and they want to do as much damage as they can: the more deaths, the more fear. So anti-terrorists have to distinguish themselves by insisting on the category of collateral damage, and by doing as little of it as they can. The same rules of *jus in bello* apply to the "war" against terrorism as to war in general: soldiers must aim only at military targets and they must minimize the harm they do to civilians. I don't believe that the doctrine of "double effect," as it is usually understood, adequately describes what is required here. It isn't enough that the first effect, the damage to military targets, is intended and the second one, the harm to civilians, is unintended. The two effects require two intentions: first, that the damage be done and, second, that the harm be avoided. What justice demands is that the army take positive measures, accept risks to its own soldiers, in order to avoid harm to civilians.[7] The same requirement holds for anti-terrorists—holds more strongly, I think, insofar as it is mostly police rather than soldiers who are at work in this "war" (or, the soldiers are doing police work), and we impose much higher standards of care for civilians on the police than we do on armies in combat.

This need for care also governs the practice that has come to be called "targeted killing." It is the Israelis who made this practice famous, but I am going to look at an American example. First, though, a general word. The killing of the political leaders of the enemy state is ruled out by just war theory, as it is by international law, because of the assumption that the war will end, and should end, with a peace agreement negotiated with those same leaders, who are taken to be representative figures. Not many people would have opposed the assassination of Adolph Hitler, but that was (in part) because we had no intention of negotiating with him. But this argument applies only to *political* leaders, the heads of the civilian collective; it doesn't apply at all to army officers, who are part of a military collective.

We should probably try to make this same distinction in the "war" against terrorism, even when it is blurred or non-existent in fact. In Ireland, the political party, Sinn Fein, managed to separate itself from the IRA—an "army" whose members were vulnerable to attacks from which the politicians were exempt. If the separation was a pretense, as the British claimed for a long time, it was a useful pretense, as they acknowledged in the end when they negotiated with the leaders of Sinn Fein—who were by then in a tense relationship with IRA militants. It is harder to figure out how to deal with organizations that hardly bother to pretend that they have separate political and military "arms," like Hamas in Palestine, where the claim to separation is made only after an Israeli attack and then forgotten. Still, it might be prudent to support the pretense in the hope that it will one day take on some reality and open a path to negotiation. But this is prudence, it seems to me, not a moral requirement (except insofar as political leaders ought to be prudent).

In any case, the vulnerability of military leaders is clear. If a couple of British commandos in World War II had crossed German lines in North Africa (or if a couple of German commandos had crossed British lines), made their way to army headquarters, and killed a colonel, a brilliant tactician, let's say, who was planning, but wasn't going to be engaged in, the next tank attack, that would have been a "targeted killing," but not a wrongful assassination.

Now consider the case of the five Al Qaeda militants (so they were described by US officials) traveling in a van in the Yemini desert, who were killed by a Hellfire missile in November, 2002. Imagine that the same attack had taken place ten months earlier in Afghanistan. It would have been an act of war and, assuming that the people killed were correctly identified, we would not have thought the attack wrong or even problematic. It is part of the awfulness of war that people actively engaged on the other side can legitimately be killed without warning. Sometimes it is possible to offer them a chance to surrender but often, in night raids, ambushes, and air attacks, for example, it isn't possible.

Now imagine that the same Hellfire attack on the same people in the same van had taken place not in Afghanistan but on a street in Philadelphia. It would not be an act of war, and it would not be legitimate. We would be horrified; the attack would be a political crime, and we would look for the officials responsible. In Philadelphia, the (suspected) terrorists would have to be arrested, arraigned, provided with lawyers, and brought to trial. They could not be killed unless they were convicted—and many Americans, opposed to capital punishment, would say: not even then.

Yemen is somewhere between Afghanistan and Philadelphia. It isn't a war zone, but it also isn't a zone of peace—and this description will fit many, not all, of the "battlefields" of the "war" against terrorism. In large sections of Yemen, the government's writ doesn't run; there are no police who could make the arrests (14 soldiers had already been killed in attempts to capture the Al Qaeda militants) and no courts in which prisoners could expect a fair trial. The Yemini desert is a lawless land, and lawlessness provides a refuge for the political criminals called terrorists. The best way to deal with the refuge would be to help the Yemini government extend its authority over the whole of its territory. But that is a long process, and the urgencies of the "war" against terrorism may require more immediate action. When that is true, if it is true, it doesn't seem morally wrong to target Al Qaeda militants directly—for capture, if that's possible, but also for death. Yemen in this regard is closer to Afghanistan than to Philadelphia.

But there are two moral/political limits on policies of this sort, and the limits are critically important because governments, once they learn to kill, are likely to kill too much and too often. The first limit is implied by the word "targeted." We have to be as sure as we can be, without judge or jury, that the people we are aiming at are really Al Qaeda militants or, more generally, that they are engaged in planning and carrying out terrorist attacks. Targets have to be identified, and the work of identification must be careful and precise.

The second limit is at least equally important. We have to be as sure as we can be that we are able to hit the targeted person without killing innocent people in his (or her) vicinity. Here I think that we have to adopt standards that are closer to Philadelphia than to Afghanistan. In a war zone, collateral damage cannot be avoided; it can only be minimized. The hard question in war is what degree of risk we are willing to accept for our own soldiers in order to reduce the risks we impose on enemy civilians. But when the police are chasing criminals in a zone of peace, we rightly give them no latitude for collateral damage. In the strongest sense, they must intend not to injure civilians—even if that makes their operation more difficult and even if the criminals get away.

That seems to me roughly the right rule for people planning targeted killings. Like the police, they are not actually engaged in a battle; they plan their attack in advance and they can call it off if they discover, say, that their target is holding a child on his lap (as in Albert Camus's play *The Just Assassins*[8]), or has moved into a crowd, or is sitting in an apartment that isn't empty—as it was expected to be. They can't avoid imposing some degree of risk on innocent people, and the risks will certainly be greater than those imposed by police in a city at peace, but we must insist on a strenuous effort to minimize the risks. The American attack in the Yemini desert may have met this standard; I don't know enough about the people killed, or about other people in the vicinity, or about the tactical choices that had to be made, to arrive at a firm judgment. Some of Israel's targeted killings have met the standard; some almost certainly have not. A car on a busy street is not a permissible target—no more than a single table in a crowded café would be. If terrorists use other people as shields, then anti-terrorists have to find their way around the shields, just as we would want the police to do. The case of the one ton bomb dropped on an apartment house in Gaza, where the target was one person but almost twenty were killed, is a paradigmatic example of what should not be done. I don't think that it could be justified even by wartime rules of "taking aim."

When killing takes precedence over targeting, the anti-terrorists look too much like the terrorists, and the moral distinction that justifies their "war" is called into question. The same thing happens in domestic society when the line between police and criminals is blurred by the brutality or corruption of the police. But it is important to stress that when that happens, we defend the line as best we can by criticizing and reforming the police; we don't join the criminals. Similarly, whatever goes wrong in the "war" against terrorism doesn't affect the wrongness of terror. In fact, it confirms the wrongness: what we learn is that we have to condemn the murder of innocent people wherever it occurs, on both sides of the line.

This condemnation works best, it seems to me, if we start from just war theory with its recognition of non-combatant immunity. But as the last part of this essay should have made clear, we can't stop with just war theory. We need to maneuver between our conception of combat and our conception of police work, between international conflict and domestic crime, between the zones of war and peace. *Jus in bello* represents an adaptation of morality to the circumstances of combat, to the heat of battle. We may need further adaptations, to the circumstances of terror. But we can still be guided, even in these new circumstances, by our fundamental understanding of when fighting and killing are just and when they are unjust.

NOTES

1. Aristotle, *The Politics*, 1311a, 1312a–1314a.

2. Edmund Burke, *Reflections on the Revolution in France* (London: J. M. Dent [Everyman's Library], 1953), 75.

3. See Maria McGuire, *To Take Arms: My Year with the IRA Provisionals* (New York: Viking Press, 1973).

4. I discuss these excuses in "Terrorism: A Critique of Excuses," in *Arguing about War* (New Haven: Yale University Press, 2004), 51–66.

5. The opponents included General Dwight Eisenhower and Admiral William Leahy. See Gar Alperowitz's definitive study *The Decision to Use the Atomic Bomb* (New York: Knopf, 1995).

6. I rely here on Noble Frankland, *The Bombing Offensive against Germany* (London: Faber, 1965), Gavin Lyall, ed., *The War in the Air: The Royal Air Force in World War II* (New York: Ballantine, 1970), Dudley Saward, *Bomber Harris* (Garden City, N.Y.: Doubleday, 1985), C. P. Snow, *Science and Government* (The Godkin Lectures at Harvard University) (New York: New American Library, 1962), and John C. Ford, S.J., "The Morality of Obliteration Bombing," in Richard Wasserstrom, ed., *War and Morality* (Belmont, Calif.: Wadsworth, 1970), 15–41.

7. I defend this revision of the doctrine of double effect in more detail in *Just and Unjust Wars* (New York: Basic Books, 1977), 152–59.

8. "The Just Assassins," Act II: "There were children in the Grand Duke's carriage." The play is included in *Caligula and 3 Other Plays*, trans. Stuart Gilbert (New York: Vintage, 1958), 253.

CHAPTER SEVENTEEN

Political Action

The Problem of Dirty Hands

In an early issue of *Philosophy and Public Affairs* there appeared a symposium on the rules of war which was actually (or at least more importantly) a symposium on another topic.[1] The actual topic was whether or not a man can ever face, or ever has to face, a moral dilemma, a situation where he must choose between two courses of action both of which it would be wrong for him to undertake. Thomas Nagel worriedly suggested that this could happen and that it did happen whenever someone was forced to choose between upholding an important moral principle and avoiding some looming disaster.[2] R. B. Brandt argued that it could not possibly happen, for there were guidelines we might follow and calculations we might go through which would necessarily yield the conclusion that one or the other course of action was the right one to undertake in the circumstances (or that it did not matter which we undertook). R. M. Hare explained how it was that someone might wrongly suppose that he was faced with a moral dilemma: sometimes, he suggested, the precepts and principles of an ordinary man, the products of his moral education, come into conflict with injunctions developed at a higher level of moral discourse. But this conflict is, or ought to be, resolved at the higher level; there is no real dilemma.

I am not sure that Hare's explanation is at all comforting, but the question is important even if no such explanation is possible, perhaps especially so if this is the case. The argument relates not only to the coherence and harmony of the moral universe, but also to the relative ease or difficulty—or impossibility—of living a moral life. It is not, therefore, merely a philosopher's question. If such a dilemma can arise, whether frequently or very rarely, any of us might one day face it. Indeed, many men have faced it, or think they have, especially men involved in political activity or war. The dilemma, exactly as Nagel describes it, is frequently discussed in the literature of political action—in novels and plays dealing with politics and in the work of theorists too.

In modern times the dilemma appears most often as the problem of "dirty hands," and it is typically stated by the Communist leader Hoerderer in Sartre's play of that name: "I have dirty hands right up to the elbows. I've plunged them in filth and blood. Do you think you can govern innocently?"³ My own answer is no, I don't think I could govern innocently; nor do most of us believe that those who govern us are innocent—as I shall argue below—even the best of them. But this does not mean that it isn't possible to do the right thing while governing. It means that a particular act of government (in a political party or in the state) may be exactly the right thing to do in utilitarian terms and yet leave the man who does it guilty of a moral wrong. The innocent man, afterwards, is no longer innocent. If on the other hand he remains innocent, chooses, that is, the "absolutist" side of Nagel's dilemma, he not only fails to do the right thing (in utilitarian terms), he may also fail to measure up to the duties of his office (which imposes on him a considerable responsibility for consequences and outcomes). Most often, of course, political leaders accept the utilitarian calculation; they try to measure up. One might offer a number of sardonic comments on this fact, the most obvious being that by the calculations they usually make they demonstrate the great virtues of the "absolutist" position. Nevertheless, we would not want to be governed by men who consistently adopted that position.

The notion of dirty hands derives from an effort to refuse "absolutism" without denying the reality of the moral dilemma. Though this may appear to utilitarian philosophers to pile confusion upon confusion, I propose to take it very seriously. For the literature I shall examine is the work of serious and often wise men, and it reflects, though it may also have helped to shape, popular thinking about politics. It is important to pay attention to that too. I shall do so without assuming, as Hare suggests one might, that everyday moral and political discourse constitutes a distinct level of argument, where content is largely a matter of pedagogic expediency.⁴ If popular views are resistant (as they are) to utilitarianism, there may be something to learn from that and not merely something to explain about it.

[1]

Let me begin, then, with a piece of conventional wisdom to the effect that politicians are a good deal worse, morally worse, than the rest of us (it is the wisdom of the rest of us). Without either endorsing it or pretending to disbelieve it,

I am going to expound this convention. For it suggests that the dilemma of dirty hands is a central feature of political life, that it arises not merely as an occasional crisis in the career of this or that unlucky politician but systematically and frequently.

Why is the politician singled out? Isn't he like the other entrepreneurs in an open society, who hustle, lie, intrigue, wear masks, smile and are villains? He is not, no doubt for many reasons, three of which I need to consider. First of all, the politician claims to play a different part than other entrepreneurs. He doesn't merely cater to our interests; he acts on our behalf, even in our name. He has purposes in mind, causes and projects that require the support and redound to the benefit, not of each of us individually, but of all of us together. He hustles, lies, and intrigues *for us*—or so he claims. Perhaps he is right, or at least sincere, but we suspect that he acts for himself also. Indeed, he cannot serve us without serving himself, for success brings him power and glory, the greatest rewards that men can win from their fellows. The competition for these two is fierce; the risks are often great, but the temptations are greater. We imagine ourselves succumbing. Why should our representatives act differently? Even if they would like to act differently, they probably can not: for other men are all too ready to hustle and lie for power and glory, and it is the others who set the terms of the competition. Hustling and lying are necessary because power and glory are so desirable—that is, so widely desired. And so the men who act for us and in our name are necessarily hustlers and liars.

Politicians are also thought to be worse than the rest of us because they rule over us, and the pleasures of ruling are much greater than the pleasures of being ruled. The successful politician becomes the visible architect of our restraint. He taxes us, licenses us, forbids and permits us, directs us to this or that distant goal—all for our greater good. Moreover, he takes chances for our greater good that put us, or some of us, in danger. Sometimes he puts himself in danger too, but politics, after all, is his adventure. It is not always ours. There are undoubtedly times when it is good or necessary to direct the affairs of other people and to put them in danger. But we are a little frightened of the man who seeks, ordinarily and every day, the power to do so. And the fear is reasonable enough. The politician has, or pretends to have, a kind of confidence in his own judgment that the rest of us know to be presumptuous in any man.

The presumption is especially great because the victorious politician uses violence and the threat of violence—not only against foreign nations in our defense but also against us, and again ostensibly for our greater good. This is a point emphasized and perhaps overemphasized by Max Weber in his essay

"Politics as a Vocation."[5] It has not, so far as I can tell, played an overt or obvious part in the development of the convention I am examining. The stock figure is the lying, not the murderous, politician—though the murderer lurks in the background, appearing most often in the form of the revolutionary or terrorist, very rarely as an ordinary magistrate or official. Nevertheless, the sheer weight of official violence in human history does suggest the kind of power to which politicians aspire, the kind of power they want to wield, and it may point to the roots of our half-conscious dislike and unease. The men who act for us and in our name are often killers, or seem to become killers too quickly and too easily.

Knowing all this or most of it, good and decent people still enter political life, aiming at some specific reform or seeking a general reformation. They are then required to learn the lesson Machiavelli first set out to teach: "how not to be good."[6] Some of them are incapable of learning; many more profess to be incapable. But they will not succeed unless they learn, for they have joined the terrible competition for power and glory; they have chosen to work and struggle as Machiavelli says, among "so many who are not good." They can do no good themselves unless they win the struggle, which they are unlikely to do unless they are willing and able to use the necessary means. So we are suspicious even of the best of winners. It is not a sign of our perversity if we think them only more clever than the rest. They have not won, after all, because they were good, or not only because of that, but also because they were not good. No one succeeds in politics without getting his hands dirty. This is conventional wisdom again, and again I don't mean to insist that it is true without qualification. I repeat it only to disclose the moral dilemma inherent in the convention. For sometimes it is right to try to succeed, and then it must also be right to get one's hands dirty. But one's hands get dirty from doing what it is wrong to do. And how can it be wrong to do what is right? Or, how can we get our hands dirty by doing what we ought to do?

[2]

It will be best to turn quickly to some examples. I have chosen two, one relating to the struggle for power and one to its exercise. I should stress that in both these cases the men who face the dilemma of dirty hands have in an important sense chosen to do so; the cases tell us nothing about what it would be like, so to speak, to fall into the dilemma; nor shall I say anything about that here. Politicians often argue that they have no right to keep their hands clean, and that may well be true of them, but it is not so clearly true of the rest of us. Probably we do have a right to avoid, if we possibly can, those positions in which we might be forced to do terrible things. This might be regarded as the moral equivalent of our legal right not to incriminate ourselves. Good men will be in no hurry to surrender it, though there are reasons for doing so sometimes, and among these are or might be the reasons good men have for entering politics. But let us imagine a politician who does not agree to that: he wants to do good only by doing good, or at least he is certain that he can stop short of the most corrupting and brutal uses of political power. Very quickly that certainty is tested. What do we think of him then?

He wants to win the election, someone says, but he doesn't want to get his hands dirty. This is meant as a disparagement, even though it also means that the man being criticized is the sort of man who will not lie, cheat, bargain behind the backs of his supporters, shout absurdities at public meetings, or manipulate other men and women. Assuming that this particular election ought to be won, it is clear, I think, that the disparagement is justified. If the candidate didn't want to get his hands dirty, he should have stayed at home; if he can't stand the heat, he should get out of the kitchen, and so on. His decision to run was a commitment (to all of us who think the election important) to try to win, that is, to do within rational limits whatever is necessary to win. But the candidate is a moral man. He has principles and a history of adherence to those principles. That is why we are supporting him. Perhaps when he refuses to dirty his hands, he is simply insisting on being the sort of man he is. And isn't that the sort of man we want?

Let us look more closely at this case. In order to win the election the candidate must make a deal with a dishonest ward boss, involving the granting of contracts for school construction over the next four years. Should he make the deal? Well, at least he shouldn't be surprised by the offer, most of us would probably say (a conventional piece of sarcasm). And he should accept it or not, depending on exactly what is at stake in the election. But that is not the candidate's view. He is extremely reluctant even to consider the deal, puts off his aides when they remind him of it, refuses to calculate its possible effects upon the campaign. Now, if he is acting this way because the very thought of bargaining with that particular ward boss makes him feel unclean, his reluctance isn't very interesting. His feelings by themselves are not important. But he may also have reasons for his reluctance. He may know, for example, that some of his supporters support him precisely because they believe he is a good man, and this means to them a man who won't make such deals. Or he may doubt his own motives for considering the deal, wondering whether it is the political campaign or his own candidacy that makes the bargain at all tempting. Or he may believe that if he makes deals of this sort now he may not be able later on to achieve those ends that make the campaign worthwhile, and he may not feel entitled to take such risks with a future that is not only his own future. Or he may simply think that the deal is dishonest and therefore wrong, corrupting not only himself but all those human relations in which he is involved.

Because he has scruples of this sort, we know him to be a good man. But we view the campaign in a certain light, estimate its importance in a certain way, and hope that he will overcome his scruples and make the deal. It is important to stress that we don't want just *anyone* to make the deal; we want *him* to make it, precisely because he has scruples about it. We know he is doing right when he makes the deal because he knows he is doing wrong. I don't mean merely that he will feel badly or even very badly after he makes the deal. If he is the good man I am imagining him to be, he will feel guilty, that is, he will believe himself to be guilty. That is what it means to have dirty hands.

All this may become clearer if we look at a more dramatic example, for we are, perhaps, a little blasé about political deals and disinclined to worry much about the man who makes one. So consider a politician who has seized upon a national crisis—a prolonged colonial war—to reach for power. He and his friends win office pledged to decolonization and peace; they are honestly committed to both, though not without some sense of the advantages of the commitment. In any case, they have no responsibility for the war; they have steadfastly opposed it. Immediately, the politician goes off to the colonial capital to open negotiations with the rebels. But the capital is in the grip of a terrorist campaign, and the first decision the new leader faces is this: he is asked to authorize the torture of a captured rebel leader who knows or probably knows the location of a number of bombs hidden in apartment buildings around the city, set to go off within the next twenty-four hours. He orders the man tortured, convinced that he must do so for the sake of the people who might otherwise die in the explosions—even though he believes that torture is wrong, indeed abominable, not just sometimes, but always.[7] He had expressed this belief often and angrily during his own campaign; the rest of us took it as a sign of his goodness. How should we regard him now? (How should he regard himself?)

Once again, it does not seem enough to say that he should feel very badly. But why not? Why shouldn't he have feelings like those of St. Augustine's melancholy soldier, who understood both that his war was just and that killing, even in a just war, is a terrible thing to do?[8] The difference is that Augustine did not believe that it was wrong to kill in a just war; it was just sad, or the sort of thing a good man would be saddened by. But he might have thought it wrong to torture in a just war, and later Catholic theorists have certainly thought it wrong. Moreover, the politician I am imagining thinks it wrong, as do many of us who supported him. Surely we have a right to expect more than melancholy from him now. When he ordered the prisoner tortured, he committed a moral crime and he accepted a moral burden. Now he is a guilty man. His willingness to acknowledge and bear (and perhaps to repent and do penance for) his guilt is evidence, and it is the only evidence he can offer us, both that he is not too good for politics and that he is good enough. Here is the moral politician: it is by his dirty hands that we know him. If he were a moral man and nothing else, his hands would not be dirty; if he were a politician and nothing else, he would pretend that they were clean.

[3]

Machiavelli's argument about the need to learn how not to be good clearly implies that there are acts known to be bad quite apart from the immediate circumstances in which they are performed or not performed. He points to a distinct set of political methods and stratagems which good men must study (by reading his books), not only because their use does not come naturally, but also because they are explicitly condemned by the moral teachings good men accept—and whose acceptance serves in turn to mark men as good. These methods may be condemned because they are thought contrary to divine law or to the order of nature or to our moral sense, or because in prescribing the law to ourselves we have individually or collectively prohibited them. Machiavelli does not commit himself on such issues, and I shall not do so either if I can avoid it. The effects of these different views are, at least in one crucial sense, the same. They take out of our hands the constant business of attaching moral labels to such Machiavellian methods as deceit and betrayal. Such methods are simply bad. They are the sort of thing that good men avoid, at least until they have learned how not to be good.

Now, if there is no such class of actions, there is no dilemma of dirty hands, and the Machiavellian teaching loses what Machiavelli surely intended it to have, its disturbing and paradoxical character. He can then be understood to be saying that political actors must sometimes overcome their moral inhibitions, but not that they must sometimes commit crimes. I take it that utilitarian philosophers also want to make the first of these statements and to deny the second. From their point of view, the candidate who makes a corrupt deal and the official who authorizes the torture of a prisoner must be described as good men (given the cases as I have specified them), who ought, perhaps, to be honored for making the right decision when it was a hard decision to make. There are three ways of developing this argument. First, it might be said that every political choice ought to be made solely in terms of its particular and immediate circumstances—in terms, that is, of the reasonable alternatives, available knowledge, likely consequences, and so on. Then the good man will face difficult choices (when his knowledge of options and outcomes is radically uncertain), but it cannot happen that he will face a moral dilemma. Indeed, if he always makes decisions in this way, and has been taught from childhood to do so, he will never have to overcome his inhibitions, whatever he does, for how could he have acquired inhibitions? Assuming further that he weighs the alternatives and calculates the consequences seriously and in good faith, he cannot commit a crime, though he can certainly make a mistake, even a very serious mistake. Even when he lies and tortures, his hands will be clean, for he has done what he should do as best he can, standing alone in a moment of time, forced to choose.

This is in some ways an attractive description of moral decision-making, but it is also a very improbable one. For while any one of us may stand alone, and so on, when we make this or that decision, we are not isolated or solitary in our moral lives. Moral life is a social phenomenon, and it is constituted at least in part by rules, the knowing of which (and perhaps the making of which) we share with our fellows. The experience of coming up against these rules, challenging their prohibitions, and explaining ourselves to other men and women is so common and so obviously important that no account of moral decision-making can possibly fail to come to grips with it. Hence the second utilitarian argument: such rules do indeed exist, but they are not really prohibitions of wrongful actions (though they do, perhaps for pedagogic reasons, have that form). They are moral guidelines, summaries of previous calculations. They ease our choices in ordinary cases, for we can simply follow their injunctions and do what has been found useful in the past; in exceptional cases they serve as signals warning us against doing too quickly or without the most careful calculations what has not been found useful in the past. But they do no more than that; they have no other purpose, and so it cannot be the case that it is or even might be a crime to override them.[9] Nor is it necessary to feel guilty when one does so. Once again, if it is right to break the rule in some hard case, after conscientiously worrying about it, the man who acts (especially if he knows that many of his fellows would simply worry rather than act) may properly feel pride in his achievement.

But this view, it seems to me, captures the reality of our moral life no better than the last. It may well be right to say that moral rules ought to have the character of guidelines, but it seems that in fact they do not. Or at least, we defend ourselves when we break the rules as if they had some status entirely independent of their previous utility (and we rarely feel proud of ourselves). The defenses we normally offer are not simply justifications; they are also excuses. Now, as Austin says, these two can *seem* to come very close together—indeed, I shall suggest that they can appear side by side in the same sentence—but they are conceptually distinct, differentiated in this crucial respect: an excuse is typically an admission of fault; a justification is typically a denial of fault and an assertion of innocence.[10] Consider a well-known defense from Shakespeare's *Hamlet* that has often reappeared in political literature: "I must be cruel only to be kind."[11] The words are spoken on an occasion when Hamlet is actually being cruel to his mother. I will leave aside the possibility that she deserves to hear (to be forced to listen to) every harsh word he utters, for Hamlet himself makes no such claim—and if she did indeed deserve that, his words might not be cruel or he might not be cruel for speaking them. "I must be cruel" contains the excuse, since it both admits a fault and suggests that Hamlet has no choice but to commit it. He is doing what he has to do; he can't help himself (given the ghost's command, the rotten state of Denmark, and so on). The rest of the sentence is a justification, for it suggests that Hamlet intends and expects kindness to be the outcome of his actions—we must assume that he means greater kindness, kindness to the right persons, or some such. It is not, however, so complete a justification that Hamlet is able to say that he is not *really* being cruel. "Cruel" and "kind" have exactly the same status; they both follow the verb "to be," and so they perfectly reveal the moral dilemma.[12]

When rules are overridden, we do not talk or act as if they had been set aside, canceled, or annulled. They still stand and have this much effect at least: that we know we have done something wrong even if what we have done was also the best thing to do on the whole in the circumstances.[13] Or at least we feel that way, and this feeling is itself a crucial feature of our moral life. Hence the third utilitarian argument, which recognizes the usefulness of guilt and seeks to explain it. There are, it appears, good reasons for "overvaluing" as well as for overriding the rules. For the consequences might be very bad indeed if the rules were overridden every time the moral calculation seemed to go against them. It is probably best if most men do not calculate too nicely, but simply follow the rules; they are less likely to make mistakes that way, all in all. And so a good man (or at least an ordinary good man) will respect the rules rather more than he would if he thought them merely guidelines, and he will feel guilty when he overrides them. Indeed, if he did not feel guilty, "he would not be such a good man."[14] It is by his feelings that we know him. Because of those feelings he will never be in a hurry to override the rules, but will wait until there is no choice, acting only to avoid consequences that are both imminent and almost certainly disastrous.

The obvious difficulty with this argument is that the feeling whose usefulness is being explained is most unlikely to be felt by someone who is convinced only of its usefulness. He breaks a utilitarian rule (guideline), let us say, for good utilitarian reasons: but can he then feel guilty, also for good utilitarian reasons, when he has no reason for believing that he *is* guilty? Imagine a moral philosopher expounding the third argument to a man who actually does feel guilty or to the sort of man who is likely to feel guilty. Either the man won't accept the utilitarian explanation as an account of his feeling about the rules (probably the best outcome from a utilitarian point of view) or he will accept it and then cease to feel that (useful) feeling. But I do not want to exclude the possibility of a kind of superstitious anxiety, the possibility, that is, that some men will continue to feel guilty even after they have been taught, and have agreed, that they cannot possibly *be* guilty. It is best to say only that the more fully they accept the utilitarian account, the less likely they are to feel that (useful) feeling. The utilitarian account is not at all useful, then, if political actors accept it, and that may help us to understand why it plays, as Hare has pointed out, so small a part in our moral education.[15]

[4]

One further comment on the third argument: it is worth stressing that to feel guilty is to suffer, and that the men whose guilt feelings are here called useful are themselves innocent according to the utilitarian account. So we seem to have come upon another case where the suffering of the innocent is permitted and even encouraged by utilitarian calculation.[16] But surely an innocent man who has done something painful or hard (but justified) should be helped to avoid or escape the sense of guilt; he might reasonably expect the assistance of his fellow men, even of moral philosophers, at such a time. On the other hand, if we intuitively think it true of some other man that he *should* feel guilty, then we ought to be able to specify the nature of his guilt (and if he is a good man, win his agreement). I think I can construct a case which, with only small variation, highlights what is different in these two situations.

Consider the common practice of distributing rifles loaded with blanks to some of the members of a firing squad. The individual men are not told whether their own weapons are lethal, and so though all of them look like executioners to the victim in front of them, none of them know whether they are really executioners or not. The purpose of this stratagem is to relieve each man of the sense that he is a killer. It can hardly relieve him of whatever moral responsibility he incurs by serving on a firing squad, and that is not its purpose, for the execution is not thought to be (and let us grant this to be the case) an immoral or wrongful act. But the inhibition against killing another human being is so strong that even if the men believe that what they are doing is right, they will still feel guilty. Uncertainty as to their actual role apparently reduces the intensity of these feelings. If this is so, the stratagem is perfectly justifiable, and one can only rejoice in every case where it succeeds—for every success subtracts one from the number of innocent men who suffer.

But we would feel differently, I think, if we imagine a man who believes (and let us assume here that we believe also) either that capital punishment is wrong or that this particular victim is innocent, but who nevertheless agrees to participate in the firing squad for some overriding political or moral reason—I won't try to suggest what that reason might be. If he is comforted by the trick with the rifles, then we can be reasonably certain that his opposition to capital punishment or his belief in the victim's innocence is not morally serious. And if it is serious, he will not merely feel guilty, he will know that he is guilty (and we will know it too), though he may also believe (and we may agree) that he has good reasons for incurring the guilt. Our guilt feelings can be tricked away when they are isolated from our moral beliefs, as in the first case, but not when they are allied with them, as in the second. The beliefs themselves and the rules which are believed in can only be *overridden,* a painful process which forces a man to weigh the wrong he is willing to do in order to do right, and which leaves pain behind, and should do so, even after the decision has been made.

[5]

That is the dilemma of dirty hands as it has been experienced by political actors and written about in the literature of political action. I don't want to argue that it is only a political dilemma. No doubt we can get our hands dirty in private life also, and sometimes, no doubt, we should. But the issue is posed most dramatically in politics for the three reasons that make political life the kind of life it is, because we claim to act for others but also serve ourselves, rule over others, and use violence against them. It is easy to get one's hands dirty in politics and it is often right to do so. But it is not easy to teach a good man how not to be good, nor is it easy to explain such a man to himself once he has committed whatever crimes are required of him. At least, it is not easy once we have agreed to use the word "crimes" and to live with (because we have no choice) the dilemma of dirty hands. Still, the agreement is common enough, and on its basis there have developed three broad traditions of explanation, three ways of thinking about dirty hands, which derive in some very general fashion from neoclassical, Protestant, and Catholic perspectives on politics and morality. I want to try to say something very briefly about each of them, or rather about a representative example of each of them, for each seems to me partly right. But I don't think I can put together the compound view that might be wholly right.

The first tradition is best represented by Machiavelli, the first man, so far as I know, to state the paradox that I am examining. The good man who aims to found or reform a republic must, Machiavelli tells us, do terrible things to reach his goal. Like Romulus, he must murder his brother; like Numa, he must lie to the people. Sometimes, however, "when the act accuses, the result excuses."[17] This sentence from *The Discourses* is often taken to mean that the politician's deceit and cruelty are justified by the good results he brings about. But if they were justified, it wouldn't be necessary to learn what Machiavelli claims to teach: how not to be good. It would only be necessary to learn how to be good in a new, more difficult, perhaps roundabout way. That is not Machiavelli's argument. His political judgments are indeed consequentialist in character, but not his moral judgments. We know whether cruelty is used well or badly by its effects over time. But that it is bad to use cruelty we know in some other way. The deceitful and cruel politician is excused (if he succeeds) only in the sense that the rest of us come to agree that the results were "worth it" or, more likely, that we simply forget his crimes when we praise his success.

It is important to stress Machiavelli's own commitment to the existence of moral standards. His paradox depends upon that commitment as it depends upon the general stability of the standards—which he upholds in his consistent use of words like good and bad.[18] If he wants the standards to be disregarded by good men more often than they are, he has nothing with which to replace them and no other way of recognizing the good men except by their allegiance to those same standards. It is exceedingly rare, he writes, that a good man is willing to employ bad means to become prince.[19] Machiavelli's purpose is to persuade such a person to make the attempt, and he holds out the supreme political rewards, power and glory, to the man who does so and succeeds. The good man is not rewarded (or excused), however, merely for his willingness to get his hands dirty. He must do bad things well. There is no reward for doing bad things badly, though they are done with the best of intentions. And so political action necessarily involves taking a risk. But it should be clear that what is risked is not personal goodness—*that is thrown away*—but power and glory. If the politician succeeds, he is a hero; eternal praise is the supreme reward for not being good.

What the penalties are for not being good, Machiavelli doesn't say, and it is probably for this reason above all that his moral sensitivity has so often been questioned. He is suspect not because he tells political actors they must get their hands dirty, but because he does not specify the state of mind appropriate to a man with dirty hands. A Machiavellian hero has no inwardness. What he thinks of himself we don't know. I would guess, along with most other readers of Machiavelli, that he basks in his glory. But then it is difficult to account for the strength of his original reluctance to learn how not to be good. In any case, he is the sort of man who is unlikely to keep a diary and so we cannot find out what he thinks. Yet we do want to know; above all, we want a record of his anguish. That is a sign of our own conscientiousness and of the impact on us of the second tradition of thought that I want to examine, in which personal anguish sometimes seems the only acceptable excuse for political crimes.

The second tradition is best represented, I think, by Max Weber, who outlines its essential features with great power at the very end of his essay "Politics as a Vocation." For Weber, the good man with dirty hands is a hero still, but he is a tragic hero. In part, his tragedy is that though politics is his vocation, he has not been called by God and so cannot be justified by Him. Weber's hero is alone in a world that seems to belong to Satan, and his vocation is entirely his own choice. He still wants what Christian magistrates have always wanted, both to do good in the world and to save his soul, but now these two ends have come into sharp contradiction. They are contradictory because of the necessity for violence in a world where God has not instituted the sword. The politician takes the sword himself, and only by doing so does he measure up to his vocation. With full consciousness of what he is doing, he does bad in order to do good, and surrenders his soul. He "lets himself in," Weber says, "for the diabolic forces lurking in all violence." Perhaps Machiavelli also meant to suggest that his hero surrenders salvation in exchange for glory, but he does not explicitly say so. Weber is absolutely clear: "the genius or demon of politics lives in an inner tension with the god of love . . . [which] can at any time lead to an irreconcilable conflict."[20] His politician views this conflict when it comes with a tough realism, never pretends that it might be solved by compromise, chooses politics once again, and turns decisively away from love. Weber writes about this choice with a passionate high-mindedness that makes a concern for one's soul seem no more elevated than a concern for one's flesh. Yet the reader never doubts that his mature, superbly trained, relentless, objective, responsible, and disciplined political leader is also a suffering servant. His choices are hard and painful, and he pays the price not only while making them but forever after. A man doesn't lose his soul one day and find it the next.

The difficulties with this view will be clear to anyone who has ever met a suffering servant. Here is a man who lies, intrigues, sends other men to their death—and suffers. He does what he must do with a heavy heart. None of us can know, he tells us, how much it costs him to do his duty. Indeed, we cannot, for he himself fixes the price he pays. And that is the trouble with this view of political crime. We suspect the suffering servant of either masochism or hypocrisy or both, and while we are often wrong, we are not always wrong. Weber attempts to resolve the problem of dirty hands entirely within the confines of the individual conscience, but I am inclined to think that this is neither possible nor desirable. The self-awareness of the tragic hero is obviously of great value. We want the politician to have an inner life at least something like that which Weber describes. But sometimes the hero's suffering needs to be socially expressed (for like punishment, it confirms and reinforces our sense that certain acts are wrong). And equally important, it sometimes needs to be socially limited. We don't want to be ruled by men who have lost their souls. A politician with dirty hands needs a soul, and it is best for us all if be has some hope of personal salvation, however that is conceived. It is not the case that when be does bad in order to do good be surrenders himself forever to the demon of politics. He commits a determinate crime, and he must pay a determinate penalty. When he has done so, his hands will be clean again, or as clean as human hands can ever be. So the Catholic Church has always taught, and this teaching is central to the third tradition that I want to examine.

Once again I will take a latter-day and a lapsed representative of the tradition and consider Albert Camus's *The Just Assassins*. The heroes of this play are terrorists at work in nineteenth-century Russia. The dirt on their hands is human blood. And yet Camus's admiration for them, he tells us, is complete. We consent to being criminals, one of them says, but there is nothing with which anyone can reproach us. Here is the dilemma of dirty hands in a new form. The heroes are innocent criminals, just assassins, because, having killed, they are prepared to die—*and will die*. Only their execution, by the same despotic authorities they are attacking, will complete the action in which they are engaged:

dying, they need make no excuses. That is the end of their guilt and pain. The execution is not so much punishment as self-punishment and expiation. On the scaffold they wash their hands clean and, unlike the suffering servant, they die happy.

Now the argument of the play when presented in so radically simplified a form may seem a little bizarre, and perhaps it is marred by the moral extremism of Camus's politics. "Political action has limits," he says in a preface to the volume containing *The Just Assassins,* "and there is no good and just action but what recognizes those limits and if it must go beyond them, at least accepts death."[21] I am less interested here in the violence of that "at least"—what else does he have in mind?—than in the sensible doctrine that it exaggerates. That doctrine might best be described by an analogy: just assassination, I want to suggest, is like civil disobedience. In both men violate a set of rules, go beyond a moral or legal limit, in order to do what they believe they should do. At the same time, they acknowledge their responsibility for the violation by accepting punishment or doing penance. But there is also a difference between the two, which has to do with the difference between law and morality. In most cases of civil disobedience the laws of the state are broken for moral reasons, and the state provides the punishment. In most cases of dirty hands moral rules are broken for reasons of state, and no one provides the punishment. There is rarely a Czarist executioner waiting in the wings for politicians with dirty hands, even the most deserving among them. Moral roles are not usually enforced against the sort of actor I am considering, largely because he acts in an official capacity. If they were enforced, dirty hands would be no problem. We would simply honor the man who did bad in order to do good, and at the same time we would punish him. We would honor him for the good he has done, and we would punish him for the bad he has done. We would punish him, that is, for the same reasons we punish anyone else; it is not my purpose here to defend any particular view of punishment. In any case, there seems no way to establish or enforce the punishment. Short of the priest and the confessional, there are no authorities to whom we might entrust the task.

I am nevertheless inclined to think Camus's view the most attractive of the three, if only because it requires us at least to imagine a punishment or a penance that fits the crime and so to examine closely the nature of the crime. The others do not require that. Once he has launched his career, the crimes of Machiavelli's prince seem subject only to prudential control. And the crimes of Weber's tragic hero are limited only by *his* capacity for suffering and not, as they should be, by *our* capacity for suffering. In neither case is there any explicit reference back to the moral code, once it has, at great personal cost to be sure, been set aside. The question posed by Sartre's Hoerderer (whom I suspect of being a suffering servant) is rhetorical, and the answer is obvious (I have already given it), but the characteristic sweep of both is disturbing. Since it is concerned only with those crimes that ought to be committed, the dilemma of dirty hands seems to exclude questions of degree. Wanton or excessive cruelty is not at issue, any more than is cruelty directed at bad ends. But political action is so uncertain that politicians necessarily take moral as well as political risks, committing crimes that they only think ought to be committed. They override the rules without ever being certain that they have found the best way to the results they hope to achieve, and we don't want them to do that too quickly or too often. So it is important that the moral stakes be very high—which is to say, that the rules be rightly valued. That, I suppose, is the reason for Camus's extremism. Without the executioner, however, there is no one to set the stakes or maintain the values except ourselves, and probably no way to do either except through philosophic reiteration and political activity.

"We shall not abolish lying by refusing to tell lies," says Hoerderer, "but by using every means at hand to abolish social classes."[22] I suspect we shall not abolish lying at all, but we might see to it that fewer lies were told if we contrived to deny power and glory to the greatest liars—except, of course, in the case of those lucky few whose extraordinary achievements make us forget the lies they told. If Hoerderer succeeds in abolishing social classes, perhaps he will join the lucky few. Meanwhile, he lies, manipulates, and kills, and we must make sure he pays the price. We won't be able to do that, however, without getting our own hands dirty, and then we must find some way of paying the price ourselves.

NOTES

An earlier version of this paper was read at the annual meeting of the Conference for the Study of Political Thought in New York, April 1971. I am indebted to Charles Taylor, who served as commentator at that time and encouraged me to think that its arguments might be right.

1. *Philosophy and Public Affairs* 1:2 (Winter 1971/72): Thomas Nagel, "War and Massacre," 123–44; R. B. Brandt, "Utilitarianism and the Rules of War," 145–65; and R. M. Hare, "Rules of War and Moral Reasoning," 166–81.

2. For Nagel's description of a possible "moral blind alley," see "War and Massacre," 142–44. Bernard Williams has made a similar suggestion, though without quite acknowledging it as his own: "Many people can recognize the thought that a certain course of action is, indeed, the best thing to do on the whole in the circumstances, but that doing it involves

doing something wrong" (*Morality: An Introduction to Ethics* [New York: Cambridge University Press, 1972], 93).

3. Jean-Paul Sartre, *Dirty Hands* in *No Exit and Three Other Plays*, trans. Lionel Abel (New York: Vintage Books, 1955), 224.

4. Hare, "Rules of War and Moral Reasoning," 173–78, esp. 174: "The simple principles of the deontologist . . . have their place at the level of character-formation (moral education and self-education)."

5. Max Weber, "Politics as a Vocation" in *From Max Weber: Essays in Sociology*, trans. and ed. Hans H. Gerth and C. Wright Mills (New York: Oxford University Press, 1946), 77–128.

6. See Niccolò Machiavelli, *The Prince*, chap. 15; cf. Niccolò Machiavelli, *The Discourses*, bk. 1, chaps. 9, 18. I quote from the Modern Library edition of the two works (New York, 1950), 57.

7. I leave aside the question of whether the prisoner is himself responsible for the terrorist campaign. Perhaps he opposed it in meetings of the rebel organization. In any case, whether he deserves to be punished or not, he does not deserve to be tortured.

8. Other writers argued that Christians must never kill, even in a just war; and there was also an intermediate position which suggests the origins of the idea of dirty hands. Thus Basil the Great (bishop of Caesarea in the fourth century AD): "Killing in war was differentiated by our fathers from murder. . . nevertheless, perhaps it would be well that those whose hands are unclean abstain from communion for three years." Here dirty hands are a kind of impurity or unworthiness, which is not the same as guilt, though closely related to it. For a general survey of these and other Christian views, see Roland H. Bainton, *Christian Attitudes Toward War and Peace* (New York: Abingdon Press, 1960), esp. chaps. 5–7.

9. Brandt's rules do not appear to be of the sort that can be overridden—except perhaps by a soldier who decides that he just *won't* kill any more civilians, no matter what cause is served—since all they require is careful calculation. But I take it that rules of a different sort, which have the form of ordinary injunctions and prohibitions, can and often do figure in what is called "rule-utilitarianism."

10. J. L. Austin, "A Plea for Excuses," in *Philosophical Papers*, ed. J. O. Urmson and G. J. Warnock (Oxford: Oxford University Press, 1961), 123–52.

11. William Shakespeare, *Hamlet*, act 3.4.178.

12. Compare the following lines from Bertold Brecht's poem "To Posterity": "Alas, we / Who wished to lay the foundations of kindness / Could not ourselves be kind" (Bertolt Brecht, *Selected Poems*, trans. H. R. Hays [New York: Grove Press, 1959], 177). This is more of an excuse, less of a justification (the poem is an *apologia*).

13. Robert Nozick discusses some of the possible effects of overriding a rule in his "Moral Complications and Moral Structures," *Natural Law Forum* 13 (1968), 34–35 and notes. Nozick suggests that what may remain after one has broken a rule (for good reasons) is a "duty to make reparations." He does not call this "guilt," though the two notions are closely connected.

14. Hare, "Rules of War and Moral Reasoning," 179.

15. There is another possible utilitarian position, suggested in Maurice Merleau-Ponty's *Humanism and Terror*, trans. John O'Neill (Boston: Beacon Press, 1970). According to this

view, the agony and the guilt feelings experienced by the man who makes a "dirty hands" decision derive from his radical uncertainty about the actual outcome. Perhaps the awful thing he is doing will be done in vain; the results he hopes for won't occur; the only outcome will be the pain he has caused or the deceit he has fostered. Then (and only then) he will indeed have committed a crime. On the other hand, if the expected good does come, then (and only then) he can abandon his guilt feelings; he can say, and the rest of us must agree, that he is justified. This is a kind of delayed utilitarianism, where justification is a matter of actual and not at all of predicted outcomes. It is not implausible to imagine a political actor anxiously awaiting the "verdict of history." But suppose the verdict is in his favor (assuming that there is a *final* verdict or a statute of limitations on possible verdicts): he will surely feel relieved—more so, no doubt, than the rest of us. I can see no reason, however, why he should think himself justified, if he is a good man and knows that what he did was wrong. Perhaps the victims of his crime, seeing the happy result, will absolve him, but history has no powers of absolution. Indeed, history is more likely to play tricks on our moral judgment. Predicted outcomes are at least thought to follow from our own acts (this is the prediction), but actual outcomes almost certainly have a multitude of causes, the combination of which may well be fortuitous. Merleau-Ponty stresses the risks of political decision-making so heavily that he turns politics into a gamble with time and circumstance. But the anxiety of the gambler is of no great moral interest. Nor is it much of a barrier, as Merleau-Ponty's book makes all too clear, to the commission of the most terrible crimes.

16. Cf. the cases suggested by David Ross, *The Right and the Good* (Oxford: Oxford University Press, 1930), 56–57, and E. F. Carritt, *Ethical and Political Thinking* (Oxford, 1947), 65.

17. Machiavelli, *The Discourses*, bk. 1, chap. 9, 139.

18. For a very different view of Machiavelli, see Isaiah Berlin, "The Question of Machiavelli," *New York Review of Books*, (November 4, 1971).

19. Machiavelli, *The Discourses*, bk. 1, chap. 18, 171.

20. Weber, "Politics as a Vocation," 125–26. But sometimes a political leader does choose the "absolutist" side of the conflict, and Weber writes (127) that it is "immensely moving when a *mature* man . . . aware of a responsibility for the consequences of his conduct . . . reaches a point where he says: 'Here I stand; I can do no other.' " Unfortunately, he does not suggest just where that point is or even where it might be.

21. Albert Camus, *Caligula and Three Other Plays* (New York: Vintage Books, 1958), x. (The preface is translated by Justin O'Brian, the plays by Stuart Gilbert.)

22. Jean-Paul Sartre, *Dirty Hands* in *No Exit and Three Other Plays*, trans. Lionel Abel (New York: Vintage Books, 1955), 223.

CHAPTER EIGHTEEN

The United States in the World—
Just Wars and Just Societies

An Interview with Michael Walzer

You've been highly critical of the Bush administration's policy toward Iraq and especially of their attempt to legitimate a doctrine of preventive war. At the same time, you have suggested that European critics of the U.S. administration—especially the French and German governments—have failed to take seriously their own responsibility for the maintenance of a peaceful international order and have undermined international efforts to contain Saddam Hussein. Could you say something about how these criticisms are connected to the account of just war you defend in Just and Unjust Wars? *In your view, how should European powers see their international role in a world in which the United States is as militarily dominant as at present?*

The criticisms I have made of the Bush administration's doctrine of pre-emptive war follow pretty closely, I think, the argument in *Just and Unjust Wars* (see the chapter on "Anticipations"). But my critique of French and German policy doesn't have much to do with just war theory. It is a much more general moral/political critique, having to do with hypocrisy and irresponsibility rather than with injustice. France and Germany did not refuse to fight or wrongly resist a just war; they refused to provide what was in their power to provide: a serious alternative to an unjust war. I continue to believe, even at this late date, that had France and Germany (and Russia too) been willing to support, and had the UN Security Council been willing to authorize, a strongly coercive containment regime for Iraq, the war would have been, first, unnecessary, and second, politically impossible for the American government to fight. But this would have involved giving up the notion that force was a "last resort," as the French said, or morally impermissible, as the Germans said. For containment depended on force from the beginning: the no-fly zones and the embargo required forceful actions every day, and the restoration of the inspection regime depended on a credible American threat to use force. Now imagine the no-fly zones expanded to include the whole country; imagine the very porous embargo replaced by "smart sanctions," which actually shut down the import of military equipment (while permitting materials needed by the civilian population); imagine the inspectors strengthened by UN troops, who could patrol installations once they had been inspected, and by unannounced surveillance flights. Given all that, it would have been very difficult to make a case that Iraq was still a threat to its neighbors or to world peace. But the US did not want a regime of that sort, having settled on war early on; and France and Germany were not willing to support anything close to this: they had, in fact, decided that the appeasement of Saddam was the best policy.

What should be the role of Europe in a future international order? European states together could create a new balance of power, but that would require military expenditure on a scale that none of them, with the exception of the UK, seems willing to contemplate. Even so, some increase in their military budgets seems to me necessary if they are to play the part that I would like them to play in deciding when war is just and necessary. They can't claim such a role and then, if the decision is made to go to war, insist that the US (or the US and the UK) do all the fighting. That's not a morally tenable position. The US needs partners, real partners, who can say "yes" and "no" to our government— but these have to be partners who are ready to take responsibility for the way the world goes. Iraq would have nuclear weapons today, had Europe alone been making decisions about the inspection regime, the embargo, and the no-fly zones. And there would be many fewer Kosovars alive in Kosovo today had Europe alone been making decisions there. It is easy to criticize American unilateralism; I do that all the time. But European irresponsibility is an equally serious problem.

You make some very cogent points about the attitude of the European powers, but the analysis leaves two kinds of question outstanding. First, you are obviously implying that military action to implement a "strongly coercive containment regime" would have been justified. But is it in your view ever justified to intervene militarily in order to effect regime change? I am reminded of the doctrine of double effect in relation to chronically sick patients, whereby

pain relief can be given even if it will cause death, so long as causing death is
not the primary purpose of the treatment. It is clear that some elements within
the US administration have on the contrary seen regime change as the primary
purpose of intervention, to liberate the Iraqi people regardless of their
preferences in the matter. How do you see this problem in relation to the
justice of the conflict?

Humanitarian interventions to stop mass murder and "ethnic cleansing" will obviously aim at regime change, since the regime's criminal behavior is the reason for the intervention. Thus Vietnam replaced the Khmer Rouge regime in Cambodia when its army shut down the killing fields, and Tanzania replaced Idi Amin's government in Uganda. Had there been a UN intervention in Rwanda, as there should have been, it would surely have resulted in the overthrow of Hutu Power. In the case of Iraq, the northern no-fly zone was something like a humanitarian intervention on behalf of the Kurds, and it produced something like a regime change, in the form of Kurdish autonomy. But the safety and success of the Kurds undermined any argument that might have been made for a war for regime change in Baghdad. I don't mean that this wasn't an awful regime, the worst example of third world fascism. And so I accept what your question suggests: if it happened that a regime of coercive constraint weakened and eventually brought down the Baathist regime, that would have been a desirable side-effect, but only a side-effect, of the constraint.

A second area concerns the problem of what should have been done given the
attitude of the French, Germans and Russians, no matter how reprehensible the
latter's attitudes are held to be. British public opinion is apparently judging the
legitimacy of the war within two distinct frames of reference. On the one hand,
there is the (more or less clearly articulated) perspective of just war principles:
just cause, proportionality, last resort and so on. On the other hand, there is the
pragmatic frame of reference, which renders a war legitimate only if a) the
House of Commons votes in favor, b) there is relatively unified public support,
with a large majority in favor of war, and c) the intervention conforms with
international law. The current political anguish in Britain derives not only
from the fact that Britain's leadership appears to be crushed between the rock of
the Pentagon and the hard place of Europe, but because neither condition b) nor
condition c) appears to be met. This is why the issue of the second UN resolution
assumed a significance on this side of the water that it perhaps did not possess in
the US. A second resolution would have made the war more clearly legal
(condition c)), thereby swinging a large majority of public opinion behind it

(condition b)). The questions are: would a Security Council resolution conferred legitimacy on the war in your view? And should either the US or the UK have gone ahead without it? More generally: what is the relationship between the philosophical principles of just war and the pragmatics of law and political consent?

It is a good idea to strengthen the UN and to take whatever steps are possible to establish a global rule of law. It is a very bad idea to pretend that a strong UN and a global rule of law already exist. Most of the just uses of military force in the last thirty or forty years have not been authorized by the UN: the Vietnamese and Tanzanian interventions I just mentioned; the Indian war against Pakistan that resulted in the secession of Bangladesh and the return of millions of refugees; the Israeli pre-emptive strike against Egypt in 1967, after the abject withdrawal of UN forces from the Sinai; the Kosovo war in 1999. So far as justice, that is, moral legitimacy is concerned, if the Iraq war was unjust before the Security Council voted, it would have been unjust afterwards, however the vote went. It can't be the case that when we try to figure out whether a war is just or unjust, we are predicting how the Council will vote. Indeed, justice would be independent of UN decision-making even if the UN were a global government, though then, assuming the democratic legitimacy of this government, we would be bound to respect its decisions.

As for your condition b), I doubt that you would want to defend the proposition that democratic decisions should be made via opinion polls or mass demonstrations rather than by parliamentary majorities. We organize demonstrations to influence the parliamentary majority, and if we don't do that, we wait until the next election. Watching from the US, and thinking about the virtual withdrawal of Congress from the American debate about the war, I had to feel that Blair's necessary appearance before the Commons on the eve of war was a memorable democratic moment.

You have been very critical of the American left's opposition to the war in Afghanistan, especially the left's refusal to see it as a just war on terror. Do you think that there are other countries in which the US should intervene militarily in order to combat terror, as President Bush has suggested?

I supported the war in Afghanistan because I believed that this was a defensive war (the paradigmatic case of just war) against a regime that did not merely harbor terrorists but was an active partner of the terrorist organization that attacked New York and Washington on 9/11. The Taliban regime provided Al

Qaeda with all the advantages of sovereignty, most importantly, a territorial base. It was entirely legitimate for the US to attack that territorial base and to overthrow the regime that provided it. I have reservations about the way we fought the war, and I have criticized our behavior in Afghanistan after it was over. But the war itself was eminently defensible. And should there be other countries that enter into a partnership of the same kind with Al Qaeda, I would think, other things being equal, they would be subject to a similar attack. But, right now, there are no such other countries. As for countries that harbor terrorist organizations, they can and should be dealt with through non-military means: diplomacy and, in extreme cases, international sanctions. Of course, if there were a visible readiness to apply international sanctions, there would be many fewer countries harboring terrorist organizations.

> *In* Just and Unjust Wars *you take a strong stand on the issues of war crimes, guerrilla war, reprisals, and terrorism in general. How do you view the current crisis in Israel in the light of what you wrote in that book? How do your insights regarding the history of anti-Semitism contribute to an analysis of how radical politics is understood within both sets of national identities?*

This is a hard question for me to answer with any sort of brevity, given my long involvement in Zionist politics in the Jewish diaspora and in Israeli politics too, as a frequent visitor. I recently published an article in *Dissent*, "The Four Wars of Israel / Palestine," explaining my position, which I will try to summarize here. These are the four wars: there is a Palestinian war to destroy and replace the state of Israel, which is unjust, and a Palestinian war to establish a state alongside Israel, which is just. And there is an Israeli war to defend the state, which is just, and an Israeli war for Greater Israel, which is unjust. When making particular judgments, you always have to ask who is fighting which war, and what means they have adopted, and whether those means are legitimate for these ends, or for any ends. Most of the people attacking Israel or defending it, and most of the people attacking the Palestinians or defending them, don't even begin to do the necessary work. I can't do that work here, but I will suggest some of the judgments that I think it leads to—most crucially these two: Palestinian terrorism, that is, the deliberate targeting of civilians, should always and every-where be condemned. And Israeli settlement policy in the occupied territories has been wrong from the very beginning of the occupation. But this second wrongness doesn't mitigate the first: Palestinian attacks on the occupying army or on paramilitary settler groups are justified—at least they are justified whenever there is an Israeli government unwilling to negotiate; but attacks on settler families or schools are terrorist acts, murder exactly. (I want to insist that this is not special pleading: I am old enough to have made similar arguments at the time of the Algerian war: FLN attacks on French soldiers or on OAS militants were justified; putting a bomb in a café or a supermarket in the French section of Algiers was murder.) And similarly, Israeli attacks on Hamas or Islamic Jihad fighters are justified; dropping a bomb on an apartment house in Gaza was a criminal act.

Since I have often been a critic of Israeli governments, I am reluctant to call such criticism anti-Semitic. But it does seem to me that there is an oddly disproportionate hostility toward Israel on the European left, which requires some explanation. I know, for example, people my own age who indignantly refuse even to consider a visit to Israel, but who had no trouble visiting France at the height of the Algerian war and have no trouble visiting China today despite its brutal policy in Tibet (which includes a far more massive settlement program than Israel has attempted in the West Bank). Indeed, much of the criticism directed at Israel has more to do with the existence of the state than with the policies of any of its governments—which was, again, never the case with France or with Germany after World War Two or with China today. Something is seriously wrong here.

A number of US intellectuals have been reassessing their commitment to civil liberties, which they now see as a liability to security, post–September 11. This reassessment has led to torture being placed on the political agenda, as in the case of Alan Dershowitz. What are your views and feelings with respect to this new climate of debate?

I don't think that I have changed my position—except perhaps in the way I distribute the burden of argument. After 9/11, those of us who want to defend civil liberties have to accept a greater burden than before. It isn't enough to point to the Patriot Act and scream "Fascism!" We have to make the case to our fellow citizens that the government can defend them against terrorism within the constitutional constraints, whatever they are, that we believe necessary to personal freedom and democratic politics. Only if we can't make that case would we have to consider modifying the constitutional regime. Right now, I think that we can make the case; I only regret that so many people on the left don't believe that they have to make it. They talk about this question as if the last thing they want to worry about is the safety of their fellow citizens.

Back in the early 1970s, I published an article called "Dirty Hands," that dealt with the responsibility of political leaders in extreme situations, where the safety of their people seemed to require immoral acts. One of my examples was the "ticking bomb" case, where a captured terrorist knows, but refuses to reveal, the location of a bomb that is timed to go off soon in a school building. I argued that a political leader in such a case might be bound to order the torture of the prisoner, but that we should regard this as a moral paradox, where the right thing to do was also wrong. The leader would have to bear the guilt and opprobrium of the wrongful act he had ordered, and we should want leaders who were prepared both to give the order and to bear the guilt. This was widely criticized at the time as an incoherent position, and the article has been frequently reprinted, most often, I think, as an example of philosophical incoherence. But I am inclined to think that the moral world is much less tidy than most moral philosophers are prepared to admit. Now Dershowitz has cited my argument in his defense of torture in extreme cases (though he insists on a judicial warrant before anything at all can be done to the prisoner).

But extreme cases make bad law. Yes, I would do whatever was necessary to extract information in the ticking bomb case—that is, I would make the same argument after 9/11 that I made 30 years before. But I don't want to generalize from cases like that; I don't want to rewrite the rule against torture to incorporate this exception. Rules are rules, and exceptions are exceptions. I want political leaders to accept the rule, to understand its reasons, even to internalize it. I also want them to be smart enough to know when to break it. And finally, because they believe in the rule, I want them to feel guilty about breaking it— which is the only guarantee they can offer us that they won't break it too often.

More generally, in Thick and Thin *you offered an account of universal ideals of justice—such as "human rights"—which sought to explain how people with different histories and political traditions can come to share a commitment to these ideals even though they are not foundational for, or even integral to, their diverse understandings of justice. Your claim there was that such ideals are minimalist, or "thin," and that their reiteration across political traditions explains why we can understand what people in contexts utterly different from ours are calling for when they march carrying signs simply stating "Truth" or "Justice." If this account is correct, then if commitment to, for example, human rights is eroded within a significant number of powerful political traditions—as was suggested by the last question—does it become legitimate for the ideal of human rights to disappear from the landscape of international justice?*

The people carrying signs in my account are Czechs in 1989, during the "Velvet Revolution." They hadn't been able to defend truth or justice in public for many years, yet Czechs watching the demonstration knew what the words meant, and so did we know, watching from farther away. If civil liberties are curtailed in the US, there will soon be a movement to defend and restore them. And when we march with signs saying "Liberty," Americans watching us will know what the word means, and so will you in Britain, and so will people in China, who have never enjoyed anything like our civil liberties. A full-scale cultural inquiry would surely reveal significant differences in American, British, and Chinese understandings of liberty, but some minimal sense, sufficient for mutual comprehension, would be common to all three.

But your question is really just another invitation to make the relativist/anti-relativist argument of Philosophy 101. So let me restate the question in the strongest possible form. Suppose that the Nazis had conquered the world, and that the Third Reich lasted the full thousand years that Hitler promised. Would the ideal of human rights, at the end of that time, have disappeared "from the landscape of international justice?" I don't know the answer to that question, and I don't think that anyone else does. But I hope that people in different parts of the world would resist the Nazis and when they did (I am paraphrasing my argument in *Thick and Thin* now) they would discover that though they had different histories and cultures, their experience of tyranny was similar, and so was their response to it. And out of these commonalities they would fashion a minimal morality that would serve the purposes of their struggle. "It would be a jerry-built and ramshackle affair—as hastily put together as the signs for the Prague march."

> *You are also well-known for your influential work on "complex equality" in* Spheres of Justice. *Elizabeth Anderson has recently asked the following hypothetical question: "if much recent academic work defending equality had been secretly penned by conservatives, could the results be any more embarrassing for egalitarians?" How do you view current philosophical work on equality, especially with respect to its relevance for the left?*

I think that Anderson's article is right on target. I agree with many of her positive arguments, but I am especially sympathetic to her critique. She is right to say that much contemporary philosophical writing about equality fails to address or even to recognize "the concerns of the politically oppressed" and the actual "inequalities of race, gender, class, and caste." Maybe there is a natural disconnect between academic philosophy and political struggle, and maybe it is a good thing if philosophers are disengaged, looking on from afar. I don't want to argue that academic work is the same as work in the political arena. Still, there are reasons that we are interested in equality and inequality, and Anderson is right to insist that philosophers today don't always have a good grasp of those reasons. There are, however, contemporary writers whose grasp is very good indeed: consider the work of Ian Shapiro (*Democratic Justice*), Anne Phillips (*Which Equalities Matter?*), Charles Beitz (*Political Equality*), David Miller (*Principles of Social Justice*), and Iris Young (*Inclusion and Democracy*). It is interesting that these people are not working in philosophy departments; they are political theorists and feminist theorists, and they take their starting point from politics-on-the-ground.

For myself, I think that one great mistake of contemporary academic philosophers, starting with Rawls himself, is the claim that our natural endowments are "arbitrary from a moral point of view" and should not be allowed to have effects in the social world—or, better, the effects they have should never be philosophically ratified. As Rawls wrote, we have to "nullify the accidents of natural endowment." This puts philosophy radically at odds with ordinary morality. Sometimes, of course, that is a useful conflict, but in this particular encounter, philosophy does not fare well. Our natural endowments make us what we are, and what we are necessarily has consequences in the social world, and some, at least, of these consequences must be legitimate. John Rawls deserved the honors he won by writing *A Theory of Justice*—even if his intelligence was an accidental effect of the natural lottery. Beautiful men and women may not deserve the sexual and marriage offers that they get (we have different, but not entirely different, ideas about intelligence and beauty); still, they cannot be obliged to share their wealth or, as Phillipe Van Parijs has suggested, to compensate the losers in love. This last is one of Anderson's most telling examples, and she goes on to point out that those of us who are not beautiful have never organized to demand such compensation. There is something to learn even from political struggles that never happened!

How does your view of complex equality relate to the contemporary tendency (in the US and Europe) for policy on the welfare state to move away from a focus on need to a much more conditional conception of welfare?

I don't think that is the right way to describe the current debate. Conservative critics of the welfare state claim that many of the people receiving welfare don't "need" it in any reasonable sense of that word. These people, it is said, are capable of working, and society would be better served if they were enabled, or even required, to work. Now, there is an old left argument remarkably similar to this: that the first priority of a socialist state should be to provide decent jobs for all its citizens; welfare is necessary only for people who cannot work. "From each according to his ability," is as important as "to each according to his need." It is much better to be an independent worker than a client of the state. Two things are wrong with the conservatives' version of this argument: first, they are not willing to regulate the economy, or subsidize sectors of it, so as to provide the necessary decent jobs; they have a radical, and I think radically implausible, view of market capabilities. And, second, they have no sense of solidarity or, indeed, common citizenship with people who can't find work, or who haven't been prepared by the state schools for decent jobs, or who have obligations (to children above all) that prevent them from looking for work. All these people need help from the state, that is, from their fellow citizens, in exactly the way, and for exactly the reasons, that I described in the chapter on welfare in *Spheres of Justice*. Conservatives generally don't deny the legitimate claims of "need," but most of them have no sense of what it means to be needy. I doubt that you can address this lack with a philosophical argument alone; you also need to evoke the sense of compassion. Here politics follows the affiliative or sympathetic emotions.

Given your influential discussion of "blocked exchanges" in Spheres of Justice, *what do you think of the emerging or possible markets in human organs and tissues, genetic material, and so on? How should we think about goods like this, which seem tightly bound up with personhood, on the one hand, and are easily commodifiable on the other?*

What things are there in the world that are not "easily commodifiable?" It is in the nature of the sphere of money and commodities that its extent is unlimited —until we limit it. Consider the debate in the US today about whether guns are commodities. They are certainly easy to manufacture for sale. But it seems to me an obvious argument, though it is often resisted, that guns are significantly different from bicycles and breakfast cereals and rare books and dress shirts. I am fairly sure that we will eventually win this argument (indeed this blocked exchange may be one of the restrictions on American liberty that comes, though not soon, in the aftermath of 9/11). I don't have any similar assurance on how the argument about human organs and tissues is going to turn out. Given my own sense of what "personhood" means in our culture, I think that the best outcome would be the one that Titmuss defended in the case of blood. Organs should be donated to some kind of public "fund," and then dispensed in accordance with one or another fairness principle.

But maybe people will turn out to be remarkably detached from their organs (we've never seen them, after all), and that will make an organ market fairly easy to defend. And then the problems we will face will have less to do with "personhood" than with distributive justice in a more immediate sense. For it is likely to be only the very poor, in the third world as well as at home, whose organs are collected, and there are sure to be patterns of coercion and pressure that will make the collection exploitative. Commodities are legitimately distributed only in a free market. Whenever inequalities of power interfere with that freedom, the market requires, as this market surely will, extensive regulation.

The left in the US has suffered defeat after defeat, and the Democratic Party has moved purposefully to the right over the past twenty years. Because of the design of the electoral and campaign financing systems third party efforts (like the New Party and the Labor Party) often seem either quixotic, or (as in the case of Nader's Presidential candidacy) can be portrayed as efforts to spoil the chances of Democratic candidates. What are the strategic options available to the US left in the next decade, and which of those options do you favor?

I take it this is not a philosophical question. The picture is not quite as bleak as you describe. The feminist movement continues to make progress in the US today or, at least, women continue to make progress, in political life, in the professions, even in corporate America. The movement for gay rights is stronger, I think, than it has ever been. Blacks continue to "arrive" in the upper reaches of American society (even as the crisis of the black underclass deepens). The incorporation of previously marginalized groups into American life is a feature of our times. But it is especially depressing that this does not have the effect that we expected: moving the country leftwards. Perhaps we should not have expected this. I remember the first year (it was sometime in the 1980s) when a majority of the delegates at the Republican Party convention were women, and I thought: It is certainly good that they are there, but why are they *there?*

People on the left can work, with varying degrees of hopefulness, in a number of different places over the next decade. The first is the Democratic Party, where we have to be engaged because that is where the largest number of

"our" people are. The New Party was a good idea because it involved supporting Democratic candidates while seeking, at the local level, to organize a base of
our own. But that strategy has now failed. The Green Party campaign in 2000
was a very bad idea, the product in part of Ralph Nader's narcissism and in part
of old left sectarianism. The sharp right turn of American politics is the direct
result of that campaign.

The second place is the labor movement. This is a very old-fashioned
recommendation, I suppose, but there are still significant sectors of the American economy where organizing is possible, and this remains the best way of
expanding the base of the left. The politics of welfare and redistribution still
depend in significant ways on the labor movement. And as Seattle 2000 demon-
strated, any move toward a global version of social democracy requires the
support of organized labor.

The third place is the famous but not always easy to locate "civil society,"
where organizations of all sorts proliferate, and some of them are ours: environ-
mentalists, feminists, defenders of civil liberties, advocates on behalf of minority groups, and so on. These are the "fragments" of a left politics that still has
not come together and may not come together anytime soon. But the fragments
are important in themselves, the more the better, and the people who work in
them constitute a kind of civil service of the left. Anything we can do to expand
these groups is worth doing, even if many of them are wholly engaged in a rear-
guard, defensive politics.

*Do you think that the recent deaths of John Rawls and Robert Nozick have
marked the end of an era for political philosophy in the US? What are your
memories of doing political philosophy at Harvard in the late 1960s and 1970s?*

I spent much of the 1960s and early 1970s learning to "do" political philosophy
rather than doing it, and Rawls and Nozick were two of my teachers. There was
a discussion group that met every month in those years, in Cambridge and New
York, that included those two and Ronnie Dworkin, Tom Nagel, Tim Scanlon,
Judy Thomson, Charles Fried, Marshall Cohen, and a few others: a peer group
for most of them, a school for me. In 1971, Nozick and I taught a course together called "Capitalism and Socialism," which was a semester-long argument
—out of which came his *Anarchy, State, and Utopia* and my *Spheres*. Rawls,
Nozick, Nagel, and Dworkin were, I suppose, the leaders of the return of
philosophers to "public affairs." For me, there was no return; I had never been

interested in anything else. But I did make an effort to write about politics in a more philosophical way. I don't think that I ever managed real philosophy. I couldn't breathe easily at the high level of abstraction that philosophy seemed to require, where my friends in the group were entirely comfortable. And I quickly got impatient with the playful extension of hypothetical cases, moving farther and farther away from the world we all lived in. I was writing *Just and Unjust Wars* in the middle 1970s, and my decision to work the argument through historical examples was in part a reaction against the hypothetical cases of my friends. The current state of the philosophical argument about justice, as described and criticized by Anderson, follows from too much abstraction, too many hypotheticals, too great a distance from the real world.

The Rawls / Nozick debate was, I think, pretty much over even before their deaths. In the philosophical world, Rawls and the Rawlsians won decisively; in the political world, I am afraid, the Nozickians won, but it isn't philosophers, it is economists, who relish the victory. Right now, the forces aren't engaged: consider how little criticism of the market model is carried in the journal that came out of our discussion group: *Philosophy and Public Affairs.*

In a sense, the key argument now, or the one that seems central to me, though I stand at a distance from it, takes place within the Rawlsian camp: between those, including Charles Beitz and Thomas Pogge, who would extend the principles of *A Theory of Justice*, and especially the difference principle, to global society and those, including Rawls, who resist the extension. For myself, I think that a strong critique of global inequalities and a persuasive claim that we are obligated to help the poorest countries can be derived from an historical account of how the world economy developed, and from an account of what Rawls called our "natural duties." I am a little dubious about the global reach of moral commitments that grow up within, and seem dependent on the solidarity of, a particular political community. One day, maybe . . .

You say that you support Anderson's critique of recent academic egalitarian writings on equality. You also comment on the welcome return of philosophy to public affairs in the 1970s. Do you think that the engagement of philosophy with public affairs is still not engaged enough?

As I suggested before, I do respect, though I don't always admire, academic philosophy in its more detached and abstract modes. It may even be the case that philosophical innovation is most likely to take place at very high levels of abstraction, even if most of what goes on up there isn't particularly innovative. But when philosophers write about public affairs, I believe that they must attend to the political and moral realities of the world whose affairs these are. Thomas Pogge's recent writings on global justice provide a useful model: he has gone to school with the political economists and writes knowledgeably about international terms of trade and the political context in which states borrow money and sell natural resources. That is the sort of work we have to do if we want to call ourselves "engaged."

What are you working on now?

I am just finishing up a little book with the working title *The Exclusions of Liberal Theory*.[1] This will be a critique of standard liberalism, though not in any sense a rejection of it. My argument is that liberalism would be a more effectively egalitarian doctrine if it acknowledged the power of involuntary association; accommodated group life, even in its more intense forms; and recognized the role of passion in political conflict. It is a plea for a more sociologically and psychologically sophisticated liberal political theory. An even littler version of this book has already appeared in Germany under the title *Vernunft, Politik und Leidenschaft: Defizite liberaler Theorie*—my Horkheimer lectures in 1999. But I have now added a lot more stuff, trying to address some of the arguments about multiculturalism.

I am also involved in a big collaborative project that will eventually produce four volumes of texts and commentaries that represent (our version of) *The Jewish Political Tradition*. Volume One, dealing with all the arguments about authority and legitimacy, came out in 2000; Volume Two, on membership, deals with the attempts, over three thousand years, to answer the question, Who is a Jew? It has just come out (April 2003). On my part, the project is an effort to deny that the tradition "belongs" exclusively to orthodox Jews or even to religious Jews. I am also arguing that Jewish political experience, above all, the experience of statelessness, of collective survival without territory or sovereignty, should be of interest to anyone interested in politics, whatever their religion or ethnicity (or lack thereof).

Finally, *Dissent* magazine takes a lot of my time. It is hard work trying to sustain an oppositionist politics in the US today—especially when part of what I feel I have to oppose is the idiocy of many of my fellow oppositionists: knee-jerk anti-Americanism, old left dogmatism, and the rejection of any fellowship larger than the sect of the politically correct and the morally pure. I live on the left, but quarrel with some of my neighbors, and in the aftermath of 9/11 the quarrels have gotten more intense. But I would resist the idea that I am "working" on these quarrels. They are just occasionally necessary engagements.

NOTES

Interview with the *Imprints* editorial collective, 2003.

1. Published as Michael Walzer, *Politics and Passion: Toward a More Egalitarian Liberalism* (New Haven: Yale University Press, 2005).

Works by Michael Walzer

Note: To conserve space, this bibliography records only the first printings of Michael Walzer's books and articles; it does not include material published in languages other than English; and it excludes some shorter pieces of topical commentary from *Dissent*, *New Republic*, and elsewhere. These exclusions apart, all of Walzer's published work is listed here.

Books, Articles, Essays, and Published Lectures

1956–60

"The Travail of the U.S. Communists." *Dissent* (Fall 1956), 406–10.
"Hungary and the Failure of the Left." *Dissent* (Spring 1957), 157–62.
"John Wain: The Hero in Limbo." *Perspective* 10 (Summer–Fall 1958), 137–45.
"Politics of the Angry Young Men." *Dissent* (Spring 1958), 148–54.
"When the Hundred Flowers Withered." *Dissent* (Fall 1958), 360–74.
"Education for a Democratic Culture: I." *Dissent* (Spring 1959), 107–21.
"The American School: II." *Dissent* (Summer 1959), 223–36. (Second part of above.)
"A Cup of Coffee and a Seat." *Dissent* (Spring 1960), 111–20.
Exchange with H. Brand. "Classless Education in Class Society?" *Dissent* (Winter 1960), 86–89.
"The Idea of Resistance." In "Politics of Non-Violent Resistance: A Discussion." *Dissent* (Fall 1960), 369–73.
"In Place of a Hero." *Dissent* (Spring 1960), 156–62.
"The Politics of the New Negro." *Dissent* (Summer 1960), 235–43.

1961

Pamphlet. "Cuba: The Invasion and the Consequences." *Dissent* (June 1961). Exchange with Joyce Kolko. "Cuba and Radicalism." *Dissent* (Fall 1961), 517–19. Exchange with Tom Kahn. "The Idea of Revolution." *Dissent* (Spring 1961), 180–84.

1962

"The Mood and the Style." *Dissent* (Winter 1962), 29–33.
"Students in Washington: A New Peace Movement." *Dissent* (Spring 1962), 179–82.
"The Young Radicals: A Symposium." *Dissent* (Spring 1962), 129–31.

1963

"In Defense of Spying." *Dissent* (Fall 1963), 398–99.
"Puritanism as a Revolutionary Ideology." *History and Theory* 3 (1963), 59–90.
"Revolutionary Ideology: The Case of the Marian Exiles." *American Political Science Review* 57 (1963), 643–54.

1964

"The Only Revolution: Notes on the Theory of Modernization." *Dissent* (Fall 1964), 432–40.
"Paul Goodman's Community of Scholars." With response by Paul Goodman. *Dissent* (Winter 1964), 21–28.

1965

The Revolution of the Saints: A Study in the Origins of Radical Politics. Cambridge: Harvard University Press, 1965. Translations: French, Italian; forthcoming in Spanish.
With John Schrecker. "American Intervention and the Cold War." *Dissent* (Fall 1965), 43–46.
With Michael Rustin. "Labor in Britain: Victory and Beyond." *Dissent* (Winter 1965), 21–31.
"Report from America." *Views* (Summer 1965), 12–13.

1966

"Democracy and the Conscript." *Dissent* (January–February 1966), 16–22.
Exchange (coauthored with John Schrecker) with Henry Pachter. "Ideology and Power in Foreign Affairs: Comments on John Schrecker and Michael Walzer,

'American Intervention and the Cold War' in *Dissent,* Autumn 1965." *Dissent* (March–April 1966), 198–207.
"On the Nature of Freedom." *Dissent* (November–December 1966), 725–28.
"Options for Resistance Today." In symposium, "The Draft: Reflections and Opinions." *Dissent* (May–June 1966), 318–19.

1967

Exchange with Lewis Coser. "Anti-Communism and the CIA." *Dissent* (May–June 1967), 274–80.
"The Condition of Greece: Twenty Years After the Truman Doctrine." *Dissent* (July–August 1967), 421–31.
"The Exodus and Revolution: An Exercise in Comparative History." *Mosaic* 8 (1967), 6–21.
"Moral Judgment in Time of War." *Dissent* (May–June 1967), 284–92.
"The Obligation to Disobey." *Ethics* 77 (1967), 163–75.
"On the Role of Symbolism in Political Thought." *Political Science Quarterly* 82 (1967), 191–204.

1968

"Civil Disobedience and 'Resistance.' " *Dissent* (January–February 1968), 13–15.
"The New Left." In *The University and the New Intellectual Environment: The Frank Gerstein Lectures, York University 1967–68,* 29–48. Toronto: Macmillan of Canada, 1968.
"Politics in the Welfare State." *Dissent* (January–February 1968), 26–40.

1969

"Civil Disobedience and Corporate Authority." In *Power and Community: Dissenting Essays in Political Science,* edited by Philip Green and Sanford Levinson, 223–46. New York: Random House, 1969.
"Prisoners of War: Does the Fight Continue After the Battle?" *American Political Science Review* 63 (1969), 777–86.

1970

Obligations: Essays on Disobedience, War and Citizenship. Cambridge: Harvard University Press, 1970. Translations: Spanish, Portuguese, Japanese.
"A Journey to Israel." *Dissent* (November–December 1970), 497–503.
"The Revolutionary Uses of Repression." In *Essays in Theory and History: An Approach to the Social Sciences,* edited by Melvin Richter, 122–36. Cambridge: Harvard University Press, 1970.

1971

Political Action. Chicago: Quadrangle Books, 1971.
"'Citizens' Politics': How to Do It." *Dissent* (June 1971), 252–57.
"Violence: The Police, the Militants, and the Rest of Us." *Dissent* (April 1971), 119–27.
"World War II: Why Was This War Different?" *Philosophy and Public Affairs* 1 (1971), 3–21.

1972

"Notes for Whoever's Left." *Dissent* (Spring 1972), 309–14.

1973

"In Defense of Equality." *Dissent* (Fall 1973), 399–408.
"The Peace Movement: What Was Won by Protest?" *New Republic* 168 (February 10, 1973), 24–26.
"Political Action: The Problem of Dirty Hands." *Philosophy and Public Affairs* 2 (Winter 1973), 160–80.
"Regicide and Revolution." *Social Research* 40 (1973), 617–42.

1974

Regicide and Revolution. London: Cambridge University Press, 1974. Translation: French; new ed. with introduction by author, Columbia University Press, 1992.
"Civility and Civic Virtue in Contemporary America." *Social Research* 41 (1974), 593–611.

1975

"Consenting to One's Own Death: The Case of Brutus." In *Beneficent Euthanasia,* edited by Marvin Kohl, 100–05. Buffalo, N.Y.: Prometheus Books, 1975.
Exchange with J. Bowyer Bell and Roger Morris. "Terrorism: A Debate." *New Republic* 173 (December 27, 1975), 12–15.

1976

"Israeli Policy and the West Bank." *Dissent* (Summer 1976), 234–36.
"The Memory of Justice: Marcel Ophuls and the Nuremberg Trials." *New Republic* 175 (October 9, 1976), 19–23.
"Thoughts on Democratic Schools." *Dissent* (Winter 1976), 57–64.

1977

Just and Unjust Wars. New York: Basic Books, 1977. Second edition, 1992, third edition 2000, fourth edition, 2006. Translations: Hebrew, Spanish, Italian, German, French, Portuguese, Dutch.

Radical Principles. New York: Basic Books, 1977.

"War Crimes: Defining the Moral Culpability of Leaders and Citizens." *New Republic* 177 (November 5, 1977), 17–23.

1978

Symposium. "Capitalism, Socialism, and Democracy." *Commentary* 65 (April 1978), 70–71.

"Israel in Lebanon: Just and Unjust Responses to Terrorism." *New Republic* 178 (April 8, 1978), 17–18.

"Teaching Morality: Ethics Makes a Comeback." *New Republic* 178 (June 10, 1978), 12–14.

"Town Meetings and Workers' Control: A Story for Socialists." *Dissent* (Summer 1978), 325–33.

Symposium. "Vietnam and Cambodia." *Dissent* (Fall 1978), 390–91.

Exchange with Robert L. Heilbroner. "What Is Socialism?" *Dissent* (Summer 1978), 341–60.

1979

"The Islam Explosion: Religion is Reemerging as a Political Force Throughout the Third World." *New Republic* 181 (December 8, 1979), 18–21.

"The Moral Problem of Refugees: The Boat People Are an Easy Case. How Will We Handle a Tough One?" *New Republic* 180 (February 10, 1979), 15–17.

"The Pastoral Retreat of the New Left." *Dissent* (Fall 1979), 406–11.

"Socialism and Self-Restraint: The Moral Equivalent of War Requires the Moral Equivalent of Wartime Equality." *New Republic* 181 (July 7 and 14, 1979), 16–19.

"A Theory of Revolution." *Marxist Perspectives* 52 (Spring 1979), 30–44.

With Irving Howe. "Were We Wrong About Vietnam?: Reconsidering the Antiwar Movement." *New Republic* 181 (August 18, 1979), 15–18.

1980

Symposium. "Liberalism and the Jews." *Commentary* 69 (January 1980), 76–77.

"The Moral Standing of States: A Response to Four Critics." *Philosophy and Public Affairs* 9 (1980), 209–29.

"Pluralism: A Political Perspective." In *Harvard Encyclopedia of American Ethnic Groups,* edited by Stephan Thernstrom, Ann Orlov, and Oscar Handlin, 781–87. Cambridge: Belknap Press of Harvard University Press, 1980.

"Political Decision-Making and Political Education." In *Political Theory and Political Education*, edited by Melvin Richter, 159–76. Princeton: Princeton University Press, 1980.
"Revolution-Watching: The Iranian Captivity." *New Republic* 182 (March 29, 1980), 14–16.

1981

"The Courts, the Elections, and the People." *Dissent* (Spring 1981), 153–55.
"Democracy vs. Elections: Primaries Have Ruined Our Politics." *New Republic* 184 (January 3 and 10, 1981), 17–19.
"The Distribution of Membership." In *Boundaries: National Autonomy and Its Limits*, edited by Peter G. Brown and Henry Shue, 1–35. Totowa, N.J.: Rowman and Littlefield, 1981.
Exchange with Paul Fussell. "An Exchange on Hiroshima: Michael Walzer and Paul Fussell on the Moral Calculus of the Bomb." *New Republic* 185 (September 23, 1981), 13–14.
"Philosophy and Democracy." *Political Theory* 9 (1981), 379–99.
"Response to Chaney and Lichtenberg." In *Boundaries: National Autonomy and Its Limits*, edited by Peter G. Brown and Henry Shue, 101–05. Totowa, N.J.: Rowman and Littlefield, 1981.
"Totalitarianism vs. Authoritarianism: The Theory of Tyranny, the Tyranny of Theory." *New Republic* 185 (July 4 and 11, 1981), 21, 24–25.
"Two Kinds of Military Responsibility." *Parameters* 11 (March 1981), 42–46.

1982

"The Community: Wanted: Moral Engagement." *New Republic* 186 (March 31, 1982), 11–12, 14.
"Dirty Work Should Be Shared: In a Society of Equals, Garbage is Everyone's Business." *Harper's* 265 (December 1982), 22–31.
"Political Alienation and Military Service." In *The Military Draft: Selected Readings on Conscription*, edited by Martin Anderson, 153–70. Stanford: Hoover Institution Press, 1982.
"Response to Lackey." *Ethics* 92 (1982), 547–48.
"Socialism and the Gift Relationship." *Dissent* (Fall 1982), 431–41.

1983

Spheres of Justice. New York: Basic Books, 1983. Translations: Italian, German (second edition with new preface, 2006), Swedish, French, Spanish, Japanese, Korean, Chinese, Portuguese.
"On Failed Totalitarianism." *Dissent* (Summer 1983), 297–306.

"Notes from an Israel Journal: What the Students Taught the Teacher about Just and Unjust Wars." *New Republic* 189 (September 5, 1983), 13–17.

"The Politics of Michel Foucault." *Dissent* (Fall 1983), 481–90.

Exchange with Ronald Dworkin. "'Spheres of Justice': An Exchange." *New York Review of Books* (July 21, 1983), 43–44.

"States and Minorities." In *Minorities: Community and Identity*, edited by C. Fried, 219–27. Berlin: Springer-Verlag, 1983.

1984

"Commitment and Social Criticism: Camus's Algerian War." *Dissent* (Fall 1984), 424–32.

"Deterrence and Democracy: In a Nuclear Age We Need Both 'Normal' and 'Abnormal' Politics." *New Republic* 191 (July 2, 1984), 16–21.

"*Dissent* at Thirty." *Dissent* (Winter 1984), 3–4.

"Liberalism and the Art of Separation." *Political Theory* 12 (1984), 315–30.

"The Politics of the Intellectual: Julien Benda's *La Trahison des Clercs* Reconsidered." In *Conflict and Consensus: A Festschrift in Honor of Lewis A. Coser,* edited by Walter W. Powell and Richard Robbins, 365–77. New York: Macmillan, 1984.

1985

Exodus and Revolution. New York: Basic Books, 1985. Translations: French, German, Italian, Japanese, Hebrew, Spanish.

Exchange with Joseph Frank and Lionel Abel. "Camus and the Algerian War." *Dissent* (Winter 1985), 105–10.

"Hold the Justice: At McPrison and Burglar King, It's . . . " *New Republic* 192 (April 8, 1985), 10–12.

"Panel Discussion: The Arts, the Humanities, and Their Institutions." *Art and the Law* 9 (1985), 179–214.

1986

"Cheap Moralizing." In symposium, "The Jeweler's Dilemma: How Would You Respond?" *New Republic* 195 (November 10, 1986), 20.

Introduction. *The Hedgehog and the Fox*, by Isaiah Berlin. New York: Simon and Schuster, Touchstone, 1986.

"Justice Here and Now." In *Justice and Equality Here and Now*, edited by Frank S. Lucash, 136–50. Ithaca: Cornell University Press, 1986.

"The Long-Term Perspective." *Bulletin of the New York Academy of Medicine* 62 (January–February 1986), 8–14.

"Pleasures and Costs of Urbanity." *Dissent* (Fall 1986), 470–75.

"The Reform of the International System." In *Studies of War and Peace*, edited by Øyvind Østerud, 227–50, 276. Oslo: Norwegian University Press, 1986.

"Toward a Theory of Social Assignments." In *American Society: Public and Private Responsibilities*, edited by Winthrop Knowlton and Richard Zechhauser, 79–96. Cambridge: Harper and Row, Ballinger 1986.

"What's Terrorism–And What Isn't?" *Dissent* (Summer 1986), 274–75.

1987

Interpretation and Social Criticism. Cambridge: Harvard University Press, 1987. Translations: French, German, Italian, Japanese, Spanish.

"Israel's Great Victory: A War of Survival or Conquest?" *New Republic* 196 (June 8, 1987), 22–25.

"Notes on Self-Criticism." *Social Research* 54 (1987), 33–43.

1988

The Company of Critics. New York: Basic Books, 1988. Second edition, 2002. Translations: Italian, German, French, Spanish, Lithuanian, Russian.

"The Ambiguous Legacy of Antonio Gramsci." *Dissent* (Fall 1988), 444–56.

Published lecture. "Emergency Ethics." The Joseph A. Reich, Sr. Distinguished Lecture on War, Morality, and the Military Profession, no. 1 (November 21, 1988).

"The Green Line: After the Uprising, Israel's New Border." *New Republic* 199 (September 5, 1988), 22–24.

Published lecture. "Interpretation and Social Criticism." In *The Tanner Lectures on Human Values*, edited by Sterling M. McMurrin, vol. 8, 1–80. Salt Lake City: University of Utah Press, 1988.

"Socializing the Welfare State." In *Democracy and the Welfare State*, edited by Amy Gutmann, 13–26. Princeton: Princeton University Press, 1988.

"Terrorism: A Critique of Excuses." In *Problems of International Justice*, edited by Steven Luper-Foy, 237–47. Boulder: Westview Press, 1988.

1989

"Citizenship." In *Political Innovation and Conceptual Change*, edited by Terence Ball, James Farr, and Russell L. Hanson, 211–19. Cambridge: Cambridge University Press, 1989.

"The Critic in Exile: Breyten Breytenbach and South Africa." *Dissent* (Spring 1989), 177–85.

"A Critique of Philosophical Conversation." *Philosophical Forum* 21 (Fall–Winter 1989–90), 182–96.

"The Sins of Salman: The Do's and Don't's of Blasphemy." *New Republic* 200 (April 10, 1989), 13–15.
"Socialism Then and Now." *New Republic* 201 (November 6, 1989), 75–78.

1990

"The Communitarian Critique of Liberalism." *Political Theory* 18 (1990), 6–23.
"The Constitution and Social Change: A Comment." In The *Constitutional Bases of Political and Social Change in the United States,* edited by Shlomo Slonim, 353–56. New York: Praeger, 1990.
Published lecture. "Nation and Universe." In *The Tanner Lectures on Human Values,* edited by Grethe B. Peterson, vol. 11, 507–56. Salt Lake City: University of Utah Press, 1990.
"What Does It Mean to Be an 'American'?" *Social Research* 57 (1990), 591–614.

1991

"Constitutional Rights and the Shape of Civil Society." In *"The Constitution of the People": Reflections on Citizens and Civil Society,* edited by Robert E. Calvert, 113–26. Lawrence: University Press of Kansas, 1991.
"On Distributive Justice." Preface in *The 1990 American Education Finance Association Yearbook: Spheres of Justice in Education,* edited by Deborah A. Verstegen and James G. Ward, v–viii. New York: HarperCollins, HarperBusiness, 1991.
"Education." In *The 1990 American Education Finance Association Yearbook: Spheres of Justice in Education,* edited by Deborah A. Verstegen and James G. Ward, 239–68. New York: HarperCollins, HarperBusiness, 1991.
"Good Aristocrats/Bad Aristocrats: Thomas Hobbes and Early Modern Political Culture." In *In the Presence of the Past: Essays in Honor of Frank Manuel,* edited by Richard T. Bienvenu and Mordechai Feingold, 41–53. Dordrecht, The Netherlands: Kluwer Academic Publishers, 1991.
"The Idea of Civil Society: A Path to Social Reconstruction." *Dissent* (Spring 1991), 293–304.
"Perplexed: Moral Ambiguities in the Gulf Crisis." *New Republic* 204 (January 28, 1991), 13–15.
"Introduction." In *Toward a Global Civil Society,* edited by Michael Walzer, 1–4. Providence, R.I.: Berghahn Books, 1991.

1992

What It Means to be an American. New York: Marsilio, 1992. Published in Italian and English. Translation: Japanese.
Civil Society and American Democracy. Berlin: Rotbuch Verlag, 1992. Selected essays, in German.

"The Idea of Holy War in Ancient Israel." *Journal of Religious Ethics* 20 (1992), 215–28.
"Justice and Injustice in the Gulf War." In *But Was It Just?: Reflections on the Morality of the Persian Gulf War,* edited by David E. DeCosse, 1–17. New York: Doubleday, 1992. Walzer essay copyright 1992 by Basic Books, Inc., and is an adaptation of the Foreword to his 1992 edition of Basic Books' *Just and Unjust Wars.*
"The Legal Codes of Ancient Israel." *Yale Journal of Law and the Humanities* 4 (1992), 335–49.
"Moral Minimalism." In *From the Twilight of Probability: Ethics and Politics,* edited by William R. Shea and Antonio Spadafora, 3–14. Canton, Mass.: Watson Publishing International, Science History Publications, 1992.
"The New Tribalism: Notes on a Difficult Problem." *Dissent* (Spring 1992), 164–71.
"Scenarios for Possible Lefts: Where Can We Go?" *Dissent* (Fall 1992), 466–69.
"Two Kinds of Institute." *Cambridge Review* 113 (June 1992), 55–56.

1993

"Between Nation and World: Welcome to Some New Ideologies." *The Economist.* Special issue, *150 Economist Years* (September 11, 1993), 51–54.
"Exclusion, Injustice, and the Democratic State." *Dissent* (Winter 1993), 55–64.
"Objectivity and Social Meaning." In *The Quality of Life,* edited by Martha C. Nussbaum and Amartya Sen, 165–77. Oxford: Clarendon Press, 1993.

1994

Thick and Thin: Moral Argument at Home and Abroad. Notre Dame: Notre Dame Press, 1994. Translations: Italian, German, Spanish, Slovak, Greek, French, Japanese.
"Shared Meanings in a Poly-Ethnic Democratic Setting: A Response." *Journal of Religious Ethics* 22.2 (1994), 401–05.

1995

Pluralism, Justice, and Equality, with David Miller. Oxford: Oxford University Press, 1995. Translation: Spanish.
Toward a Global Civil Society, editor. Providence, R.I.: Berghahn Books, 1995. Translation: Japanese.
"Education, Democratic Citizenship, and Multiculturalism." *Journal of Philosophy of Education* 29 (1995), 181–89.
"The Civil Society Argument." In *Theorizing Citizenship,* edited by Ronald Beiner, 153–74. Albany: State University of New York Press, 1995.
Symposium. "Fifty Years After Hiroshima." *Dissent* (Summer 1995), 330–31.

"The Politics of Rescue." *Dissent* (Winter 1995), 35–41.
"The Public Impact of the Christian-Jewish Dialogue." *New Theology Review* 8 (May 1995), 79–83.

1996

"For Identity." *New Republic* 215 (December 2, 1996), 39.
Exchange with Cornel West. "The Million Man March." *Dissent* (Winter 1996), 97–99, 101.
"On Negative Politics." In *Liberalism Without Illusions,* edited by Bernard Yack, 17–24. Chicago: University of Chicago Press, 1996.
"What's Going On?: Notes on the Right Turn." *Dissent* (Winter 1996), 5–11.

1997

On Toleration. New Haven: Yale University Press, 1997. English edition in India by Frank Bros. & Co. (Publishers) Ltd. Translations: French, German, Italian, Spanish, Portuguese, Dutch, Swedish, Estonian, Greek, Bulgarian, Hebrew, Russian, Polish, Chinese, Japanese, Romanian, Slovak, Ukrainian; forthcoming in Lithuanian, Turkish.
Arguments from the Left. Stockholm: Atlas, 1997. Selected essays, in Swedish.
Pluralism and Democracy. Paris: Éditions Esprit, 1997. Selected essays, in French.
"Blacks and Jews: A Personal Reflection." In *Struggles in the Promised Land: Toward a History of Black-Jewish Relations in the United States,* edited by Jack Salzman and Cornel West, 401–09. New York: Oxford University Press, 1997.
Symposium. "Campaign Financing: Four Views." *Dissent* (Summer 1997), 5–6.
"The Politics of Difference: Statehood and Toleration in a Multicultural World." In *The Morality of Nationalism,* edited by Robert McKim and Jeff McMahan, 245–57. Oxford: Oxford University Press, 1997.
"The Underworked American." *New Republic* 217 (September 22, 1997), 29.
Special issue. "Zionism at 100: A Symposium." *New Republic* 217 (September 8 and 15, 1997), 22.

1998

"The Big Shrug." *New Republic* 218 (February 2, 1998), 9–10.
"Crass Demos." *New Republic* 218 (June 8, 1998), 11–12.
"Disunited." *New Republic* 219 (July 27, 1998), 10–11.
"On Involuntary Association." In *Freedom of Association,* edited by Amy Gutmann, 64–74. Princeton: Princeton University Press, 1998.
"Michael Sandel's America." In *Debating Democracy's Discontent: Essays on American Politics, Law, and Public Philosophy,* edited by Anita L. Allen and Milton C. Regan, Jr., 175–82. Oxford: Oxford University Press, 1998.
"Multiculturalism and the Politics of Interest." In *Insider / Outsider: American Jews*

and Multiculturalism, edited by David Biale, Michael Galchinsky, and Susannah Heschel, 88–98. Berkeley: University of California Press, 1998.
"Pluralism and Social Democracy." *Dissent* (Winter 1998), 47–53.

1999

Reason, Politics, and Passion. Frankfurt: Fischer Taschenbuch Verlag, 1999. The Horkheimer Lectures, in German; also published in Spanish, French, Italian, and Korean.
"Deliberation, and What Else?" In *Deliberative Politics: Essays on Democracy and Disagreement*, edited by Stephen Macedo, 58–69. New York: Oxford University Press, 1999.
Published lecture. "Drawing the Line: Religion and Politics." *Utah Law Review* 1999, no. 3: 619–38.
"Kosovo." *Dissent* (Summer 1999), 5–7.
"Rescuing Civil Society." *Dissent* 46 (Winter 1999), 62–67.

2000

The Jewish Political Tradition. Volume 1: *Authority*, coedited with Menachem Lorberbaum, Noam Zohar, and Ari Ackerman. New Haven: Yale University Press, 2000.
"Governing the Globe: What Is the Best We Can Do?" *Dissent* (Fall 2000), 44–51.

2001

Exilic Politics in the Hebrew Bible. Tübingen, Germany: Mohr Siebeck, 2001, in German.
War, Politics, and Morality. Barcelona: Ediciones Paidos, 2001. Selected essays, in Spanish.
"Double Effect." In *The Doctrine of Double Effect: Philosophers Debate a Controversial Moral Principle*, edited by P. A. Woodward, 261–69. Notre Dame: University of Notre Dame Press, 2001.
"Excusing Terror: The Politics of Ideological Apology." *American Prospect* 12 (October 22, 2001), 16–17.
"History and National Liberation." *Journal of Israeli History: Politics, Society, Culture* 20 (Summer–Fall 2001), 1–8.
"Liberalism, Nationalism, Reform." In *The Legacy of Isaiah Berlin*, edited by Ronald Dworkin, Mark Lilla, and Robert B. Silvers, 169–76. New York: New York Review Books, 2001.
"Nation-States and Immigrant Societies." In *Can Liberal Pluralism Be Exported?: Western Political Theory and Ethnic Relations in Eastern Europe*, edited by Will Kymlicka and Magda Opalski, 150–53. Oxford: Oxford University Press, 2001.
Published lecture. "Universalism and Jewish Values." *The Twentieth Morgenthau*

Memorial Lecture on Ethics and Foreign Policy (May 15, 2001.) New York: Carnegie Council on Ethics and Foreign Policy, 2001.

2002

The Thread of Politics: Democracy, Social Criticism, and World Government. Reggio Emilia, Italy: Edizioni Diabasis, 2002. Selected essays, in Italian.
"The Argument about Humanitarian Intervention." *Dissent* (Winter 2002), 29–37.
"Can There Be a Decent Left?" *Dissent* (Spring 2002), 19–23.
"Equality and Civil Society." In *Alternative Conceptions of Civil Society,* edited by Simone Chambers and Will Kymlicka, 34–49. Princeton: Princeton University Press, 2002.
"Five Questions about Terrorism." (Followed by exchange with Leo Casey, Michael Kazin, James B. Rule, and Ann Snitow.) *Dissent* (Winter 2002), 5–16.
"The Four Wars of Israel/Palestine." *Dissent* (Fall 2002), 26–33.
"The 9/11 License." *Renewal* 10:3 (2002), 28–31.
"No Strikes." *New Republic* 227 (September 30, 2002), 19–22.
"Passion and Politics." *Philosophy and Social Criticism* 28 (November 2002), 617–33.
"The Triumph of Just War Theory (and the Dangers of Success)." *Social Research* 69 (2002), 925–44.

2003

Erklärte Kriege—Kriegserklärungen. Hamburg: Europäische Verlagsanstalt, 2003. Selected essays, in German.
The Jewish Political Tradition. Volume 2: *Membership,* coedited with Menachem Lorberbaum, Noam Zohar, and Ari Ackerman. New Haven: Yale University Press, 2003.
"Is There an American Empire?" *Dissent* (Fall 2003), 27–31.
"What Rights for Illiberal Communities?" In *Forms of Justice: Critical Perspectives on David Miller's Political Philosophy,* edited by Daniel A. Bell and Avner de-Shalit, 123–34. Lanham, Md.: Rowman and Littlefield, 2003.
"The United States in the World—Just Wars and Just Societies: An Interview with Michael Walzer." Interview by *Imprints: A Journal of Analytical Socialism* 7:1 (2003), 4–19.

2004

Arguing About War. New Haven: Yale University Press, 2004. Selected essays and articles. Translations: Spanish, French, Italian, Polish; forthcoming in Japanese.
Published lecture. "Beyond Humanitarian Intervention: Human Rights in Global Society." Original: "Una lista breve di casi da difendere a oltranza." Translated by René Capovin. *Reset* (July–August 2004), 42–45.
"Can There be a Moral Foreign Policy?" In *Liberty and Power: A Dialogue on*

Religion and U.S. Foreign Policy in an Unjust World, series editors E. J. Dionne, Jr., Jean Bethke Elshtain, Kayla Drogosz, 34–52. Washington, D.C.: Brookings Institution Press, 2004.

"A Liberal Perspective on Deterrence and Proliferation of Weapons of Mass Destruction." In *Ethics and Weapons of Mass Destruction: Religious and Secular Perspectives,* edited by Sohail H. Hashmi and Steven P. Lee, 163–67. Cambridge: Cambridge University Press, 2004.

"Zionism and Judaism." In *Judaism and Modernity: The Religious Philosophy of David Hartman,* edited by Jonathan W. Malino, 308–25. Hampshire, England, and Burlington, Vermont: Ashgate Publishing, 2004.

2005

Politics and Passion: Toward a More Egalitarian Liberalism. New Haven: Yale University Press, 2005. Translation: Polish; forthcoming in Chinese, Japanese. (Expanded version of *Reason, Politics, and Passion.*)

"All God's Children Got Values." *Dissent* (Spring 2005), 35–40.

"The Good Society." In *Marx and the Future of Socialism,* edited by Uri Zilbersheid, 260–67. Tel Aviv: Resling, 2005.

2006

"Moral Education and Democratic Citizenship." In *To Restore American Democracy: Political Education and the Modern University,* edited by Robert E. Calvert, 217–30. Oxford: Rowman and Littlefield, 2006.

"Morality and Politics in the Work of Michael Wyschogrod." *Modern Theology* 22:4 (October 2006), 687–92.

"Political Theology: Response to the Six." *Political Theology* 7:1 (January 2006), 91–99.

"Regime Change and Just War." *Dissent* (Summer 2006), 103–08. Reprint of Preface to the 4th edition, *Just and Unjust Wars: A Moral Argument with Historical Illustrations.* New York: Basic Books, 2006.

Published lecture. "Terrorism and Just War." *Philosophia* 34:1 (January 2006), 3–12.

Published lecture. "Who Is an American Jew?" *Occasional Papers on Jewish Civilization, Jewish Thought, and Philosophy* (February 2006), 8–15. The Program for Jewish Civilization, Edmund A. Walsh School of Foreign Service, Georgetown University (November 19, 2003).

Credits

---

1. "Philosophy and Democracy." *Political Theory* 9 (1981), 379–99.
2. "A Critique of Philosophical Conversation." *Philosophical Forum* 21 (Fall–Winter 1989–90), 182–96.
3. "Objectivity and Social Meaning." In *The Quality of Life*, edited by Martha C. Nussbaum and Amartya Sen, 165–77. Oxford: Clarendon Press, 1993.
4. "Liberalism and the Art of Separation." *Political Theory* 12 (1984), 315–30.
5. "Justice Here and Now." In *Justice and Equality Here and Now*, edited by Frank S. Lucash, 136–50. Ithaca: Cornell University Press, 1986.
6. "Exclusion, Injustice, and the Democratic State." *Dissent* (Winter 1993), 55–64.
7. "The Communitarian Critique of Liberalism." *Political Theory* 18 (1990), 6–23.
8. "The Civil Society Argument." In *Theorizing Citizenship*, edited by Ronald Beiner, 153–74. Albany: State University of New York Press, 1995.
9. "Deliberation, and What Else?" In *Deliberative Politics: Essays on Democracy and Disagreement*, edited by Stephen Macedo, 58–69. New York: Oxford University Press, 1999.
10. "Drawing the Line: Religion and Politics." *Utah Law Review* 3 (1999), 619–38.
11. "The Politics of Difference: Statehood and Toleration in a Multicultural World." In *The Morality of Nationalism*, edited by Robert McKim and Jeff McMahan, 245–57. New York: Oxford University Press, 1997.

12. "Nation and Universe." In *The Tanner Lectures on Human Values,* edited by Grethe B. Peterson, 11:507–56. Salt Lake City: University of Utah Press, 1990.

13. "The Moral Standing of States: A Reply to Four Critics." *Philosophy and Public Affairs* 9 (1980), 209–29.

14. "The Argument about Humanitarian Intervention." *Dissent* (Winter 2002), 29–37.

15. "Beyond Humanitarian Intervention: Human Rights in Global Society." Original: "Una lista breve di casi da difendere a oltranza." Translated by René Capovin. *Reset* (July–August 2004), 42–45.

16. "Terrorism and Just War." *Philosophia* 34:1 (January 2006), 3–12.

17. "Political Action: The Problem of Dirty Hands." *Philosophy and Public Affairs* 2 (Winter 1973), 160–80.

18. "The United States in the World: Just Wars and Just Societies: An Interview with Michael Walzer." Interview by *Imprints: A Journal of Analytical Socialism* 7:1 (2003), 4–19.

Index